HERMENEUTISCHE UNTERSUCHUNGEN ZUR THEOLOGIE

Herausgegeben von
HANS DIETER BETZ · GERHARD EBELING
MANFRED MEZGER

19

Julius Africanus
and the Early Christian
View of Magic

by

Francis C. R. Thee

J. C. B. Mohr (Paul Siebeck) Tübingen 1984

CIP-Kurztitelaufnahme der Deutschen Bibliothek

Thee, Francis C. R.:
Julius Africanus and the early Christian view
of magic / by Francis C. R. Thee. – Tübingen:
Mohr, 1984.
    (Hermeneutische Untersuchungen zur Theologie;
    19)
    ISBN 3-16-144552-X
    ISSN 0440-7180

NE: GT

© J. C. B. Mohr (Paul Siebeck) Tübingen 1984.
Printed in Germany. Satz und Druck: Gulde-Druck GmbH, Tübingen. Einband: Heinrich
Koch, Großbuchbinderei, Tübingen.

To Paul and Yetta

and

To Mary

and

Paul

TABLE OF CONTENTS

LIST OF ILLUSTRATIONS

ACKNOWLEDGMENTS

Professor Robert M. Grant first suggested Africanus and the concentration of the study on the magic in Africanus to me. I have appreciated his advice--both positive and negative, whether taken immediately or not--and his restraint over the years. His efforts in the processing of the paper made possible the meeting of the final deadlines.

Professors Hans Dieter Betz and Bernard McGinn deserve special thanks for consenting, on short notice, to serve as readers of the paper.

Professor Betz further suggested this series to me and kindly recommended this study to its publisher and the other editors.

INTRODUCTION

Statement of the Problem

Aspects of the Problem

Julius Africanus suffers the peculiar fate of being, perhaps, best known today for his shortest work, a letter to Origen, which the ancients preserved mainly as a preface to Origen's reply, while his major works fell victim, in a sense, to their popularity, being absorbed into larger works, and surviving solely as only partially identifiable fragments. This, at least, is one way of describing the fate of his Chronography--it built a tidy edifice of Christian chronology, but then was dismantled to provide materials for those who built otherwise on his foundation.[1] With the Kestoi, though, perhaps the opposite is more true--here was gathered a great and miscellaneous mass of materials which shortly sank under its own disordered weight, and so perished, except for a few items picked out here and there as useful, or at least curious, matter, and so preserved.[2]

_____

[1]Note especially Eusebius's Chronicon and the Byzantine chronologists; on the latter see Heinrich Gelzer, Sextus Julius Africanus und die Byzantinische Chronographie, 2 vols. in 1 (Leipzig: J. C. Hinrichs'sche Buchhandlung, 1898).

[2]They are found mainly in the Byzantine collections of tactical, veterinary, and agricultural writers, with other fragments elsewhere, e.g., among the alchemical writers. The quick demise of the Kestoi is illustrated by its sole surviving direct fragment: less than a half century after the writing of the Kestoi, a professionally produced copy had been discarded and cut up for more practical

1

As to the man himself, certain clear traits appear from his
writings. He was a Christian of unquestioned faith, with keen critical abilities, of broad wisdom and learning, versed in history, in
the Scriptures, and in the traditions of the Jewish church, especially
the desposynē; on the other hand, he was a man of purely pagan interests, of incredible credulity, and a paragon of superstition and
superficial pedantry, steeped in Hellenic traditions and literature,
especially magic. The one side of the portrait is that commonly
drawn from his "Christian" writings (his letters To Origen and To
Aristides, and the Chronography), the other from the Kestoi.

But, are these portraitures drawn in too-broad strokes? Are
the differences between the "Christian" and the "secular" Africanus
really so clear-cut? And, if a properly balanced sketch of Africanus
can be produced, how sharply does it stand out from its Christian
background? Specifically, how does the "magical" Africanus blend
into the rest of the portrait?

Most recent discussions of Africanus assume that a synthesis
is possible, since it is necessary, but do not deal with its specifics (or sometimes, even refer to a problem).[1] Those who deal with

---

uses of its blank verso, in the case of the surviving fragment, a copy
of a will; Bernard P. Grenfell and Arthur S. Hunt, The Oxyrhynchus
Papyri, part III (Egypt Exploration Fund: Graeco-Roman Branch; London:
Egypt Exploration Fund, 1903), no. 412, pp. 36-41, and plate V, for
the fragment, and part VI (1908), no. 907, pp. 247-53, concerning the
copy of the will.

[1]Earlier studies (to be dealt with in Chapter I, the history
of the study of Africanus) had solved the problem in various ways,
postulating two or more Africani, attributing the Kestoi to Africanus's pagan youth, or to a postulated period of lapse, or, again, ignoring it.

the specifics consider only part of the problems as stated above.

The only two recent scholars to deal with Africanus to any extent are J. R. Vieillefond and Gudmund Björck, with the former standing alone as far as individual attention to Africanus is concerned.
Björck, though presenting some valuable ideas, dealt with Africanus
extensively only as one part of one study[1]; Vieillefond has devoted
over 30 years to Africanus, producing a definitive edition of the
surviving Kestoi fragments, and an extensive introductory study of
the man himself.[2] But Vieillefond himself recognizes that his work is
incomplete;[3] and, concentrating as it does on the Kestoi and the
"secular" Africanus, it assumes, rather than really proves, that a
unified picture is possible. Further, his picture may be inaccurate
in some points: he argues, for example, for a Jewish background for
Africanus and the Kestoi.[4] He does this mainly on the basis of the
more recently found fragments, especially that from Oxyrhynchus, setting aside the past inference from Africanus's other writings, and
from Origen's letter to him.[5]

---

[1]Gudmund Björck, "Apsyrtus, Julius Africanus et l'hippiatrique
grecque," Uppsala Universitets Årsskrift, 1944, no. 4, esp. chap. 2.

[2]Jean-René Vieillefond, Les "Cestes" de Julius Africanus: Etude
sur l'ensemble des fragments avec édition, traduction et commentaires,
Publications de l'Institute Français de Florence, Ière Série, no. 20
(Florence: Edizioni Sansoni Antiquariato, and Paris: Librairie Marcel
Didier, 1970); note esp. the "Introduction," pp. 5-9, and the "Etude
générale," pp. 13-70. His publications began with Jules Africain:
Fragments des Cestes provenant de la collection des tacticiens grecs,
Nouvelle collection de textes et documents publiée sous le patronage
de l'Association Guillaume Budé (Paris: Société d'Edition "Les Belles
Lettres," 1932).

[3]Les Cestes, p. 23.   [4]Ibid., pp. 41-42.

[5]This matter will be dealt with in the history of the study of
Africanus and his writings (Chapter I, below).

A major element in the problem of reconciling Africanus to himself and to his background is the "magical" strain in the Kestoi. This is not the whole problem—the Kestoi is written from a consistently secular, pagan viewpoint—but it lies near the heart of the problem and is frequently used as the main, or at least leading, element in characterizing the Kestoi.[1] Further, it provides one, fairly objective, way of marking off a feasible segment of the problem for study. For this reason the present study will be concerned with the "magical" elements in the writings of Africanus and with the question of how they compare to the attitudes of the early church toward magic.

But there is a further problem: exactly what constitutes magic is difficult to define or describe, either in general, or in regard to a particular culture. For this reason, the study includes a fairly extensive study of magic in the early Christian writers,[2] to provide a background against which to compare and assess the magical elements in Africanus. This study is intended to define the segment of their belief systems relating to magic, specifically to identify

---

[1]Starting with Syncellus (Georgius Syncellus et Nicephorus CP, ed. Guilielmus Dindorfius, Corpus Scriptorum Historiae Byzantinae, ed. B. G. Niebuhrius, 2 vols. [Bonn: Ed. Weber, 1829], 1:676[=P359B (=ed. Paris, 1652, by Jacob Goarus)], expanded in the Suidas (Suidae Lexicon, ed. Ada Adler, Lexicographi Graeci, vol. 1 [Leipzig: B. G. Teubner, 1928], part 1, pp. 433-34, entry no. A4647), and continuing into the modern encyclopediae (most recently in The New Columbia Encyclopedia [ed. William H. Harris and Judith S. Levey (New York and London: Columbia University Press, 1975)] which concludes its article on "Africanus, Sextus Julius": "and an anthology, mostly of materials on magic").

[2]For the purposes of this study, confined to the group commonly known as the "Ante-Nicene Fathers," representing writers contemporary with Africanus, and those of, approximately, the preceding and following centuries.

the terms they use of magic, to define what they mean by them, to note
what actions, materiel, etc., they associate with the idea, to describe
their attitude(s) toward magic, or the various specific items involved, and to consider, briefly, how this element fits into their
total belief system. Several partial studies have been made in this
area, notably Richard Ganschinietz, "Hippolytos' Capitel gegen die
Magier,"[1] and Gustave Bardy, "Origène et la magie,"[2] but no complete
survey of the whole area has been made.

      Preceding this study, but partially anticipating its results
as a general guide in identifying the magical elements, is a study of
Africanus. Major attention is directed, naturally, to the Kestoi
(with a translation of the full text, as edited by Vieillefond, provided), but it includes a consideration of relevant or questionable
references in his other writings. From this a summary view of Africanus's knowledge and attitudes is drawn, and this is compared, in a
concluding chapter, to that of the writers previously mentioned.

Statement of the Thesis

The thesis

      The difference in the attitudes of the early church fathers
and of Africanus toward magic is to be explained by the fact that
the former regarded magic as a religious matter (i.e., as being anti-
religious), while Africanus regarded the items he presented as being,

---

[1] Texte und Untersuchungen vol. 39, no. 2 (1913). (Cited hereafter as TU.)

[2] Recherches de science religieuse 18 (1928):126-42.

by and large,[1] matters of science (or technology--_techne_) and thus
unrelated to his religious beliefs.

Amplification of statement

In terms of the overlapping areas distinguished by moderns into
Religion, Magic, and Science (with magic as a middle term sometimes
regarded as closer to the one, sometimes to the other), Africanus regarded the items he presents as being in the area we would call Science, and thus not related to Religion (except insofar as each of
these areas, including Science, might involve some sort of mysterious,
transhuman force), whereas the early Christian writers regarded most
such things as Magic, and thus related to Religion as its antithesis.
Africanus would probably take much the same view of "Magic," but
would differ in his opinions as to what fit into that category.

Related aspects

The study will show that the belief-systems of Africanus and
the other writers largely overlap,[2] but that there are significant
portions of his belief-system that lie outside the circle of Christian
beliefs. These areas, however, while outside the circle of Christian
acceptance (and perhaps specifically rejected or even attacked by
them), can be regarded as logically consistent with (or even, derived
from) beliefs of Africanus that he holds in common with other

---

[1]The apparent exceptions are generally cases in which Africanus,
as a litterateur, connected his presentation with some aspect of Greek
mythology.

[2]Otherwise Africanus would not have been considered by himself
and by others to be a Christian, and especially would not have been so
highly regarded by his contemporaries and later generations among the
Christians.

Christians. The major points of conflict are in their religious and
moral evaluation of certain items, Africanus holding as morally neutral and/or as scientifically valuable, certain procedures or concepts which his Christian contemporaries regard as evil, and possibly
demonic. In most of these cases a closer examination will show that
Africanus can be intellectually justified by current views of (i.e.,
his belief-system will be found to coincide with many current belief
systems in regard to) physics, physiology, etc., any excess being due
to his more liberal, empirical approach. Further, most of these
items could probably be more accurately described as "popularly superstitious" than as "actively magical."

Most, if not all, of the material in Africanus that appears to
be magical to men of today (and to many of his day) should be regarded
from the perspectives of his writing as (1) a litterateur,[1] and (2) a
dilettante at empirical science. Yet his relation to it is in contrast
and, indeed, in opposition to the attitudes of the church leaders of
his period, and of the centuries immediately before and after. This
difference in view is in line with other aspects of Africanus's thinking in regard to the relations between Christianity and the culture

---

[1]While Vieillefond's strictures on Björck's view of the Kestoi
as a pastiche (Les Cestes, pp. 52-56) are probably correct, it still
must be recognized that one of the goals of Africanus was to entertain,
and some of his statements may well fall into the "tall tale" category.
Björck himself was probably justified in questioning Vieillefond's
earlier reference to Africanus as "conseille le plus sérieusement du
monde les incantations magiques" (Vieillefond in Jules Africain, p. xv,
cited by Björck, "Apsyrtus," p. 22). W. W. Tarn notes this characteristic of Africanus in a review of Jules Africain (Classical Review 46
[1932]:238), referring to "his queer farrago of sense and nonsense,
history and tall stories."

of his day; it is a result of his practical, rather than philosophical
or theological, bent of mind.

Working Definition of Magic

Introduction

There is no universally accepted definition of magic, or view
of its relation, on the one side, to religion, or to science, on the
other.[1] There seems to be a growing consensus, however, that magic is
to be more closely linked with religion than with science,[2] and they
are frequently defined together by comparison and/or contrast.

Definition, and Related Terms

For the purposes of this study, magic is defined as the use of

-----

[1]For magic, this can be demonstrated from numerous studies of
magic, and from many of religion, e.g.: Edward Norbeck, Religion in
Primitive Society (New York: Harper and Row, 1961), esp. chapters 1,
3,   and 4; the articles on "Magic" by R. R. Marett in Encyclopedia
of Religion and Ethics, ed. James Hastings (Edinburgh: T. & T. Clark,
1925), 8:245-52 (as well as the area studies by King [Babylonian],
Gardiner [Egyptian], Smith [Greek and Roman], etc., which follow it);
by Nur Yalman in International Encyclopedia of the Social Sciences, ed.
David L. Sills (n.p.: Macmillan, 1968), 9:521-28; by John F. M. Middleton in the New Encyclopaedia Britannica, 15th ed. (1974), Macropaedia,
11:298-302; and Murray Wax and Rosalie Wax, "The Notion of Magic,"
Current Anthropology 4 (December 1963):495-518. Apparent exceptions
are usually cases in which the author attempts no definition, assuming
a common understanding of the term based on common speech usage, or
gives his own ad hoc definition, frequently colored by what has been
termed "Western ethnocentric views" (e.g., by Middleton, p. 298; cf.
also Norbeck, pp. 4-13, and Wax and Wax, p. 495). The same situation
obtains in regard to religion: note Norbeck, above, and Hans H.
Penner and Edward A. Yonan, "Is a Science of Religion Possible?"
Journal of Religion 52 (April 1972):107-33.

[2]Thus following somewhat in the line established by Edward
Tylor (Primitive Culture), and not that of James Frazer (Golden Bough).
All of the sources in the first part of the preceding note trace the
main lines in the development of the consideration of magic and its
place in the world.

irrational means to try to obtain (or compel) some result, operating
by means of some presumed supernatural (or transhuman) causal relationship. This relationship (and the associated means) may be viewed
as existing in two, not necessarily exclusive, varieties, impersonal
or personal, resulting in a possible distinction of "direct" (compulsive, manipulative), and "indirect" (supplicative) magic.[1] (More
specific guidelines, related to the areas being considered, are given
at the beginnings of Chapters III and IV.)

Closely related to magic is the use of charms, used here as a
general term to include both spells ("words," spoken or written; if
spoken, incantations); and amulets (objects, including copies of written spells). Charms are viewed as efficacious largely on the basis
of association, that is, either "sympathetic" or "contagious" magical
power.

Magic, as defined above, can thus be broadly distinguished from
science and religion, though the distinction is not always clear-cut.
In contrast to magic, science can be defined, for the present purposes,
as the use of rational, natural (physical) cause and effect relation-
ships, either known or hypothesized.[2]   Religion, on the other hand,
uses personal appeal based on a relationship with the/a supernatural
power (deity) to obtain (request) the desired result.

The preceding definitions are designed specifically for the

---

[1]Cf. Kirby Flower Smith, "Magic (Greek and Roman)," Encyclopedia of Religion and Ethics, ed. Hastings (1925), 8:279.

[2]Those hypothesized being supported by "reasonable," explicitly formulated, supporting evidences and suggested rationale.

present study, and are not necessarily applicable to greatly differ-
ing cultures. It is also recognized that, even in their own areas,
they are somewhat loose. This will allow for variations among the
writers studied, while these studies, in turn, will produce the possibility of greater precision in defining the terms for their culture.
Also, the preceding definitions are expressed, necessarily, from the
modern vantage point, especially in the use of the terms "irrational"
and "rational," and "supernatural."

CHAPTER I

THE STUDY OF JULIUS AFRICANUS

AND HIS KESTOI

The question of Julius Africanus, while not subjected to the
definitive studies such as the affairs of many of the other church
fathers have received, has been considered and contested and debated
at varying periods over the centuries. In order to prepare for the
consideration of the problem of the relation of Africanus to magic,
an attempt will be made to put it in perspective by tracing the history of the discussion of Africanus from the earliest literary references to him to the development of a modern semi-consensus. The discussion will emphasize those items relating to the magical aspect of
the question, but will not be restricted to it, especially in the earlier periods.

The discussion will begin with a presentation, in historical
order, of the references to Africanus in the ancient and Byzantine
sources, generally exclusive of those which only became known to
scholars in the later stages of the history of the problems.

Following this, consideration will be given to studies prior
to the appearance of Vieillefond's Jules Africain in 1932. These
early studies will be further divided, chronologically, into two
periods. The first period spans the discussion from the first published reference to Africanus to the end of the eighteenth century.

11

During this period scattered contributions were made to the study,
largely in the form of the publication of short texts, or the presentation of suggestions as to a solution of the problem. These items
appeared mainly as sidelines to other studies, or as sections in works
surveying early church history or Christian writers, but, despite
the occasional nature of the references, most of the solutions that
have been suggested for the problem originated in this period. The
second period, from the early nineteenth century to the first decades
of the twentieth, differs from the preceding one largely in the increased emphasis on the discovery and publication of all possible ancient texts, and in increasingly self-conscious efforts to find a
place for Africanus in the history of human thought. Some major
studies of various aspects of Africanus were produced, but no really
new solutions were suggested. Near the end of the period, the presentation of these studies cannot be organized strictly chronologically,
but is partially organized according to major writers who dealt with
the question.

The final section of this chapter deals with more recent contributions to the problem, especially the longer studies by Vieillefond[1] and Björck.[2] The former, in a sense, sums up previous study
and presents the closest approach to a consensus; the latter suggested
a largely new solution (though it too had some embryonic anticipations
in earlier periods).

---

[1] Jules Africain, and Les Cestes.

[2] "Apsyrtus."

Ancient and Byzantine References

Greek and Related Ecclesiastical Sources

Other than in Origen's reply to the letter concerning Susanna, Africanus is not mentioned in extant literary sources before Eusebius. This, of course, is already a gap of approximately a century between Africanus's lifetime and our major sources, but this is partially compensated for by the location and nature of this first source.

Eusebius

As a long-time resident of Caesarea in Palestine, Eusebius would have been in one of the best possible locations to have access to copies of Africanus's literary efforts; and the references in his own writings seem to indicate that he had utilized the opportunity. His Chronicle has as one of its basic sources the Chronography of Africanus, and he cites or names all the other works attributed to Africanus by modern scholars, i.e., the letters to Origen and to Aristides, and the Kestoi.

In the Chronicle, Eusebius refers to Africanus three times. In the Preface, he lists Africanus between Clement and Tatian as among those who place Moses in the time of Inachus,[1] and under the first year of Macrinus he cites, as an opinion of Africanus, that at this point, "Abgar, a venerable man (vir sanctus) ruled

---

[1] Eusebius Werke, siebenter Band, Die Chronik des Hieronymus, ed. Rudolf Helm, Die Griechischen Christlichen Schriftsteller der ersten Jahrhunderte, 2d ed. (Berlin: Akademie-Verlag, 1956), p. 7, lines 10-18. (Hereafter cited as Chronik, followed by page and line numbers.)

Edessa."[1] The third reference is more substantial. At Olympiad 250, 1,

Heliogabalus III (=an.Abr. 2237, p. Chr. 221), Eusebius testifies,

> In Palestine, Nicopolis, which was formerly called Emmaus, was
> constituted a city, a legation having been diligently undertaken
> for it by Julius Africanus, the chronological writer (scriptore
> temporum).[2]

Further information is provided in the Ecclesiastical History.

The most important reference occurs in 6. 31, where Eusebius briefly

describes Africanus and his writings. It occurs in the general con-

text of the discussion of the life, works, and associates of Origen

(which extends through most of book 6). This chapter, headed "Con-

cerning Africanus," says,

> About this time also, Africanus, the writer of the work en-
> titled Kestoi became known. A letter of his, written to Origen,
> is preserved, questioning whether the story concerning Susanna
> in Daniel is spurious and fictitious. Origen wrote a most full
> reply to this. And of the same Africanus also another work, the
> five in number of the Chronographia, came to us; an accurately
> produced labor. In it he says he himself undertook a journey to
> Alexandria on account of the great fame of Heraclas (who indeed
> in philosophical matters and in the other Greek learning really
> was most distinguished, the oversight of the church there being
> put in his hands as we have shown). And also a further work of
> the same Africanus is preserved, a letter to Aristides, concern-
> ing the apparent dissonance of the genealogies of Christ in
> Matthew and Luke.

In an earlier book, 1. 6. 2, Eusebius mentions an opinion of

---

[1]An. Abr. 2234,   p. Chr. 218; Chronik, 214. 5-6. (The
English translation here, and elsewhere in this chapter, is by the
present writer.)

[2]Chronik, 214. 20-24. Besides these, Eusebius gives long
extracts from Africanus's Chronographia in his Preparation for the
Gospel (10. 10--periods of history before the Olympiads), and in the
Proof of the Gospel (8. 2--an extract from the Fifth Book, concerning
Daniel's prophecy of the Seventy Weeks [Daniel 9:24-27]). Eusebius
cites these opinions with respect, though he goes on to differ with
them.

Africanus, describing him in passing as "not the ordinary historian."[1]

Jerome

Jerome produced a Latin edition of Eusebius's Chronicle
(which today forms our major source for it), and in addition refers
to Africanus in three passages in his own writings.

In one of his epistles, (no. 70) Ad Magnum, in section 4,
Jerome lists the writers of the church from Quadratus to the Cappa-
docians. After naming Hippolytus and Apollonius, he says, "There
are extant also Julius Africanus's books, which he wrote a history of
the times."[2]

---

[1]Shortly thereafter, in 1. 7, Eusebius gives a long extract
from Africanus's letter To Aristides. This citation is our major source
for the text of that letter. Further sections of this work are provided in Eusebius's Quaestiones evangelicae ad Stephanam, a work which
partially survives in an epitome. Here also, Eusebius cites Africanus's opinion as worthy of attention, though he does not completely
agree with him.
    The section of To Aristides concerning Herod's origins was
cited about the same time by Athanasius (?) ("Athanasii Alexandrini
ex interpretatione in Matthaeum," in Bernardo de Montfaucon, Collectio
nova patrum et scriptorum Graecorum, 2 vols [Paris: Claudius Rigaud,
1706], 2:27). But this seems to be Athanasius's only reference to Africanus, if this work is genuine; it is quite possibly mediated
through Eusebius, in any case, and not directly from Africanus.
    Possibly about a half century later, Basil the Great,
in the De spiritu sancto, chapter 29 (sec. 73), defends the use of
the phrase "with (syn) the Spirit" in doxologies by citing, among
various earlier examples of its use, such a usage by "Africanus the
historiographer . . . in the 5th of the Epitome of the
Times."
    The Quaes. ev. ad Steph. were first printed by Angelo Mai,
Scriptorum veterum nova collectio e Vaticanis codicibus edita, vol.
1 (Rome: Typis Vaticanis, 1825); the epitome begins on p. 1, the
citation from Africanus is in Quaes. IIII, pp. 21-23. (In an 1831
reprint of this volume, the extract is on pp. 17-19.)

[2]Sancti Eusebii Hieronymi Stridonensis presbyteri operum,
tomus prima, pars prima, ed. Dominicus Valarsius, editio altera
(Venice: G. Zerletti, 1766).

A more extensive account is given in his <u>De viris illustribus</u>, chapter 63:

> Julius Africanus, whose five volumes <u>Concerning Times</u> are extant, under emperor Marcus Aurelius Antonius [i.e., Elagabalus], who succeeded Macrinus, undertook a mission for renewal of the city of Emmaus which afterward was called Nicopolis. From him is a letter to Origen over the question of Susanna, in which he says this fable not to be contained in the Hebrew, nor the line <u>apo tou prinou prisai kai apo tou schinou schisai</u> to coincide with the Hebrew etymology; against whom Origen wrote a learned letter. Another letter of his, to Aristides, is extant, in which he argues at great length concerning the <u>diaphōnia</u> which appears to exist in the genealogies of the Saviour according to Matthew and Luke.[1]

Much of the <u>De vir. ill.</u> and <u>Comm. Dan.</u> references, probably not unnaturally, seems simply to echo Eusebius, but with some significant additions and deletions. Notably, there is no reference to the <u>Kestoi</u>; this omission suggests disapproval of either the work or its attribution to Africanus. Either idea supposes some knowledge of the work by Jerome.

Rufinus of Aquileia and Philip of Side

Two other writers, in passages based on Eusebius, present individual modifications.

In his translation of Eusebius's <u>Church History</u>, Rufinus makes one notable change, the omission of the reference to the <u>Kestoi</u>

---

[1] <u>Hieronymus Liber de viris inlustribus . . .</u>, ed. Ernest Cushing Richardson, <u>TU</u> 14, no. 1 (1896):36-37.
    In his Commentary on Daniel, Book 3, at Daniel 9:24, Jerome also gives (or repeats from Eusebius <u>Proof Gosp</u>. 8. 2?) a lengthy extract concerning the "Seventy Weeks" from Africanus's fifth volume <u>Of Times</u> (compare Eus. <u>Proof Gosp</u>. 8. 2).

in the chapter on Africanus (6. 31.1).[1] The same considerations that apply to Jerome's omission apply here also.

Philip of Side, in a surviving fragment not generally known to modern scholars before its publication by de Boor in 1889, makes a significant addition to Eusebius's description of Africanus in H.E. 1. 7 (Eusebius's comment forms the essence of its first half):

> Most excellently Africanus wrote through a letter to Aristides concerning the apparent discord in the genealogy regarding the generations by the evangelists Matthew and also Luke. But Africanus was from Emmaus the village in Palestine into which Cleopas and those with him journeyed, and which later receiving the right of a city in accordance with the embassy of Africanus, was renamed Nikopolis.[2]

As the editor of the fragment points out, the last sentence forms a middle ground between the reference to Emmaus in the Eusebius-Hieronymus Chronicle (cf. also, the Chronicon Paschale, below), and the report by Syncellus (see below also).[3]

Moses of Chorene

In the fifth century, in the East but following the Greek (Eusebian) tradition, Africanus's work was utilized by Moses of

---

[1] See, e.g., Theodor Mommsen, ed., Die lateinische Übersetzung des Rufinus, included in Eusebius Werke, zweiter Band: Die Kirchengeschichte, ed., Eduard Schwartz, Die Griechischen Christlichen Schriftsteller der ersten drei Jahrhunderte, 3 parts (Leipzig: J. C. Hinrichs'sche Buchhandlung, 1903-9), 2:585.

[2] C. de Boor, "Neue Fragmente des Papias, Hegesippus und Pierius in bisher unbekannten Excerpten aus der Kirchengeschichte des Philippus Sidetes," TU 5, no. 2 (1889): 169.

[3] Ibid., p. 174. In this same tradition, a pair of fifth century church historians, Socrates Scholasticus (H.E. 2. 35) and Sozomen Salaminus (H.E. 1. 1) have passing references to Africanus, classing him among the most learned of the early Christian writers.

Chorene in his <u>History of Armenia</u>. In book 2, chapter 10, Moses turns

to a new source (the end of chapter 9 had announced the termination

of use of another source), saying:

> We will commence to describe the events according to the
> fifth book of Africanus the Chronologist whose testimony is con-
> firmed by Josephus, Hippolytus, and many other Greek writers;
> for he excerpted the documents and [/of?] the archives of
> Edessa, that is Urha, all that concerned the history of our
> kings (those books had been brought from Medzpin); he also used
> the histories of the temples of Sinope of Pontus. No one should
> doubt this, for we ourselves have seen these archives with our
> own eyes. Further testimony of this is provided by the Church
> History of Eusebius of Caesarea . . . in the first book, chapter
> 13. . . .[1]

There is, unfortunately, no further indication of how closely, nor how

far, Moses followed Africanus.

In the following century, in the West, a different kind of

reference began to appear with Fulgentius. This new line of tradi-

tion will be discussed below, under the heading "Secular Sources."

Meanwhile, the "Eusebian" line continued also during this same

period.[2]

---

[1] <u>Moïse de Khorène, auteur du Ve siècle, Histoire d'Armenie,</u>
Texte Armenien et traduction Française, par P. E. LeVaillant de
Florival, 2 vols. (Venice: Typographie arménienne de Saint-Lazare,
1841), 1:168-71; <u>Des Moses von Chorene Geschichte Gross-Armeniens</u>, aus
den Armenischen übersetzt von Dr. M. Lauer (Regensburg: G. J. Manz,
1869), p. 70; the English translation given here has been made from
the French translation compared with the German.

[2] The <u>Chronographia</u> of Malalas (later sixth century) continued
the tradition of dependence on Africanus (albeit in a somewhat cor-
rupt form). Extant copies, however, give no specific data concerning
Africanus's life, since they lack the period from Caracalla to
Valerian (<u>Joannis Malalae Chronographia</u>, ed. Ludovicus Dindorfius,
Corpus Scriptorum Historiae Byzantinae, ed. B. G. Niebuhrius [Bonn:
Ed. Weber, 1831]).

Chronicon Paschale

The anonymous seventh century work known as the Easter Chronicle (Chronicon paschale) has several references to Africanus. The
last, which concerns us most, seems to be derived from Eusebius's
Chronicle (an. Abr. 2237). Dated in the 250th Olympiad [A.D. 221-224],
under Indiction 14, [year of the emperor] 3, during the consulships
of Maximus and Aelianus [=A.D. 223[1]], it says, "Nikopolis of Palestine, previously Emmaus, was made a city, Julius Africanus, who wrote
a history of the times, serving as ambassador on behalf of it and
being leader"[2]; the next year notes the death of Antoninus Elagabalus
(this placement corresponds with that of Eusebius).[3]

Georgius Syncellus

Syncellus, of the late eighth and early ninth centuries in
Constantinople, has numerous references to Africanus in his Chronography. These include one of the more informative ones in this
period.[4]

---

[1]E. J. Bickerman, Chronology of the Ancient World (Ithaca,
N.Y.: Cornell University Press, 1969), p. 189.

[2]Chronicon paschale, ed. Ludovicus Dindorfius, Corpus Scriptorum Historiae Byzantinae, ed. B. G. Niebuhrius, 2 vols. (Bonn:
Ed. Weber, 1832), 1:499, lines 5-7.

[3]Other references to Africanus which occur earlier in the
work relate to his views on the dating of the first Olympiad (ibid.,
p. 193), and on the Seventy Weeks of Daniel (pp. 307 and 311).
Later (1:479, 1-2), the writer notes the death of an Africanus in
Olym. 231, Ind. 15, [yr. of emp.] 11, consulship of Torquatus II
and Julianus (=A.D. 148), but this would have to be one of the
numerous earlier Africani.

[4]Most of the references, however, consist of citations of
data (ranging in length from a short line to several pages) taken
from Africanus's Chronography. These commonly alternate with supporting or contrasting opinions from Eusebius and/or other sources.

Four references relate directly to the life and times of

Africanus. The first two date his historical writing to the time of

Antoninus (Elagabalus).[1] The third occurs in the account of the

reign of Septimius Severus: "Africanus, a Christian historian,

flourished."[2] The fourth such passage consists of three paragraphs

partly derived from Eusebius's Chronicle (an. Abr. 2237 and 2234)

and partly from some other source, possibly personal knowledge. It

reads,

> Emmaus, the village in Palestine, concerning which report is
> made in the Holy Gospels, was given the honor to be named Nikop-
> olis by the emperor Alexander, Africanus, who wrote the his-
> tories in his five book work, serving as ambassador.
>   Africanus, having inscribed the nine-book treatise of the
> Kestoi, comprising formulae [powers?, prescriptions?] of medi-
> cine and of nature and of agriculture and of alchemy [metallurgy?],
> dedicates it to this Alexander.
>   Africanus says that Abgar, a devout man, namesake of the
> previously named Abgar, rules Edessa about these times.[3]

This passage occurs shortly after a reference to the takeover of

Persia by Artaxerxes (A.D. 226), being separated from it only by an

updating reference to the occupants of the bishoprics of Rome

(Urbanus), Antioch (Philetos or Philippos, and Zebennus), and

Jerusalem (Narcissus).

---

[1] Georgius Syncellus et Nicephorus CP, ed. Guilielmus Dindorfius, Corpus Scriptorum Historiae Byzantinae, ed. B. G. Niebuhrius,
2 vols. (Bonn: Ed. Weber, 1829), 1:201 and 400. The second reference
specifies the third year of Antoninus as the terminus of Africanus's
chronological calculations.

[2] Ibid., p. 669. It is more closely dated only by its position, immediately following references to Clement and Pantaenus, and
immediately preceding a reference to the martyrdom of Leonidas, father
of Origen.

[3] Ibid., p. 676.

A fifth reference, from earlier in the work, gives insight

into Africanus's literary interests. Syncellus quotes Africanus's

lists of the Egyptian dynasties, and, under the fourth, Memphitic,

dynasty appears the notation:

> 2. Souphis, 63 years, who raised the greatest pyramid, which Herodotus says to have been done by Cheops. This man also became haughty toward the gods and wrote the holy book, which, as a great value, I procured while in Egypt.[1]

Photius

Somewhat over a half century later, Photius, in his Biblio-

theca (or Myriobibloi), describes the works of Africanus:

> Africanus's historical work was read. (This is the one who also composed the so-called Kestoi in 14 sections.)

> And it is in fact a summary, but nothing of the necessities fail to be recorded. He begins with the Mosaic world-creation, and comes down to the appearance of Christ. And he cursorily handles also the events from Christ until the reign of Macrinus the king of the Romans, because with him, as is said, this history was also completed, totalling 5723 years. The book is five volumes.

> He also writes to Origen concerning the narrative about Susanna as not being read by him among the Hebrew writings, and as not following the Hebrew etymology, neither the apo tou prinou prisai nor the apo tou schinou schisai; which also Origen having received wrote in reply.

> And Africanus writes also to Aristides in which he adequately showed the harmony in the supposed dissonance between Matthew and Luke concerning the genealogy of our Savior.[2]

---

[1]Ibid., p. 105. Eusebius modified this somewhat, according to Syncellus's report, "Who also having become haughty toward the gods, when he had repented, wrote the holy book, which the Egyptians treat as a great treasure" (ibid., p. 107).

[2]Codex 34 in Photius Bibliothèque, text establ. and trans. by Renè Henry, Collection byzantine publiée sous le patronage l'Association Guillaume Budé, 2 vols. (Paris: Société d'Edition "Les Belles Lettres," 1959, 1960), 1:19, 20; Photii Bibliotheca, ed. Immanuelus Bekkerus, 2 vols. in 1 (Berlin: G. E. Reimer, 1824, 1825), 1:7a.
On the relationship of Photius, and also of the Suidas, to

Somewhat later, Africanus appears as one of the sources of

another work read by Photius:

> Vindanius Anatolius Berytus's collection of agricultural
> pursuits was read. The book was assembled by him both out of
> the paradoxa of Democritus, and of Africanus, and of Tarentinus,
> and of Apuleius, and of Florentinus, and of Valens, and of Leon,
> and of Pamphilus, and finally also out of Diophanes; and the
> book is 12 volumes.[1]

Suidas

New, though quite possibly somewhat erroneous, information is

provided by the tenth century Lexicon that bears the name "Suidas."

Under the name "Africanus" appears the following entry:

> Africanus, styled Sektos, a Libyan philosopher, who wrote
> The Kestoi in 24 books. They are a kind of natural history hav-
> ing healings [remedies?] both from words and charms [spells?]
> and writings of certain characters, and also from other (sorts
> of) operations. Against him Origen wrote submitting a rejoinder
> concerning the book of Susanna which is in Daniel.[2]

Some time later a marginal entry, based on this one, was

added: "Susanna: That against Africanus Sextus, Origen wrote

Jerome (and Eusebius), see Georg Wentzel, "Die Griechische Übersetzung der viri inlustres des Hieronymus," TU 13, no. 3 (1895): esp. pp.
1-4, and 44-46. He suggests a common source behind Photius and the
Suidas, with Photius's figure of 14 books varying only textually from
the Suidas' 24 (p. 46 [Wentzel wrote before the Oxyrhynchus Papyrus
demonstrated which was the correct figure]). Photius knew personally
only Africanus's "History" (pp. 44-45).

[1]Codex 163 (Henry, 1:163; Bekker, 1:106b-107a). The lines
"out of the paradoxa of . . ." could be construed in other ways.
Paradoxa could be taken as a personal title ("out of the Admirables
[Illustrious] Democritus, and . . ."), or as the title of a work of
only the last named individual ("out of Democritus, . . . and finally
also out of Diophanes' Paradoxa").

[2]Suidae Lexicon (ed. Adler), part 1, p. 433, line 30 to p.
434, line 3, entry no. A4647; or Suidae Lexicon, ed. Thomas Gaisford,
2 vols. (Oxford: Typographeo Academica, 1834), 1:683B.

submitting a rejoinder concerning the book of Susanna, which is in
Daniel."[1]

Georgius Cedrenus

In his <u>Synopsis historiōn</u>, which comes down to the mid-
eleventh century, Cedrenus provides a few references to Africanus.
The major one goes back to Eusebius as its basic source, though it is
somewhat confused in transmission.

In his account of the reign of Commodus, Cedrenus cites
"Africanus the Chronographer" as placing "Clement the Stromatist" in
this time, with the following clause making Origen a pupil of Clement.[2]
The next paragraph, describing the reign of Pertinax, cites Eusebius
as placing the <u>floruits</u> of Symmachus, Porphyry, and Africanus, and the
martyrdom of Leonidas, father of Origen, in this reign.[3]

---

[1]Gaisford, 2:3374B; a marginal note on p. 3373 indicates its
questionable status ("Hunc art. habet A in marg. om. V. Et male huc
illatus videtur ex. p. 683B"); it is omitted from the critical text
of Adler. It may be noted that while the original entry in MS A
still retained the form <u>Sektos</u>, the marginal annotator understood it
as <u>Sextos</u>.

[2]<u>Georgius Cedrenus Ioannis Scylitzae Ope</u>, ed. Immanuelus Bekkerus, Corpus Scriptorum Historiae Byzantinae, ed. B. G. Niebuhrius,
2 vols. (Bonn: Ed. Weber, 1838, 1839), 1:441. Such chronological mis-
placements were not unusual: two centuries earlier, Georgius Hamar-
tolos (alias Monachus), in his <u>Chronicon syntomon</u>, erred in the opposite direction, putting Africanus's <u>floruit</u> under "Maximus and
Gordian" (bk. 3, chap. 149, item 4), and, along with Clement the
Stromatist, Gregory Thaumaturgus, and the presbyter Novatus, under
Decius (bk. 3, chap. 157, item 2) (J.-P. Migne, ed., <u>Patrologiae
cursus completus . . . series Graeca</u>, 162 vols. [Paris: Garnier
Fratres, 1857-66; reprinted 1880-1904], vol. 110, cols. 545/546B,
and 551/552C, respectively. [This work is hereafter cited as <u>PG</u>.]).

[3]<u>Cedrenus</u>, ed. Bekker, 1:441. These events are all included
in Eus. <u>H.E.</u>, book 6 (chaps. 17, 19, 31, 1, resp.), but without indication of the emperor; his <u>Chronicle</u> puts Leonidas's martyrdom under

Nicephorus Callistus

This line of tradition ends as it began--with Eusebius. The
fourteenth century Ecclesiastical History of Nicephorus presents Africanus in book 5, chapter 21, a slight rearrangement and re-working of
Eusebius H.E. 6. 31 (compare also Nicephorus 1. 11 and Eusebius 1. 7).
He includes the reference to the Kestoi, "And he, being also the author
of the books entitled Kestoi, sent an offhand letter to Origen,"[1] but
gives it less prominence, having moved the references to the Chronography and to Heracles to a position before it.

Syriac Ecclesiastical Sources

In the East, a somewhat different line of tradition was being
maintained or developed. This view presented Africanus as a biblical
commentator and bishop (of Emmaus). Possible origins of these views
are noted in the discussions below.

This line of tradition relates only indirectly to the question
of Africanus, the Kestoi, and magic, as stressing the Christian aspect
of his life and writings, and ignoring the secular side (from which
the questions arose).

Septimius and discusses Africanus under Caracalla.
    Earlier in his work Cedrenus had cited Africanus's opinion
regarding the interpretation of the first day of creation (Bekker,
1:7). Other items (e.g., the description of the Dead Sea) are probably to be traced to Africanus's Chronography (cf., e.g., the verbal
agreement of the account regarding the Dead Sea [Bekker, 1:51] with
that of Syncellus [Dindorfius, 1:188-189]), but are not identified
as such by Cedrenus.

    [1]Nicephorus Callistus Xanthopulus Ecclesiasticae historiae
5. 21, in PG 145: col. 1109C.

Moses Bar-Cepha

According to Assemani's summary, among the sources of the
first part of the De paradiso commentarius ad Ignatium of Moses Bar-
Cepha (died A.D. 913) was "Julius Commentar. in Evangelium Joannis."[1]
Assemani attempts to clarify this by reference to the testimony of
Ebed-Jesu and Bar-hebraeus.[2]

Bar Ṣalibi

Dionysius Jacobus bar Ṣalibi (died 1171), bishop of Amida,
provides a further testimony to knowledge of Africanus in the East.
In his commentary on Matthew, he cites Africanus in the discussion
of 1:15 and 17, on the genealogies, and of 17:9, on the appearance
of Moses on the Mount of Transfiguration. In the discussion of 1:17,
Africanus is listed (in the introductory paragraph but not in the
following discussion) along with Eusebius in contrast to various other
(possibly Syriac) sources.[3] The source of the comments on the first
two passages (1:15 and 17) is clearly the letter to Aristides, that
for the third (17:9) is possibly the Chronography.[4] In all cases,

_____

[1]Joseph Simonius Assemani, Bibliotheca Orientalis Clementino-
Vaticana, 3 vols. in 4 (Rome: Typis Sacrae Congregationis De Propa-
ganda Fide, 1719-28), 2 (1721): 129.

[2]On both of these men, see below (esp. p. 26, n.2, re the latter).

[3]Dionysii bar Ṣalibi Commentarii in evangelica, trans. I.
Sedlacek, aided by I.-B. Chabot, vol. 1, Corpus Scriptorum Christian-
orum Orientalium, ed. I.-B. Chabot, et al., Scriptores Syri, Versio,
series secunda, tomus 98 (Rome: Karolus de Luigi, 1906; Leipzig: Otto
Harrassowitz, 1906), pp. 37, 44, 289. On 1:17 see also Assemani,
Bibl. Or., 2:161-62.

[4]See below, p. 28, with n. 1, for a related Syriac item attributed to the "Scholia on the Gospel of Matthew" by Africanus.

bar Ṣalibi refers to the writer simply as Africanus.[1]

Bar-Hebraeus

Gregory Abu'l Faraj, called Bar-Hebraeus, a learned Syriac
scholar and ecclesiastic of the thirteenth century, utilized the work
of Africanus of Emmaus[2] (and also of Pope Julius[3]), among many others,
in his commentary on the Holy Scriptures the Syriac title of which is
Latinized as Horreum mysteriorum (The Granary of Mysteries). In two
chronologies also attributed to him, the Chronicon Arabicum (or Liber
Dynastiarum) and the Chronicon Syriacum, Africanus is used; in the

---

[1]Assemani, however, probably as a carry-over from his study
of later Syriac writers (esp. Ebed Jesu) and the views of scholars of
his own time (cf. his discussions of the sources of Bar-Cepha, 2:129),
refers to bar Ṣalibi's sources as including "Africanus Episcopus Emmaus Comment. in Evangel." (2:158). For this reason bar Ṣalibi is
frequently cited (usually with a reference to Assemani, as e.g., by
Vieillefond, Les Cestes, p. 22, n. 23 [the point is emphasized by an
attempt to explain the origin of bar Ṣalibi's error]) as one of the
Syriac writers who make Africanus a bishop. It is, however, Assemani,
not bar Ṣalibi, speaking at this point.

[2]Wilmot Eardley W. Carr, trans. and ed., Gregory Abu'l Faraj
Commonly Called Bar-Hebraeus, Commentary on the Gospels from the Horreum Mysteriorum (London: SPCK, 1925), pp. liii, and 6. The references to Africanus occur in discussions of Matthew's genealogy of
Christ (pp. 6, 102, 103, 105), and, at one point, Africanus is referred to as "a compiler of genealogies" (p. 102). The last three
references seem clearly to be from the letter to Aristides; the first,
which concerns the omission of the names of Ahaziah, Joash, and Ama-
ziah by Matthew, could well be from a lost portion of the letter (or
from the Chronography).

[3]Assemani, Bibl. Or., 2:283. Though he lists both, Assemani
does not take sufficient cognizance of the fact, and elsewhere wonders
whether Gregory does not cite the one writer as both Africanus and
Julius in various passages of the Horreum (2:129, while discussing
"Julius Commentar. in Evangelium Joannis" which he finds as a source
of Bar-Cepha's de paradiso).

latter, Africanus (according to the evaluation of Assemani) is "often (saepe)" favorably cited.[1]

Ebed Jesu

This line of tradition reaches its climax in the Catalogus librorum omnium ecclesiasticorum of Ebed Jesu. Chapter 6, between the chapters on Clement of Rome and on Hippolytus, presents "Africanus Episcopus Emmaus," saying: "The blessed Africanus, Bishop of Emmaus, has a commentary on the New Testament, and a Chronicle."[2]

Summary

The two peculiar features of this line of tradition are the identification of Africanus as a bishop and the attribution of a New Testament commentary to him. Gelzer speculates that the former may derive from Eusebius's reference to him as proïstamenos,[3] though it is

---

[1] Bibl. Or., 2:310, 313.

[2] Ibid., 3, part 1 (1725):14; cf. Jo. Albertus Fabricius, Bibliotheca Graeca, sive notitia scriptorum veterum Graecorum, 3d ed., 14 vols. (Hamburg: Christian Liebezeit, and Theodor. Christoph. Felginer, 1718-28), 5 (1723):270 (=Fabricius-Harles, 4th ed., 4 [1795]: 245; = PG 10:42D).

[3] Gelzer, Sextus, 1:10, re Eusebius Chronik, an Abr. 2237, via Chronicon paschale, ed. Dindorf (1:499.6). It may be noted, however, that the Latin compiler or translator of pseudo-Abdias (an Easterner?) makes Africanus, the alleged translator of the work, a bishop in one reference (Gelzer, Sextus, 1:18, and note 5). Another source of the idea may be confusion with the "Julius Episcopus" who appears at least once in the catena on John, at 17:5 (see Balthasar Corderius, Catena patrum Graecorum in sanctum Joannem [Antwerp: Ex Officina Plantiniana Balthasaris Moreti, 1630], p. 409). Assemani, in discussing Bar-Cepha, identifies this catena item as from the supposed "Julius Commentar. in Evangelium Joannis" which he postulates as one of Africanus's works (2:129); Gelzer suggests it as a scribal error for Julianus (i.e., of Halicarnassus) (1:18). Since, however, the passage and quotation involved (John 17:5) deal with the relationship of the persons

sometimes supported by Origen's addressing him as "Brother," in his

reply to the letter concerning Susanna. The supposition of a New

Testament commentary is probably based on an incorrect deduction

from the prominent citation of Africanus in other commentaries, i.e.,

at Matthew 1 (and on a few other passages besides). Similar to this

supposition of a commentary by Africanus, is the attribution of a

Scholia on Matthew's Gospel to him.[1]

---

of the Godhead, could this not perhaps be from one of the writings of
Julius I, of Rome? He was, after all, deeply concerned with this very
question (note also the appearance of "Julius Paps" among the sources
of Bar-Hebraeus [Assemani, Bibl. Or., 2:283; see above, p. 26, with
n. 3]).

   [1]E.g., a chapter, "Concerning the appearance of Moses and
Elias to our Lord in the mountain; from Africanus's scholia which he
composed on Mátthew's Gospel," first published by Joannes Baptista
Pitra, Analecta sacra spicilegio Solesmensi, 8 vols. (various places,
1876-91; 1st ed., 4 vols., 1876-84, republished, Farnborough, Hants.,
England: Gregg Press Ltd., 1966), 2 (Typis Tusculanis, 1884): 292, in
a Latin translation communicated to him by P. Martin (as from "cod.
Syriaco 15155 Musei Britannici, fol. 56 a tergo col. 2"); it was republished in vol. 4 (Paris: Ex Publica Galliarum Typographeo, 1883),
with both the Syriac text ("ex codice additionali Musaei Britannici
12155, fol. 56 v? col. 2") (p. 71) and a new Latin translation (p.
337).
   In the West, Africanus was utilized in various Greek catenae
and scholia. Pitra published, immediately following the Syriac item
just noted, an example of the latter (2:292; from codex Coislinianus
276, fol. 162, from a collectanea by John, an unknown seventh century
monk [concerning Manasseh's repentance and escape]; cf. Martin Joseph
Routh, Reliquiae sacrae, editio altera, 5 vols. [Oxford: E Typographeo
Academico, 1846-48], 2:288, Afr. Chron., frag. XL). As an example
of the use in the catenae, see: Spyr. P. Lambros, Catalogue of Greek
Manuscripts on Mount Athos, 2 vols. (Cambridge: University Press,
1895, 1900), 2:99 re the contents of the Iviron MS 371; or, Petrus
Lambecius, Commentariorum de Augustissima Bibliotheca Caesarea
Vindobonensi, 8 vols., ed. Adamus Franciscus Kollarius (Vienna: Joan.
Thomae Nob. de Trattnern, 1766-82), vol. 3, cols. 163-68, re codex
Th. Gr. XLII (note esp. cols. 164-65 and 167); both of these are examples of catenae on Luke.
   These, and other such items that I have seen, relate to areas
of the Bible that are prominent among the surviving fragments of Africanus's known works; thus, they do not require the postulating of any
other, lost, writing of Africanus, either commentary or scholia.

Secular Sources

A third line of evidence, mainly Greek, though sometimes represented by translations into other languages, presents a different
view of Africanus. Of these, the authentic fragments found in the
various Byzantine collections of military and veterinary writers form
the main basis of the surviving fragments of the Kestoi, and are
dealt with extensively in the following chapters. They are therefore
presented rather summarily here.

Fulgentius

In the middle of the sixth century, in the West, a different
type of reference to Africanus appears in our sources. Fulgentius,
in his Mythology, book 3, chapter 7, dealing with the fable of Peleus
and Thetis, in the latter part of the chapter, refers to the dipping
of Achilles by Thetis. In discussing the significance of his being
grasped by the heel, Fulgentius relates this to the fact that the
vein from the heel and toe runs to the kidney, thigh, and male organs.
In support of this, he cites an Africanus "hiatrosofistes": "For
also a stimulating [aphrodisiac?] plaster which Africanus the professor of medicine called stisidem, he prescribed applying to the big
toe and heel."[1]

Agricultural and veterinary writers

Photius, discussed above, in his second item listed there,

---

[1] Fabii Planciadis Fulgentii V. C. Opera . . . , ed. Rudolf
Helm (Leipzig: B. G. Teubner, 1898), p. 71. In the textual notes,
the editor suggests that "stisidem" may relate to the Greek stȳo.

refers to Africanus's <u>paradoxa</u> (?) as a source used by Vindonius
Anatolius Berytus. His work, in turn, was one of the principal
sources of the Byzantine compilation commonly known as the <u>Geoponica</u>,
in which the name of Africanus figures in the listing of sources,
both at the beginning of the work and in the headings of certain individual chapters. Africanus's name turns up similarly in certain
forms of the Byzantine veterinary collection known today as the <u>Hip-</u>
<u>piatrica Graece</u>, with some slight overlap with the <u>Geoponica</u>. There
are, however, textual problems which raise questions as to the antiquity and authenticity of the specific attributions in both collections, especially those in the <u>Geoponica</u>.[1] In both works, Africanus's
name is usually connected with some of the more bizarre or questionable remedies and procedures.

Suidas

On Suidas, see the discussion above, under "Greek and Related
Ecclesiastical Sources."

Military collections

The Byzantine military collections contain, as part of their
tactical sections, a number of chapters attributed to Africanus.
Vieillefond[2] and, especially, Alphonse Dain[3] have thrown light on the

---

[1]Note the discussions of these collections later in this chapter.

[2]<u>Jules Africain</u>, pp. xxxvi-xli; "Adaptations et paraphrases du
Commentaire d'Enée le Tacticien," <u>Revue de philologie, de litterature
et d'histoire anciennes</u>, 3rd series, 6 (58 of the collection; 1932):
24-36; <u>Les Cestes</u>, pp. 77-83, 189-98.

[3]<u>La "Tactique" de Nicephore Ouranos</u> (Paris: Société d'Edition
"Les Belles Lettres," 1937); <u>Sylloge Tacticorum, quae olim "Inedita</u>

lines of descent and interrelationships of the varying collections.

The chapters involved here make up the bulk of the material traceable

to the Kestoi, and, indeed, is so attributed (specifically to Kestos

7)[1] in some of the manuscripts.

Psellus

In the eleventh century, Michael Psellus, in his "Concerning

paradoxical readings," devotes a considerable proportion of his space

to a summary of the curiosities dealt with by Africanus in his Kestoi.

Because of the length of the passage, and since the full text is given

below (in Chapter II), only a selection of lines is given here to il-

lustrate Psellus's views:

> God and nature produce conception, as I indeed believe, but
> Africanus says that generation is a kind of craft, and one will
> beget in a craftsmanlike manner, if the man . . . , a secret
> charm . . . antipathies . . . paradox . . . paradoxes . . . by
> certain charms and enchantments . . . craftsmanlike, or rather
> sorcerous . . . and various other such like things this man in
> his Kestoi tells as marvels and recounts in detail.[2]

Summary

These three lines of tradition overlap, but each has distinc-

tive features corresponding to the nature of the interests of the

writers in it. The first line discussed, the Greek ecclesiastical,

---

Leonis Tactica" dicebatur (Paris: Société d'Edition "Les Belles Lettres," 1938.
Le "Corpus Perditum" (Paris: L'Auteur, 1939); also various periodical
articles and other works.

[1] Vieillefond, Jules Africain, pp. xxxiv-xxxvi.

[2] Antonius Westermann, ΠΑΡΑΔΟΞΟΓΡΑΦΟΙ--Scriptores rerum
mirabilium Graeci (Braunschweig: Georgius Westermann, 1839; London:
Black & Armstrong, 1839), pages (and lines) 143.14-144.2; 144.16-17,
20, 22; 145.3, 14, 17-18; 146.12-13.

deals largely with the ecclesiastical writings of Africanus, but in the interest of completeness keeps alive the knowledge of the existence of the Kestoi, though with varying degrees of evidence of personal knowledge of it. The second line, the Syriac ecclesiastical, is solely concerned with Africanus's ecclesiastical writings, and, as noted above, enlarges his ties with the church and the scope of his religious writings, but betray no knowledge of the Kestoi. On the other side of the ledger, the third line is concerned exclusively with Africanus's secular work, the Kestoi, and even more exclusively, with specialized areas of information within it. The exceptions are the work of Photius, and the Suidas, which provide links between the two major interests shown by lines one and three.

Of these three lines of tradition, the first seems to be the most useful, as being, relatively, the most complete and accurate, but it is unbalanced without the evidence of the third line. The second line appears to have little of value to contribute to a knowledge or understanding of Africanus, apart from providing some fragments of his letter to Aristides or of the Chronography.

Early Studies

The references to Africanus by Eusebius and other early writers have kept his name before the literate world, and the variety of items drawn from his writings which appeared in Greek manuscripts known or reported added to the intrigue of the subject. Thus there was (and is) a perennial, though fluctuating, interest in Africanus and his affairs. This was fed by the persistent hope that "soon" the world would have a complete publication of his works, gathered from all the various sources.[1] Meanwhile, those who, for whatever reason, came into contact with the question, did their best to illuminate the matter, either by publication of fragments, or by speculation. The latter approach was the most common.

Sixteenth to Eighteenth Centuries

In the early centuries, these references, of whatever sort, were all incidental to, or just a small part of, some more important or larger task.

The first printed references to Africanus

The incidental nature of the references to Africanus are well illustrated by the references to him in his first century in print. (These early references usually involved publication of fragments, or summaries of parts, of the _Kestoi_.)

Possibly the first appearance of the name of Africanus in print is, appropriately enough, in a work entitled _Miscellaneorum centuria prima_.[2] In chapter 15, concerning the Sybarites, Politian gives in Latin translation a passage cited from Africanus _in Cestis_ (= the first paragraph of I. 11 in Vieillefond's editions of Africanus).

---

[1] This hope, though now considerably advanced by the work of Vieillefond, still remains unfulfilled in its entirety.

[2] Angelus Politianus (Florence, 1489); reference to this first edition from Vieillefond, _Jules Africain_, p. xxv, n. 2; the earliest edition available to me was the _Omnium Angeli Politiano operum_ (2 vols. in 1 [Paris: I. Badius Ascensius, 1512]).

About a quarter century later, Calvus de Ravenna published
a Latin translation of a tract, De ponderibus et mensuris, attributed
to Aphricanus medicus,[1] which seems to be from the Kestoi. (This
tractate was the object of frequent reference or citation of lines or
isolated items in the following period.) Shortly thereafter, in 1530,
Africanus's name appears, apparently falsely, in connection with certain added chapters in a Latin translation of the Hippiatrica by
Joannes Ruelle. It was included by Grynaeus, in 1537, with a publication of the Greek text in which the name of Africanus appears only
at the beginning, in the list of authors used in the collection.[2]

About a quarter century later, Calvus de Ravenna published

Almost at the end of this first century, Joannes Lang published his Latin translation, with notes, of Nicephorus's Ecclesiastical History. In the marginal note on the mention of the Kestoi in
5. 21, Lang referred to the Suidas article on Africanus with no indication of any question regarding the ascription.[3]

Developing theories: Suggestions of
multiple authorship

The simple acceptance and publication of items attributed to
the Kestoi continued in the next century as well, but along with this

---

[1]M. Fabius Calvus Rhavennatis, Hippocratis Coi, octoginta
volumina (Rome, 1525), p. 697 (also, Basel, 1526, p. 471), cited in
Fridericus Hultsch, Metrologicorum scriptorum reliquiae, 2 vols.
(Leipzig: B. G. Teubner, 1864, 1866), 2:14, with nn.1 and 2.

[2]Veterinariae medicina libri II (Basle); on this edition and
the sources of the chapters attributed to Africanus, see Vieillefond,
Les Cestes, pp. 215, 216, and esp. n. 3.

[3]Nicephori Callisti Xanthopuli: Scriptoris vere Catholici,
Ecclesiasticae historiae libri decem et octo, ed. and trans. Joannes
Lang (Frankfurt: Impensis Sigismundi Feyerabendii, 1588), p. 250.

approach appeared a greater attention to questions relating to Africanus and his writings. This resulted in the presentation of suggestions on various points, the foremost suggestion being that there
was more than one Africanus involved.

Isaac Casaubon, in his Commentary on Suetonius, used a passage
concerning lanterns for night-fighting, [then] attributed to Africanus[1]
whose "elegantissimum librum de bellico apparatu" had not yet been
published. He concluded the reference by stating his intention, D.V.,
of carefully considering elsewhere the writings of Africanus "and
whether those mentioned by the ancients under Africanus's name, were
of one writer or many."[2] (This is perhaps the first of many such
declarations of intent which followed over the next centuries.)

In the same year as Casaubon's question, a brief, but decided,
answer was published. Joseph Justus Scaliger, in explicit opposition

---

[1]Cited as chapter 70 (=69 in the Thevenot-Boivin edition, to
be presented below), one of a section of chapters which scholars from
Boivin to the present reject as non-Africanian.

[2]Originally, Geneva, 1595; republished in C. Suetonii Tranquilli opera, Textu ad Codd. MSS. recognito cum Jo. Aug. Ernestii anim-
adversionibus nova cura auctis emendatisque et Isaac Casauboni Com-
mentario, ed. Frid. Aug. Wolfius, 4 vols. (Leipzig: Impensis Casp.
Fritsch., 1802), 3:141, in "Julius Caesar," cap. 31, on the line "cum
luminibus exstinctis decessisset via." Casaubon notes that Politian
had referred to this work as the Cestes in accord with an old codex
in the royal library, but that his own codex (purchased from Darmarius!)
calls it Polemon paraskeuai. Casaubon did return to the subject of
Africanus, but not to solve the basic problem (Aeneae vetustissimi
scriptoris Commentarius tacticus et obsidionalis quomodo obsessum
resistere oporteat ... recensuit publicavit et notis illustravit
[orig. publ., Paris, 1609], republished as pages 387-600 of vol. 3
of: Polybii Lycortae F. Historiarum quae supersunt, 3 vols.
[Leipzig and Venice: Ioann. Paul. Krausium, 1763-64], 3 [1763]: 389,
393, and 493-550 passim). (Concerning Darmarius, see Vieillefond,
Les Cestes, p. 29, continuation of n. 31.)

to the testimony of Photius, Eusebius, and Suidas, denied the possi-

bility of a unity of authorship: the author of the Kestoi should have

been Sextus Africanus (Photius erred on this point, as Suidas erred

in making Sextus the author of the Chronographia and the letter to

Origen).[1]

     It was over a half-century later before this idea was accepted

in print by another writer;[2] in the meantime, the idea was either re-

jected or ignored. Gerard Jan Voss praised Scaliger's work on the

Chronography, but questioned the distinction of authorship.[3] Denis

Petau (Petavius) also rejected Scaliger's suggestion, at one point

even confusing the Kestoi with the Chronography.[4] A few years later,

Gabriel Naude included a paragraph of summary of military chapters

from the Kestoi (from what he believed to be the fifth and sixth

---

[1]Thesaurus temporum Eusebii Pamphili Caesareae Palestinae epis-
copi chronicorum canonum (Leiden: Thomas Basson, 1606; also, reprinted,
Osnabrück, Zeller, 1968), part 2, "Animadversiones in chronologica
Eusebii," p. 212b.

[2]Robert Cardinal Bellarmin, however, omitted any reference to
the Kestoi from his summary of Africanus's writings in his De scriptoribus ecclesiasticis, liber unus (Coloniae Agrippinae: I. Kalcovii,
1645 [orig. publ. 1613]), pp. 53–54.

[3]De historicis Graecis liber IV, editio altera (Leiden: Ex
Officinâ Joannis Maire, 1651 [orig. publ. 1624],), p. 237 (book 2,
chap. 15).

[4]Opus de doctrina temporum, 3 vols. (Antwerp: Georgius Gallet,
1703 [vols. 1 and 2 orig. publ. Paris, 1627; vol. 3 orig. publ. separately as Uranologium sive systema variorum auctorum . . . variarum
dissertationum libri VIII, 1630]), 2:275 (book 12, chap. 40), with
correction, 3:156 (book 8, chap. 2). The correction gives the original statement as book 12, chap. 42, as does Fabricius, Bibl. Gr.,
3d ed., 2:598 (but correctly as 12, 40, in 5:269). The confusion of
works was due to a misreading of Photius, missing the parenthetical
nature of the reference to the Kestoi.

books) in his <u>Syntagma de studio militari</u>,[1] while Saumaise (Salmasius)
cited various passages from Africanus much in the manner of the preceding century. The citations were from both the <u>Kestoi</u> and the
<u>Chronography</u>;[2] in the first instance Saumaise identifies the author
as Julius Africanus, elsewhere referring to him simply as Africanus.
In another context, Saumaise joined Causabon as identifying the <u>De
bellico apparatu</u>, extant in manuscripts but then still unpublished,
as being part of the <u>Kestoi</u>.[3] The same year as Saumaise's <u>Exercita-
tiones</u>, Miraeus, in his comments on Jerome's "De scriptoris ecclesiasticis," chap. 63, accepted the <u>Kestoi</u> as Africanian. He further
suggested that the name came either "à deae illius fabulosae baltheo,"
or "à pugilum armis."[4]

Support for part of Scaliger's theory came finally in the notes
by Henry Valois to his 1659 edition and translation of Eusebius's

[1](Rome, 1637), book 2, chap. 4, sec. 8, pp. 520-21, cited
in Vieillefond, <u>Les Cestes</u>, p. 84, n. 12. For the identification as
the fifth and sixth books, see Fabricius-Harles, <u>Bibl. Gr.</u>, 4th ed.,
4:241 (=Migne, <u>PG</u>, 10, col. 38), where the reference in Naude is
given as 2, <u>8</u>, cap. 8, p. 520.

[2]Claude Saumaise, <u>Plinianae exercitationes in Caii Julii
Solini Polyhistora</u> (Trajecti ad Rhenum: Johannem vande Water, 1689
[orig. publ., Paris, 1629], 1:163bB, 327bB, 417aG; 2:689aF, 847aB,
867aF, 872aE. The first five items are from the fragment, <u>peri metron</u>,
cited either by that designation or some variant of it, or simply as
from Africanus (in the fifth instance, 2:847aB, the designation is
more full, being "Africanus in Cestis, capite <u>peri metron kai sathmon</u>
[sic]"). The last two references, from the <u>Chronography</u>, relate to
the successors of Belus in Babylon.

[3]Epist. 123 ad Isaacum Vossium; see Fabricius, <u>Bibl. Gr.</u>,
3rd ed., 5(1723):270.

[4]Aubertus Miraeus, <u>Bibliotheca ecclesiastica sive nomenclatores VII. veteres</u> (Antwerp: Apud Jacobum Mesium, 1639), p. 21.

Ecclesiastical History.[1] He would delete the words, "the writer of
the work titled Kestoi" from Euseb. H.E. 6. 31, because they are not
mentioned by Rufinus or Jerome, because it is ridiculous in dealing
with a church writer to mention first a work of such a nature as
Suidas and Syncellus show the Kestoi to be (and the very title "à
Veneris cesto ita dicti"[2] confirms this character), and finally, because the backgrounds of the writers appear to be different: Africanus
Chronographus (called Julius Africanus by Scaliger) was from Palestine (from Emmaus, specifically) and was a Christian, while Africanus
Cestus (incorrectly called Sextus Africanus by Scaliger) was from
Libya (as Suidas testifies) and was a "Gentile" (as the topic of his
book sufficiently shows). In regard to the name of the latter writer,
Scaliger erred in interpreting Suidas's sektos as Sextus; it should
be emended to Kestos as a designation of Africanus just as Clement was
called Stromateus. Further, Valois concluded, there was another
Julius Africanus, author of the De bellico apparatu known to him from
a manuscript in the royal library and by Politian's citation. Valois
assumes that it was a Greek custom to call such works of diverse content Kestoi, from its meaning of variegated girdle, just as Clement's

---

[1] Eusebii Pamphili ecclesiasticae historiae libri decem (Paris:
A. Vitré, 1659), "Annotationes in Historiam Ecclesiasticam Eusebii
Caesariensis," p. 127, cols. 1D-2B. H.E. 6. 31 appears on p. 230 of
the text section; text and "annotations" are numbered separately.

[2] Valois adds the explanation, "eo quod amatoria praecipuè
complecterentur," an explanation not usually repeated by those who
echoed the preceding dictum.

work was called Stromateis. The suggestion of a third Africanus
found few, if any, supporters, but his other points have been adopted
in varying combinations by later scholars down to the present. Especially frequently repeated were the derivation of the name Kestoi
"à veneris cesto," the points of distinction between Africanus Chronographus and Africanus Cestus, and the emendation of the Suidas's
sektos to kestos.

The next year Philip Labbe made a similar suggestion concerning
a Sektos-Kestos metathesis. But in the addenda to his work, after due
consideration, he rejected Valesius's other suggestions on the basis
of the ancient testimonies. He further suggested there that the title,
tōn Kestōn, is likely in aemulatione of Clement's tōn Strōmateōn.[1]

Peter Lambeck (Lambecius) noted the idea of a metathesis as
part of a process of piling error on error following the original "care-
less and absurd" change of the praenomen Sextos to the false cognomen
Sektos.[2] Thus Lambeck favored Scaliger's original suggestion concerning
this name, but at the same time rejected the distinction of authors
and specifically rejected Valois's arguments on this point, calling
attention to the fact that Eusebius only says he was an ambassador
for Emmaus, not that it was his patria, and that the magia naturalis

---

[1]Phil. Labbe, Dissertationes philologicae de scriptoribus
ecclesiasticis quos attigit Eminentiss. S. R. E. Card. Robertus
Bellarminus, 2 vols. (Paris: Sebastian Cramoisy, 1660), 1:659, 830.

[2]Lambeck-Kollar, Commentarium, 7: col. 427, also col. 428,
with note 2 (re cod. Gr. Phil. MS CXI, part 4, containing the de re
militari from the Cestus). (Lambeck's first edition appeared 1665-
79; see Vieillefond, Les Cestes, p. 312, n. 4.)

in the _Cestoi_ shows that he was a Gentile.[1] Lambeck also argued that

the _Kestoi_ contained only nine books, Photius's 14 (ιδ΄) being an

easy corruption from 9 (θ΄), from which Suidas's 24 was a further de-

velopment of the error.[2] Later in the same volume Lambeck included

the text of Michael Psellus's resume of part of the _Kestoi_.[3]

Johann Rudolf Wettstein, in his edition of Origen's works,

dealt with the question in connection with Africanus's letter to

Origen. After considering the ancient references and the views of

Scaliger and Valois, he was "inclined to believe, with Lambeck, that

Sextus Julius Africanus was that one and celebrated writer rather

than two."[4] He judged Rufinus's omission of reference to the _Kestoi_

as explainable, Rufinus may have either questioned the fact, or he may

have judged the work unworthy of Africanus.[5] Wettstein himself adds a

conjecture in an attempt to reconcile the statements of Syncellus

---

[1]Lambeck-Kollar, _Commentarium_, 7: col. 429.

[2]Ibid., cols. 426-27; cf. also the index entry for _Sexti Julii Africani_, col. 637, where the work is called _Enneabiblo_. In the same entry the title is described as "metaphora a variegato Veneris cingulo desumpta," similarly to Valois's statement.

[3]Lambeck-Kollar, _Commentarium_, 7: cols. 476-78 (= 1st ed., vol. 7, cols. 222ff). In earlier volumes, he also notes manuscripts containing other of Africanus's works (1:254-55; 3:103, 167, 202; and, on 5:623-24, the falsely ascribed "_Narratio . . . in Perside_").

[4]_Origenis dialogus contra Marcionitas, sive De recta in Deum fide: Exhortatio ad martyrum: Responsum ad Africani epistolam de historia Susannae . . . additis notis . . ._ (Basel: J. Bertschius, 1674), "Notae," cols. 149-54. It might be noted that he uses Scaliger's reconstruction for Eusebius's _Chronicon_ and thus falsely credits some items to Eusebius; e.g., Syncellus's statement regarding Emmaus and the _Kestoi_ is credited to Eusebius "_in Chronicis pag. 70_" (=Scaliger, _Thes. temp._ 1, Greek section, p. 70) (col. 151).

[5]Wettstein, _Origenis_, "Notae," col. 152.

(credited also to Eusebius, see preceding note), that Africanus's embassy was to Alexander, and of Eusebius in "Chron. Can. p. 204" (i.e., of Scaliger, Thes. temp., 1, Greek section), followed by Jerome, etc., that the embassy was under Elagabalus. He proposes,

> What if that Africanus undertook two successive legations, first to Elagabalus to obtain the building of the city, then to Alexander to give as thanks for benefit received the presentation of the book [the Kestoi], and to ask other benefits? This certainly easily reconciles Eusebius with himself and with the others.[1]

Isaac Voss continued and sharpened the views of his father. After a discussion of the alleged epistle of Hadrian to Servianus (occasioned by a reference to Serapis in a poem of Catullus), he concludes that there is no reason to make three Africani of one. The writer of the Chronography, the Kestoi, and the strategika are the same (indeed, extant fragments of the last constitute the sixth and seventh books of the Kestoi), but he was a Syrian of Emmaus, not a Libyan (a mistake, due to his name Africanus). The Kestoi is named à cesto Veneris and this fits its contents, but nothing hinders Africanus from being a Christian. The reported contents of the Kestoi and the Ad Servianum illuminate each other: many Christians were addicted to magic arts, nativities, etc. In sum, persons mentioned, age, patria, and the ancient testimonies, all confirm his identity.[2]

---

[1]Ibid., col. 153; see also the end of col. 151 and top of 152. Scaliger had attempted to solve the problem (compounded by his failure to clearly distinguish Syncellus's testimony from Eusebius's), by charging Eusebius with error (Thes. temp., 2: "Animadversiones,"p. 212), the year of the end of the Chronography and of the embassy was the third year of Elagabalus.

[2]Isaac Vossius, Cajus Valerius Catullus: Observationes (London: Isaac Littlebury, 1684), p. 30. Some years earlier, in Justini historiarum ex Trogo Pompeio lib. XLIV (Amsterdam: Ex Officina Elzeviriana,

About the same time, Ducange presented a variation on this

view: if the _Kestoi_ was indeed dedicated to a pagan prince, its

pagan character, with no Christian marks, is little surprise.[1]

Collections and descriptions: More theories

William Cave presented a new theory, but then wavered. He

surveyed the information available about Africanus's writings, includ-

ing the various theories regarding the _Kestoi_, and asked if there was

not a middle way, "the work of our Africanus, but from before he em-

braced the Christian faith?"[2] After actually becoming acquainted with

the texts, in Thevenot's edition (see next paragraph), he doubted its

derivation from _Africani nostri_; it seemed more recent (but he later

dropped this suggestion).[3]

Meanwhile, the year before Cave's first volume was published

in Geneva, a large portion of the extant text of the _Kestoi_ was

---

1664), p. 305 (book 2, chap. 10), he had referred to a supposed chapter of
Africanus (chap. 54, _peri kryphias epistolōn_, actually from Aeneas).

[1]Carolus du Fresne, D. du Cange, ed. and trans., ΠΑΣΧΑΛΙΟΝ
seu Chronicon paschale (Paris: Typographia Regia, 1688), p. 537b.
Ducange's notes are also reprinted in Dindorf's edition of the
Chronicon paschale (2:331 for this note).

[2]Guilielmo Cave, _Scriptorum ecclesiasticorum historia literaria_
(Geneva: Samuel de Tournes, 1694), p. 54. Though this is a later
edition, at least this part of the text must be the same as the original
London edition of 1688-89, for Cave knows of the _Kestoi_ only in manuscripts in the library of Isaac Vossius and elsewhere.

[3]_Scriptorum ecclesiasticorum historia literaria_, pars altera
(Geneva: Fratres de Tournes, 1699), p. 29; omitted from the combined
discussion in later editions (Oxford: Sheldon, 1740-43; Basel: Joh.
Rudolph. Im-Hoff., 1741, 1745), 1:112. (But these later editions do
introduce the Syrian line of tradition, adding a reference to Hebediesu
and making Africanus a city bishop [1:110].)

published, as part of a larger production, by Thevenot.[1] Included

was a judicious set of notes on the Kestoi section by Joannes Boivin.[2]

Boivin briefly stated the problem, tending to favor the identity of

authorship. He based this largely on the acceptance of the ascrip-

tion to Africanus of Geoponica 7 [i.e., 7. 14] which contains a line

from Holy Scriptures (Ps. 34:8). Though tending to favor authorship

by a single Africanus, he suggested that the author was not entirely

orthodox: he was condemned Gelasio papa (= a late addition to the

Decretum Gelasianum), and even the Chronology (sic) had not been trans-

mitted integram by the ancients. Further, in the notes on Pasithea,

etc. (=Vieillefond, I. 17), he considers that the author could not

yet have been a Christian when he wrote this and similar things.[3]

Boivin also suggested good reasons to believe that, at most, 44 of the

77 chapters published actually came from the Kestoi, several having

been added from Aeneas and other, later, sources.[4]

The same year, Dupin, who knew that the Kestoi cited by Poli-

tian was "lately published," denied that it was the same as Photius

described; and, in any case, he simply repeated the main points of

Valesius as his view.[5]

---

[1]Melchisedech Thevenot, ed., Veterum mathematicorum . . .
opera (Paris: Typographia Regia, 1693), pp. 275-316 (280-89 were
omitted in the page numeration).

[2]Ibid., pp. 339-60.   [3]Ibid., pp. 339, 340, 348-49.

[4]Ibid., pp. 339, 353-55 (chs. 38, 45, 46, and 48-59), and 357.

[5]L. Ellies du Pin, Nouvelle bibliotheque des auteurs eccles-
tiques, 3d corr. and rev. ed., 21 vols. (Paris: Chez André Prallard
1693-1715), 1:117, and note g.

Tillemont took Dupin's word on the difference between the works known to Politian and to Photius, but otherwise his conclusion (as much as he came to one) was more like Cave's: the Kestoi must have been written while Africanus was a pagan, though that eliminated the possibility of its dedication to Alexander Severus.[1]

Fabricius's massive and ever-growing Bibliotheca Graeca provided a complete survey of the literature to his day (including many manuscripts).[2] For his own part, he could not accept Valois's and Labbe's suggestion to change the name from Sextus, nor Scaliger's and Valois's suggestions of other Africani,[3] but he did believe that Africanus was a Syrian of Emmaus.[4] The evidence was too little to allow a good judgment on Africanus's Christian status, but there were many Christian sects involved in various types of superstition, and the Psalms quotation in Geoponica 14. 5 (sic) supports his status as a Christian.[5]

---

[1] [Sebastian] Lenain de Tillemont, Memoires pour servir a l'histoire ecclesiastiques des six premiers siecles, 16 vols. (Paris: Charles Robustel, 1693-1712), 1:682-83 (the main discussion of Africanus is on pp. 254-58, but the discussion of the Kestoi was banished to the notes at the end of the volume).

[2] First edition, 1705-28, but with the 2nd and 3d eds. overtaking it (3d ed., 1718-28); 2 (2nd ed.?, 1716): 572, 595-600 (=Lib. III, caps. 23,24. 7-9); 5 (1723): 268-71 (Lib. V, cap. 1. 3), and some minor references at 3:213 (IV. 5. 20); 5:222 (V. 1. 26); 6:112 (V. 4. 28); 7:765, 787 (V. 17. 10); 9:386 (V. 38. 9); 12:775 (VI. 8. 4); 13:629 (VI. 10. 24. 14). (This work was continued in a 4th ed., 12 vols., ed. Gottlieb Christophorus Harles [Hamburg: Carolum Ernestum Bohn, 1790-1809]; an index vol., vol. 13, was added in a later reprint of this edition [Leipzig: C. Cnobloch, 1838].)

[3] Fabricius, Bibliotheca Graeca, 2 (1716): 597 and note.

[4] Ibid., 5 (1723): 268.   [5] Ibid., 2:598.

With the appearance of the second volume of Assemani's <u>Bib-</u>
<u>liotheca Orientalis</u> came the celebration of Africanus's elevation to
bishop and New Testament commentator.[1]

The results of this last work were soon forthcoming, in 1725.
Basnage said there were two contemporary Africani, one a gentile from
Libya, writer of the <u>Cestis</u>, the other a Christian from Nicopolis
(Emmaus of the Gospels), writer of the <u>Chronicon</u>, "whom <u>many</u> [<u>plur-</u>
<u>imi</u>] make a bishop."[2]

Lardner vacillated on the question of two Africani, tending
to favor the idea, but concluding it was "of no great importance."
On the other hand, he was reasonably sure Africanus did not write any
New Testament commentaries. He also became the first in a long line
of writers to credit Dionysius bar-Salibi with making Africanus a
bishop, citing Assemani, 2:129 and 158, as evidence.[3]

Other eighteenth century works related to Africanus were mainly

----

[1] 2 (1721): 129, 158, 283; see also, 3 (1725): 14. In vol. 1
(1719), Africanus appears simply as the source concerning Edessa in
Eusebius's <u>Chronicon</u> (p. 391, n. 1). As Assemani notes (2:129),
however, "Masius in Praefatione" and Fabricius had already mentioned
one or both of these points. Fabricius himself cites Cordier's <u>Catena</u>
<u>in Joannem</u> as a prior notice of them (5:270 in a note on Hebed Iesu).
He also adds a reference to Moses Barcepha and Paulus Colomesius, <u>De</u>
<u>scriptoribus Ecclesiasticis paralipomena</u> (ibid.).

[2] Jacobus Basnage, <u>Thesaurus monumentorum ecclesiasticorum et</u>
<u>historicum, sive Henrici Canisii Lectiones antiquae ad saeculorum</u>
<u>ordinem digestae variisque opusculis auctae, quibus praefationes</u>
<u>historicas, animadversiones criticas, et notas in singulos auctores</u>
<u>adjecit</u>, 4 vols. (Antwerp: n.p., 1725), 2:148 ("Jacobi Basnagii in
Anonymi collectionem chronologicam observationes").

[3] <u>The Works of Nathaniel Lardner</u>, with a Life by [Andrew]
Kippis, vol. 2, <u>The Credibility of the Gospel History</u>, part 2 (London:
William Ball, 1838), pp. 457-60 [<u>Credibility</u> was originally published
as 2 vols. in 14, London: J. Chandler, 1727-55]).

concerned with publication of texts, most with limited relation to

the Kestoi. In 1704, Peter Needham published an edition of the

Geoponica which was re-edited by Niclas in 1781. It included a dis-

cussion of authors cited which follows the ancient testimonies con-

cerning Africanus; the only unusual point by Needham was his accept-

ance of the figure of nine books for the Kestoi, attributing this

first to Eusebius and Syncellus, and then to Eusebius alone.[1] Carolus

and Carol. Vincent. de La Rue published an edition of Origen's works

which included the exchange of letters with Africanus. In the intro-

duction to these letters they followed Scaliger's distinction of Af-

ricani. This work was in turn shortly reprinted in Gallandi, who

followed their lead.[2]

Near the mid and three-quarter points of the century, there

appeared two works somewhat more useful: Giovanni Lami's edition of

Joannis Meursii Opera, including a text of Africanus from the mili-

tary collections;[3] and a paraphrase of certain chapters by Ch.

---

[1] Geoponicorum sive de re rustica libri XX, ed. and illus. Jo.
Nicolaus Niclas, 4 vols. (Leipzig: Caspar Fritsch, 1781), 1:xlv, xlvi.

[2] Origenis opera . . . , originally published in 4 vols.
(Paris, 1733-59); reprinted in Andreas Gallandi, Bibliotheca
veterum patrum antiquorumque scriptorum ecclesiasticorum Graeco-Latina
in XIV. tomos distributa, editio novis (Venice: Albritiana, 1788
[orig. ed., Venice, 1765-81]), 2:xxxviii. In the nineteenth century
this line continued: the de La Rues' work was again reedited by
Carol. Henric. Eduard. Lommatzsch, 23 vols. (Berlin: Haude et Spener,
1831-47), vol. 17 (1844); and both Gallandi and the de La Rues re-
appear in Migne, P.G., 10: cols. 45-50; and 11 (cols. 37-42 for Africanus); respectively; as does Fabricius (P.G., 10: cols. 35-46).

[3] Vol. 7 (Florence, 1746), cols. 897-980, cited by Vieillefond,
Les Cestes, p. 85.

Guischard.[1] Within this period there also appeared a work with only

minor references to Africanus, but including one which was to have

some effect on the discussion of the length of the Kestoi. Volume 2

of Bandini's Catalogue notes the presence of part of the Kestoi in Lau-

rent. Plut. LV, Cod. IV, pp. 231-244, and warns of the danger of con-

fusing Julius Africanus, the author of the Kestoi and the Chronography,

with others of the same name from earlier times.[2] Volume 3 prints a

short item, Ek tou Aphrikanou kestōn hoper esti keston ig'. keph. kb'.

kathartika hapla, from Laurent. Plut. LXIV, Cod. XXIII, p. 204.[3]

Finally, Rosenmüller seemed to identify Julius Africanus as a priest

(Presbyter Nicopolitanus), and mentioned Valesius's view, perhaps

favorably, but concluded that the dispute was foreign to his present

purpose.[4]

---

[1]Memoires critiques et historiques sur plusiers points d'antiquité militaire, vol. 3 (1774), cited by Vieillefond, Les Cestes, p.
88, n. 16. Vieillefond here corrects a commonly repeated statement
that Guischard's work was a translation. During this period at least
three attempts at translating Africanus were made, but few were completed and none were published (see the survey in Vieillefond, Les
Cestes, pp. 86-89, 91, 93-99).

[2]Angelo Maria Bandini, Catalogus codicum manuscriptorum bibliothecae mediceae Laurentianae varia continens opera Graecorum patrum,
3 vols. (Florence: Typis Caesariis, 1764; Typis Regiis, 1768, 1770;
repr. 3 vols. in 2, Leipzig: Zentral-Antiquariat der Deutschen Demo-
kratischen Republik, 1961), 2 (1768): cols. 232-33.

[3]Ibid., 3 (1770): col. 127.

[4]Jo. Georg. Rosenmüller, Historia interpretationis librorum
sacrum in ecclesia Christiana, 5 vols. in 4 (Leipzig: Jo. Gottfr.
Hanisch, 1795-1814 [but orig. publ. earlier; a German trans. was publ.
at Leipzig in 1791]), Pars tertia continens periodum II. ab Origene
ad Jo. Chrysostomum et Cypriano ad Augustinum (1807), p. 157, with
note 1. He therefore concentrated attention on Africanus's interpre-
tational writings, the letters. In this context he penned the famous
line of tribute to Africanus's critical ability as shown in the

The fortunes of Africanus, ancient encyclopedist, in this
period are somewhat reflected by his relationship to a modern insti-
tution, the Encyclopaedia Britannica. He failed to make the first
two editions,[1] and when he finally appeared in "Moore's Dublin ed."
(1791), there was no reference to the Kestoi.[2]

Nineteenth and Early Twentieth Centuries

As stated above, in the introduction to the chapter, this
period was especially concerned with publication of ancient fragments
and more self-conscious attempts to explain Africanus.

The early decades

The century opened rather slowly in the realm of Africaniana.
Routh's Reliquiae sacrae made available most of Africanus's Christian
writings, but omitted the Kestoi as semi-ethnicum and incerti auc-
toris.[3] Then, near the quarter century mark, Augustus Neander

---

epistle To Origen: "In haec una Epistola, quae vix duabus paginis
constat, plus est verae eruditionis exegeticae, quam in omnibus
Origenis Commentariis et Homiliis" (3:161). This view became somewhat standard for the next century, and even to the present.

[1]First ed., 3 vols. (Edinburgh, 1768-71); 2d ed., 10 vols.
(Edinburgh, 1778-83).

[2]Eighteen vols. (Dublin: J. Moore, 1791-97), 1 (1791): 228.
This seems to be the same as the 3d ed., 18 vols. (Edinburgh, 1797).
(The article also introduces Julius Caesar [rather than Jesus Christ;
an incorrect expansion of an abbreviated "J.C."?] as the climax of
Africanus's 5500 year era from creation.)

[3]Second ed., 2:502. Routh's work, programmatically sub-titled
Sive auctorum fere jam perditorum secundi tertiique saeculi post Chris-
tum natum quae supersunt, remains in use in this second edition. It
was originally published in four volumes at Oxford, 1814-18. Routh's
collection still remains the only real one for the Chronography
fragments.

presented a tribute similar to Rosenmüller's to Africanus's critical

ability, and added what was in essence a modification of the view of

Cave and Tillemont. He suggested that the divergent character of

the _Kestoi_ was because it was probably written by Africanus "before

his habits of thinking had become decidedly Christian"[1] (or "before

he had devoted himself to religious subjects"[2]).

Fragments of the Kestoi

In 1839, there appeared Westermann's _Paradoxographoi_, which

included Michael Psellus's p̄eri paradox̄on anaḡnosmat̄on. Psellus, in

turn, had included summaries of many of the more "magical" items in

the _Kestoi_.[3] Westermann accepted the ancient testimonies as to

authorship, and further accepted the attribution of various excerpts

in the _Geoponica_ to Africanus, noting that they were twin to those

in _Psellus_.[4]

In 1841 and for several years thereafter, A. J. H. Vincent

devoted part of his attention to the publication and explication of

---

[1]_General History of the Christian Religion and Church_, 9 vols.,
trans. Joseph Torrey, rev. ed. (London: George Bell and Sons, 1890),
2:479 and note. (The first German edition appeared in 6 volumes, Hamburg, 1825-52). Despite the perpetuation of a variant of this quotation by the _Encyclopaedia Britannica_ (see next note), this version
seems to be subject to the same disability as the original suggestion
of Cave and Tillemont: the _Kestoi_ cannot be dated earlier than the
Chronography, and certainly not that much earlier.

[2]_Encyclopaedia Britannica_, 9th ed. (1875; and continuing
through subsequent editions to 1969), s.v. "Africanus, Julius."

[3]Westermann, pp. xliii-xlvii, and 143-46.

[4]Ibid., pp. xlvi-xlvii.

certain of the <u>Kestoi</u> texts, especially those relating to music and
to geometry.[1]

In 1864, Hultsch published most of the <u>peri metrōn kai stathmōn</u>
as two separate fragments going back to first century(?) Alexandrian
authors, one a Jew.[2] A dozen years later, full texts, with ascription
to Africanus, were published in rapid succession by Duchesne and Lagarde.[3]

_____

[1]Letter to the President of the Academie des Inscriptions et
Belles-Lettres de Paris, <u>L'Institut,</u> II[e] section, 6 (1841): 173-75.
The main part of the letter was a translation of parts of chapters 2
(pentagon and musical notes in a poison recipe) and 76 (fire signals)
of Thevenot's edition of the <u>Kestoi</u>. The latter chapter is no longer
credited to Africanus and Vincent notes its questionable status at the
end of the letter. This letter was reprinted (without a P.S. included
in <u>L'Institut</u>) under the heading "Histoire du Mathematics," <u>Comptes
rendus hebdomadaires des séances de l'Academie des Sciences (Paris)</u>,
14 (1842): 43-44 (and as the last item in the following work). The
full range of musical signs in the <u>Kestoi</u> was discussed in "Extraits
des Cestes de Jules l' Africain" (part of a longer article, "Notice
sur trois manuscrits grecs relatifs à la musique, avec une traduction
française et des commentaires"), in <u>Notices et extraits des manuscrits
de la Bibliotheque du roi et autres bibliotheques</u>, vol. 16, part 2
(Paris, 1847 [part 1 published in 1858]): 344-63, accompanied by
"Addition: communiquée par M. le Docteur Roulin relativ aux animaux
mentioné par Jules l'Africain," pp. 561-64. This was followed by
"Extrait des Cestes de Jules l'Africain" (part of "Extraits des manuscrits relatifs à la géométrie pratique des Grecs"), <u>Notices et ex-
traits</u> 19, part 2 (1858 [part 1 published in 1862]): 407-15. This
latter contained a text and translation of "To find the width of a
river or the height of a wall" (ch. 21, Thevenot; = Vieillefond, I. 15).

[2]Fridericus Hultsch, <u>Metrologicorum scriptorum reliquiae</u>, 2
vols. (Leipzig: B. G. Teubner, 1864, 1866), 1:257-59 (no. 81), and
300-2 (no. 95), with introductory material, pp. 20-21, 80-81, 138-40,
158-61. Vol. 2 gave the Latin translation of Calvus de Ravenna (pp.
142-46, with introduction, pp. 14-16, 39-43).

[3]L. Duchesne, "III. Fragments métrologiques," <u>Archives des
missions scientifiques et litteraires</u> (Paris) 3d series, 3 (1876):
378-85; Paul de Lagarde, <u>Symmicta</u> 1 (Göttingen: Dieterich'sche Verlagsbuchhandlung, 1877): 166-73.

Reference works

Meanwhile, Africanus received notice in various encyclopedias, dictionaries, and other reference works, secular as well as religious. Generally, the number of books in the Kestoi was held to be nine (even by those who were aware of the kathartika hapla fragment from Kestos 13),[1] though sometimes the alternatives, 9, or 14, or 24, were simply given. The preference for this figure was mainly based on two arguments: the projection of Syncellus's enneabiblon back to Eusebius (à la Scaliger), and a form of the "lectio originalis" text critical canon, it seemed easier to explain the ιδ´ as an error from θ´, and κδ´ from ιδ´, than to reverse any part of the sequence.[2] Most of the writers accepted the unity of authorship of the Kestoi and the Chronography and letters,[3] but several tried to put the Kestoi in an earlier,

---

[1]Th. Henri Martin, "Recherches sur la vie et les ouvrages d'Héron d'Alexandrie," Mémoires présentés par divers savants a l'Académie des Inscriptions et Belles-Lettres de l'Institut Imperial de France, premiére série, tome 4 (Paris, 1854): 343; H. Köchly and W. Rüstow, Griechische Kriegsschriftsteller, zweiter Theil: Die Taktiker, zweite Abtheilung: Des Byzantiner Anonymus Kriegswissenschaft (Leipzig: Wilhelm Engelmann, 1855), p. 7; Duchesne, p. 380; George Salmon, "Africanus, Julius," Dictionary of Christian Biography, Literature, Sects and Doctrines, ed. William Smith and Henry Wace, 4 vols. (Boston: Little, Brown, and Co., 1877-87), 1:56. Martin knew of the kathartika hapla fragment (p. 355, with n. 3) from Lami; and Köchly and Rüstow specifically reject any significance for the book number in Bandini's notice in decisions on the question (p. 7, n. 1).

[2]Lambeck (Commentary, ed. Kollar, 7: cols. 426-27) seems to have been the first to so argue.

[3]The exceptions were: Ernst H. F. Meyer, Geschichte der Botanik, 4 vols. in 2 (Königsberg: Gebrüder Bornträger, 1854-57), 2 (1855): 220-26; J. B. Pitra, Spicilegium Solesmense complectens sanctorum patrum scriptorumque ecclesiasticorum anecdota hactenus opera, selecta e Graecis Orientalibusque et Latinis codicibus, 4 vols. (Paris: F. Didot Fratres, 1852-58), 3 (1855): lvii and n. 9; and especially, John M'Clintock and James Strong, Cyclopaedia of Biblical,

pagan period of Africanus's life, even if this meant giving up the

dedication to Severus Alexander.[1]

One significant advance was the recognition by Martin of the

composite nature of the military collections. This resulted in a

separation between chapters actually coming from Africanus and some-

what similar chapters, drawn more or less directly from earlier writ-

ers such as Aeneas Tacticus, which followed them in the manuscript

traditions and in the edition of Thevenot.[2]

Opinion was somewhat divided as to Africanus's churchly con-

nections, only a few writers accepting the idea of an episcopal

status, but several allowing for a possible presbyterate. Opinion

---

Theological and Ecclesiastical Literature, 10 vols. (New York: Harper
and Brothers, 1867-81), 4:1092-93, s.v. "Julius Africanus." The last
item distinguished between Julius Africanus and Julius Sextus (!),
crediting the suggestion to Dupin.

[1]Martin, "Recherches sur Heron," noting that he was "peu or-
thodoxe"(p. 343), dated it 210-17, but with the chapter on arms, which
mentions Persians rather than Parthians, added between 226 and 232 (pp.
349-52); A. Sevestre, Dictionnaire de patrologie, 5 vols. (=Nouvelle
encyclopédie théologique, vols. 20-23 bis; Paris: J.-P. Migne, 1851-
55), 3 [22] (1854): cols. 932-37, s.v. "Jules Africain"; L.-F. Guerin,
Dictionaire de l'histoire universelle de l'Eglise, 6 vols. (=Encyclo-
pédie théologique, vols. 51-56; Paris: J.-P. Migne, 1854-73), 5 [55]
(1865): cols. 598-602, s.v. "Jules Africain." Similarly, Th. Pressel,
"Julius Africanus," Real-Encyklopädie für protestantische Theologie und
Kirche, ed. J. J. Herzog, 22 vols. (Stuttgart and Hamburg: R. Besser,
1854-68), 7 (1857): 155-56, followed Neander's view.

[2]Martin, "Recherches sur Heron," pp. 351-64, esp. 355-61.
Martin regarded only 37 chapters as authentic, attributing the addition of the others to the compiler (whom he tentatively called Hero
of Constantinople [p. 361]). This view had been anticipated by Boivin,
who had denied certain chapters to Africanus, accepting only 44 as
authentic (see the discussion above in connection with the presentation of Thevenot's edition). (See further below, at the discussion
of Vieillefond, Jules Africain, 1932).

was equally divided as to his homeland, Africa or Syria. The state

of knowledge during this period can, perhaps, be represented by two

contrasting articles. Salmon's article in Smith and Wace is a full,

careful presentation (albeit with some errors, as e.g., the number of

books in the Kestoi, and the likelihood of commentaries by Africanus)

of scholarly knowledge to that time.[1] Meanwhile, the Encyclopaedia

Britannica updated its article somewhat, but it was still brief, gen-

eral, and inconclusive; the Kestoi was introduced tentatively and

this was followed by (a distortion of?) Neander's suggestion.[2] The

latter article is probably more broadly representative of the views

of the times.

Gelzer and Harnack

The discussion for the next decades, beginning in 1880, was

dominated by two names, Heinrich Gelzer and Adolf Harnack. Gelzer

appeared on the scene as the author of an authoritative work on Af-

ricanus (especially concerning the Chronography),[3] while Harnack's

---

[1]"Africanus, Julius."

[2]Encyclopaedia Britannica, 9th ed. (1875), 1:273. (On
Neander, see above, p. 49 with nn. 1 and 2.) This article also
tentatively introduced the by-name Sextus ("AFRICANUS, JULIUS, called
also SEXTUS by Suidas, . . .") and suggested that he was probably a
priest.

[3]Heinrich Gelzer, Sextus Julius Africanus und die Byzantinische Chronographie, erster Theil: Die Chronographie des Julius
Africanus (Leipzig: B. G. Teubner, 1880); zweiter Theil, erste Abtheilung: Die Nachfolger des Julius Africanus (Leipzig: B. G. Teubner,
1885); zweiter Theil, zweite Abtheilung: Nachträge (Leipzig: J. C.
Hinrichs'sche Buchhandlung, 1898); also, an article, "Zu Africanus,"
Jahrbücher für protestantische Theologie 7 (1881): 376-78.

position was developed more slowly in a continuing series of articles
and studies.[1]

Gelzer answered most of the critical questions of his day,
and his views became dominant in the following years. There was only
one Africanus involved, Sextus Julius Africanus, a Christian from
Latin Africa, associate of kings and emperors, who accompanied Septimius Severus on his Osrhoenian campaign, a military man, not an ecclesiastic, and a widely travelled man.[2] The Kestoi, dedicated to
Alexander Severus, was probably completed in the first half of his
reign. It was a sort of "Realencyclopädie," though not exclusively
natural science, especially characterized by thaumasia, probably having Paradoxa as a sub-title. Valesius's explanation of the main title
is incorrect, rather it is "Tapestry" or "Embroidery," in reference
to its miscellaneous (vermischt) contents. The number of books
was either 14 or 24, Syncellus probably having an incomplete copy.[3]
The combination of the sharp, critical sense of the letter concerning
Susanna, and the crass superstition of the Kestoi is explainable in a
contemporary of Septimius Severus; Voss correctly compared the situation to that described in Hadrian's letter.[4] Remains of the Kestoi

---

[1]Beginning with the article, "Julius Africanus," in Real-
Encyklopädie für protestantische Theologie und Kirche, ed. J. J. Herzog and G. L. Plitt, 2d ed., 18 vols. (Leipzig: J. C. Hinrichs, 1877-
88), 7 (1880): 296-98; and continuing to at least 1925.

[2]Gelzer, Sextus, 1:1-11.   [3]Ibid., p. 12.

[4]Ibid., pp. 16-17. Also, the prized book Africanus purchased
in Egypt was one of the Hermetic books (p. 4).

are found among the Byzantine tactical, agricultural, and veterinary
collections, as well as some other fragments, and in Psellus's excerpt.[1]

The year following the publication of his first volume, Gelzer
published a brief article amplifying and clarifying certain points,
only two relating to the Kestoi. The first documents the rejection of
the nine-book total for the Kestoi (1:12), citing a communication from
K. K. Müller regarding the fragment from Keston 13 (corrected by
Gelzer, as by others of his time to Kestōn 13); the second called attention to examples of numerous manuscripts (of the military writers)
besides Codex Regius 2706 (cited in Sextus 1:13) which included the
inscription Iouliou Afrikanou kestos Z'.[2] (K. K. Müller published the
text of the Kestos 13 fragment, kathartika hapla, with a German translation, in a later number of the same volume.[3]) The later parts of
Gelzer's work are chiefly of interest here as announcing and then
postponing plans for publication of the fragments of Africanus.[4]

Harnack's first systematic presentation concerning Africanus
appeared in the same year as Gelzer's first volume, and agreed with
Gelzer in many points (even suggesting the need for such a basic
study as Gelzer was about to supply). Sextus Julius Africanus was

---

[1]Ibid., pp. 13-16.

[2]"Zu Africanus," Jahrbücher für protestantische Theologie 7
(1881): 376-78.

[3]"Zu Julius Africanus," Jahrbücher für protestantische Theologie 7 (1881): 759-60.

[4]Sextus, zweiter Theil, erste Abtheilung, p. vi, and zweite
Abtheilung, p. 429, respectively.

likely a Libyan, as Suidas asserted, had contacts with various royal
houses, and was probably the author of the _Kestoi_ (a "reichhaltigen
Sammelwerkes"), but he was also probably a presbyter.[1] Probably by a
misprint, he credited Syncellus with reporting 19 books (but followed
a few lines later by the _enneabiblon_ passage). He further credited
Du Pin with first suggesting the two Africanus hypothesis, a view he
himself regarded as doubtful.[2] The following year, in a review of
Gelzer's first volume, Harnack reported, apparently approvingly, Gelzer's view that Africanus was a layman, a former officer in the forces
of Septimius Severus.[3]

Eleven years later, Harnack suggested two more items for Africanus's repertoire--he was a translator and medical writer. Starting from Gelzer's argument that Africanus knew Latin, having used
Suetonius's _De regibus_ in his _Chronography_, Harnack argued for Africanus as the translator of a Greek version of Tertullian's _Apology_
which was apparently used by Eusebius. Further, Africanus and the
translator fit the same general place and time, and Africanus was
credited by later tradition as a translator (from Greek into
Latin).[4] His title to a place among the medical writers comes from

---

[1] "Julius Africanus," pp. 296 and 298. Africanus's year and
place of birth were unknown, but he was still alive after 240 (p. 296).

[2] Ibid., p. 298.

[3] Review of _Sextus Julius Africanus und die Byzantinische Chron-
ographie_, erster Theil, by Heinrich Gelzer, in _Theologische Literatur-
zeitung_ 6 (1881): cols. 278-83, esp. col. 278.

[4] "Die griechische Uebersetzung des Apologeticus Tertullianus,"
_TU_ 8, no. 4 (1892): 32-36.

the Kestoi, which further serves to show the breadth of his interests,
and their secular, even superstitious, character, alongside the theological interests and critical abilities shown in his other works.[1]

Africanus appears twice in Harnack's Geschichte der altchristlichen Litteratur bis Eusebius, the first account by his assistant
E. Preuschen, the second by Harnack himself. Preuschen's views are
much the same as Harnack's, but more definite on some points. Africanus is "Sextus(?) Julius Africanus, ein Arzt," and the Kestoi contains 24 books. The two Africanus theory is traced back to Scaliger
and Valois, but both it and the "pre-conversion" view are impossible.
Rather, the Kestoi results from the period of excessive syncretism in
which Africanus lived.[2] Preuschen also cited Rosenmüller's comparison
of the critical abilities of Africanus and Origen.[3] He also presented
Harnack's theory of Africanus as translator of Tertullian's Apology,
and added Pitra's two fragments (the Syriac "Caput" concerning Moses
and Elijah, and the Scholion concerning Manasseh's escape from Assyrian
bondage) to the list of possible Africanian items.[4] By the time
Harnack's account appeared in the second part of the work, Grenfell
and Hunt's discovery of the end of the eighteenth book had settled
the question of the number of books in the Kestoi (thus justifying
the conclusion of Preuschen), but, besides the confirmation of unity

---

[1]"Medicinisches aus der ältesten Kirchengeschichte," TU 8,
no. 4 (1892): 43-44 (in part 1, "Christliche Ärtze").

[2]Erster Theil: Die Überlieferung und der Bestand der altchristlichen Litteratur bis Eusebius (Leipzig: J. C. Hinrichs'sche
Buchhandlung, 1893), pp. 507, 508, 511.

[3]Ibid., p. 512.   [4]Ibid., p. 513.

of authorship, not otherwise affecting any of the conclusions. Har-

nack here also suggested Paradoxa as a second title for the Kestoi,

which is characterized as "eine Art von technischer Enzyklopädie und

Kuriositätensammlung."[1] This article also repeated and amplified

Gelzer's suggestion that Sextus Julius Africanus was a Latin-speaking

officer who had accompanied Severus on his Osrhoenian expedition of

A.D. 195. In this connection, Harnack noted Africanus's report of

having seen both alleged sites of Noah's ark, Mt. Ararat and Celaenae

in Phrygia.[2]

In the meantime, Harnack's revised article in the third edi-

tion of the Realencyklopädie für protestantische Theologie und Kirche

had appeared two years too early to benefit from the Oxyrhynchus dis-

covery,[3] but otherwise the views were essentially the same as those

to appear in the Geschichte: this included the introduction of the

reference to the Osrhoene campaign, with date, and the questioning of

Africanus's clerical status, a possibility no longer even mentioned in

_____

[1]Zweiter Theil: Die Chronologie der altchristlichen Litteratur bis Eusebius, zweiter Band: Die Chronologie der Litteratur von
Irenaeus bis Eusebius (Leipzig: J. C. Hinrichs'sche Buchhandlung, 1904),
p. 91.

[2]Ibid., p. 89. The specification of the year of the campaign
in this connection (Gelzer gives the date [Sextus, 1:5], but separated
from this part of the account [p. 8] by several pages of discussion)
is Harnack's addition, and becomes characteristic for later summaries
of Africanus's life. (By a slip of the pen, Harnack transferred
Celaenae from Phrygia to Phoenicia.) Meanwhile, Gelzer's collection
of fragments had still not appeared (pp. 90-91).

[3]Founded by J. J. Herzog, ed. Albert Hauck, 24 vols. (Leipzig:
J. C. Hinrichs'sche Buchhandlung, 1896-1913), 9(1901): 627-28, s.v.
"Julius Africanus Sextus" (sic).   This was followed by a date of
death of "nach 140" (but given correctly in the body of the article).

the later article. Africanus's lifespan was given as from about 160

to soon after 240.[1] There was also a somewhat fuller characterization

of the Kestoi ē Paradoxa:

> eine Art von Encyklopädie der realistischen Wissenschaften, der
> angewandten Mathematik und der Technik gewesen zu sein, z. T.
> angefüllt mit kuriösen, läppischen, mirakulösen, und anstössigen
> Dingen (wesshalb A. als Verfasser in Zweifel gezogen ist). Ver-
> öffentlicht sind bisher Abschnitte zum Landbau, zur Messkunde,
> zur Taktik, zur Medizin und Veterinär-Medizin, zur Geheimmittel-
> kunde u.s.w. [2]

Harnack's last pronouncements concerning Africanus came more

than a decade and a half later, and presented some modification of

view. They will, therefore, be presented below, after consideration

of other developments which had occurred in the intervening period.

Geoponica and Hippiatrica

The last two decades of the nineteenth century saw discus-

sions concerning various suggested sources of additional fragments

from the Kestoi. The most notable of such sources was the Geoponica,

---

[1]Ibid., p. 627.

[2]Ibid., p. 628. An abbreviated form of this article appeared
in English in The New Schaff-Herzog Encyclopedia of Religious Knowledge,
ed. Samuel Macauley Jackson, 12 vols. (New York and London: Funk &
Wagnalls, 1908-12), 6 (1910): 264-65, s.v. "Julius Africanus, Sextus."
There is no reference to the Oxyrhynchus papyrus, even in the Bibliography. By an interesting mistranslation, this version also makes
Africanus a writer on "liturgiology" (for the original "Messkunde"--
"surveying"). It also tones down the description of the Kestoi somewhat, and eliminates a reference to Africanus as a possible translator
of Tertullian's Apology.
    Harnack's Militia Christi: die Christliche Religion und der
Soldatenstand in den ersten drei Jahrhunderten (Tübingen: J. C. B.
Mohr, 1905) includes Africanus and the tactical sections of the Kestoi
as (exceptional) examples of involvement of early Christians with the
military (p. 73 and n. 3), but does not contain any advancement of the
study of the Kestoi.

on one chapter of which, book 7, chapter 14, interpreters since Boivin

had relied to show the Christian status of the author of the Kestoi.

In 1884, Wilhelm Gemoll, while holding to the identity of authorship,

argued that the compiler of the Geoponica had not used Africanus di-

rectly, so that the chapter attributions were suspect.[1] But compari-

sons of Psellus and the Thevenot-Boivin text with the Geoponica also

suggested that there were probably in the Geoponica numerous items

from the Kestoi not so identified and thus impossible to distinguish

now.[2]

Eugen Oder, though presenting a different view of the over-

all development of the Geoponica, reached the same conclusion on the

last two points: only one passage is identified in the text itself

as from Africanus (Geop. 5. 45. 2), and comparison with Psellus and

Thevenot-Boivin show, contra Gelzer, that the passages ascribed to

Africanus in the lemmata cannot be accepted without question; but

neither should the Geoponica be completely eliminated as a source for

Africanus.[3] On other points of Africaniana, Oder argued for the

identity of authorship, for 24 books in the Kestoi (Syncellus's "nine

books" must have been an epitome, and one would hardly make a 9-book

---

[1]Untersuchungen über die Quellen, den Verfasser und die Abfassungszeit der Geoponica, Berliner Studien für classische Philologie
und Archaeologie, ed. Ferdinand Ascherson (Berlin: S. Calvary & Co.),
1 (1884): 85, 88, 91-92, 228 (also published separately by Calvary,
1883). Gemoll also felt that the Thevenot-Boivin text was not just
from books 6 and 7 of the Kestoi, but was an extract from the whole
work (p. 86).

[2]Ibid., pp. 87-92.

[3]"Beiträge zur Geschichte der Landwirthschaft bei den Griechen,"
Rheinisches Museum für Philologie n.s. 45 (1890): 82-83.

epitome of a 14-book work), divided into four divisions of six books
each, corresponding to the contents as given by Syncellus (i.e.,
iatrikōn, physikōn, geōrgikōn, and chymeutikōn).[1] While the sources
correctly connect the title paradoxa with the Kestoi, this is probably
the title of one of the divisions (the Georgika) not a second title
of the whole work as Gelzer suggested.[2] Oder mentioned Gelzer's proposed edition of the fragments of Africanus,[3] but in a later addition
to the discussion, he noted a division of the publication, the Kestoi
fragments would not be edited by Gelzer, but by K. K. Müller in his
edition of the Greek military writers (Kriegsschriftsteller).[4]

Oder's views were seconded by Max Ihm, who suggested that the
chapter ascriptions in the companion compilation, the Hippiatrica,
were as trustworthy as those of the Geoponica were untrustworthy or
even fraudulent.[5]

Antonius Baumstark, in addition to presenting a still different view of the development (and reconstruction of the text) of
the Greek Geoponica, especially emphasizing the role of the Oriental
versions, was more sanguine about the Africanian elements in the

---

[1]Ibid., p. 82.   [2]Ibid., pp. 81, 82.

[3]Ibid., p. 82.

[4]"Beiträge zur Geschichte der Landswirthschaft bei den
Griechen. III," Rheinisches Museum für Philologie n.s. 48 (1893): 2,
in the continuation of note 1 from p. 1.

[5]"Die Hippiatrica," Rheinisches Museum für Philologie n.s.
47 (1892): 314.

Geoponica. However, he simply emphasized their presence, rather than suggesting any real method of identifying them specifically.[1]

The study of the Geoponica reached something of a plateau in the following year with the publication of a new text by Beckh.[2] Though continuously criticized for a too-narrow manuscript base and failure to adequately consider the evidence of the Oriental versions, it has not been replaced.

Two years later Oder himself turned to the Hippiatrica, calling attention to additional chapters credited to Africanus in the Cambridge codex of the Hippiatrica.[3]

Alchemy

A year after Gemoll's study, Africanus's name turned up in the history of alchemy.[4] His membership in this fraternity was vouched for by his purchase of the book of Souphis while in Egypt,[5] by Suidas's description, and by the appearance of his name in various alchemical works, especially in the list of "the philosophers of the divine knowledge and art" at the beginning of an alchemical manuscript

---

[1]"Lucubrationes Syro-Graecae," Jahrbücher für classische Philologie [Annalium Philologicorum] 21er Supplementband (1894): 404-5.

[2]Geoponica sive Cassiani Bassi scholastici de re rusticae eclogae, ed. Henricus Beckh (Leipzig: B. G. Teubner, 1895).

[3]Eugenius Oder, "De hippiatricorum codice Cantabrigiensi," Rheinische Museum für Philologie n.s. 51 (1895): 57-58.

[4]M[arcel Pierre Eugene] Berthelot, Les origines de l'alchemie (Paris: Georges Steinheil, 1885).

[5]Reported by Syncellus (Dindorf 1:105).

which Berthelot studied at the library of St. Mark (Codex Marc. 299).[1]

Aside from this, Berthelot's view of Africanus was somewhat atypical:

he was a Syrian, who composed geographical works, as well as a his-

tory of Armenia drawn from the tabularia of Edessa, and a military

work, the Kestoi. The latter name is analogous in meaning to the

word "anthology."[2] Elsewhere Berthelot named Africanus among the

pagan writers, before going on to discuss the Christian majority

among alchemical authors.[3] Africanus also appeared briefly in Ber-

thelot and Ruelle's collection of alchemical writings. There, he

was dated as roughly contemporaneous with the more prominent (Chris-

tian) alchemical writer Zosimus, as were the pseudonymous writings

attributed to Souphis (Cheops).[4]

---

[1] Berthelot, Origines, p. 187. See also Catalogue des manuscrits alchimiques grecs, 8 vols. in 3 (Brussels: M. Lamertin, 1924-
32), 3 (1924):14 for the same list in an Oxford codex (Bodl. Libr.
D'Orville 401[Auct. X. 2. 4. 31] [17279], p. 126 of MS).

[2] Origines, p. 187. The reference to Armenia and Edessa suggests Moses of Chorene as a partial source; the "geographical works"
are perhaps a reference to parts of the Chronography. (The relation
of Africanus to Hippolytus's "Liber generationis" and, especially,
his "Diamerismon tēs gēs" had been much discussed in the preceding
two or three decades.)

[3] Ibid., pp. 98-99.

[4] M[arcel Pierre Eugene] Berthelot and Ch.-Em[ile] Ruelle,
Collection des anciens alchimistes grecs, 3 vols. (Paris: Georges
Steinheil, 1888; also, repr., 3 vols. in 1, London: Holland Press,
1963), 1:202. The Greek text, with facsimile of the St. Mark's MS
list of "philosophers" appear on pp. 110-11 (Figure 5--Planche III),
and a French translation of a second list, a chapter list not exactly
corresponding to the actual contents of the manuscript, is given on
pp. 174-75. Africanus appears after Hermes, Zosimus, and Nilus in
item no. 32 of that list. Africanus's name also appeared in connection with brief statements in the Greek text in vol. 2 (pp. 75 and
169, with translation in vol. 3). (Also see below, Chapter II, in
the translation of Vieillefond's IX. 2 and 3.)

Religious writings

In 1889, de Boor published several fragments from Philip of
Side's church history. The first of them was the account of Africanus
which was presented earlier in this chapter.[1] As de Boor pointed out,
the account stands mid-way between that of Eusebius (Chronicon, Greek
text as reflected in the Chronicon paschale) and Syncellus: it presents the change in status of Nicopolis somewhat more clearly than
Eusebius ("a village . . . which later received the right [dikaia]
of a city," compared to the "was founded [ektisthē] a city" of
Eusebius, omitted by Syncellus), but shares with Syncellus the double
error of identifying Emmaus with that of the Gospels, and of dating
the change of the name to Nicopolis to this time.[2] At the same time,
Philip's statement, "was from Emmaus" (apo Emmaous ēn), indicated that
Emmaus-Nicopolis was Africanus's home. This seems to provide the first
direct support for Valesius's hypothesis.[3] The Suidas's statement concerning Africanus's Libyan origin is open to the suspicion that it is
a misunderstanding, or a false deduction, from the name Africanus, and
Gelzer's attempts to support it are not conclusive. Even assuming
Africanus's knowledge of Latin, this does not prove an origin in Latin
Africa. Knowledge of Latin by an Easterner is much less striking than
a Westerner who wrote in Greek and knew Hebrew and Syriac. Besides
this, his interest in Hermetic books and the secret wisdom of the
Egyptians[4] is in keeping with the mystical-speculative interests of the

---

[1]"Neue Fragmente," p. 169.   [2]Ibid., p. 174.

[3]Ibid. This point, however, was only part of Valois's view.

[4]Cf. Gelzer, Sextus, p. 4.

East. Lacking some witness besides the Suidas, or at least some traces
in Africanus's works showing an exact knowledge of the West, the fragment's evidence for Emmaus as Africanus's birthplace seems to be
authenticated.[1]

Charles Cruttwell provides something of the combination of
common sense and the absurd which is characteristic not only of Africanus, but of the study of him. He concluded that Africanus was born
a pagan, about A.D. 170, and, after he became a Christian, was a philosopher, interested in scientific subjects, not a bishop nor New Testament commentator. Thus there was no reason to doubt Africanus's
authorship of the Kestoi, though it "obviously" belonged to his pagan
days.[2] Despite this conclusion, however, he finds it "odd that the
mere fact of a book's contents being of a secular kind should be evidence that it was not written by a Christian."[3]

At the end of the century, Bratke finalized the separation of
one work, the so-called "Persian Narrative," from Africanus's name
with the publication of the text, with a full study of its background.[4]
Of concern here is the demonstration that the connection of the work

---

[1]"Neue Fragmente," p. 175.

[2]Charles Thomas Cruttwell, Literary History of Early Christianity, 2 vols. (N.Y.: Scribner's, 1893), 2:514, 516.

[3]Ibid., p. 516, n. 1. This statement had been anticipated in
the Introductory Essay ("on the sole ground that it deals with secular
topics," p. 1, n. 1). Apart from the question of whether Cruttwell
could have made such a statement if he had read any of the Kestoi, is
the further oddity of a character sufficient to clearly prove something
pagan, but not to prove it non-Christian.

[4]Eduard Bratke, "Das Sogenannte Religionsgespräch am Hof der
Sasaniden," TU 19 (n.s. 4), no. 3 (1899).

with Africanus in some manuscripts was the result of a misinterpreta-
tion of an earlier abbreviation, Aphr (for Aphroditianos). Bratke
credited Usener with first recognizing the nature and source of the
error.[1]

Oxyrhynchus and beyond

The answers to several questions were provided by a 1903 publication,[2] though the results were not always immediately apparent.
A fragment of the Kestoi, containing the conclusion of Book 18, provided an immediate answer to two questions: the author was Julius
Africanus, not Scaliger's Sextus Africanus, and the number of books
was 24, not 14.[3] The fragment also provided further evidence of Africanus's varied interests, here literary (Homeric) criticism and
magical incantations,[4] as well as personal information about the
author. The papyrus seems to confirm Gelzer's view of Africanus's
friendly connection with the imperial house, presenting Africanus as
having "arranged" a library in the Pantheon for the emperor.[5] A

---

[1]Ibid., p. 51, citing Usener, "Religionsgeschichtliche Untersuchungen" (1899), pp. 32-37. Usener had earlier communicated this
information to Gelzer (see Gelzer, "Zu Africanus," p. 377).

[2]A minor part of finds of Egyptian papyri that have had major
effects on ancient philology, it was published by Grenfell and Hunt,
Oxyrhynchus Papyri, III,   papyrus no. 412, pp. 36-41, and plate
5. The preserved text consists of 2 columns numbered 35 and 36, the
latter concluding "Iouliou Afrikanou/Kestos/iē." The verso, the Will
of Hermogenes, was published in part VI (1908), pp. 247-53, as papyrus
no. 907.

[3]Ibid., III, p. 36.   [4]Ibid.

[5]Ibid., p. 37. A translation in the notes to the text uses
the word "designed" in relation to the library (p. 40). The text is
ērchitektonēsa (line 67).

reference to "the ancient _patria_" Aelia Capitolina, might suggest a
Syrian origin for Africanus, though the editors were reluctant to
contravene Suidas.[1]

    This fragment rekindled interest in Africanus, and various
articles appeared over the next decade, many short items suggesting
textual improvements of the Oxyrhynchus fragment, or other Africaniana.
Before the year was out, Arthur Ludwich contributed a number of suggestions toward the completion and understanding of the text, in a
general framework of comment on traditions in the textual transmission
of Homer.[2] In the second part, he defended the credibility of Africanus's report of the sources of his variant text, but presented a
sharply contrasting picture of Africanus as a critic.[3]

    Some months thereafter, in review articles, Weil suggested an
Egyptian provenance for the Odyssey interpolation,[4] and Wilamowitz
drew the conclusion that Africanus was from Jerusalem.[5] Friedrich

---

[1]Ibid., pp. 40-41.

[2]"Iulius Africanus und die Peisistratos-Legende über Homer,"
Berliner philologische Wochenschrift 23 (1903): cols. 1467-70, 1502-4.

[3]Ibid., cols. 1502-3.

[4]Henri Weil, "Textes grecs trouvis récemment en Egypte," a
review of _The Oxyrhynchus Papyri_, part III, in _Journal des savants_,
n.s. 2d année (1904): 108.

[5]U. v. Wilamowitz-Möllendorf, review of _The Oxyrynchos_ [sic]
Papyri, part IV, in _Göttingische gelehrte Anzeigen_, 166. Jahrgang,
zweiter Band (1904): 659-78. A brief review of Oxyrhynchus III appeared at the beginning, with Africanus on p. 659, n. 2. He further
pictured Africanus as a man without culture; superstitious; but a
polyhistor with occasional admirable opinions, and touchs (or "fits"--
Anwandelungen) of critical ability.

Blass reached a conclusion similar to the latter, though even more spe-

cific: Africanus was a Jew from Jerusalem.[1] In addition, this and

other articles suggested completions or corrections of individual

points, but in 1909, Richard Wünsch subjected the entire Odyssey in-

terpolation to a more thorough, systematic study.[2] Lines 14 and 21

of the fragment (ha dei poiēsai irēken; ha dei epạsai legei), whether

added by Africanus, or marginal glosses taken over with his manu-

scripts, indicate that whoever wrote them was aware that invocations

of the dead, like most magical operations, consisted of two major

parts: praxis and epǭdē.[3] The interpolation itself divides easily

into three parts, lines 15-20, 22-36, and 37-42, of which the first

and third are "homeric," while the middle is entirely different, more

like the magical or orphic hymns.[4] This provides reasonable bases

for filling in the incomplete line beginnings of the first column of

the papyrus,[5] as well as suggesting some basis for a history of the

interpolation. Lines 13-20 and 37-42 fit well together and represent

an older interpolation, in essentially homeric style and freedom of

meter, that suggest the pre-Christian era.[6] This was later expanded

by the insertion (lines 22-36) of a true magical composition ("ein

---

[1]"Literarische Texte mit Ausschluss der christlichen,"
Archiv für Papyrusforschung und verwandte Gebiete, ed. Ulrich Wilcken,
3 (1906): 255-99; item no. 250, "Pap. Oxyrh. 412," pp. 297-98, esp.
297.

[2]"Deisidaimoniaka," Archiv für Religionswissenschaft 12
(1909): 1-45; pp. 2-19 are devoted to "Der Zaubersang in der Nekyia
Homers."

[3]Ibid., p. 3.   [4]Ibid., pp. 4, 6, 14.

[5]Ibid., pp. 4-14.   [6]Ibid., pp. 15-16.

fertiger Zaubersang unverändert").[1] Its extremely syncretistic nature and prosody suggest the first or second centuries A.D.[2] The
thirteen lines to be found in the copy at Rome must be counted from
the beginning of the interpolation (line 15), not from the beginning
of the Odyssey citation, thus it runs through line 28; but lines 29-
42 are the same in viewpoint and expression as the preceding, so
there is no reason to separate lines 22-36 into two separate interpolations: the Roman copyist, for some reason, simply did not include the second half of the Hymn.[3] The reference to Nysa in Caria
in line 62, and a reading of Kareiē (as an epithet of Hecate) in
line 29, might suggest Nysa as its place of origin, though Weil had
suggested Alexandria and this would fit the reference to euplokamos
Zeus katachthonios (line 24).[4]

In relation to other fragments connected with the Kestoi,
contrasting opinions prevailed. Africanus's name appeared in connection with an ancestor of "Greek fire," though the "automatic fire"
text (Thevenot's chap. 44) was credited by the writer to a late
seventh century interpolation into the Kestoi.[5] Conversely, the

[1]Ibid., p. 16. This section (lines 22-36) later appeared in
two major collections of magical papyri: Theodor Hopfner, Griechisch-
Ägyptischer Offenbarungszauber, Studien zur Palaeographie und Papyrus-
kunde, ed. Carl Wessely, vols. 21 and 23, 2 vols. (Leipzig: H. Haessel,
1921, 1924), 2:150-52 (secs. 334-38); and Karl Preisendanz, Papyri
Graecae Magicae: Die griechischen Zauberpapyri, 2 vols. (Leipzig and
Berlin: B. G. Teubner, 1928-31), 2:150-51 (P xxiii).

[2]Wünsch, "Deisidaimoniaka," p. 17.   [3]Ibid., p. 18.

[4]Ibid., p. 19; also, p. 10, re Carian Hecate. On Weil see
above, p. 67, and n. 4.

[5]Edmund O. von Lippmann, Abhandlungen und Vorträge zur
Geschichte der Naturwissenschaften, 2 vols. (Leipzig: Verlag von Veit

excerpts from Aeneas which followed Africanus in the manuscript

tradition of the military writers (published by Thevenot-Boivin)

were treated by Schoene as genuine parts of the Kestoi (derived

from Aeneas by Africanus).[1] Ganschinietz suggested that the

Kestoi, viewed as a whole, certainly (s i c h e r) belonged to the

category of magia naturalis.[2]

   Meanwhile, the division of Africanian studies into secular

and religious continued; studies related to his more "religious"

side continued much as before, based essentially on Gelzer, with,

perhaps, some reference to Preuschen-Harnack. Reichardt published

an edition of the letters with extensive introduction. Such a pub-

lication did not involve areas that would require a reference to the

Oxyrhynchus papyrus (or to the Kestoi at all), but included several

testimonials to Africanus's sharp critical ability.[3] Duchesne's

---

& Comp., 1906, 1913), 1:130 (in chap. 9, "Zur Geschichte des Schiess-
pulvers und der älteren Feuerwaffen," pp. 125-89).

[1]Richardus Schoene, Aeneae Tactici: de obsidione toleranda
commentarius, Bibliotheca Scriptorum Graecorum et Romanorum Teubner-
iana (Leipzig: B. G . Teubner, 1911), pp. x-xi, xiv, 115-23. This
procedure was continued in Aeneas Tacticus, Asclepiodotus, Onasander,
trans. Illinois Greek Club, Loeb Classical Library (Cambridge: Harvard University Press, 1923; London: Wm. Heinemann, 1923), pp. 206-
25, which also reprinted Schoene's text with certain noted changes
from Boivin (p. 206, n. 2); and by L. W. Hunter, ΑΙΝΕΟΥ ΠΟΛΙΟΡΚΗΤΙΚΑ:
Aeneas on Siegecraft, rev. S. A. Hanford (Oxford: Clarendon Press,
1927), pp. 240-51, "Appendix I, Julius Africanus." (Concerning the
authenticity of these chapters, see the discussion of Martin, above,
and, especially, of Vieillefond, Jules Africain, 1932, below.)

[2]Richard Ganschinietz, "Hippolytos' Capitel gegen die Magier:
Refut. Haer. IV 28-42," TU 39, no. 2 (3d series, 9, no. 2) (1913): 29.

[3]Walter Reichardt, "Die Briefe des Sextus Julius Africanus
an Aristides und Origenes, " TU 34, no. 3 (3d series, 4, no. 3)
(1909). Note esp. pp. 1, 3, 63; note 1, on the last page cited, also
includes a quotation of Rosenmüller's contrast of Africanus and Origen.

history of the early church (first published in English in 1909, but
with original preface dated 1905), though incorporating details from
the Kestoi (following Gelzer's lead but somewhat "embroidering" the
picture),[1] did not include reference to the Oxyrhynchus papyrus until
the second French edition (1906).[2] Even then, only a couple of biographical details were included.[3] The picture presented by Fortescue
was more complete, and generally more restrained, but essentially the
same, following Gelzer and Harnack (and Jerome, with whom the article
concludes), but with no reference to Oxyrhynchus.[4]

The state of knowledge at this time (at least among the
"theological" writers) can again be approximated by the Encyclopaedia

---

[1]Louis Duchesne, Early History of the Christian Church from
Its Foundation to the End of the Third Century, trans. from the 4th
ed., 3 vols. (New York: Longman, Green & Co., 1909-24), 1:333-34.
Africanus, "a great hunter, . . . had scoured the forests" of Edessa,
saw "the remains of Noah's ark" (italics mine) at Apamea, and "obtained a copy of the Hermetic books" in Alexandria (p. 333). His
Kestoi contained "many thousand observations and precepts" (shades
of Pliny!), but was tainted by magic and Africanus's familiarity with
the Hermetic and similar books (p. 334).

[2]Ibid., p. xi, note to the second edition regarding the added
material.

[3]Birth at Aelia, and arrangement of "a library near the Pantheon" (ibid., p. 333; italics mine). A similar, but even more extreme example occurs in Otto Bardenhewer's Geschichte der altkirch-
lichen Literatur, in which the only immediate effect of the Oxyrhynchus papyrus was the settling of the question of the number of books
in the Kestoi (2d ed., 5 vols. [Freiburg im Breisgau: Herdersche Ver-
lagshandlung, 1912-32], 2 [1914]: 267 and 269). Otherwise Bardenhewer follows Gelzer.

[4]Adrian Fortescue, s.v. "Julius Africanus," The Catholic Encyclopedia, 15 vols. (New York: Appleton, 1907-12), 8:565-66. He
does, however, speak of the Kestoi as "constantly quoted and much es-
teemed by the Greek Fathers" (!) (8:565).

<u>Britannica</u> in which another, slightly revised (and again slightly ex-

panded) article appeared in the 11th edition (1910). This article

reversed the previous conclusion concerning Africanus's priesthood,

and otherwise essentially followed the views of Gelzer (and Harnack).

The article concluded with a scant line and a half reference to a new

fragment of the <u>Kestoi</u> among the Oxyrhynchus papyri.[1]

More alchemy

In 1913, Lagercrantz published an alchemical papyrus which

included two passages related to dyeing which were attributed to an

<u>Aphrikianos</u>.[2] In the introduction, Lagercrantz suggested, but with

reservations, the possible identification of Africianus with the Af-

ricanus of the list of alchemists in Berthelot's manuscripts (Cod.

Marc. 299), already identified by Berthelot with Sextus Julius Afri-

canus.[3]

The name Africanus also appears three other times in a later

publication of alchemical manuscripts. In the first, <u>Babylōnios ho</u>

---

[1]<u>The Encyclopaedia Britannica</u>, 11th ed. (1910), 1:361,
s.v. "Africanus, Sextus Julius." A five line list of "Authorities"
(Routh, ANF, Gelzer, Krüger, and Harnack) was added. (The article
also continued the [mis]quotation of Neander.)
    This article continued with only minor changes through 1969;
it was slightly condensed in the 14th edition (1929), and slightly revised (birthplace changed from Libya to Aelia Capitolina; Harnack
dropped from the "Bibliography," and <u>Oxy. Pap.</u> shifted to it) in the
1960 edition.

[2]Otto Lagercrantz, <u>Papyrus Graecus Holmiensis (P. Holm.): Recepte für Silber, Steine und Purpur</u> (Uppsala: Akademiska Bokhandeln,
1913; Leipzig: Otto Harrassowitz, 1913), pp. 32-33 and 37, with translations on pp. 216 and 226. The first is given as from <u>Aphrikianou
boublou</u>, the second from <u>Aphrikianou ek bou<b>lou g'</u>.

[3]<u>Ibid.</u>, pp. 106-7.

<u>Aphrikanos</u> appears as the authority for a non-alchemical fragment for

producing a child of the desired sex.[1] In the other two, the name

appears only in lists.[2]

Some new views

Kroll's article in Pauly-Wissowa not only gave an essentially

complete summary of scholarly views (and materials available), but

suggested some important corrections to them.[3] S. Julius Africanus

originated from Jerusalem, as shown by <u>Oxy. Pap.</u> 412, and evidence

from the same source shows the <u>Kestoi</u> to have been written after 227

(the date of the completion of the "baths of Alexander" in Rome), thus

placing it between 227 and 235.[4] Contra Gelzer, while Africanus did

have connections with the royal house of Edessa during the time of

Septimius Severus, there is really nothing to connect him with the

---

[1]<u>Catalogue des manuscrits alchimiques grecs</u> 1 (1924): 185-86.

[2]Ibid., 2:21 and 3:14. The former is the Greek text of the
chapter list from Berthelot's St. Mark's manuscript, the second is the
Oxford manuscript list of "philosophers of the divine science and art"
(see above, p. 63, and nn. 1 and 4).

[3]W. Kroll, "S. Julius Africanus," <u>Pauly's Real-Encyclopädie
der classischen Altertumswissenschaft</u>, rev. Georg Wissowa,et al., 34
vols. in 66 Halbbänder, in two series (plus supplements) (Stuttgart:
J. B. Metzlersche Buchhandlung, 1893-1972; plus Supplements, 1903-)
10 (1917): cols. 116-23, s.v., "Julius" (no. 47). Only a reference
to Lagercrantz's possible fragments seems to be lacking. Kroll's
acceptance of the by-name Sextus (indicated by the <u>S</u>. in the article
heading) is emphasized by the fact that he even wondered if the Sextus
to whom Neptunianus dedicated his <u>Physika</u> was not our Africanus (col.
121). (This work is hereafter identified by its common designation,
Pauly-Wissowa, and cited by its abbreviated form, PW.)

[4]Ibid., cols. 116-17.

Osrhoene campaign of 195.[1] Further, even if Africanus's use of

Suetonius were established, this would not prove he knew Latin.[2] A

survey of extant Kestoi fragments gives us further information about

the work and the author. The title indicates that the work is a

miscellany; Valesius's explanation of it is correct only in that

Africanus probably did think of Venus's magic girdle when seeking a

title for his work.[3] The work is a mixture of sober principles and

magical rubbish, often presenting good old home-remedies beside crass

superstitions; many belong to magia naturalis, but others can only

be understood as jokes (Scherz).[4] The Oxyrhynchus fragment generally

presents Africanus in a bad light: he is either responsible for the

forged Homeric interpolation, or, even worse for his critical reputa-

tion, was taken in by it. His hunting tales sound much like tall

stories (Jägerlatein); and though he has a good rhetorical education,

he has put it to misuse.[5] As far as Africanus's religious status is

concerned, the Kestoi must be regarded as a document of a completely

superficial Christianity, such as would be able to exist in proximity

to the imperial court.[6] As far as texts were concerned, the situation

was still in suspension, Gelzer's planned edition of the Chronography

had not yet been reassigned, but K. Müller's collection of materials

---

[1]Ibid., col. 116.

[2]Ibid., col. 117. This adds further uncertainty to Harnack's
view that Africanus translated Tertullian's Apology into Greek.

[3]Ibid., col. 120.   [4]Ibid., col. 121.

[5]Ibid., col. 122.   [6]Ibid., col. 123.

of the _Kestoi_ had been committed to F. Melzer.[1]

(J. Sickenberger contributed a supplement to Kroll's article,
dealing with Africanus's letters, which emphasized the positive aspects of Africanus's critical ability.[2])

In the first half of the next decade, Adolf Harnack made some
final suggestions concerning Africanus. In view of Africanus's literary interests, Harnack suggested that his work as architechtōn in
relation to the imperial library in Oxy. Pap. 412 was that of librarian, not architect.[3] This view attracted a certain amount of attention over the years, but what is perhaps Harnack's final judgment on
Africanus has been considerably less influential, though it has considerably more substance. Reversing the more-than-a-century-old dictum of Rosenmüller, Harnack asserted that Africanus's letter was over-
rated and Origen's answer underrated. Africanus was right, "trotz
seiner schnellfertigen Beweisführung," but the dogmatically bound
Origen "hat ein Meisterstück philologisch-historischer Gelehrsamkeit,
ja auch guter Methode geliefert."[4]

---

[1]Ibid., col. 118.   [2]Ibid., cols. 123-25.

[3]"Julius Afrikanus, der Bibliothekar des Kaisers Alexander
Severus," _Aufsätze Fritz Milkau gewidmet_ [ed. George Leyh] (Leipzig:
Karl W. Hiersemann, 1921), pp. 142-46; note esp. p. 145. Along the
line Harnack also speculated about Africanus's Christianity: was
there a period in Rome in which he left the church, or, was his
Christianity of a very secular, superstitious type? (p. 144). The
idea of Africanus as librarian was taken up, by Granger especially,
in a series of articles in 1932-34 (on which, see below).

[4]Adolf von Harnack, "Über die Sammlung der Briefe des
Origenes und seinen Briefwechsel mit Julius Africanus," _Sitzungs-
berichte der Preussischen Akademie der Wissenschaften: Philosophisch-
Historische Klasse_ (Berlin), 1925, p. 266.

The religious view again

Meanwhile, articles on Africanus as a church writer were incorporating the more recent data. Stählin, in his history of early
Christian literature, still relied heavily on Gelzer and Harnack,
but included significant information from the Oxyrhynchus papyrus and
Harnack's "Bibliothekar."[1] While Amann was not quite so up to date
bibliographically, he did include Oxyrhynchus in his data, and, in
addition, presented something of the rationale for the various conclusions concerning Africanus's life (e.g., the idea of his presence
on the Osrhoene campaign), not just repeating them on the authority
of Gelzer.[2]

Puech, like Amann, presented a discussion of Africanus,
which, though it presented much the common view, tried to sketch the
rationales for the various points.[3] In interests, Africanus was
characteristic of his era; he gave himself without restraint to the
contemporary interest in the occult sciences, and to dilettantism in

---

[1]Otto Stählin, Die altchristliche griechische Litteratur,
Sonder-Abdruck aus W. v. Christ's Geschichte der griechischen Lit-
teratur, sechste Auflage, zweiter Teil, zweiter Hälfte (Munich: C. H.
Becksche Verlagsbuchhandlung, Oskar Beck, 1924), pp. 1346-48.

[2]E. Amann, "Jules Africain," Dictionnaire de theologie catholique, 15 vols. in 23 (Paris: Librairie Letouzey et Ané, 1903-50),
vol. 8, part 2 (1925): cols. 1921-25; note esp. col. 1922, for the
biographical information.

[3]Aimé Puech, Histoire de la littérature grecque chrétienne
depuis le origines jusqu'a la fin du IVe siècle, vol. 2: Le IIe
et le IIIe siècle (Paris: Société d'Edition "Les Belles Lettres,"
1928), pp. 465-76.
Puech's summary was not, however, flawless: he spoke of
Africanus as being shown the remains (les restes) of Noah's ark at
Apamea (p. 467), and credits this and other details to fragments of
the Kestoi, rather than the Chronography (ibid., n. 2).

regard to historical curiosities.[1] The <u>Kestoi</u> reveals him as

> un caractère plus ou moins scientifique; mais . . . aussi . . .
> fassent appel à la magie, qui mêlait si largement, au IIIe
> siècle, aux éléments des sciences physiques, et plus encore aux
> premiers tâtonnements de la chimie.[2]

Africanus was a child of his syncretistic times, able to live in

close relations with princes favorable to Christianity, such as Abgar

of Edessa, or a syncretistic emperor such as Alexander Severus, but

also, apparently, to serve one hostile to the church such as Sep-

timius Severus.[3]

Recent Contributions

A New Era

Almost three decades after the last major advance in Afri-

canian studies, the publication of the Oxyrhynchus fragment in 1903,

another advance, of even greater potential significance, occurred:

the long desired publication of a major portion of the extant Afri-

caniana, in 1932.

"Nineteen thirty-two was a very good year"

That year, 1932, saw not only the appearance of Vieillefond's

<u>Kestoi</u> text,[4] but also the debut in print of possibly the next most

important name in recent Africanian studies, that of Gudmund Björck.[5]

---

[1]Ibid., pp. 466-67.   [2]Ibid., p. 474.

[3]Ibid., pp. 475-76.

[4]<u>Jules Africain: Fragments des Cestes provenant de la collection des tacticiens grecs</u> (cited elsewhere as <u>Jules Africain</u>).

[5]"Zum Corpus hippiatricorum Graecorum," <u>Uppsala Universitets
Årsskrift: Filosofi, språkvetenskap och historiska vetenskaper</u>, 1932,

It also saw the elaboration of some earlier themes, in Vincent and

Abel's Emmaüs,[1] and the appearance of the first of a series of articles

by Frank Granger spinning out various ramifications of Africanus's

hypothesized librarianship.[2]

Vieillefond

After several centuries of false starts and unfulfilled prom-

ises, the text of the major extant portion of the Kestoi appeared

rather quietly and unexpectedly. Further, it appeared in France (more

specifically Paris, also the place of origin of the Thevenot-Boivin

edition), rather than Germany, which had held something of a lead in

Africanian studies for the preceding half-century. J.-R. Vieillefond

undertook the establishment of a text for Africanus at the suggestion

of Aimé Puech,[3] beginning with the chapters preserved in the Byzan-

tine military collections. The introduction included studies of the

---

no. 5, pp. 31 and 41. This first publication, however, simply noted
the appearance of Africanus in the English hippiatrica manuscripts;
Björck's major contribution came later, in 1944.

[1]L.-H. Vincent and F.-M. Abel, Emmaüs, sa basilique et son
histoire (Paris: Librairie Ernest Leroux, 1932), esp. pp. 257-62,
331-41.

[2]"The Greek Origin of the Pantheon," Journal of the Royal Institute of British Architects 40 (1932): 57-61; "Julius Africanus and
the Library of the Pantheon," Journal of Theological Studies 34 (1933):
157-61; and, "Julius Africanus and the Western Text," Journal of Theological Studies 35 (1934): 361-68. This idea was further elaborated
by Carl Wendel, "Versuch einer Deutung der Hippolyt-Statue," Theologische Studien und Kritiken 108 (n.s. 3) (1937-38): 362-69.

[3]Jules Africain, p. v; also Puech's review of it in Revue des
études grecques 45 (1932): 447.

textual tradition of these writings[1] (carried on jointly with Alphonse
Dain, both before and after this publication), and of Africanus's
life and writings,[2] especially the Kestoi.[3]

Concerning Africanus, Vieillefond's views were not radically
different from the current views, especially as presented by Puech,
but were somewhat more cautious, with new views on a few significant
points. Concerning Africanus's name, Vieillefond argued that the
Suidas's Sektos chrēmatisas should be taken at face value, as indicating an epithet, Sectus, rather than being corrected into a praenomen, Sextus. This epithet he then interpreted as "l'émasculé."[4]
On the other hand, the Suidas's designation of him as a "Libyan
philosopher" was an error deriving from the name Africanus; actually,
he was born at Aelia Capitolina (probably between 160 and 180).[5]

The idea that Africanus was a military officer who accompanied
Septimius Severus on the Osrhoene campaign of 195, or even more specifically, was an officer in the engineer corps, is reasonable, but
has no real support.[6] On the contrary, the broad range of contents of
his writings could just as easily make him a doctor, or a countryman.
Besides, in his reports of military stratagems, he recounts no personal experiences.[7] Finally, the report of the later Syrians,

----

[1]Jules Africain, pp. xxv-liv.   [2]Ibid., pp. vii-xvii.

[3]Ibid., pp. xviii-xxv, and liv-lviii.   [4]Ibid., p. viii.

[5]Ibid., pp. viii-ix.

[6]Ibid., pp. ix, x-xi, though he constructed, or organized,
a library at the Pantheon for the emperor (p. x, with n. 2).

[7]Ibid., p. xi.

Dionysius bar Ṣalibi and Ebed Jesu, that he was a bishop probably stems from a misapplication to Africanus of Eusebius's statement concerning Heracles becoming bishop (H.E. 6. 31. 2). This is preferable to Gelzer's and Puech's interpretation of it as a misunderstanding of Eusebius's proistamenos in his notice in the Chronicon concerning Africanus's embassy for Emmaus.[1]

The author of the Kestoi was the same as the author of the Chronography and of the letters (with the Kestoi coming between them). He was thus a Christian, as stated by Eusebius, etc., but the commonly cited Psalm quotation in Geoponica is as valueless in proof of it as is the attributions of authorship in that work. More to the point is a comparison to Africanus's description of the Dead Sea in the Chronography (Migne, PG, 10:69).[2]

The title of Africanus's secular work, the Kestoi, derives from the kestos of Aphrodite, but in the sense of Talismans or Amulets.[3] Further, each book was designated as a Kestos, with accompanying number, in an explicit at the end of each (note the end of Oxy. Pap. 412);[4] this arrangement explains the form of the "titles" which had puzzled editors over the years.[5] Within the work, however,

---

[1] Ibid., p. xi, with notes 3 and 4 (cont. on p. xii). (But concerning bar Ṣalibi's supposed evidence, see above, pp. 25-26, with n. 1 on the latter page.)

[2] Ibid., pp. xvi-xvii.   [3] Ibid., pp. xiii-xiv.

[4] Ibid., pp. xxxv-xxxvii.

[5] The confusion goes at least as far back as the copyists of Vieillefond's "recueil A" who omitted the book number at the beginning of the extracts from Kestos 7 (Jules Africain, p. xxxvi); Isaac Voss who attributed the military chapters to books 6 and 7 of the Kestoi

neither the ordering of the books, nor of the chapters, was based on
logic, but followed the whim of the author, or an exceedingly loose
series of associations of ideas. There was not even a particular
subject for each book.[1]

While the work is basically scientific in intent,[2] it is also
a "literary" work characterized by various rhetorical embellishments.[3]
It also contains distinctly magical elements, themselves apparently
characteristic of another side both of the author's age and of his
wide-ranging personal interests.[4]

In the manuscript tradition, besides the main group of chapters, taken more or less en bloc from Kestos 7, there was a smaller
group of chapters, partially overlapping the preceding, apparently
drawn (and in some cases condensed) from various parts of the Kestoi.
Certain excerpts were also included in later compilations of "Tactics"
by pseudo-Leon and pseudo-Constantine.[5] On the other hand, several
chapters included in the editions of Thevenot and of Lami were to be

---

(Catullus, p. 30); and Martin and Gelzer who corrected Keston ig' to
Kestōn ig' in the introduction to the purgatives fragment (respectively, "Recherches sur Heron," p. 355, n. 3; and "Zu Africanus," p.
376).

[1] Jules Africain, p. xv.

[2] Ibid., pp. xvii, xxxix, lv.

[3] Ibid., pp. xxxvii, and liv-lv; also, lviii.

[4] Ibid., pp. xv-xvi, xxxix, and lv-lviii.

[5] These four groups make up the two parts and the two appen-
dices, respectively, of Vieillefond's text. See also the "Introduction," ibid., pp. xxxvi – xli, and xlvi-liii.

excluded on literary and textual grounds.[1]

The following year, 1933, Vieillefond made another contribution to the study of Africanus with the decipherment and publication of the text of another fragment, that concerning cinnamon.[2] Though its existence had been known for some time (Vieillefond mentions H. Diels, Die Handschriften der antiken Aertze, II, erster Nachtrag, p. 43 [1907], as first calling attention to it),[3] its condition had discouraged earlier publication. Besides the matter in the text itself, the fragment further illustrated Africanus's broad interests and critical abilities (in rejecting the account of the origin of cinnamon accepted by Herodotus [3. 111]).[4] It also provided personal

---

[1] Boivin and Martin, as noted above in the discussion of each, had questioned the authenticity of several chapters on the former basis. Their conclusions were largely based on the close verbal correspondences of certain chapters with earlier writers such as Aeneas and Polyaenus, coupled with a lack of distinguishing Africanian stylistic characteristics in these chapters. Vieillefond recognized the force, but also the limitations, of these arguments, and so, together with Alphonse Dain, sought to provide an objective solution by delineating the manuscript tradition(s) of the military collections (Jules Africain, pp. xxix-xliii; "Adaptations . . . d'Enée," pp. 25-36; also Les Cestes [1970], pp. 189-98--Vieillefond there added two more chapters to the excluded list: Thevenot's chaps. 35 and 36, which had appeared in Jules Africain as "Deuxième partie," chaps. 5 and 6 [see Les Cestes, p. 191]). For Dain's work see the note to the paragraph on the "Military Collections" (above, p. 30, n. 3), and, especially, Enée le tacticien: Poliorcétique, texte établi par Alphonse Dain; traduit et annoté Anne-Marie Bon (Paris: Société d'Edition "Les Belles Lettres," 1967), pp. xliii-liv. (Gudmund Björck further used the verbal similarity argument in rejecting a chapter from the hippiatrica tradition, Vieillefond's [1970] III. 11, as coming more or less directly from Aelian ["Apsyrtus," p. 17]).

[2] "Un fragment inédit de Julius Africanus," Revue des études grecques 46 (1933): 197-203.

[3] Ibid., p. 198, and n. 1.

[4] Ibid., pp. 201-2.

information about Africanus: Africanus changed Herodotus's <u>tous</u>
<u>Arabious</u> to <u>tous par' hēmin</u>, showing that he was "un Asiatique du
Sud-Est," and thus corroborating the evidence of <u>Oxy. Pap.</u> 412 concerning his birth in Aelia Capitolina.[1]

Reviews and results

The reviews of <u>Jules Africain</u> served to underline certain
views of Africanus, both pro and con Vieillefond. Georges Mathieu
regretted the restricting of the text to the military extracts
(though recognizing its practical basis): Africanus was a poly-
graph, and it is precisely the variety of his occupations which is
interesting.[2] W. W. Tarn characterized Africanus's work as a

> queer farrago of sense and nonsense, history and tall stories,
> . . . often both attractive and interesting, . . . important
> for the study of magic, and . . . gropes along a path which was
> to lead to poison gas and germ-carriers.[3]

In a view not really contradictory to the preceding, P. Chantraine
spoke of Africanus as being, in all truth, "un écrivain assez me-
diocre," but with his rhetoric and style being accurately evaluated
by Vieillefond, who also gave a precise indication of the place of
magic in his work. On the other hand, Vieillefond's interpretation
of the name <u>Sectus</u> as "l'emasculé" was not supported by any datum.[4]

---

[1]Ibid., pp. 202-3.

[2]Review in <u>Revue des études anciennes</u> 33 (1931[-32]): 307-9--
Vieillefond, in effect, had admitted this when he questioned [p. xi]
that Africanus was an officer (p. 309).

[3]Review in <u>The Classical Review</u> 46 (1932): 238.

[4]Review in <u>Revue critique d'histoire et de litterature</u>, n.s.
99 (1932): 199.

Similarly, Aimé Puech, in an otherwise naturally favorable review, re-asserted his preference for the older interpretation of Cestes as "Tissus brodës = Variétés" against Vieillefond's suggestion of Talismans or Amulets.[1]

Apart from the reviews, Vieillefond's work produced little direct result in stimulation of further Africanian studies. The major exception, however, appeared in the following year, in a study by Gustave Bardy entitled, "Un encyclopédiste chrétien du IIIe siècle."[2] Bardy shared with Vieillefond a similar attitude of restraint on obscure points, but sometimes with contrasting preferences. He maintained the older interpretation of Kestoi as meaning "Broderies,"[3] but allowed the reasonableness of Vieillefond's suggestion regarding Sectos as a sobriquet.[4] Born around 180, Africanus reflected the religious syncretism of his times, especially that promoted by the Syrian princesses.[5] His contacts with the Edessene court may have included acquaintance with Bardesane, with whom he shared an interest

---

[1] Review in Revue des études grecques 45 (1932): 447, n. 1.

[2] Revue apologétique 56 (1933): 257-71. (There is no reference to Vieillefond's work in either of the two other articles devoted to Africanus in the 1930s: E. H. Blakeney, "Julius Africanus: A Letter to Origen on the Story of Susanna," Theology 29 [1934]: 164-69; and, Ier. Ier. Kotsones, "Ἰούλιος ὁ Ἀφρικανός, ὁ πρῶτος χριστιανὸς χρονογράφος," Θεολογία   [Athens] 15 [1937]: 227-38.)

[3] "Un encyclopédiste," p. 257 and, esp., p. 266; talisman or amulet is too restricted to adequately represent the variety of this work.

[4] Ibid., p. 258.   [5] Ibid., pp. 258-59.

in the profane sciences, though this is questionable.[1] He may have

been an officer, but there is no proof of this; what is known is his

wide-ranging curiosity--this curiosity brought him into contact with

many places, people, and subjects.[2] It is especially shown in the

Kestoi, though also illustrated by the general topics and specific

development of his other works.[3] More specifically, Africanus seems

to have been a man of good family and of much leisure, who travelled

for his own enjoyment, and who had an untiring curiosity about every-

thing.[4] This interest included not only natural science but also

the reason for events, "la philosophie des choses."[5] But, despite

his scientific and historical interests, and his proven critical

abilities, Africanus did believe in magic. In the Kestoi, he reports

magical formulae and invocations to deities or demons, and uses

pentagons and hexagons; but a fully accurate evaluation of the Kestoi

is prevented by the fact that we only have fragments of it, fragments

chosen (and recorded) according to the special interests of other

collectors.[6] The Kestoi was written by a Christian (this is shown,

not by the Psalms citation in the Geoponica, which is probably not

authentic, but by the order of Africanus's writings), but it has no

apologetic intent: all the known fragments could have been written

---

[1]Ibid., p. 260, and nn. 2 and 3: the fragment speaks of a
Parthian called Bardesane.

[2]Ibid., pp. 260-63.   [3]Ibid., pp. 265, 261-64.

[4]Ibid., pp. 262-63.   [5]Ibid., pp. 263, 269.

[6]Ibid., pp. 266-68. Further, while the Kestoi has been compared to an encyclopedia, it was one without order (p. 265).

by a pagan.[1] The writer loved life, and was curious about all things;

he treated of science for its own sake. This last made him unique

among the Christian writers of his day, and for long afterward.[2]

A New Approach?

In 1944, Gudmund Björck presented a largely new suggestion

toward the solution of the Africanian problem: the Kestoi was a

pastiche, "un veritable travestissement."[3] At the same time, Björck

also demonstrated, on the score of Africanus's style as further de-

veloped from Vieillefond's summary,[4] that several extracts credited

to Africanus in Codex Cantabrigiensis of the Hippiatrica were as

authentic as any in the tacticians.[5]

As to the origin of the Kestoi, Vieillefond's appeal to the

strange mixture of ideas of diverse religions and contradictory tend-

encies in the third century (Jules Africain, p. xvi) is astonishing:

ideas have little place in the Kestoi, and religion none at all; it

was not a question of Africanus's Christianity, but of his good sense.[6]

---

[1]Ibid., pp. 269-70.   [2]Ibid., p. 270.

[3]"Apsyrtus," pp. 22, 24-25. Kroll bordered on this in some
statements in his article in Pauly-Wissowa ("S. Julius Africanus,"
cols. 121, 122) but he never suggested it as an over-all solution to
the problem.

[4]"Apsyrtus," p. 15. Its characteristics are: "des clausules
calculées (crétiques), des vocables recherchés et des tournures ora-
toires, des comparaisons, des circonlocutions et des réflexions
souvent assez forcées, enfin des références mythologiques et litté-
raires."

[5]Ibid. On the other hand, none of the Geoponica items, at
least in their present state, can be certainly attributed to Africanus (p. 18).

[6]Ibid., p. 20.

Similarly, Vieillefond's citation (Jules Africain, pp. xvi-xvii) of

Africanus's description of the Dead Sea in the Chronography is point-

less: that is a geographical curiosity in the ancient Hellenic his-

torical tradition, it is nothing like the prescriptions of the Kes-

toi.[1] Following a summary reference to Africanus's procedures for

poisoning the air and for driving worms from a horse by sprinkling

with water (cited also at more length before the preceding items),

Björck concludes, "si Africanus a composé 'le plus sérieusement du

monde' (VI. p. XV) les Κεστοί que nous possédons, alors nous sommes

devant un dilemme insoluble."[2] The solution: the Kestoi is a

pastiche. Besides the two examples already cited, which represent

the zoological pharmacopia of the magicians and the old popular medi-

cine, a third passage, from the philological realm, Oxy. Pap. 412,

seems to confirm this result.[3] In it, "Nous reconnaissons l'esprit

bizarre de notre auteur, la contrefaçon d'un jargon pseudo-

scientifique poussée jusqu'à la caricature, la précision détaillée

d'un imposteur."[4] This passage stands in marked contrast to his

serious discussion of the story of Susanna. An author such as the

one who wrote the letters and the Chronography, especially on the

look-out for falsifications, could hardly be taken in by a "Homeric"

---

[1]Ibid., p. 21. The linguistic argument against the authenticity of Susanna in the Epistle to Origen is more typical of Africanus as historian and theologian (p. 23).

[2]Ibid., p. 22.   [3]Ibid.

[4]Ibid., p. 23.

incantation of such content and form.[1] Before coming to his final

proposal (with which this discussion of Björck's views was begun),

Björck posed a rhetorical question which he admitted himself unable

to answer: did Africanus intend his work to be, from end to end, a

parody of the empty polymathy of his day; was part of it more legit-

imate instruction; was there an element of "l'art pour l'art," ac-

cording to the sophistic desire to present picturesque matter in an

astonishing form?[2]

Though earlier writers (especially Kroll in Pauly-Wissowa,

as noted) had called attention to the facetious element in the Kes-

toi, Björck was the first to suggest this as the explanation of all,

or large parts of the work. In a sense, this made him a successor

of the views of Valesius and of Tillemont, in that this view also

would have absolved the Christian Africanus of real advocacy of magic

and other completely secular beliefs.[3] If his view had been vindi-

cated, it would have dramatically changed the complexion of Africanian

studies. Farrington, who considered Björck's suggested solution

worthy of more study, noted that it would transform Africanus "from a

believer in magic and superstition to a subtle critic of these

---

[1]Ibid. Again Björck's analysis has similarities to Kroll's
("S. Julius Africanus," col. 122), but developed from a different
viewpoint and thus leading to different conclusions concerning Africanus's good sense.

[2]"Apsyrtus," p. 24. Part of the problem, as Björck saw it,
was the tendency toward parody within magic itself; for this he refers the reader to his later discussion on p. 56.

[3]Though, of course, the motivations were different. Björck
was attempting to fit Africanus into a more natural view of the development of human thought (p. 22; cf. also p. 20), not to defend
his Christian status.

errors."[1] On the other hand, Ludwig Edelstein, while conceding that

some passages of the Kestoi were not meant to be taken quite seriously,

rejected the idea that the Kestoi as a whole was intended as a parody

of superstition: Africanus adhered to "superstitious" beliefs, rel-

ished "sacred" books concerning the mysteries, and enjoyed relating

"secret histories." At the same time, Edelstein seems to concede

that Björck's two prime examples (poisoning air and sprinkling

against worms) fall into the category of paignia (practical jokes).

He concluded with the hope that Björck, who wrote so lucidly on

magic in the last chapter of his work, would reconsider and allow

Africanus to be "sensible" and "superstitious" at the same time--

"Many of Julius' contemporaries were of like hue."[2]

Variant Views[3]

Opposing views of the character and value of Africanus appeared

as by-products of two other works of the thirties. The first, Vin-

cent and Abel's Emmaus, appeared the same year as Vieillefond's Jules

---

[1]B. Farrington, review of "Apsyrtus, Julius Africanus et l'hippiatrique grecque," by Gudmund Björck, in Journal of Hellenic Studies
64 (1944): 121.

[2]Review of "Apsyrtus, Julius Africanus et l'hippiatrique
grecque," by Gudmund Björck, in American Journal of Philology 68
(1947): 444-45.

[3]During the period after Vieillefond, Africanus also appeared
briefly in a number of other works. The chapter automaton pyr hapsai
earned him a place in several technical works: R. J. Forbes, Bitumen
and Petroleum in Antiquity (Leiden: E. J. Brill, 1936), chap. 7,
"Petroleum and Greek Fire in Warfare," esp. pp. 95-96, and More Studies
in Early Petroleum History (Leiden: E. J. Brill, 1959), chap. 4, "Naphtha Goes to War," esp. p. 84, and chart facing p. 80; and J. R. Part-
ington, A History of Greek Fire and Gunpowder (Cambridge: W. Heffer &
Sons, Ltd., 1960), pp. 7-9, 28, 31 (but with the chapter regarded as
probably a later interpolation [pp. 7-8]).

<u>Africain</u>. It presented an expanded, and somewhat speculative, picture
of the role of Africanus. He was probably a wealthy, travelled, and
influential courtier, a true Christian, though embued with many of the
occult interests of his day, who not only secured, but also directed,
the imperial restoration of Emmaus-Nicopolis, his home by adoption or
by birth.[1] This restoration involved special attention to the
Christian quarter, including the building of a church there (comparable to the public buildings elsewhere in the city).[2] Oliver Spaulding,
on the other hand, concluded that Africanus manifested the greatest
credulity, and that, at least from the military viewpoint, the <u>Kestoi</u>
had "no real value in itself."[3] Further, as far as Africanus's character was concerned: "Nothing was unfair in his warfare; without
apology, he presents formulae for poisoning everything--weapons,
forage, rations, water, and air."[4]

Edgar J. Goodspeed's view of Africanus was essentially the
Gelzer-Harnack consensus as updated by the Oxyrhynchus papyrus; he
viewed the <u>Kestoi</u> as a "sort of notebook of strange pieces of curious
information . . . the miscellanies accumulated by a travelled and
inquiring mind."[5] His <u>History of Early Christian Literature</u>, though

---

[1] <u>Emmaus</u>, pp. 257-58, 331-38.

[2] Ibid., pp. 257-62, 338-41.

[3] Oliver Lyman Spaulding, <u>Pen and Sword in Greece and Rome</u>
(Princeton: Princeton University Press, 1937), p. 99.

[4] Ibid., p. 100.

[5] <u>A History of Early Christian Literature</u> (Chicago: University
of Chicago Press, 1942), pp. 253-56 are devoted to Africanus.

published in 1942, reflected no influence or even real knowledge of
Vieillefond's work. The text of this part of Goodspeed's History was
not changed by Grant in his enlarged edition of it (though Vieillefond's Jules Africain now appeared in the Bibliography),[1] but Grant
had commented on Africanus in two earlier studies. In his "Historical Criticism in the Ancient Church," he presented Africanus as "a
critic of Homer as well as of the Old and New Testaments."[2] While
admitting that Africanus's work in the first area (as evidenced by
the Oxyrhynchus papyrus 412) was not satisfactory, Grant commended
it for its wide ranging effort and evidence of acquaintance with the
best critical methods of the day.[3] In one of a series of short notes
entitled "Patristica," he also suggested, in contrast to Vieillefond's interpretation of Sektos, that the by-name in the Suidas
should be understood as metathesis from Kestos.[4]

---

[1] Robert M. Grant, ed. and rev. of Edgar J. Goodspeed, A History of Early Christian Literature, rev. and enl. ed. (Chicago:
University of Chicago Press, Phoenix Books, 1966), pp. 151-53, 209.

[2] Journal of Religion 25 (1945): 190.

[3] Ibid., p. 191. Apart from the presumption in Africanus's
favor created by his other efforts, even this modest compliment
might appear excessive. (Africanus's critical ability earned him
only a qualified commendation, in a single footnote, in Carl Schneider, Geistesgeschichte des antiken Christentums, 2 vols. [Munich:
C. H. Beck, 1954], 2:37, n. 1; [but Porphyry and Celsus faired little
better (ibid.)].)

[4] Vigiliae Christianae 3 (1949): 227. This view was perhaps
first suggested by Valesius (Eccl. hist., "Ann.", p. 127, col. 2A;
followed by Dupin, Nouv. biblio., 1:117 and note g), but had a history separate from the rest of his theory. Many authors who distinguished the Africani called the heathen writer Sextus Africanus; but
Labbé, who argued for a single Africanus, called him Kestos (Diss.
philol. de script., 1:659).

Other Speculations

F. Lammert challenged the line of thinking (begun at least
with Boivin, elaborated by Martin, and climaxing in Vieillefond)[1]
which restricted the number of chapters in the Greek tacticians that
were seen as coming from Africanus.[2] Lammert followed Schoene and
other editors of Aeneas in also crediting to the Kestoi the chapters
from Aeneas which follow the Kestoi fragments in the military compilations. Arguing that fragments of earlier writers may be found in
Africanus, and that later terminology might be due to "modernization"
by later editors, he suggested that the decision must be based on the
factual content of the chapters (rather than style and vocabulary).[3]
Specifically, he argued that chapter 72a (i.e., the unnumbered item
following chapter 72 in the Thevenot edition) and the three following chapters, despite some Byzantine vocabulary, were by Africanus.[4]

_____

[1] Boivin, in Thevenot, Veterum mathematicorum, pp. 339, 353,
357; Martin, "Recherches sur Heron," pp. 344, 355-61; and Vieillefond, Jules Africain, pp. xxxix-xl.

[2] "Julius Afrikanus und die byzantinishe Taktik," Byzantinische Zeitschrift 44 (1951): 362-69. Lammert included only Boivin
and Vieillefond in his discussion (pp. 362-63).

[3] Ibid., p. 363.

[4] Ibid., pp. 363-69. Both Martin ("Recherches sur Heron,"
p. 361) and Vieillefond (Jules Africain, p. xl) regard these chapters as coming from an unknown, but late, source, perhaps from the
compiler himself.

In a different area, several writers speculated on Africanus's
Homeric text. Odette Bouquiaux-Simon suggested that Africanus gives
evidence of the same type of tendentious Homeric text as that appar-
ently cited by Lucian.[1] Fridolf Kudlien went further, attempting to
credit another work to Africanus, a lost pseudo-Galenic "Concerning
Homeric Medicine."[2] Finally, Vieillefond mentioned favorably
Bouquiaux-Simon's proposal in a presentation concerning Africanus's
Nekyia text as a part of the literary ancestry of Dante's Inferno.[3]

Meanwhile, two other authors dealt with the secular side of
some of Africanus's religious contacts. Abraham Schalit traced the
report that derived Herod's family from Ascalon (given, among others,
by Africanus in his letter to Aristides) back to an original Jewish,
anti-Herodian polemic. Later generations of Jews, under the later
Herods, dropped this polemic, and it survived only in Christian
sources.[4] Drijvers, in his study of Bardaisan, identified him with
Africanus's Bardaisan the Parthian, and so made use of Africanus's
testimony (and silence) concerning Bardaisan's life (and alleged
heresy).[5]

---

[1]"Lucien citateur d'Homère," L'antiquité classique 29 (1960):
13-17.

[2]"Zum Thema 'Homer und die Medizin,'" Rheinisches Museum für
Philologie n.s. 108 (1965): 295-99.

[3]J.-R. Vieillefond, "De la Nekyia Homérique à l'Enfer de Dante,"
Revue des études italiennes n.s. 11 (1965): 439-53 (Africanus on pp.
448-51; reference to Bouquiaux-Simon, p. 451, with n. 1).

[4]"Die frühchristliche Überlieferung über die Herkunft der
Familie des Herodes: Ein Beitrag zur Geschichte der politischen Invek-
tive in Judäa," Annual of the Swedish Theological Institute [Jerusalem]
1 (1960): 109-60, esp. pp. 141-43.

[5]H. J. W. Drijvers, Bardaisan of Edessa, trans. Mrs. G. E.

Status of the Question

Johannes Quasten devoted slightly over two pages of his

Patrology to a brief sketch of Africanus's life and writings.

Though he included Vieillefond in his list of Editions, his view of

Africanus was still essentially the familiar Gelzer-Harnack synthe-

sis.[1] The brief, one-page, discussion in Altaner's Patrology (which

appeared in English form in 1960), did not materially change this

view (including terminology that at least allows, and perhaps sug-

gests, Harnack's "librarian" thesis), though it expanded the charge

of magic in the Kestoi to a belief in "magic and sorcery," explain-

ing it as "syncretism."[2] In this same year, the Encyclopaedia Brit-

annica produced the previously mentioned, slightly revised version

of its earlier article (making Africanus's birthplace Aelia Capito-

lina, but not reflecting any literature after Oxyrhynchus III).[3]

This article continued through 1969, after which it disappeared,

---

van Baaren-Pape, Studia Semitica Neerlandica, no. 6 (Assen: Van
Gorcum, 1966), pp. 167, 183-85. Drijvers cited Africanus from
Thevenot and Migne, however, with no reference to Vieillefond's
text (p. 167, n. 2).

[1]Patrology, vol. 2: The Ante-Nicene Literature after Irenaeus
(Utrecht and Antwerp: Spectrum Publications, 1948), pp. 137-40. In
addition to his description, Quasten included lists of most of the
basic sources (Editions, Translations, and Studies of each of Africanus's works) necessary for the study of Africanus (but on p. 138,
Bardy's article title should be "Un encyclopédiste chrétien . . .";
on p. 139, the second of Granger's articles should be J.Th.S. 34
[1933]; and on p. 140, J. Stroux, "Zu Quintillian," should be
omitted, it concerns a different Julius Africanus.)

[2]Berthold Altaner, Patrology, trans. Hilda C. Graef from the
5th German ed. (New York: Herder & Herder, 1960), p. 236.

[3]See above, p. 72, n. 1.

squeezed out between a more lively "African Music" and an unyielding
"African Violet."   With the advent of the New Encyclopaedia Britannica in 1974, "Africanus, Sextus Julius" reappeared, but in an oddly
distorted form: he was born "c. AD 180," he "served as prefect" in
Palestine, and was "regional ambassador to Rome" about 222. Further,
the Kestoi was not even mentioned (nor, for that matter, the letter
to Origen concerning Susanna).[1]

The New Era Renovated

In 1970, Vieillefond capped off the work begun in 1932 with
his full edition (with French translation) of the fragments of the
Kestoi.[2] In accord with his previous views, this included, in eight
sections, the texts from all verifiable sources[3] (but excluding any
texts from the Geoponica), and also included citations in a ninth
section. The "Etude générale" (70 pages) which preceded the text
also continued Vieillefond's balanced, somewhat conservative approach
to the life and works of Africanus, but added a major new element to
his interpretation: Africanus in the Kestoi was a Jew writing

---

[1]The New Encyclopaedia Britannica, 30 vols., 15th ed. (1974),
Micropaedia 1:126, col. 1. (The date, about 180, is perhaps a distorted reflection of use of Vieillefond, who gave Africanus's birth-
date as 160-180 [Jules Africain, p. ix], or before 180 [Les Cestes,
p. 18], though it might be from Bardy ["Un encyclopédiste," p. 258];
most other sources that hazard a date give it simply as ca. 170.)

[2]Les Cestes de Julius Africanus (cited elsewhere as Les Cestes).

[3]Texts from Kestos 7 (from the military collections), other
texts from the military collections, Hippiatrica, weights and measures, the Oxyrhynchus fragment, purgatives, concerning cinnamon, and
dyeing.

especially for Jews of the Diaspora.[1]

Vieillefond had indicated his belief in Africanus's Jewish
origin, in a passing reference, in his study of the Nekyia and
Dante, but had not elaborated or supported it.[2] His previously stated
view, presented in his 1933 study of the "Fragment inédit" concerning
cinnamon, had been the more general (and more correct?) view of Africanus as "un Asiatique du Sud-Est" with Aelia Capitolina as his
birthplace.[3] Vieillefond supports the more specific conclusion by
attributing it to Africanus himself: in a work addressed essentially
to the Jews, the expression tēs archaias patridos . . . (Oxy. Pap.
412) could only mean "notre ancienne patrie. . . ."[4] This argument
assumes the Jewish address of the Kestoi, a point which Vieillefond
attempts to prove later in his study.[5] In terms of specific

---

[1]Les Cestes, pp. 14, 17, 41-42.

[2]"De la Nekyia," p. 448. Blass, at least, had previously
suggested this ("Literarische Texte," p. 297), but the idea seems
not to have been taken up by later writers.

[3]"Fragment inédit," p. 203.

[4]Les Cestes, p. 17. This interpretation also means that the
phrase does not necessarily indicate that Africanus himself was born
in Jerusalem (ibid.).

[5]But a failure to clearly establish this leaves the argument
essentially circular. It is, at best, possible, and seems to be in
conflict with the indications from certain references by Africanus in
his other works, and by Origen to Africanus.
        One of Origen's comments on Africanus's linguistic argument
against Susanna might have significance here: he says, "Your reason
for affirming that there is not [a possibility of such a paronomasia
in the Hebrew language], you yourself probably know" (To Africanus 6
[end]). This could be seen as a covert reference to Africanus's Jewish origin; but, if so, the question immediately arises, "Why covert?"
In addition, the statement is quite easily understood as a polite,
though emphatic, questioning of the conclusiveness of the evidence.
Elsewhere in the letter, there is a consistent pattern of reference to

reference by Africanus, besides the Oxyrhynchus and the "Concerning
cinnamon" passages, in the chapter on metrology (Les Cestes, Part IV,
line 55), he refers to the conge, "which we call cabos," a Hebrew
term.[1] In more general evidence, the pentagon and hexagon, mentioned
in several of Africanus's procedures, are also especially connected
with Jewish magic.[2]

Vieillefond's basic principle of accepting only clearly attested items in the reconstruction of the life of Africanus is now

---

the Jews as "them," not only in contrast to Origen, but also to Africanus (4; 5; 9; 12-14).
      This same pattern is found throughout Africanus's own writ-
ings: e.g., To Origen 4, "in the Daniel received among the Jews"
[cf. Origen To Africanus 9, "in their Daniel"]; To Aristides, ". . . in
Israel, the names of their generations, . . . them, . . . they," and
later, ". . . the genealogies of the Hebrews . . . , Herod . . .
burned the registers of their families" [= Eus. H.E. 1. 7. 2 and 13,
respectively]; Chronography, Routh's fragments X, XXII, XLIX, and L
(esp. the last; within it note Rel. sacr. 2:297, 301-2, 304-5, and,
esp., p. 306, line 3).
      In all these passages, Africanus writes of the Jews as a third
party, distinct from himself and his intended readers (basically
Christians); Origen's references are consistent with this pattern.
This might be correlated with Vieillefond's view by arguing that in
these cases Africanus, a Jewish Christian, is here speaking as a
Christian, distinct from the Jews. But, if so, why the need for
Origen to allude to this covertly? One who would seemingly conceal
his Jewish background when writing and being written to as a Christian,
would hardly write as a Jew to a Jewish audience (or be accepted by
them as one). Such a situation would suggest as great an "identity
crisis" for Africanus as a Christian author as is usually seen for
him as a secular one.

[1]Les Cestes, p. 41. (But kabos is not exclusively Hebrew
[qab], it also appears in Aramaic [qaba'], and has cognates in other
Semitic languages. The force of this argument depends to some extent
on the loosening of Africanus's residential ties with Palestine,
which Vieillefond does, despite the other evidence for his ties with
Emmaus especially.)

[2]Les Cestes, pp. 42-44; but Vieillefond himself follows this
by evidence of its wider use (ranging from ancient Babylon and Egypt
to modern Italian seamen) (pp. 44-45, with n. 61 [continued on p.
46]).

extended to two other areas, his residence and his profession.
Vieillefond questions the ties of Africanus to Emmaus, seeing it
basically as a client relation (or simply the introduction of its
representatives at court), rather than as his residence.[1] Concerning Africanus's profession, Vieillefond rejects Harnack's "librarian"
hypothesis[2] (which he had left open in 1932),[3] concluding that it is
best to assume that Africanus was an architect, but also interested
in other areas such as science, letters, philosophy, and theology.[4]

Vieillefond rejects Björck's theory of the Kestoi as a
pastiche,[5] but in the discussion describes it as a work

> où la mythologie païenne, la science plus ou moins sérieuse,
> le bel esprit plus ou moins humoristique[80] et la magie plus ou
> moins juive se mêlent et se superposent. . . .

---

[80]Voir I, 17, 25; I, 19, 23.[6]

He concludes that for Africanus the Kestoi was

---

[1]Ibid., p. 19. Vieillefond does not find a residence at
Emmaus indicated in Eusebius's Chronik reference (ed. Helm, p. 214).
This is perhaps a valid rejection of Vincent and Abel's reconstruction, but seems to be an over-reaction. Besides its failure to do
justice to the other testimony besides Eusebius (which may be somewhat independent of him, e.g., Philip of Side [see above, pp. 17
and 64-65]) it leaves unasked a basic question concerning Eusebius's
report: why such a reference at all? Is it because of the significance to Eusebius of Africanus, or of Emmaus? Or is it of the two
together, and together in a somewhat substantial and lasting relationship? (The elaboration of the question implies my own answer.)

[2]Les Cestes, p. 21.   [3]Jules Africain, p. x, n. 2.

[4]Les Cestes, pp. 21-22. On p. 29, continuation of n. 31 from
p. 28, Vieillefond also rejected Kudlien's suggestion that Africanus
wrote the pseudo-Galenic "Homeric Medicine" as "bien arbitraire."

[5]Les Cestes, pp. 53-55.   [6]Ibid., p. 54.

une récréation, une distraction, où l'élément ludique, propre à toute création intellectuelle, ne peut guère se dissocier de tous les autres (fierté, sentiment d'utilité etc.) qui déterminent l'oeuvre écrite.[1]

The Kestoi is not, properly speaking, syncretistic, it is written from a purely pagan, "classic," viewpoint:

On sent même qu' Africanus se refuse à superposer les registres païen et judéo-chrétien alors que pourtant des associations d'idées l'y conduisaient naturellement.[2]

Though good taste is not the dominant quality of the Kestoi, Africanus does not violate the bounds between the sacred and the profane.[3]

The sources of the Kestoi were many and varied--the school of pseudo-Democritus, Homer, Euclid, Herodotus, the Quintilian brothers, et al.--but "en général Africanus aime à souligner son originalité."[4]

Results of the New Era

The new era, which began and, at present, ends with Vieillefond, has provided a good base for further advance in Africanian studies, but it has not solved all the problems nor answered all the questions. Indeed, it has raised another question, the alleged Jewish background of Africanus and the Kestoi. There is no longer any serious question as to the fact that the author was a Christian, though the problem of what kind of Christian remains. There also seems to be agreement that the Kestoi is, on the whole, a serious work, but one with entertainment (and even humor, in some parts) as one of its goals.

---

[1]Ibid., p. 56.   [2]Ibid., pp. 56-57.

[3]Ibid., p. 58.   [4]Ibid., pp. 58-60.

Summary and Conclusions

Some of the basic objective questions have been answered: how
many books were there in the Kestoi, are there explicit Christian (or
Jewish) references in the Kestoi, was the author from Africa, was he
a bishop (or even a priest)? But others remain: what is the author's
national (and geographical) background; what else did the Kestoi contain, and can further elements of it be recovered from known works;
what are the areas of overlap between "syncretistic Christianity"
and "syncretistic paganism" in the Severan period, and between ancient magic and ancient "science"?

Thus, despite the progress, the basic problem still remains:
how is the Christianity of Africanus to be correlated with the contents and spirit of the Kestoi? Or, perhaps better asked another way,
what do the contents and spirit of the Kestoi tell us about the
Christianity of the time of Africanus?

The question cannot be solved by ignoring it (an approach
which goes back as far as Rufinus, and continues into the present in,
for example, the New Encyclopaedia Britannica), nor by denying it (as
attempted by Scaliger and Valesius, and continued in attenuated form
by Björck). But, while Björck's suggestion apparently will not stand,
his criticisms do seem to undercut the attempts to answer the question as being simply due to "syncreticism," either personal or
culture-wide.

Our usual picture of early Christianity is drawn from the
"orthodox" side, ignoring the depth presented by the "heretical"
sources (as Bauer, especially, has shown us in his Orthodoxy and

Heresy).[1] But it is also drawn largely from a view of the clerical

"peak," with little knowledge of, or interest in, the obviously much

broader (literally and figuratively) lay base. In addition, our

usual idea of "state-church" relations in the early centuries is one

of alternating persecution and passive toleration or ignoring. Af-

ricanus shows us the existence, at times at least, of a more posi-

tive tolerance, and the possibility of a more active interrelation

of Christians and governmental, even imperial, circles. Not only

does Africanus stand as a reminder of these gaps in our usual re-

constructions, he provides some information for partially filling

them.[2]

---

[1]Walter Bauer, Orthodoxy and Heresy in Earliest Christianity,
2d German ed., trans. by a team from the Philadelphia Seminar on
Christian Origins; ed. Robert A. Kraft and Gerhard Krodel (Philadelphia: Fortress Press, 1971).

[2]This emphasizes a remaining need of a more objective sort,
a complete edition of the rest of Africanus's works, especially of
the fragments of the Chronography.

CHAPTER II

TRANSLATION OF THE KESTOI FRAGMENTS

The following pages contain a translation of the fragments of
the Kestoi as identified and edited by Vieillefond in Les Cestes (pp.
103-323). The numbers of the pages of text in Vieillefond's edition
are given in the right margin with page ends marked in the text by a
double virgule (//). The end of every fifth line has been indicated
by a virgule (omitted at paragraph ends), as exactly as the exigencies
of a translated text allow, with line numbers included on the left
margin. Vieillefond numbers the lines by chapter, not by page.

In the following chapters of this study, references to the
text are given by Vieillefond sections (in Roman numerals), chapters,
and line numbers; where page numbers are given for quicker location
of references to scattered sections, they follow the others (e.g.,
I. 2. 5, p. 111). For the sake of clarity and brevity, the abbreviation "Vi." is sometimes used in cross references; where there are
differences, the forms "Vi., 1970," and "Vi., 1932" are used to distinguish between Les Cestes (1970) and Jules Africain (1932).

In the translation, I have generally preferred to err on the
side of literalism. Occasionally, however, I have been carried away
by Africanus's rhetorical conceits and have tried to embellish the
translation similarly.

102

Figure 1 helps to visualize the form of the <u>Kestoi</u> and the limitations of our knowledge of it.

Κεστός:

```
  1
  2
  3 - . . . Mordant, dyeing - PHolm. pp. 32-33(?), 37 [Vi. VIII. 1(?),
              2] (cf. Berthelot-Ruelle, tincture [Vi. IX. 2, 3]?)
  4
  5
  6
  7 - Military matters [Vi. I; cf. also items in II and III]
  8
  9
 10
 11
 12
 13 - . . .; chap. 22, kathartika hapla [Vi. VI]
 14
 15
 16
 17
 18 - . . .; [Concl.:] literary criticism of Homer (POxy 412) [Vi. V]
 19                    Unplaceable sections:
 20
 21                       Misc. military matters - Vi. II
                          Hippiatrica - Vi. III
 22                       περὶ σταθμῶν καὶ μέτρων - Vi. IV
                          περὶ τοῦ κινναμώμου - Vi. VII
 23                       Psellus (cf. Cat. mss. alc. gr.) - Vi. IX. 1, 4
 24                       Alchemy (Berthelot-Ruelle, Coll. anc. alc. gr.)
                             - Vi. IX. 2, 3
                          Geoponica - Vi. IX. 5
                          Fulgentius - Vi. IX. 6
```

Fig. 1. Κεστοί--Known Contents

Sigla[1]

Textual

[[ ]]   – conjectural restoration of manuscript lacuna

< >   – conjectural addition where there is no manuscript lacuna

[ ]   – manuscript passage to be excluded as spurious

† †   – corrupt passage not reasonably correctable

< . . . > – conjectural lacuna (not appearing as such in extant manu-
             scripts)

. . .   – lacuna in extant manuscripts

Manuscripts and Editions (Selected)[2]

V   – <u>Vaticanus gr</u>. 1164 (X-XI cent.)

D   – <u>Barberinianus gr</u>. 276 (X-XI Cent.)

Γ   – <u>Cantabrigiensis coll. Emanuelis</u> 3, 19
             (XII cent.)   ⎤ MSS of <u>corpus</u>
                                                         ⎥ <u>hippiatricorum</u>
Λ   – <u>Londinensis bibl. Sloanianae</u> 745   ⎦
             (XIII cent.)

C.H.   – <u>Corpus hippiatricorum graecorum</u>, 2 vols. (1924, 1927)

<u>O.-H.</u>   – Eugenius Oder and Carolus Hoppe, editors of <u>C.H.</u>

Hipp. Cant. = Γ (in citations from <u>C.H.</u> 2)

"Magical Passages"

The "magical passages" discussed in the next chapter are marked
in the translation by dark vertical lines in the right margin, and are
numbered for identification by larger, bold numbers (with subdivi-
sions further identified by lower case letters in bold type).

---

[1]Following Vieillefond's system in <u>Les Cestes</u> (p. 73).

[2]Cf. ibid.

The Kestoi Fragments, I: Kestos 7

<Table>   *p. 103*

These are contained in the <7th> of the Kestoi of Africanus:

1. Concerning armor. - 2. Concerning destruction of enemies. -
3. Relating to combat. - 4. For surgery on the wounded. - 5. For the
wound from iron. - 6. Taming of a horse. - 7. That a horse may not
neigh. - 8. For catarrh of horses. - 9. That a horse may not be terrified. - 10. Concerning swiftness of horses. - 11. Horse-troubler. -
12. Against ruin of beasts of burden. - 13. For a kicking mule. -
14. Military-like hunting. - 15. To find the width of a river and the
height of a wall. - 16. Theft of sound. - 17. Producing wakefulness. -
18. For fighting of elephants. - 19. Agricultural marvels. - 20. Conclusion: Concerning arrows.

<Proem>

The issues of deeds--production and decay, changes and remedies
--occur according to reason or principle or fate or chance. It is good
to know each one of them, gathering from each various fruitful helps,
(either) treatment of ills, or secret accounts, or beautiful expressions. These, in my estimation, have been accomplished to the best of
5 my / ability both in the preceding and the following.

1. Concerning Armor   *p.*

It is good to know war also, among all other things. For many
times I wondered both about the cause of the critical difference of
the armed battles, and that, indeed, of these, the Greeks had been
conquered by the Romans, and the Persians by the Greeks. But yet the
Persians have never been conquered by the Romans, but are overconfident
of freedom and have forced equality of honor with us, the nations of
5 inner Asia claim. So, providing a rationale / to myself, I found that
it is not superiority of stratagems nor the total military strength
(for, in war, no account is taken of numbers by the valiant), but the
preparation of the arms and the form of the military gear.

For the Greeks delight in heavy, full armor: they have a
10 dou/ble helmet, scaly breastplate, a convex, bronze-covered round-
shield, held by two handles (of which the one is around the forearm to
be of use for shoving, the other being grasped by the hand), two
greaves, a javelin in the hands and a close-fighting spear equal to
those of the royal cavalry, and a sword, broad, not long. Rarely run-
15 ning with this armor, not much indeed, but sharply, and / of such sort
as may be necessary for the man eager to arrive under the trajectory
of the arrows. They knew both how to fight together, and each of them
fought by himself, so that the virtue of the soldier was double, both
in unison and alone. They cut up the barbarians in this manner: resting themselves many times in the journey, so as not to dull the zeal
20 by the length / of the road, by this means they were unwearied as long
as they remained in danger. Thus, using a sharp speed, they made effort to get inside the arrows' <range>, the longer ranged missiles

carrying over them, as they ran in under the trajectory; and, because

of the unarmored condition of the foot-soldiers, // the opponents could   *p. 107*

not endure the charge of such sort of armament; for the force of mis-

25 siles is at a distance, but / in the area close-in, security from the

combat is successfully maintained by the full armor. Therefore, in

order to suffer nothing from afar, the breastplate is proof against

all arrows by the overlap of the scales; and the cap around the head

<consisting of> leather and another, additional, covering of bronze,

that is, one helmet on another, it suffices against the shot from a

30 sling, the outside shell, indeed, being / dented all around and giving

way, so that the thing discharged is not able to reach the inner cov-

ering of the head. But the face is bare and the neck is free, to allow

looking around everywhere unhindered. Then, with the spears, the one

group checks the pikemen of the cavalry who are probing ahead before

35 attacking; but the others, having been stationed in more open / pha-

lanxes, separating, take effect against the barbarians [whither it is

necessary to strew hellebore]. They use both troops and slingers

without danger, by means of the wall of the shields placed in front

of them. In truth, even the heavy swords are useful for dexterity

and vehemence of blow.

But the succeeding Macedonians altered slightly a few of these,

40 because of the / variety of battles, refitting the common arms both

against the barbarians and against one another. As an example, the

vision of the fighters was unobstructed under the Laconian cap in the

Macedonian <armor>; and they call this usage and custom <that> of

the soldier king. Indeed, Alexander himself also commanded the

45 soldiers to shave the beards, / and someone objecting to cutting off

the adornment of the face, he answered, "Doubtless you do not know, O

civilian, // it is not prudent to take a beard into battle." There-   *p. 10?*

fore such armor being near no one, that is, a barbarian, should be

able to stand firm, however he should have been fitted out.

50   But for the Romans, a helmet of single material <leaving> / a

little opening for the face for both breathing and sight, but coming

down right upon the shoulder blades, the neck bound tight; not turning;

a chain-wrought breastplate; one greave; the broadsword long; an ob-

long shield as a defense, being borne about by the hand (it is less ef-

ficacious for the body in fighting in close order, the soldiers not

being able to get the whole shoulder covered by the armor); and their

55 spears were / shorter than the Greeks'.

          Still they fight successfully against the full armor previously

described; for they have security from those nearly equal, and they

gain an advantage by the agility, both for attacks and facile retreats,

and to assault higher positions swiftly, and in the use of the broad-

60 sword prone toward / striking into the necks of the Greeks, by the

blow gaining the advantage of the close engagement. Also, for all

close combat of front ranks, they trained themselves also in the gym-

nastic art, so that there was an equality of experience with both, but

they had an advantage by the lightness of their equipment. But, so

the keenness of their spears would not be dulled, nor be broken by the

65 assault on the Greeks' breast/plates, having placed the weapons skill-

fully, they transfixed the scales by thrusting.

          Therefore, the ones who, it could almost be said,

had always been victorious over the Greeks seldom conquered those who

were always conquered by the Greeks. The first reason was the <fail-

ure> to be eager in running into the close combat, in order not to

70 leave the pack animals / behind; <for> they were always shut in by the

square of troops of the army; and they fell to // the knee, roofing   *p. 111*

over the host by the holding up of the shields in desire to negate the

Parthians' arrows. But truly such a habit is impractical, by which

also one stands untouched, being distressed by sun and toil, the bar-

75 barians in relay attacking and withdrawing again, / while by means of

attacking successively, the nations are taking rest. Yet also not

one Roman fights by himself, nor is there anyone who excels in single

combat against the many; and the things cast from a sling at the heads,

crushing the helmet, sink in; and avoiding the thrown missile is diffi-

cult because of the cutting of the iron collar. But besides this,

80 nothing having / been selected, they loosed the javelins, spending ten

for one chance death, and they did not resist the attacking horsemen

with pikes, (they being too) short.

If at least, then, someone might bestow a Greek breastplate and

helmet on the Roman soldier, and give a longer pike, and each one of

the spears be thrown at a particular mark, and he might teach each one

85 to fight by himself, / <and> sometimes he might arrange running so that

the charge against the enemy might be quick to be within the missile

trajectory, the barbarians, being cut up, should not be a match for

the Romans.

2. Concerning Destruction of Enemies

One must not contend with the enemies entirely with conflict nor battles, nor must one make Chance mistress of the entirety of affairs. For the outcome of war is uncertain, and much is different from expectation; those, at any event, better preparing with iron and with men, weapons and walls, either wind cheats many times, <or> sun,

5 position, or stratagem, or sig//hts and apparitions, the daemon Pan   *p. 11* persevering indeed in the great defeats. The Phocians, being better prepared in every way, did not then take the Thebans; beholding them having crowned themselves with laurel, those who had not feared the war fled from the crown. Flaminius, and also Paulus, contrary wind

10 and sun for the most part cheated. Likewise Leo/nidas used the narrowness of the Gates against the fifty myriads. Pan ran together with the Athenians into Marathon against the Persians. Themistocles expelled Xerxes from Greece by ruse. Some smear the arrows with drugs, that every wound may be mortal; others placed their strength in forests.

15 Some, fleeing, destroy beforehand the pasturages; many poison the / wells. And Alexander overpowered the Alans by growing hellebore.

Thus it is not by the visible alone that one must attack the opposing forces, but really must one order the battle against the enemies by many such, and also by the unnoticed arts. At all events, there was observed by the Karchedonians this old law, that, the com-

20 manders having taken counsel, then the best, even though / not successfully accomplishing, they honored, but they used to chastise those undertaking anything rashly and achieving, not making the judgment from

the chance but from the intention; and good also is the ancient verse,
that the safe leader is more advantageous in every way than the rash.

    The arts of generals, therefore, are numerous, and there is
25 not one which is unrecorded / (for which there corresponds teaching how
they may not be done): healthfulness of encampments and well watered
areas, possessing higher places, entrenchments, outposts, night-
marches, out-riders, reconnaissances, ambuscades, spies, // well main-   *p. 115*
tained arms, foragers and likewise sufficient equipment for sleeping;
toward the enemies, before all, distrust. Indeed, the means for top-
30 ping whatever harm they / do are apparent, I consider, and well known
to those acquainted with historical narratives; drinking antidotes
for venomous beasts beforehand to defend against the poison-bearing
arrows, but also equally a remedy for the corrupting of the waters;
the drinkings of brine, on the other hand, we decline on account of
the disgust of the receiving by the many. Also cutting down trees of
the enemy, preventing the antagonists from escaping notice; and, in
35 order / to have no need for foreign pasturage, the green fodder being
brought along suffices, as well as such quantity of other things as
are estimated for the supply of the necessities for a long campaign
and for nothing difficult to be managed by the enemies. This is also
a prime exploit; for, compared to inflicting damage, not to suffer
damage is much better: Pyrrhus, at any event, though gaining an ad-
40 vantage over the Romans, was destroyed.

    By time, first, and by pressure and famine and especially
destruction, one must work against the barbarians, with whom the as-
sembling of the army is occasional and not a lasting force, but

relying on booty from raids. For also, bearing provisions measured

for a certain number of days, and a precise number of arrows also,

flight is obvious when they are exhausted. Why, therefore, will they

45 always hasten to the enemy / whom I, being patient, would see pursued

by their own appointed time? Hunger comes on them past due, the few

provisions having been vainly consumed.

Come then, let us not entrust fleeing even to their being fam-

ished; let destruction apart from iron possess them, and death apart

50 from battle. Let us conquer / them with allied air and assisting water;

with the elements let us arm ourselves against them. I am general of

a secret marshalling, I use an unseen way of battle. Let every one

of the enemies fall, taking breath, drinking, or eating; // I make all *p.11*

things dangerous to him. Let him famish if he should stay, and let him

be struck by plague that he may not flee. Let us produce a work

55 greatly desired. Populous Athe/ns was emptied, air fighting with the

Lacedaemonians, and the such-like condition mastered the Karchedon-

ians in Sicily. The victorious attribute the wars of such kind to

their peculiar gods. Those gods also we will imitate; spontaneous

fortune will be produced by our arts.

60   Food then thus: let us make loaves which nourish the / last

day, using the animals[1] which are depicted, placed at the end in

pentagon <1>, in which, according to the linear form, lie the signs

of the proslambanomenē of the Lydian mode, zeta defective and tau

reclining. Sealing up both together in a vessel, closing the cover

1

---

[1]MSS V and D add, "forest frog or toad, and viper, . . ."
(Vieillefond, Les Cestes, p. 117 mg, re line 61).

with clay, so as not to have an air vent for the animals which are
65 within being destroyed by one another; then levigating / their remains,
drop it into the water with which the food is mixed. And having done
this, smear the baking vessel with this same juice; but certainly,
this <presents(?)> a danger to those cooking. The sufficiency,
therefore, of such food having prepared, furnish to the enemies in
whatever way you can.

     And it may be done unsuspectedly, if someone should be hand-
70 ling the transport carelessly, / easy for the enemies' attack and desirable seizure of the things being brought by them; or if someone,
pretending a quick flight, might give way to attacks, the camp having
been fortified by such sorts of provisions. These do not produce
death in one day, nor immediately remove the one using it; this one
75 also overtakes the one not eating, by means of plague; / it is mingled
among all, and settles into the community; into a house, into a city,
into an army, into a nation, the plot resides. Such a surfeit //
Erinys introduces to them. These are just meals of recompense against *p. 119*
the barbarians, pouring out disease upon all, and mishap inexorably
80 overtaking the enemies.

     But if we fear lest we should have used such preparations
vainly, the loaves not being used either through suspicion or this
matter having been learned from deserters, having entertained them,
let us release toward them either the evildoers or the prisoners;
and those associating with them [the enemies], they immediately infect
85 with plague. I send a treacherous benevolence to them.

     We will give them drink likewise with such sort of loving-cup.

Three kinds of animals which lie in the second pentagon, with the signs **2**

of the hypatē of the hypatai, gamma reversed and gamma regular,[1] chop

up these so that all becomes juice, and boiling with much water until

it takes up all the grease of the things being seethed, pour in the

90 water supply of the enemies. / The bodies of the men, and also of

their beasts, having drunk, will be puffed up; then swelling, with

pain, will set upon them, and anyone seeing himself having become

otherwise, not recognizing the present form, and slow in flight and

in expiring, awaits the neighboring death; he will desire a quick,

warlike attack that he may cease both being punished by the force of

95 the inflammation,/ and being hated by himself on account of the

odious appearance, the armor which had been used by the body pre-

viously not having room for the present man, <so that> he sets it

aside and even yet appears to stand in arms.

But also to spoil the waters otherwise: filling in <the> wells

with refuse and stones, and if the water should be wide-spreading, by

100 the rancid oil being poured / into them and by the sea-purple,

which makes all // water undrinkable for a long time. For a greater   *p. 1.*

collection of waters, or a lake, myrtle spurge being cast in spoils

it; thus we may first hinder the enemies by the drink. But no one

should consider the barbarians of the east unlearned in these things;

105 and they work evil to the invaders / many times.

[Poisoning of wine.] The Pharisees prided themselves on once

having killed a phalanx of the Romans by feigning of flight. For

---

[1]MSS V and D add, "a snake, the physalos or aquatic physa, . . ."
(but they also omit the third item) (Vieillefond, Les Cestes, p. 119
mg, re line 88).

feeding well, as appeared, they then withdrew, giving way, leaving be-

hind the prepared lunch. But the wine was treacherous, poisoned by

110 lime quenched in it. Wine is poisoned / with aphronitron, with box-

wood, with hemlock, and with similar means; for these things being

eaten in sufficiency harm and adequately take care of enemies.

Now then, moreover, we have used both food and drink as al-

lies; come, let us also use air and wind against them: one is able to

be guarded not to drink, not to eat (anything) from enemies, (but) how

115 is any to guard / breathing, how shall he lock up air? Through these

I will come at them.

[Poisoning of air.] Thrissos is a Thessalian snake, red   **3**

colored, about equal to a drakontis in length, [and it is also common

in Asia; Syrians call it "Bathanērathan"] which is next written in the

third pentagon of which the signs are of the parhypatē of the hypatai,

120 beta / defective, and gamma reclining; and leōn is another serpent, of

various species, for these are both small and large; but really, the

smaller is rather to be preferred for this [and it is also abundantly

produced in Syria]. Let them both be shut up together in a vessel

very securely watertight; and let the fiercest sun shine on the ves-

125 sel. Then, whenever they are destroyed by each other, and by the /

heat and the time, according as the customary wind also continuously

bears toward them, // place the vessel opened, so that the foul smell   *p. 123*

from it will go toward the antagonists, being ferried by the breeze

into the breathing of those plotted against. Now, examples of its

power: a horse will fall while running by; and a nearby man; and a

130 bird, not getting / over, comes down from the air killed, overtaken

by fleeter wind while fleeing on the wing.

But if, by some means also, it should come on us, either by a

crafty plot of them, or also from some one of the elements, the rem-

edy[1] for escape from the plague I have anticipated, setting it forth

135 in the preceding pages.

Themistocles secured for himself beforehand the victory against

the Medes, before the occurrence of the sea battle, while the generals

were sailing around without sleep; great also being this advantage, to

steal the sleep of the enemies. The ancient Imperators of the Romans

used the thing most baldly and effectively, sending out by night to the

140 camp of the / opponents both very lightly armed foot soldiers and with

them mounted trumpeters, through whom they accomplished two different

things: for either overcoming the more negligent outposts and guards,

they destroyed those obstructing them, or injecting panic; some by

shooting bows and throwing javelins, and the others discharging // from p.

145 a sling, hurling, when they should miss, against a tent / or a horse or

armor, the din accomplishing more than the injury, the one nearby being

always shocked by fear. But the trumpeters riding around were sounding

a charge, so there was always an imagination by those arrayed against

it that the enemies were offering to attack at any moment. Then

----

[1]V and D read, "As a remedy let us array against it thus:
kindling many and also great fires round about the camp, between them
we will also make censers, close-packed, so that the (fumes) over us
will fight against the pestilential breath/wind; and order everyone
to eat ox meat very lavishly and to set up tanning pits outside of
the full camp and of the interval of the fires, at the way leading
out opposite the wind; that some least of the camp, both of the leather
tanners and of the other men, will be harmed by the corrupted air even
as also I anticipated . . . ." (Vieillefond, Les Cestes, p. 123 mg,
re line 134).

150 during the day they sent out the army, by every way contriv/ing to
    avoid contact, and the following night sending out likewise as pre-
    viously those then resting at home with complete leisure by day, or
    by sending others; but they were always being plotted against for
    sleeplessness. But who does not know how difficult the results of
    this are to deal with? Headache, lack of appetite, enervation of the
155 body by desire to sleep no matter what, the same circumstance / suc-
    ceeding both night and day. Doing this regularly, we will destroy
    the enemy by a mere shout, they being enervated by sleeplessness.

                    3. Relating to Combat

        The stones found in the stomachs of the pure-bred cocks, all   **4**
    who are skilled in these things praise, as cooperating in producing
    both excellence and victory; for being worn either in leather amulets
    or carried under the tongue, (it) keeps soldiers and athletes and
    gladiators steadfast and enduring and not thirsting. But different
  5 people ascribe a different appearance / and color to them, some as
    crystalline and rough, and the others, correctly, as black; but they
    are found at the sacrificing of the victor, as though not the virtue
    of the fowl but the nature of the stone had been the cause of the
 10 powerfulness. Since, therefore, when it is borne by mouth, or around
    // the arm, the stone either falls out or is clipped off by the op-   *p. 127*
    ponent, one must use it unseen and in a covering of great power.
        Let the victorious cock, prepared according to custom, be
    eaten whole by the one fighting, so that all the flesh is stripped

off all round and the skeleton is kept entire, unbroken; then after

the meal, let it be purged by fire. The bird is a messenger, not only

15 of day, but of coming victory,/ making the one eating a successor of

his own invincibility, by which virtue he moves into the man.

Neokles' son, fighting with the Persians, used the stone and

the food; and from this he established by law the fighting of cocks in

restored Athens, and after the Median victory, the Athenians brought

20 a / victory-offering of cocks.

4. For Surgery on the Wounded

Since many are cowardly toward the necessary remedies from

iron, fearing the pain from the treatment more than the impending

harm from the failure to be treated; come, by all means, let us en-

courage the one shrinking from pain, rendering those distressed bolder

5 for the enduring of the remedy.

Let the healing hand be light, that it may run easily over

the incision, and let the edge it bears be sharp; for the dullness

is painful. But the assistant being ready for everything, let him

also sprinkle on the brick which[1] lies in penta//gon 4, in which,

according to the pyramidal form, lie the signs, both vocal and in-

strumental, of the <lichanos of the> enharmonic hypatai, alpha re-

10 clining and gamma invert/ed having a mark after it.

_____

[1]Reading hēper with Vieillefond (and Boivin), rather than the
MSS hoper.

5

p.

5. For the Wound from Iron

Also, for the one wounded by iron, this is the cure of suf- **6**
fering: it is fitting to anoint the wounding iron, then to drive it
into[1] the wound; <and> we should say "ta ta" thrice, and, while at
the same time spitting out, a certain Latin expression which is inserted in the <fifth> pentagon set out, with the signs of the chromatic <lichanos>, alpha <reclining having a mark after it and gamma>
5 in/verted having two marks after it. The suffering then will cease;
and let the sons of the physicians treat the wound, the one suffering
subjecting himself unflinchingly to their touch.

6. Taming of a Horse

Seldom, just as among men, so also among horses, is virtue
unmixed. For malicious evil is near the good ones, so that the go//od *p. 131*
should not appear pure; one is eloquent, but not august; and another
commanding, but not temperate; and one is manly, but a braggart, not
keeping his honor untarnished for himself; and another in another way
5 both gains advantage and fa/ils. Likewise also the good and evil in
horses: fast, but amorous; hunters, but hard mouthed; trotters, but
unruly; some not receiving the riders, and others throwing them off;
some rubbing along walls or trees; one group evil doers by nature,
another having been made so by the owners; they bite and kick and shy
10 away and rear / up, either hating or scorning the masters. And I can

---

[1]Or "strike it (on)to" (epikrousai auton tō . . .)?

speak concerning many, variously killed by horses in diverse mishaps

and species of misfortunes.

The arts, therefore, of horsebreakers are of such a sort as

either to control or correct the evils: by small rations the unruly

15 ones, by castration the amorous, by muzzles / the biters, the hard

mouthed by sharp bits, by blows the disobedient. But what may one do   **7**

against the one which has withdrawn and deliberately chosen not to be

obedient in any way, to anything, neither commands nor trainings?

For even as the most wild of beasts, having been taken as adults, is

not trained, but, even if it may seem for a little to have become

20 manageable, all the same the previous // savagery has not been for-   *p.*

gotten; thus also this very creature is hard to tame, evil having

become chronic.

Seeing then, moreover, poor result to such sort of blow and

threat and art and feed, "let evil of nature by art of nature be cor-

rected." Let an inscription also tame him, which he will not fear,

25 which he will not suspect, which bearing, he will / be subdued. In

the hollow of the hoof of the left front foot, engrave with the left

hand with a bronze pen, under a sixteen day old moon, a threat of

Roman prescription; the inscription has a necessity of obedience:

it lies in the 6th pentagon, in which has been inscribed the signs

30 of the diatonic <u>lichanos</u>(?)> of the <u>hypatai</u>, <u>phi</u> and <u>digamma</u>.

7. That a Horse May Not Neigh

Horses neigh, some boasting and others only smelling the

scent which comes from mares. But both their noise and silence is
useful. For when they attack, to incite fear, they are taught to cry
aloud with their fellow sol//diers, but when they lie in wait, with   *p. 135*
them to be unnoticed. Certainly this product of craft either (the)
5 time of year, or rather the erotic nature, dulls. / Indeed, Aristo-
menes the Messenian detected the Lacedaemonians lying in wait, the
horses neighing to them, because he was leading mares. Again, he
established the ambush without danger, his horses having been compelled to silence at a band of the Spartan mares.

   The trick of the Messenian remains in remembrance. Whether
10 therefore one would pass through a robber / infested region or would
set a cavalry ambush for the enemies, let him practice what will be
set forth; and not only is this a deed of Greeks and an invention of
ancient generals, but indeed, the Parthians also lead their own
horses thus being silent into battle. The tail of the horse above
15 the hair is bound about with a well twisted cord, so that the / band
sinks deeply into the surface; for by the tension of the binding the
horse is pained; he keeps the same spirit and swiftness, he restrains
only the utterance, even though time or love should be constraining.

8. For Catarrh of Horses

   Homer reported the Trojan horses swift, and he made the Thes-
salians oracular, and a human voice he gave to them, not pointing out
daemons indeed, but a lesson reproving horsemen. Therefore, those
now commanding need clearly to learn divining from horses, but they
5 are inexperienced. //

Many things about a horse gives signs, both nod and look and   *p. I*

silence. The other matters, then, I will omit, of storms and of suc-

cess in hunt and of good seasons of fruit and of their own offspring,

but the greatest is that the approaches of the enemies they both

speak and point out; and they foretell killings also; and unseen

bands of robbers they exposed many times by tension of ears, or by

10 hesitation / in advancing, <or by> snorting. And they showed not only   **8**

evil men; believe me when I say they see even daemons, and I know of

many neighing and falling and proclaiming by voice the threat at road

junctions. But chiefly for the knowledge of such sorts those with

eyes of different color seem to be distinguished, despising both war

15 and apparitions, and / only being opposed by lions for the kingship

among beasts. Whether, therefore, it is a work of the soul, or the

nature of the eyes, both must be developed, the one by teaching and

craft, the other by attention.

Horses, just as human athletes, it is necessary to restrain

from the sexual acts; this produces harm to the eyes; but so also

20 does much cold / for a long time, bringing on dripping, and to cough-

ing also. Let either misfortune be treated [the catarrh] by the

plant of Bacchus. [Treatment of horses suffering from catarrh.]

For ivy having had the juice extracted and having been mixed with the

forementioned substance, use it as a liniment two successive days;

omitting again the succeeding day, let this be done thrice and many

25 times, until the horse recover the customary / [and] [oracular] ap-

pearance.[1] But I do not begrudge the treatment also to the animals

------

[1]Or "vision" (opsin).

secondary to horses. And I use the same sort for the cough; after a
little you will find something lying within. //

9. That a Horse May Not Be Terrified   *p.139*

A cure that the horses may not be terrified needlessly by new   **9**
sights or shadows is the attaching to the right ear of the animal of
a tail cut off of a living beast[1] itself, and it lies in pentagon
seven, above which are placed the signs of the hypatē of the mesai,
5 sigma and sigma.

10. Concerning Swiftness of Horses

Horses' swiftness is dulled and increases; †wolf - antipathy -   **10**
each one is stayed and his pair of feet grows stiff, but he is made
more swift than himself by a wolf.†[2] A possession much desired by
horsemen is a wolf's feet; and also an astragalos of the same beast
having been hung on strikes the mouth of one running. This, indeed,
is rare, since it can result in damaging and bruising. But we have
5 found / a different way for the wolf to be able to contribute swiftness
without harm of the horse. For indeed the canine teeth taken from a
living one are worked into the neckbands and produce a double benefit,

---

[1]Hippiatrica codd. Londinensis and Cantabrigiensis read lykou
oura.

[2]In the second line, the translation follows the transposition
and corrections of text suggested by Simone Follet, review of J.-R.
Vieillefond, Les "Cestes" de Julius Africanus, in Revue de philologique
49 (1975): 318-19. Vieillefond does not attempt to reconstruct or
translate these lines (but cf. the line cited from Aelian N.A. 1. 36
in Les Cestes, p. 352, n. 165).

being an unsuspected aid and an ornament for the racing bridles. Then,

indeed, it is good if, for a four-horse team, one might append it to

10 all, but, if otherwise, even the lead / horse alone having this neck-

lace suffices to make the teammates more swift. //

11. Horse-troubler

p. ?

(There is) an account that the Sybarites were once driven to

this by luxury, that after dinner they brought the horses into the

drinking party. Then, hearing the flute music, they reared up on the

pair of feet, with the forefeet as if shadow-boxing, and danced. But,

having been insulted, a flute player deserted to the Krotonians, who

5 had recently been beaten in a cavalry battle, and he promised to help /

the league greatly, for he would hand over all the Sybarite cavalry

captive; the Krotonians believed him and entrusted him to be general.

But he, mustering the flute players of the city, demonstrated the tune,

and when the time came, gave command for the expedition against the

enemy. But as the Sybarites came together in a very large group, some-

10 what insolent / because of the superiority of their horse, and the

phalanxes engaged one another, by a sign they all played the flute,

and as customary, hearing the sound, the horses, as they had been

taught at home, threw the riders, all dancing with the music. Then,

as a result, the knights were destroyed lying, and the horses were

15 taken dancing, the accustomed tunes raising them up.

But others pray, being about to fight; and not only so, but

they also sacrifice, having come to the contest, to Poseidon Horse-troubler. But we have found a drug sharper than prayer, greater than

anything whatever that you may have, of which very thing the form is

inscribed at the end in pentagon 8, above which are placed the signs

of the parhypatē of the mesai., rho and sigma reclining. It is put

20 into pus-extractors / and given to carry to light-armed men in the

front line, so that they are positioned easily under the protection

of the front rank. The opponents then advance, being emboldened by

prowess and swiftness and iron, and whether these chance to be heavily

armed, or otherwise equipped, they hasten to the same // danger.   *p. 143*

25 For when the charge against the infantry comes, those array/ed in

front bear the attack by the screen of the shields, and those having

the pus-extractors press out the drug[1] into the nostrils of the

horses. (The juice is also very fearful for harm to men.) When

therefore the horses shall receive the scent of the evil stuff, they

are maddened and snort, and suddenly rear up as if frightened by the

30 exhalations of the ground /, and (being) reared straight up they skip

about. But the riders fall from the horses to the earth, ready for

capture and also slaughter, shackled by their own armor so as to be

unable to flee, being either stomped or stricken. It is possible to

make test of this drug at leisure also, and to marvel at how great

35 the power of this stuff is, and, in war, better than arrows.

A horse may fall otherwise, the nostrils having been be-

sprinkled with the bile of a sea-turtle, and being given up to his

own concerns, the gain is ours. Indeed, he will be caused to rear up

---

[1]MSS V and D read, "the euphorbion" (Vieillefond, Les Cestes, p.
143 mg, re line 27).

if someone should discharge saffron and myrrh, having been mixed

equally with white lily, at his muzzle; also mules which have fallen

are caused to get up. But also, indeed, the juice of white hellebore

40 is exceedingly deadly to horses. / They may die both from widow

spiders and salamander and by falling foul of ivy sap and storax

juice. They are also harmed by the smoke from a menstrual rag. But   **b**

let these things be spoken of elsewhere. Derkullidas the Lacedae-

monian, bringing up an infantry phalanx against the horse of the op-

45 ponents, within the square of troops (have arranged it back to back for/

depth), he ordered those crouching in the back under shields to dig

trenches with the hand-weapons with all speed; then he brought back

the heavy-armed troops into the midst, and they were within a fence,

for the trenches are most hostile to horsemen. //

12. Against Ruin of Beasts of Burden   *p. 1*

An ailing horse is an impediment to a soldier; also a draft

animal bearing the armor in war, and a back-packing mule carrying the

necessities; to all of which, mark you, one must apply the treatment

for both pestilential misfortunes and for the others.

[Treatment of ailing beasts.] Of celery seed, three half-

xestēs; and up to a third of linseed; and of fenugreek the double of

5 the second; / and of (ground)vetch, four times as much as the

fenugreek; these by measure, but of all-heal root and of Illyrian iris

and of juniper, the Sabine plant, each eight and forty <u>drachmae</u>; and

four times as much as the combined weight of the three of old tallow,

unsalted. And each of the forementioned, dry, is brayed by itself and
10 sifted and is sprinkled with old wine and / fat, then having been
molded into little loaves, it is dried in the shade. Then, at need,
as much as a walnut in size (which, actually, weigh seven grammata)
is emulsified with three kyathoi of honey, then is dissolved in the
oldest and strongest wine--and it should be one xestēs--and the beast
having taken it in advance for three days each year will not suffer
15 the / deadly misfortune of beasts. For those already ailing, instead
of wine, an equal amount of these things as instructed is dissolved
in water. If also, from the necessity of the unhealthy constitution
there is need to use pine resin, because of the absence of the little
loaves, infuse three pellets steeped in wine, in which way many infuse
20 tallow by itself. But those by whom wolves are caught most easily,/
these thus cure the pack animals of the fore-mentioned mishaps:
stripping (the) broad ribs of a wolf carcase of the flesh, having
dried it, they cure it hanging up over smoke, just as we do those of
oxen. One must // boil at need as much of these as may be dissolved,
and mixing in the water also a half-xestēs each of wine and oil, in-
25 fuse each year. / But really also, a head cut off of a dead, already
rotted, dog releases the ailing horse from that dire suffering; but
this will heal by the effluvium of the odor while being smoked.

[A composition more manifold and requiring more materials.]
But the one, indeed, requiring most materials, which I myself have
30 tested, which the foremost Romans use, / is indispensable to learn:
about eight drachmae, pure, both of calamine and of each pepper, both
black and white, <. . .> the double amount; three times as much of

12

a

p. 147

the leaf of both pellitory and birthwort, and of wormwood and of

hyssop, and of the untrimmed iris; then the fourfold amount of gen-

tian; a fivefold amount (obviously of the first amount) of spikenard

35 and of aro/matic calamus, and along with spignel, of pellitory, of

aloes, of myrtle-berry, of <u>kostos</u>, of cassia, of ginger, of saffron

residue, and then, of saffron, of parsley, and of Aethiopic cummin.

Each of these is brayed completely and sifted with an aromatics

seive; then taking up of these with three fingers, and mixing in one

<u>xestēs</u> of best wine, and taking the least bit of oil, then somewhat

40 moderately / beat it up. Infuse the complete mixture down into the

left nostril through a horn, both into the pack mules and the mature   ?

draft animals; but for horses the half of the mix, and to three-year-

old mules, but to two-year-olds of the other beasts; to healthy ones,

thrice yearly, whenever it should be, three days in succession. But

45 also for the ailing animal, it likewise aids the deadly (disease), /

the other diligent care being given to them as is customary; for it

is necessary to provide remedies, one sort against the lesser ills,

and other sorts against the troublesome.

    [Cure of coughing horses.] For a coughing horse, a cure is

brayed lentil; it is completely ground or powdered fine apart from

50 the pods. It should be given // to drink with water; but as to the   p. 1

amount of the pulse for each animal individually, a fourth of a

<u>xestēs</u> should be exactly suitable.

    Every beast exhausted by toil or attacked by <u>orthopnoea</u> may   b

be cured thus: give to drink lice or bedbugs having been levigated

55 in wine, or raw pitch with barley groats.

But other remedies for other things are not lacking in this
very treatise, being inserted here and there.

13. For a Kicking Mule

But a healthy beast of burden is of no benefit if it is unmanageable, either generally disobedient, or even kicking. Indeed,
therefore, the Latin expression for obedience of horses is given
above; but you will stop a kicking mule by boiling off the seed of the
box-tree and water chestnuts and giving it to drink, and it will re-
5 main tractable to you for 6 months.

13

a

b

14. Military-like Hunting

But instead of exercises by the army, a hunt <of lions> may
also be engaged in. Lions indeed overtake the fleet in quickness,
and the brave they overpower in prowess. By use of strength then,
indeed, no one of men may take them living, but by time and craft and
device; for whatever may not be done by force, // these things are
accomplished by intelligence. Therefore the most regal of the beasts,
5 the nim/blest and swiftest and most warlike, is taken by various
ways, of which, in this very composition, I will set out those
serviceable <to an army>.

p. 151

Whenever the commander is exercising with the army and should
think to hunt, he leads all the infantry into the chase, the military
10 equipment being / worn. The trackers of the brave beasts will have
reported beforehand a (land)mark where the lion lurks. Quietly, for

that reason, going forward, man keeping close to man, they are set in
a circle, putting the shields around, joining both to one another and
on one another, so that their overlap has a semblance of tiling. The
15 trumpets sound vigorously and the men shout together / loudly. At
this, the disturbed beast leaps forth from the lair, and seeing both
the wall of armed men and lighted torches being exhibited (for the
men bear these instead of spears), he is quieted and remains, and
does not leap over the close array of the shields. Insofar as there
is more steepness to the region, a device is procured on which a wide
20 and spread out cag/e sits, holding a kid. Behind the lion, full-
armored men, having hides dried and whole, shout out, beating with
sticks. Wherefore he, panic-stricken by both the sound and the sight
and the shouting, hastens toward the cage at a run, both the armed
men behind the device being laid down and not easily seen by the
25 beast, and the areas around the cage / being walled by high timbers,
so that thinking to escape by that way alone, he is conquered.

Therefore, this manner of hunting is one for exercising the
phalanx; and the others I will describe elsewhere. //

15. To Find the Width of a River
and \<the Height\> of a Wall

p. 1

Those moderately skilled in the general education have dealt
with the "Elements" of Euclid to some extent, as is likely. It is
not difficult, really, through the first (book) to contrive this also:
to measure out the width of rivers, for bridging by introducing a
suitably-sized boat-bridge, the other bank being unreachable because

of the enemy being established on it; and by the same computation to
5 take the height of a wall / from a distance for the producing of an
equal-sized city-destroying machine. And this very theorem will lead
to ease in learning the demonstration:

"If of a right-angled triangle one of the <sides> adjacent to
the right angle should be bisected, and from the (bi)section a
<straight line> should be extended at a right angle, and through the
10 point at which it intersects the other side a parallel / shall be
drawn, the other sides of the triangle are also bisected."

For let there be a right-angled triangle ABG, having a right
angle B. And let AB be bisected, by D. And let DE be drawn perpen-
dicularly. And through E, let EZ be drawn parallel. I say that also
15 <the> remaining sides of the triangle are bisected, AG at E, BG / at
Z. For let DZ be joined. Then AD is equal to DB <and DB to EZ>;
therefore AD is equal and parallel to EZ. And the connectors, equal
and parallel to the same parts, are both equal and parallel. But
also, DE ZG form a parallelogram GEDZ. DZ is therefore equal to EG.
20 But it was also equal to AE. <Therefore EG is equal to AE>. / Again,   *p. 155*
since each of the (pairs) BD EZ, GE DZ is a parallelogram, DE // is
therefore equal to both BZ and ZG; for it is opposite. So also BZ
and ZG are equal. The demonstrations apply also to all triangles.

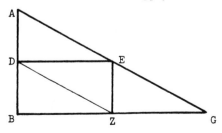

In accordance with these then, the width of a river will be
measured from a distance. Let there be banks, the opposite one, that
25 of the enemy, on which is point / A, and that toward us FH. Fix a
divided <u>dioptra</u> in the area which is toward us, at I, just so that
the space from I to the bank of the river toward us is greater than
the river; this is easily to be guessed at. At right angles, two
points are to be spied out, one on the bank opposite, either a stone
30 or a bush or any other easily seen ma/rk, and let it be A; but the
other point toward us, from the other of the cross lines, Y. And

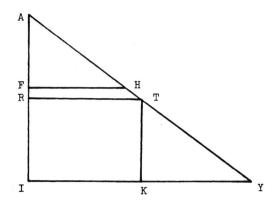

transferring the <u>dioptra</u> to Y, I spy out A and make a right angled
triangle. Let IY be bisected at K. And from K, parallel to AI let
KT be drawn, // and from T, parallel to IY, TR. Since therefore, of   *p.*
35 the right-angled triangle AIY,/ IY is bisected by K and TK is parallel
to AI <and TR to IY>, AI also is bisected at R. Measure, therefore,
the space from I to R. Therefore there is given also that from R to
A.   Subtracting from this that from R to F, we will have the remainder
40 also, this is the width of the river.

But if it is deemed to be difficult to take the interval

standing further back on our side, there being necessity of this at

that place, the sight being interrupted <and> the thing being blurred,

we may easily take, standing on the river bank, the greatness of the

45 river this way. For again, let there be on the opposite part / a

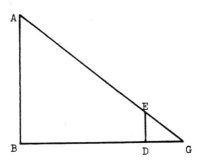

selected point A. On the part toward us let there be taken a point B,

so that AB is perpendicular to the line along the bank, BG. There is

taken some point on BG, D, at which let a rod DE be placed. At the

unsupported tip of the rod let there be a gnomon E, so that if rod DE

50 should touch the surface of the water, / the gnomon is uppermost.

Then let the rod be carried along as far as this perpendicular to BG,

until (a point) where, from someone[1] on the BG line, points EA shall

be sighted through a dioptra. Thus it will be pro//portionate, as BG   *p. 159*

to GD thus AB to ED. But the ratio of BG to GD has been given.

55 Therefore that of AB to DE has also been given. And DE is given. /

Therefore AB is given also.

By the same computation also the height of a wall will be

taken by the same figure set upright. Let the top of the breastwork

---

[1]Vieillefond, in 1970, reconstructed the text at two points
to read, "perpendicular<ly, to DE,> along BG . . ." and "some
<point, G>, on . . ." (I. 15, lines 51 and 52, Les Cestes, p. 157).

be A, and the base B, and the line from the wall to us, out of arrow

range, BG. A <u>dioptra</u> is hung from a pole (which actually is called

60 "lamp-stand") which is / fixed perpendicular at G. Now, let the line

of the pole be DG. Then, inclining the <u>dioptra</u>, I spy out the top of

the wall, which is A. Going around to the other sight, on the same

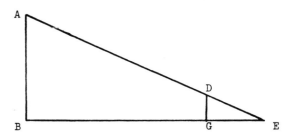

straight line I take a point <E. There will be a triangle> AEB, and

to one of the sides, AB, GD is parallel. Therefore, whatever ratio

65 EG has to GD, / this EB has to BA. But the ratio of EG to GD has been

given, for each of them has been given. Therefore, there has also

been given the <ratio> of EB <to AB. But EB also has been given>, as

was demonstrated on the river. Therefore BA is also given, which it

was necessary to demonstrate. //

16. Theft of Sound   *p. I*

The Mauretanians see most sharply of all, and anyone approach-

ing, they discover from afar; and they hear equally, though the hear-

ing is more slow than the seeing. But their vision is long by prac-

tice and nature; for besides these, they exercise in the courses, in-

haling the lightest air, yet also abstaining from both everything hot

5 and from salt, as being causes of weak sight /. But so that they

should not be taken sleeping at some time, and an attack of the enemy
should not be undetected by night, these, leaning the neck on the
wood which is a bed to them, leave the ear unhindered for hearing;
they dig a little pit underneath and from both they hear from afar
10 both sound and cries. I have heard the thieves of the western Gaul do
the same thing also /. This hunting of sound is ready to hand. Thus,
should anyone in a great camp wish to learn the plans of his own soldiers or the secrets of the enemy, [Art of prognostication of coming
things] digging a deep well, let whoever he wishes go down into it,
covering up the mouth with an ordinary garment; nothing will escape
15 the one sitting within, but he will describe to you the / things said
or the sounds as one divining. Let everyone trust my word, one
crouched down seeking for a distant sound, another on a dark night
seeking to discover something of the hidden things on the surface,
naturally, without a fire. For the higher air is full of sounds, and
the earth, per se, drives away the sight by the density and dulls the
20 hearing by the clamour. //

17. Producing Wakefulness   *p.163*

The poets lull Zeus to sleep, having been outwitted by Hera
and by Sleep, that either the Hellenes should have respite or that
Heracles might be injured. They also stay rivers many times. But
certainly, we ourselves also have apprehended how the stream is quiet
by night, that one might claim to find the water sleeping. Of winds
5 also, the airs of the night are more gentle; / by sleep, therefore,

perhaps these also are soothed. For Heroes, superfluous to say, have

been conquered by a swooping down of Sleep. He holds sway over all,

men, birds, plants, billows, winds, gods; all-subduing and limb-

relaxing, souls from the concerns of the body releasing. His brother

is Death and his accomplice Toil, toasting to each other in turn the

10 evil fortunes / of those about to sleep.

Indeed, the Ilian chief expected to take the Achaian "with

toil sated and also with sleep," but he withstood equally the atten-

tion of that one. However much the Thracians honored the sleepless-

ness of Rhesus, the noble king was betrayed by labor and sleep. No

15 one was panic-stricken by his / beautiful armor, nor feared the swift

horses; but one hour's sleep overturned hope of how great successes

also? The stratagem has descended thence to the newer forms: they

abandon much wine in camp to the pursuing enemy by appearance of

flight, that even if any was not weary, yet if drinking might fall

20 asleep; then others, com/ing up from elsewhere by night, destroy those

rising up while still asleep. Panic also many times occurs in armies

from being frightened in sleep. The fortunes of men we pity; let us

assuage the abuses from untimely sleep // by a daemon's misfortune.

The Phrygian king found Silanos sleeping and bound him; and another

25 fortunate chieftain found a satyr. I do not deem myself / unworthy

of the equality of privilege with them; they conquered earthbound and

humble spirits who had fallen asleep, I seek to take the one who

bound them: I desire Sleep to become subservient to my practice, that

with me alone this master and all-subduer may dwell. Let wake with

me both king taking counsel and general keeping watch, and noble who

30 is toiling. I set myself / against you, Sleep; as you against all,
so also I against you will wage war.

      There is a membrane-winged flyer, living in dusky places, <of   **15**

which alone> among the egg-laying winged creatures the offspring are   **a**

fed with milk. The head of this creature, dried and sewn up in a

35 leather amulet, makes the / one fastening it on sleepless as long as

he may wear it. Let one, removing a whole wing from it while alive,

use it as a spoon for taking up liquids, a few times if for a little

while, and many times and with both wings if he should desire a long

period of wakefulness. But if someone uses this drinking vessel

greedily, he will remain sleepless to eternity. But if somehow also

you should wish to play a prank by inducing sleeplessness, removing

40 the head of a liv/ing one, sew it up in the pillow where it is cus-

tomary for him to sleep, and he will not sleep, as if he were wearing

the whole creature itself; for also it will keep the one who wears

it thus sleepless through everything.

      Night's son you are, O Sleep; night's bird conquers you;   **b**

though winged you chance to be, even I forestall you by another wing.

45 Thus were the nuptials of Pasithea / to Sleep: Eros indeed was

sleepless, but a surety of this by Hera was the theft of the wing.

And what wonder Hera received even this from the Gra//ces; for even   *p. 167*

from Aphrodite she borrowed the embroidered girdle.[1]

      If in fact you knew from the signs the animal (for it is not   **a,**
                                                                       cont.
50 set out obscurely or hard / to comprehend), you should, perhaps, be

praised; but if otherwise, you will find it lying at the end, in

---

[1] Tous kestous.

pentagon 9, with the signs of the <lichanos of the> enharmonic mesai
of the Lydian mode [it is with the last ones], pi and sigma inverted.

18. For Fighting of Elephants

The ancients considered the elephants a great profit for battles, to shock unaccustomed horses and men by the first sight; and
they were furnished with a tower to be a cause of terror, as if a
wall were marching before the phalanx. Their trumpetting is sharp
and their charge unbearable. For the tusks also are self-sufficient,
5 in any case, for overthrow of every multitude; but they also used to /
fit out spears for them, proportionate to the hugeness; and they bar-
ricaded the greatest part with broad corselets; and they also gave
javelins to the beasts to throw with the trunk. It was a portable
phalanx, a manifold image of military advantage; from men sitting in
a lofty position, loosings of many arrows from above, but those at
the feet unable to fight back; and in front, enemy flights even. The
10 battle was not one of equal / opportunity; against the elephant it was
necessary to conduct siege operations. The troops being routed--the
front rank always having been broken through--they were easily yielding to ruin, the array demolished by those opposing them. It was as
if a ship having been shattered by a bronze beaked trireme, the rough
wave, by the least shock, destroyed the whole. Who will support the
15 weight of a cliff having broken loose? A fighting elephant // is   p.
like a mountain; he upsets [like], he overthrows, he shatters, he
completely destroys; and he does not even overlook the fallen one,
a habit of noble beasts, but being pulled in by the trunk, both

horse and man and chariot, and brought down with force and turned up-

side down, he drags them right up to his feet; and being leaned upon

20 by the knees, pressed down not only by its / own weight, especially,

but then also made more weighty by the addition of the tower, so that

one is not pressed by one elephant alone, but is destroyed by a great

assemblage of weight.

      How may one ward off a beast difficult to fight, and fully

armed both by the great advantages of nature and by the arts of men?

25 He over/throws the one who makes a stand, the one who flees he over-

takes, the fallen one he crushes, and he alarms the horseman, the

charioteers he hits from a tower. First then, agile men, both javelin

throwers and archers, must be set in opposition <and> no longer cav-

alry set against them, so that the army is not thrown into confusion

30 by the horses' <fear> of the strangeness; and the trum/peters are to

sound fearfully, so that the din of the opposing instruments may

blunt the trumpetting threatening of the beast. The light troops,

then, aiming at the elephant, must not attack the target aimlessly,

and let the archers shoot fire-bearing arrows at the towers. For

the chance arrow sticking in suffices for the destruction of the

35 whole; for the / beast taking notice of the flame, and fearing the

danger of the fire, he shakes off the battlements set on him, and one

might compare it with a tower falling in a city which has been be-

sieged. But if he may be wounded in the unarmored parts, he imme-

diately fears the enemy, and turning upon the friends, he rages more

dangerously. For like a mountain flame, or a steep winter stream,

40 thus being angered, // especially, he kills, injures, takes up,   *p. 171*

casts down, tramps, and hates the dead themselves, heaping up corpses

and blocking the ways of the fleeing, as though requiting the friends

because he suffers these things on their account.

45   I certainly better advise the leader not to with/stand the

elephant, nor, at the same time, to give way to the much multiplied

danger, but to anticipate his threats, his charges, his battles, his

fallings; for he will destroy many, having been encircled and falling.

Iron _triboloi_ are forged, sharp, steady, heavy. These, according to

the path of the beasts, are thickly cast [. . .][1] by those feigning

50 retreat, and being / trodden on they halt the elephant, sinking into

the pads of the feet, for by what weight he treads on the others, by

this he himself is ruined, treading with his whole self. The advan-

tage of this is double, for either, being pained, he destroys the

ones soothing his incurable pain, <or>, not being able to stand, he

55 utterly falls.

        Really then, all the spoils of war are worthy, but an elephant

presents the most worthy of all; for a captive living elephant, or

the choice spoils of an elephant, is an honor to a victorious king

not comparable to a shield of a general or a corselet of a slain

noble.

19. Agricultural Marvels

        Neither here indeed, nor anywhere, will the fair measure of

agricultural matters be neglected, for they will have some value even

---

[1]"They halt within," apparently a dittography from the next
line (see Vieillefond, _Les Cestes_, p. 347, n. 124.

to those who are making war. It is good to till a land which is all-
productive in time of peace, receiving variegated fruit of various //
seasons, picking, reaping, gathering in, receiving liberal wealth   *p. 173*
from one region, not needing goods from foreigners, nor enduring a
5 dis/tant hope. But now, <all regions do not bear> all things; some,
by an excess of cold, bear only grains; others, being sandy, gather
in vine or olive; but the much extended plains rarely possess and
produce the wine, and those which may, a poor quality only. Therefore let us procure an artificial means for both: to find what is
10 not, and the changing of the poor into the better.

     Let there be, with water, a ten-fold measure of wine; then
let it be boiled with a great fire, until the tenth of the mixture
shall be spent; there is a loss of the water, but a gain of the wine
having become better, a virtue of which the flame is mother. Doing
15 this, the ancients reported that Fire delivered Dio/nysus at birth.

     But all those who do not have vines, and have not obtained
the fruit from these plants, have imitated wine from other things,
either from seeds or by a production from fruits or by a combination
of roots, deprecating the drinking of plain water. For, indeed,
20 Egyptians drink zuthos, kamos Paeonians, Celts ker/bēsia, sikera Babylonians. For Dionysus forsook them, having been angered, and gave
nothing of viniculture to those peoples, reserving the victory feasts
for only the Greek husbandmen [boastful statement!]. Let us imitate
Dionysus, let us present to men the cup of friendship apart from
25 grapes; I know other wine-producing fruit.

     [Preparing of wine.] This then is a preparation of wine: of dried figs one <u>mna</u>, of pure sea-water three <u>choes</u>, two bunches of

liquorice root. Having brayed the roots, and putting some of the figs

into a jar, then again in turn, of the roots, alternat//ing for three   *p. 1:*

times, and then pouring in the sea-water [and let there be under the

vessel about two bunches of horse-fennel] and allow it to be steeped

30 five days and pour / off through a strainer [and let it be sweet];

then add fresh water, the same amount, and allow to be steeped five

days, and filtering this, mix with the former; then covering, put

aside in the shade and it will be good wine.

      But if, having poured in water, you should allow it to be

steeped seven days, and having filtered off you should put in the

35 dregs from the jars and having covered it / for ten days [Preparing

of vinegar], you will make vinegar [and make it in winter]. But also,

one must not neglect the vinegar itself. Vinegar is multiplied if,

having boiled a beet in a <u>chous</u> of water, you should add four <u>drach-</u>

<u>mae</u> of Hellenic <u>nitron</u>; with this preparation is mixed to one part of

40 vinegar, the / double of water. But all vinegar is strengthened, if

there is mixed in also five <u>drachmae</u> of pepper and the equal of juni-

per to the amphora. The ways, therefore, which involve only corrup-

tion of wine are a slow hope, and not desirable to a husbandman; and

vinegar is turned quickly by all sorts of means I know, turning

45 forthwith and changing about in one's hand. For some put in scorched /

barley, but others burned pottery, and others iron; many times honey

is also put in. But I produce natural vinegar, and sweet, yielding

use and pleasure, apart from the damaging of wine. For the grape

stone, being squeezed out, suffices; together with the squeezings,

they are well steeped in water, the water taking a quality as of
50 grape must; then being put into a kettle, a fire is lighted under it /
and it is boiled down to the half, and also being cooled is poured
into another vessel. Therefore it is changed since it has been mixed
with water, but remains sweet like grapejuice boiled down.//

There may also be vinegar apart from grapes: pitch last   *p. 177*
55 year's whole pine cones with pitch and scorch until the pitch / shall
be completely burned; then coat them entirely with honey, with a
feather. Let there be water in a great tub, and about ten pine cones
for each chous of water; casting these into the liquid, heat so as
to warm it; but let the tub be lacking six kotyla. Covering this
tightly, let it stand in the sun three days; then, uncovering, take
60 away as much of the vinegar as you wish and add / the equal amount of
water; thus, for a great while, you will have vinegar unfailing.

[Preparation of oil.] Of course, the oil is also to be sought
zealously. The Iberian, this is how: of wild olive leaves, a handful,
and dried fenugreek, four drachmae, and one of wormwood and two drachmae of baked wine lees which Romans call "fekla," all brayed and being
65 made into a mass filling the hand; then / having wrapped up in a rag,
drop into the jar and after nine days draw out for use.

If you would have Istrian, having chopped up green leaves of
bitter almond and made a ball and put it into the vessel, stirring
70 it up and then leaving it alone to settle.

Mastic(-oil) is prepared thus: the ripe berry of the mastic
being put into a mortar, it is brayed with a wooden pestle; then it is
poured off into pails--having been steeped for a long time with

boiling water and having been taken up with a strainer, it is squeezed
out. Some, having brayed it and kneaded it with water, put it away
75 in ovens until it should be boiled, and they press it out thus.

Furthermore the terebinthine is prepared similarly to the
mastic. But others, having chopped it up, put it into earthen pots
having a little water over it, // then they boil it and take off the   *p. 1?*
oily substance which comes to the top. (Useful oil settles out into
80 the bottom of the jar, if green dill and salt have been dropped in.)

You thus clarify black and dirty oil: one *litra* of *litron*
having been baked, brayed, sifted, cast it into the jar.

If you should also wish to make it like that from unripe
olives, braying bark and leaves of a wild olive tree, make a mass and
85 cast a *litra* by weight into a jar.

But if you should wish to make what they formerly called the
Iberian, which now we name "Spanish," put well chopped leaves of wild
olive, tied up in a suitable amount of linen and suspended into completely clear oil of Side, allow to steep as many days as you wish;
90 and thus the Iberian quality is gained.

You may cure turbid oil, having poured it into a wide mouthed
container and set it out in a steady sun and sprinkled on a sufficient
amount of roasted salt until it is warmed up; and as soon as it settles change into containers.

The foul-smelling thus: having chopped up green olives without the pits, put as much as a half-choenix into the amphora; and
95 having set it out in the sun / and heated it sufficiently, then take
out what was cast in and pour into many containers.

Oil, odorless oil even, may come from calf suet; put <. . .> chous of pickling brine into a copper (kettle) and ten mnae of the fat in a basket [a creel]; and let it have a weight so as not to float
100 on the surface, / a stone lying in it, and heat it underneath with a slow fire; and what boils up take away, put it at once into a newly emptied oil jar; and the residue of the fat which is melted out, thoroughly filtering with a strainer, pour down into the container, and separating it, leave it for twenty days; then thereafter use it.//
105   But also garum from one part of pure brine and two of the /   *p. 181* sweet wine. The best is from Lydia; but that named "sokkios" is what is praised more than all sauces. Ten xestes of the so-called "abdō̄-miōn," and the same amount of Libyan aromatic sap from Libya Felix (which indeed the natives called "phriton"), and a handful of Cretan
110 hyssop, and the Roman apple (call/ed indeed "orbiklaton"); mixing these with sixteen kotylae of honey, boil with a fig branch for three days, or for three hours each day, with a slow fire, and that kind will result.

20. Conclusion: Concerning Arrows

Now let this composition also be concluded by an old and instructive tale, corresponding to the things preceding, a tale of a bow and of an arrow.

One arrow, flying for one whole night and day, could go as far as two myriad <and five thousand> stades, if the motion might be continuous. Now concerning the flight of the arrow, it might be thus:

men (some suitable number, not more than ten) standing opposite a

5 target,/ a plethron distance having been measured; having bows pre-

pared, let each place an arrow upon the string, so that, when the

first strikes the target, at that the second also immediately shoots

and the third in turn and the others likewise, the second always re-

10 leasing the shot when / the arrow of the first impacts with the target.

I saw certain ones trying it, and I have the account from experience.

The number of the stades is arrived at in this manner; a stade is

equivalent to six plethra, and one arrow was shot for each plethron, //

and the arrows for one hour being counted, not more than six thousand   p.

15 arrows were discharged in the hour. (Now consider the number / of

the arrows and reckon it as the flight of one arrow, giving the atten-

tion to the distance, not to the number of those being discharged.)

Surely then one arrow (for let the many measured be considered one

for the force of the distance) travelled six thousand plethra from

the beginning to the ending of the hour, which makes a thousand

stades. But the distances, of course, for the night and the day be-

20 ing revolved into twenty / and four hours, are to be fixed as two

myriad and four thousand. A thousand is also added to these, being

allowed for the delay in the individual preparation, so that not

even the reaction time should be unaccounted for. Yet doubtless

there is always inequality in the hours of days and of nights, and,

indeed, considerable. If someone, therefore, keeping a standard

25 hour, / might make the trial of the shooting according to it, the

stades will turn out to him to be two myriad <and five thousand>.

Both Syrmos the Scythian and Bardesanes the Parthian made

this trial, and perhaps many others also. I myself also observed, in

(the court) of Abgar the king, Mannos his son trying it many times,

30 myself / instructing. He was so skillful an archer that, being on a

hunt with us once about midday (actually, I myself happened also to be

riding along, not being any hunter, but a spectator of the hunt), a

forest bear starting up out of a certain lair, formidable to attack,

something terrible to behold, impossible also to shoot quickly; and

35 everyone being terrified and seeking ways for flight, Man/nos, en-

couraging us to be bold, dissolved all the fear, shooting two arrows;

for shooting into the eyes of the bear, he rendered it easily over-

come, not even seeing the hunters. //

　　　　But then Bardesanes was a skilful archer, even if somewhat   *p. 185*

different, and, I know, shooting a man just like a painter. The

40 way was this: he once stood a man / opposite to him, a handsome and

strong youth whom an artist also might grow weary imitating; and the

youth placed the buckler before himself, for Bardesanes prescribed

this, displaying his skill to us spectators. But he, like a good

painter, transferred the one holding it onto the shield; first then

45 he drew the head, with straight arrows / mimicking the circle of the

head, then the flashes of the eyes, harmony of lips, symmetry of

cheeks, and the rest of the man followed in the arrangement of the

body. He prided himself on composing a drawing by shooting, both

drawing with shots, and shooting drawings; and we marvelled, while

watching, how the shooting was not a warlike pursuit, but it was both

50 a somewhat delightful and dan/gerous pleasure. But he, putting down

the shield, saw himself drawn on his own shield, and he was pleased, having a warlike portrait; this incident then, I recall with marvel.

   But Syrmos, how may I describe him? Syrmos also was a skilled archer, not painting with arrows as Bardesanes, but contriving for
55 arrow / to make war with arrow. The sight is novel, but not unbelievable. I saw arrow by arrow being conquered. Syrmos took a position, being equipped with the quiver and an arrow being readied, <he was> prepared to shoot; and there stood opposite him, at a certain distance, another counter-archer; but the contest of the archery was unequal; for the one fought with an armed arrow, but the other
60 with a naked one. Moreover the go/al was to bring arrow together with the other arrow; but the one was coming only as an unarmed soldier to meet a full armed foe; and bold he was, <but the other>, which had not been stripped, was shattering the one meeting it, and it was dragging it along, // hanging upon it, like an enemy prisoner; but the *p. I* one that had been stripped, having been seized, was no longer an ar-
65 row, but an arrow's spoil.

Julius Africanus's Kestos 7

[Appendix]

Another way to dye <like> ebony right through

   Leeches having been boiled in sharp vinegar, soak the wood and it shall be <dyed> through the depth, and after this polish with oil in which leeches were boiled likewise. //

The Kestoi Fragments, II:

Extracts Concerning Military Matters

<Table>   *p. 201*

1. How one may work through wine that those having drunk are put to sleep for three days. - 2. Concerning destruction of fields. - 3. Concerning destruction of trees. - 4. Concerning making horses unable to move out of the same place. - 5. Anointing for arrows. - 6. Concerning health of the soldiers. - 7. For not being conquered by poison. - 8. For one to close the wound without suture. - 9. For a hemorrhage difficult to control. - 10. For the horses not to be ill. - 11. To kindle fire spontaneously. - 12. Hunting of sounds.

1. How One May Work through Wine That Those Having Drunk Are Put to Sleep for Three Days

The one not lacking this sort of drug is to be envied: for if he can manage to prepare wine from it, those using this drink fall asleep, so that those who have drunk are overcome by the enemies while they sleep for up to three days; but they are roused if someone anoints their noses with vinegar. This is the preparation of it: of
5 Theb/an poppy juice, about two parts in amount, levigating these with one part of henbane juice and having levigated with wax from the right **16** ear of an ass, put it into the wine. //

2. Concerning Destruction of Fields

p. 2

Sometimes, passing through hostile territory, you should attempt to destroy its fields, cultivating hellebore; for even Alexander the Macedonian, making use of this means, destroyed the Alans. Fields are also destroyed by salt being both sown on them and covered over

5   by ploughs; this can render them entirely bad for a long time.

3. Concerning Destruction of Trees

Destroying the trees which bear fruit, as well as the fields, should seem good to you, so that the enemies, being often at a loss for provisions, will not find the fruits for provision. In any case,   1"
you will dry up every tree except apple, if you fix the sting of the sea ray into the root crown of the tree. The Quintilii assert that

5   the shells of beans being put on their roots / dry them up. But to me, it is better that you amend all which has grown well, commanding them to be cut down; for these having been handled thus, in the cut areas, no enemy will be hidden, no bird for their hunting will perch; this, indeed, is a perfect destruction.

4. Concerning Making Horses Unable to Move Out of the Same Place

While industriously working on the production of the present composition, I read in the "Physica" of Neptunianus that a wolf's astragalos of the right // forefoot being cast before a four-horse team brings the chariot to a stand. If indeed therefore, four are

caused to stand, how much better would it be, if, when in battle line,
we should give them individually to a few slingers? They, throwing
5 these into the enemy / horse, will not injure just one horse with the
one <u>astragalos</u>, but as many as happen to ride near it.

5. Anointing for Arrows

The Scythians anoint arrows, the so-called "toxic," for quick
destruction of the ones wounded. But by my inquiring into this, a
certain trustworthy man has given the following drug to accomplish
the same operation: and it is this: wood spurge of the type which
grows up into stalk-like branches--taking this, put into a new-made
5 earthenware pot and / heat with water until all of its oil is discharged into the hot water; then taking up the stalks of the plant
which were put in, put other fresh ones into the same water; again
take up and, putting in others, heat until the water from this juice
becomes like honey. But I do not have confidence if it has actually
10 been done. Some of the ancients say / that venom of vipers and asps,
and of salamanders, is also infallible for this.

19

6. Concerning the Health of the Soldiers

That a physician in the camp is good, is undeniable; but in
order that a soldier may not fall ill, being struck by sun and toil,
for this it is necessary to distribute their provisions not just once
or twice, but for them to eat many times during the day, at short
periods, and especially when not engaged in battle; for this is //

5 salutary and useful for digestion. It is necessary to take rue / and *p. 2(*

marsh mallow boiled down and mixed with sour wine, in the midst of

the meals; as also, mixing milk and water and pouring in a small

amount of sour wine, to take before eating. It is necessary for this

to be done from the beginning of spring until the end of the autumn.

10 Again, wormwood wine is drunk for the same, not only / before a meal,

but also after a meal, and with the meal itself. But if we should not

have the wormwood wine, we would give wormwood with hot water. But

the squill wine does the same also. They also prepare squill vine-

gar; but if one takes the squill wine, do it before eating, but if

the vinegar, with dinner. The marsh wine also, i.e., what is produced

15 in the /marsh-meadows, is exceedingly healthy. The pan bread also,

simply formed and dried in the sun, is most useful for health. But

also, if the available water should be unwholesome [should be pulse],

let it boil until the tenth of it is spent, then let it cool; and it

20 will thus be harmless.

7. For Not Being Conquered by Poison

In order that we may suffer nothing from poison (for there

are two remedies, being healed and working so as not to suffer the

necessity),--every application being fasting--if any will take 20

leaves of rue, two dried figs, and nuts equal to the figs, he will

be unassailable by every drug; and let a lump of salt be added to

5 them.[1] Many, indeed, / testify by experience; but those compounding

---

[1]Cf. Pliny N.H. 23. 149 (=Mithridates secret antidote or
"theriac"); see also below, III. 23.

more precisely, dou//ble the salt and the rue, and add 20 peppercorns. *p. 209*
But the more complete, which makes every drug unprofitable and which
is easily produced in the camp, is this: of oily dried figs, and
likewise of kernels, the best looking, and of dry rue, and also of
10 ripe juniper-/berry, and also of Lemnian "certified," equal amounts;
grind in a mortar and make balls the size of hazel-nuts and take one
each day.

8. For One to Close the Wound without Suture

Since in war many times individuals are injured, the separa-   **20**
tion from the iron weapon being large, they are usually handled with
sutures. For this we have found a natural remedy capable of the closing without suture; it is this: having pounded fine a bulb of the
5 edible type, lay it on, and it will heal by first intention.

9. For a Hemorrhage Difficult to Control

Taking human blood either from a phlebotomy or from some
other source, of whatever such sort as there may chance to be, and
putting into a wide-mouthed container, dry it in the sun and on the
first day you will find coming to the top a watery substance. It
is necessary to remove this and to make the rest dry, and at need
to plaster it on and to bandage. Thus it will be stayed, even though
5 it / should have been difficult to control. //

10. For the Horses Not to Be Sick

p. 2.

The horses will not be sick if one takes a small piece of
deer antler, and, making it like an ornament, fastens it around the
neck.

11. To Kindle Fire Spontaneously

Kindle fire spontaneously also by this composition: it is
prepared, indeed, thus: of native sulfur, of rock salt, of ashes,
of thunder stone, of pyrites, pounding equal amounts fine in a black
mortar, the sun being at the zenith; also there is mixed together
black mulberry sap and Zacynthian asphalt, liquid and free flowing,
an equal amount of each, so as to become sooty colored; then there
5 is added to / the asphalt the least bit of quicklime. But it is
necessary to knead it carefully with the sun at the zenith, and to
protect the face, for it ignites unexpectedly. But, being put together, it is necessary to seal it in some copper container, thus
having it at readiness in a box, and also no longer exposing it to
the sun. But at night, if you should wish to enflame the armament
10 of the enemy, smear it on them or some other things, / but secretly;
for when the sun appears, all will be burned.

12. Hunting of Sounds

I read something incredible to many, and doubted by me, but
on account of the marvel, I brought this up also: some people say
that the Mauretanians // [this is a nation], resting their necks on

p.

wood, leave the ear free, unhindered for hearing, digging a little
trench underneath and lying down. But the thieves of the western
5 Gaul also do the same, it / is reported. This hunt of sounds is ready
to hand. So if anyone in a great camp should wish to learn either
the purposes of his own soldiers [and] or the purposes of the enemies, having dug a deep well, let him send down whomever he wishes,
covering up the mouth with an ordinary garment. Nothing will escape
the one sitting within, but he will recount to you the things said
10 or the things making noise as though / divining. //

The Kestoi Fragments, III:

Extracts Concerning Hippiatrica

1. Concerning a Horse Having Elephantiasis: *p.22.*
of Africanus
[C.H. 2:130, Hipp. Cant. 3. 1]

The liver of the land hedgehog dried in the sun cures the   **22**

horses suffering from elephantiasis.

2. Of Africanus: An Ophthalmic
[C.H. 2:136-38, Hipp. Cant. 8. 6-9]

The swallow bears the juice of a certain plant, from which,

if it should drop to the ground, from the drop another plant is pro-

duced, which is named from the bird which let it fall. They come up

even if the bird's young, partaking of it, excrete it onto the ground.

But this juice is a marvelous and active drug for dim-sightedness,

5 and in a short while it thins even the leucomas from injuries and re-/

stores the eye to the appearance of the uninjured. But the plant

coming from it is more "lazy" and only corrects weakly; nevertheless,

being ground, it keeps glaucomas away, and its ash, with water, per-

forms entirely as well as the former. Indeed, if anyone had chanced

10 to find the first plant, he would have opened even the blind eyes.

The two stones which are found in the gizzards of the nest-   **2**

lings when they are opened up with a sharp reed--for they, black and   **a**

white, are found in each--, after a white dove has been sacrificed

and Aphrodite herself invoked, are put into a gold necklace and keep
off all ophthalmia.

 Anyway, cutting open the spring nestlings, one lights upon
15 stones in the gizzards, / of which the one is multi-colored and the
other clear. Therefore, before they touch earth, bind them up in //
fawn or calf skin for the "grand mal," and perhaps you will cure, or,
at any rate, lessen the epileptic seizure. But for this use, it is
necessary to wait to cut it open during the moon's beginning and increasing phase.

 They say the bile of a partridge, mixed with Attic honey, is
20 also a cure of dim sight and of cataract, / a fact which is also known
to many. The eyes of the vulture, bound up in pure linen and applied
to the eyes each day, does not permit dim-sightedness, and, truly,
will not even allow cataract to develop. But its eye being worn in
a dog skin does not permit ophthalmia. Its bile with horehound juice
25 and Attic honey, / used as an ointment, removes every darkening and
mist of the eyes and does not permit cataract to begin to form.

 The eyes of a living frog, removed and appended in a linen
rag, worn on the left shoulder or the neck, guard the eyes unaffected;
30 and if it should even be attached to one suffering, it destroys the /
misfortune. But it is necessary to release the frog where it was
taken. Its bile also is used as an ointment for eye irritation[1] and
cataract. But nothing is greater than the following for eye irritation: having made a sort of salve of ivy root, put it into a box

---

[1]Or, "sharpness of sight" (oxyōpia).

b

p. 227

c

d

e

of red copper with urine from a young infant, and tying it up se-

curely, bury in horse manure for 40 days. Then, drawing it out, rub

35 it off / on a whetstone and make like a salve with the liquid con-

tained in it; you will be amazed at the action, and you will stop

cataracts even beginning.

      3. Of Africanus: Concerning Production of Horses   <u>Bj</u>.[1]
           [<u>C.H</u>. 2:142, Hipp. Cant. 10. 8]

      If, therefore, you should wish a male to be borne, turn the

horses toward the east, that they may see the sun while mating; for

the west bears the females, as Maurousios the horse-raiser describes.

For also, as // everyone reports, the stallions are harnessed by the

Sun, and the flame is believed to be drawn by them, but the mares

5 draw Night, they say. / And properly, indeed, for the Sun favors

birth of males, but the Moon happens to be mother of those of like

nature.

      4. Of the Same: Restoratives of Power   <u>Bj</u>.
           [<u>C.H</u>. 2:142-43, Hipp. Cant. 10. 9]

      The (sweet) cicely is a plant entirely similar to the hem-

lock except for the flowers, which indeed are similar to it, but much

smaller. It has a root somewhat longish, extremely sweet smelling

and most pleasant in the eating. It is found in the arable regions.

These, having carefully ground whole, it is necessary to put into

---

[1]The <u>hippiatrica</u> passages accepted by Björck as being authen-
tically Africanian ("Apsyrtus," pp. 15-16) are marked with the notation "<u>Bj</u>." after the title as above.

5 pure, very well boiled, barley gruel / and to boil together, stirring

carefully. Then put in such a quantity of the most fragrant wine as

not to saturate the gruel too much, and fasting, to infuse. No one

may find a better remedy than this for this purpose. But if he is

without the root, having boiled together pig's marrow, especially

the spinal, with gruel, and adding wine similarly, he will have a

10 second remedy for the / foregoing.

5. Of Africanus: For Having Intercourse
Much and without Difficulty
[<u>C.H</u>. 2:145, Hipp. Cant. 10. 15]

It is necessary to infuse the animal with skink's flesh in   **26**

mixed wine. //

6. An Altogether Excellent Aid for Birth   <u>Bj</u>.   *p. 231*
[<u>C.H</u>. 2:145, Hipp. Cant. 10. 16]

Polygonum is a plant abundant everywhere, which is also   **27**

called <u>drosa</u> ; which, having been bound in dog's afterbirth, rubbed

with ointment and cleansed as necessary, and appended, becomes a

cause of conception. But in order that the animal may conceive what

you wish, either male or female, mercury and vervain plants are con-

sidered to be male and female, the upright male, the spreading the

5 opposite. / Make the animal to wear these with the former preparation;

if one wishes to produce a male, male; if a female, female.

7. Of the Same: For Abundance of Milk   B̲j̲.
    [C̲.H̲. 2:145, Hipp. Cant. 10. 17]

The milk stone fastened around the udder of the animal draws   **28**

down however much milk is needed. But in order that she may also

supply more milk, infuse the levigated milk stone itself with wine

and water.

8. Of the Same: For the Embryo Not to Miscarry   B̲j̲.
      [C̲.H̲. 2:145-46, Hipp. Cant. 10. 18]

Sailors, taking the remora fish, preserve it, using it as a   **29**

powerful drug both to prevent miscarrying and for conception. This

being levigated, the animal infused with it keeps the embryo safe in

the womb. // But if one should also bear it living to the belly of   *p. 2*

5 the mare when the stallion couples with her, both then and thereafter

she will conceive / and will not suffer the forementioned mishap.

9. Of Africanus: For Earache   B̲j̲.
    [C̲.H̲. 2:149, Hipp. Cant. 11. 12]

I wish to aid ears in a double manner: that they may both

cease being pained, and ceasing, may not be pained again. For when-

ever the condition around the ear may become insufferable and past

bearing, becoming like ulcers and producing evil smelling pus and

maggots, the pain around it becoming intolerable, the pellitory

5 plant, easily obtained and growing everywhere, / as though nature

gloried in its abundance, is chopped up thoroughly so that it pro-

duces much juice. Then a little bit of Attic honey is taken, and

not much strong vinegar, and a small amount of sea weed. These,
being mixed and warmed, become salvation to the one afflicted.

         10. Of Africanus: For Ozaenas and Polyps
                   [Concerning a Cough]
             [C.H. 2:151, Hipp. Cant. 13. 5]

    Use the root of the winter-cherry mixed equally with butter.

         11. Of Africanus: Concerning Dysurea[1]
             [C.H. 2:161, Hipp. Cant. 24. 6]

    If the urine of a horse is held back, a virgin, having loosed | **30**

the girdle which she wears, let her strike it about the face with

the girdle, and immediately it will urinate much and the pain will

cease. //

         12. Of Africanus: For a Dropsical Animal
             [C.H. 2:164-65, Hipp. Cant. 29. 2]   *p. 235*

    Infuse crow fat with 20 ounces of heated wine; or, a hedgehog | **30 A**

having been burned, infuse the ashes with wine.

         13. Of Africanus: Concerning Color of Horses   B̲j̲.
             [C.H. 2:177-78, Hipp. Cant. 44. 5-6]

    Colors of horses, also, like their virtues, are different;

but color is also a stroke of luck, and the proper hide gives

----

[1]Björck, "Apsyrtus," p. 17, rejects this passage specifically,
attributing it to Aelian directly, despite the attribution in the
British manuscripts.

stateliness to the animal. Some of them, indeed, are natural, but
others, certain persons change for the better, working artfully.
Some of them are fashioned by drugs, but others embellished with
cauteries. Therefore, a horse from a tawny color may become black
by having been plastered over by squill with vinegar and levigated
5 pumice stone /; but white would result from the drug being boiled.
But tawny may come from white, if lime and litharge emulsified in
water and boiled until it becomes a thick gum should be plastered
over it for two hours. But if the ointment remains on for more
hours, black will result from the white. Also, apart from colors,
10 the fire forges the hair to a different appearance on the animal, /
and the horse's spottedness is simulated. A whitish-gray [This is
the name of a color] horse is marked over this way: having taken a
fired, round cautery, open in the middle, like the roundness of the
letter o, apply it to the horse, which has been bound fast, alternately applying and removing. Therefore the outer ring is black,
15 but the original color remaining apart from that / simulates a leop-
ard body, having been suitably disposed on both the legs and the
neck. You may see even its face like a wild beast's. But it is
good to mark a high-spirited horse this way, that the swiftness may
match the skin. //

             14. Of Africanus: A Dye for Hair Which
                     Remains Permanently
                 [C.H. 2:178, Hipp. Cant. 46. 8]   *p.*

   Of wine lees, of black acacia, of round alum, of true

maidenhair, each 6 ounces; of oak-gall, 2 stat(ers), 6 kerat(ia);
1 green nut; of black myrtle without the juice, 1 1/2 pound; of
ladanum, 6 ounces; of old dark wine, 5 pounds. Boil all with the
wine until it is boiled down to a third, and, having cleansed the
hair beforehand, dip it three days and nights, and you will be
5 amazed.

15. Of Africanus
[C.H. 2:189, Hipp. Cant. 57. 10]

The body of a sea-urchin smeared on a body having the mange | **31**
produces soundness.

16. Of Africanus
[C.H. 2:193, Hipp. Cant. 62. 2]

Dog's brain unites a fracture in 14 days, being smeared into | **32**
a linen bandage and applied, wool being wound over it.

17. Of Africanus: Concerning Tumors and   B.j.
Warts and Acrocordons
[C.H. 2:198, Hipp. Cant. 67. 1]

Irritating warts are outgrowths of the body resembling rough
studs; they occur to many in many places. They call the condition
"Myrmēkiai," // which many superstitious persons also regard as signs *p. 239*
of something which is going to happen to them. The relief from them
is manifold and proven by all. Some, indeed, watching for <a dog> | **33**
5 urinating on the ground, having mixed the dirt up well, / put it on | **a**

the place and shut up the cause in the clay. But others, having

crushed the squirting cucumber and put it on, thus overcome it; or,

chicory flower, which is properly called "Heliotrope," picking be-

fore the rising of the sun <. . .> thrice circumscribe the place and

the wart will cease irritating.

18. Of Africanus
[C.H. 2:199, Hipp. Cant. 67. 7]

   If you feed any of the animals the cast skin of a serpent

hidden in a date, you will clear away his acrocordons.

19. Of Africanus
[C.H. 2:203, Hipp. Cant. 70. 3]

   To cast maggots out with a drench without drugs, clear water

suffices for me, being taken in this way: having drawn it up with

the thumb and the "physician's" finger drawn back, thrice besprinkle

"by a stream of pure water" the place suffering the worms. They will

5 all come pushing one another out, not one being left within. //

20. Of Africanus
[C.H. 2:205, Hipp. Cant. 70. 11]

   (")The ass, of all the animals, bears neither lice nor

ticks.(")

21. Of Africanus: Concerning Those Bitten by a
Mad Dog and Hydrophobics and Other
Bites from Reptiles
[<u>C.H.</u> 2:205, Hipp. Cant. 71. 3]

The present infusion has its composition from four things:
gentian, myrrh, round birthwort, and bay-berry. Chop up and sift
equal amounts of these, mixing with raw honey. The dose is of the
size of an Egyptian bean. But for snake bites give in water, and
for scorpion stings in first quality wine, for three days.

22. Of the Same
[<u>C.H.</u> 2:206, Hipp. Cant. 71. 4]   <u>Bj</u>.

Treatment for asps' bites: many bedbugs, being taken by the   **36**
one bitten by asps, are believed to be a great cure, or tortoise
urine being soaked up and dropped on the bite, both by itself and
with many bedbugs. But the physician Phobios gives to those bitten
by asps the serpent called <u>Hemorrhoïs</u>, cooking and levigating it
5 and soaking it in wine /, and conversely, he said to make use likewise of the asp for those bitten by the <u>hemorrhoïs</u>. For he asserts
Inaron the Libyan to have transmitted that they are a remedy of one
another. //

23. An Easily Procured Counter Measure: *p. 243*
of the Same
[<u>C.H.</u> 2:206, Hipp. Cant. 71. 5]

Rue leaves, 20; walnuts, 2; salt granule, 1; dried figs, 2;
having been given beforehand in an infusion to a fasting horse, you

will procure that it will be harmed by no drug or any other poison.

But for it not to be struck by a scorpion, inscribe <u>abbas</u> on a tin

sheet and tie this around the throat of the animal.

3̄

24. Of Africanus: For the Bite of Every Beast
[<u>C.H</u>. 2:207, Hipp. Cant. 71. 9]

Having levigated nose-smart, plaster on with linen; or the

seed of this plant, steeped and levigated, put on in like manner

with linen.

25. Of the Same: For Checking Inflammation
of a Wound by Poisonous Aquatic Animals
[<u>C.H</u>. 2:207, Hipp. Cant. 71. 10]

Lemnian earth is suitable for the wounds from poisonous sea

creatures, being given with wine; and mountain (spotted) dead-nettle

with vinegar, plastered over, heals similarly. //

26. Of the Same: Prophylactic for Not Being
Injured by Any Poisonous Bite
[<u>C.H</u>. 2:207, Hipp. Cant. 71. 11]

p. 2̄

Of oil from unripe olives, 2 pounds; of marrow of a freshly

slaughtered stag, 4 ounces; of bees wax, a sufficient amount; having

melted all together and strained, use against all venomous things.

27. Of the Same: Concerning Scolopendrids   <u>Bj</u>.
[<u>C.H</u>. 2:207, Hipp. Cant. 71. 12]

The scolopendrid injures badly, but, by smearing the antidote

for the venomous bite on any part, you will heal the gashed place.
The fruit and the flowers of asphodel, being drunk with wine, are
opposed to it, and the summer fruit of figs with wine and vetch,
5 having been plastered over, cause the suffering to cease.

28. Of the Same: Concerning Spiders
[C.H. 2:207-08, Hipp. Cant. 71. 13]

The kinds of spiders are many; but those of them that are
able to harm are two, the maddening and the copper. Therefore, for
those bitten by the maddening type, levigate 4 ounces, 4 stat(ers)[1]
of hyssop or of oregano, and an equal amount of roasted salt, and put
on with honey; or infuse a three finger pinch of cummin and an equal
amount of the fruit of the agnus (castus) with 3 ounces of wine.
5 Also, give barley-cake and / garlic and †taking by mouth is useful†
<. . .>. //

29. Of the Same: For Bees
[C.H. 2:208, Hipp. Cant. 71. 14]

p. 247

For the insects, wasps, bees, hornets, burrowing wasps,
bumblebees, and buzzing insects, plaster over with the leaves of
sweet-bay, or of mallow, or (wild) water-mint, or of coriander. Use
also cow dung smeared over, and juice of the fig with leaves of the
mulberry or catnip or lentil smeared with oil. Roots of wild cucum-
5 ber having been boiled together with oil keeps the animals unbitten, /

---

[1]Vieillefond, following MS Cant.; Oder-Hoppe, C.H., reads
hexag(ia).

<. . .> whence it is necessary to anoint them with galbanum juice with
oil. Likewise, this also having been burned before one opens the bee-
hive, he remains unharmed, or anointing with balm crushed with oil,
or burning cow dung or salvia. Further, every insect which has been
sprinkled with oil is done away with.

30. Of the Same: Concerning the Dipsas   Bj.
[C.H. 2:208, Hipp. Cant. 71. 15]

The dipsas itself has many names also: for it is called
"burning" and "bloater" from the result it causes, and "black-tail"
and "sand-burrower" both from its habit and its appearance, (it is)
a beast smaller than the viper and more grievous. For it produces
burning and an intensified thirst in those bitten, until one bursts
5 from drinking. Now, for the bite of the dipsas, a sedge infu/sion,
with wine and water, helps; and ladanum, levigated and given with
wine; and besides these, the western fruit called kitrion being
given beforehand as a potion opposes it, and being given afterward
as a potion gives aid, and especially the golden part of it. //

31. Concerning the Dryīnes   p.
[C.H. 2:209, Hipp. Cant. 71. 16]

The serpent dryīnes, passing his life in the roots of oaks
and roaming near other trees, thus also is injurious for the destruction in an evil manner, as, if one treads on it, the feet become excoriated and swellings begin affecting the whole legs. And yet more
strange: if also anyone wishes to treat them, his hands also become

5 excoriated. / Therefore the juice of the leaves of (manna) ash is

very useful, being infused before all food and drink.

32. Of the Same: Concerning Various <Bites> and Wounds
[C.H. 2:209-10, Hipp. Cant. 71. 17-19]

Specifics, then, for bites and stings of the poisonous animals

are what were given above, but some general remedies are these: iris

being drunk with vinegar, seed of Christ's thorn or juice of myrtle

with wine, cardanum in the same way, or fruit of the tuberous spurge

or of clover, 1/2 ounce; asphodel root, 2 stat(ers), 6 kerat(ia),

wine; either juice of laserwort or grains of barley; and an infusion

5 of hulwort decoction; and / centaury, dittany, castor, rue, salvia,

catnip, agnus. Besides, for these also, plaster over afterward with

bran with vinegar or wine, or with radishes, or with bulbs. Many,

having mentioned these things already, prefer one to another, commend-

ing the approved one by experience. But besides these, someone (sug-

gests) juice // of leek to drink afterward, but another, having taken   *p.251*

10 out the brains of a living hen, / soaking with unmixed wine, gave to   **38**
                                                                            a
the endangered one; another administered urine of a child having been   **b**

mixed with wine also, another, having ripped up a mouse, put it on

the wound and drew up the poison into the mouse. But, of the many, I

prefer that very one which I set out for those bitten by mad dogs and

stung by scorpions, the secret Parthian remedy, which is made from

15 four things equally: myrrh, birthwort,/ gentian, bay-berry [centaury].

Therefore, having taken these together and crushed with wine and boiled, infuse. The most readily procured are these: goat's milk

being given by itself or with 5 ounces of wine, frogs boiled with   c

wine and infused, both for all venomous beasts and toads. Also lev-

20 igating wormwood with wine, and agaric likewise and agnus' / fruit

likewise; Ethiopic ajowan and Italian cummin being infused with wine;

or oak acorns being eaten, are suitable; and fruit of St. John's

wort; mandrake roots with mixed honey. Also leeches applied to the

25 bite assist and draw out. Goat droppings / with oregano applied to

the venomous wounds help, and the dry dung of an elephant. Also,

agnus' leaves being plastered over, barley-groats likewise, with

must and bitter wine or sea-water, being liberally infused, are

suitable for all venomous animals that destroy by chilling.

Then, whatever sort of animal should bite, having removed the   d

30 head ap/ply it to the bites, and having fastened it on, you will heal

without inflammation. Or, having burned the wounding head, apply the

ashes. Or, put crushed edderwort root on the wounded place, having

scarified it beforehand. Juice of hyacinth // being infused works   p

against all poisonous animals. The root of the wild vine being hung   e

35 around, and the fruit being infused, is suitable for / every animal

bite and for stings.

33. Of Africanus: For Herds Not to Be Harmed   Bj.
by Being Blown upon by Toads by Night or
Lurking in Dusky Places
[C.H. 2:212, Hipp. Cant. 71. 27]

The toad is accustomed to blow on the herd most grievously,

if he should escape notice somewhere in the stable by night or in a darkish spot, and from it follow diseases most pestilential to the animals and tumors most difficult to treat, so as to render useless every aid for the suffering. It is necessary, therefore, so that he

5 can never do thus, to kindle a lasting fire in the stables; / for this very animal, as though convicted by himself, fears the fire.

34. Of Africanus: To the Soothing <of Inflammation of Feet> and of Other Parts [C.H. 2:222, Hipp. Cant. 80. 24]

39

Seven figs, soaked beforehand in sweet wine until soft, crush with sufficient rose oil so as to be very smooth. Then having boiled equal amounts of bees-wax and of fresh hog fat and of bread, with rose oil, pour in a little over the levigated figs and mixing in a mortar, make moist so as to be like a plaster, and placing it

5 on the inflammation, you will do away with it immediately. //

Of Africanus: Taming of Horses (See above, I. 6, Vi. pp. 129-33)[1] [C.H. 2:224-25, Hipp. Cant. 81. 8-10]

Bj.

35. Of Africanus: For <the Same> [Concerning Colics, or Rather, Diseases of the Colon] [C.H. 2:248, Hipp. Cant. 105. 5]

p. 255

The right testicle of a swan having been appended, the distress ceases.

40

---

[1]Vieillefond omits this and the second item following from this Part because of their identity with the listed item in Part I. The item following this one in the hippiatrica (C.H. 2:225-26, Hipp. Cant. 81. 11), "Another, of the same: For stopping a kicking mule," is substantially the same as the title and lines 4-5 of Vi. I. 13, p. 149.

Of Africanus: For Horses Not to Be Frightened   Bj.
or Spooked on the Road (See above,
I .9, Vi. p. 139)
[C.H. 2:249-50, Hipp. Cant. 108. 5]

36. Of Africanus: Removal of Markings of Horses   Bj.
[C.H. 2:250, Hipp. Cant. 108. 8]

This is a theft of valuable horses, changing the markings,

to remove the marks branded on the bodies and to hide the former

tokens by another color and to make unknown to the late owner. It is

thus: a pulse, of which the form is inscribed at the end in hexagon   4)

seven, being well boiled, at the first moon, at the third hour, plas-

5 ter on to whatever / part you should wish to hide [blackberry].[1] For,

ulcerating by the burning, it produces white hair; but if also it is

plastered on many places, the formerly solid color will be dappled.

This art (works) against all other colors, except white only, because

of the same nature of the growth of the hairs; it will eradicate the

10 mark, but will preserve the original color.

_____

[1]Apparently a misplaced gloss misidentifying the item pictured in the hexagon (see Vieillefond, Les Cestes, p. 360, n. 240.

The Kestoi Fragments, IV:

Concerning Weights and Measures

From the <Kestoi> of Africanus: Concerning weights and   *p. 267*
measures[1]

1. Whereas in many places I have mentioned both weights and
measures, and it is necessary to be exact concerning the proportion
of these, so that no person being mistaken in the quantity should
discredit the remedies compounded of them, of necessity I decided to
show what and what sort it is necessary to use, and to set out their
differences from one another. There is, in fact, in common use both
5 the / Attic and the Italian, and by some, a Syrian and an Egyptian,
which is also called the "Ptolemaic." These, then, one must compare
to one another.

2. In general, every talent as a whole has 60 mnai of its
own, and every mna (obviously of those aforementioned) has 25 statēres; and the statēr 4 drachmai, that is, holkai; therefore every
10 talent has 60 mnai, 1500 statēres, and / 6000 drachmai. The drachmē
has 6 obols, and the obol 8 coppers. The drachmē therefore has 48
coppers.

3. But the Attic talent is equivalent to the Ptolemaic and

---

[1]Also published by Duchesne, "Fragment metrologique" (1876),
pp. 378-85 (text, pp. 381-85, "A different account concerning measures
and weights from the . . . of Africanus.") Paragraph numbers given
in the translation are from Duchesne (they are not included in
Vieilleford).

to the Antiochian, and equal in number in everything, except in value;

according to current coinage, it is fourfold of the Ptolemaic, and

15 greater by a third than the Syrian and Antiochian, / but equal to

the Tyrian. Accordingly, by the mentioned difference concerning the

talent, the others will be used also: for both mna from mna and

stater from stater and drachme from drachme will differ by the same

amount as the difference concerning the talent.

20   4. I also know another wooden talent in Antioch which // has   *p. 2*

60 mnai, but in weight it is nearly six times as much as that of the

coinage; but the wooden one in Alexandria differs, exceeding the

forementioned usage by a fifth.

          5. But the talent in Homer could be equated to the later

daric, as is obvious from the prizes of the games for Patroclus.

25 Since for the / first a woman and an immense caldron, and for the

second a mare in foal was set as a prize, and for the third a caldron

of 4 measures; but for the fourth was set two gold talents. <Which>

would not be if it should be more valuable that the first ones,

†and of the fifth a vessel set further down the scale† which was the

"two-handled urn" <. . .>. But the gold (daric), hence the Homeric

30 talent, / weighs 2 Attic drachmai, 6 scruples, and, obviously, four

quarters.

          6. It does not escape me also that there are many differ-

ences of drachmai; for the Delian and Aegenean, and the Rhodian and

the <. . .> is five times as much as the Ptolemaic, and what is

35 called the "insular," six times as much.

          7. Therefore one must use the Attic for weight and coin,

since it is equal-value and equal-weight to the Italian which is
called "denarius," inasmuch as many now commonly   use the Italian.

    8.   The Attic mna has 25 stateres; and the Italian litra is
24 stateres; and there are myriad differences of the remaining mnai
40 and none / necessary for us to present now. //

    9.   The litra makes 12 ounces, and the ounce 8 drachmai;   *p. 271*
and the drachme is 3 grammata; and the gramma has 2 obols; again the
gramma (is) 3 thermoi, the thermos 2 keratia, thus the litra consists
of 1728 keratia.

    10.   Additionally the denarius is divided according to the
45 Romans into / 1152 parts; for it has two tropaïka, four noumoi, 16
assaria; and the noumos contains an ounce by weight. The assarion
is divided into a half, and third, and fourth, and sixth, and eighth,
and ninth, tenth, twelfth, sixteenth, twentyfourth, thirtysixth,
50 fortyeighth, seventysecond; and these parts have their own names /
among the Roman accountants.

    11.   The amphoreus of wine, which the many also call
metretes,   has 2 hemiamphoria which they call   kadoi by common
name, but Romans urnas, and it has 4 prouchoi, 8 chous, which in
fact they call congia, but we call kaboi.   And the chous is
55 equal to 6 xestai (and the xestes / the Egyptians call hinion);
so the amphoreus is 48 xestai.

    12.   But the Antiochian metretes is double the Italian.

    13.   Then the xestes is divided into two kotylai, which we
call hemina, the kotyle is divided into two oxybapha, and the oxy-
baphon is split into three kyathoi and the kyathos makes 4 mystra

60 which, in fact are / called listria many times, and a kochliarion

is the half of the mystron, and the xestēs therefore is resolved into

96 kochliaria. And those for oil similarly, except that it begins

from what is called kentēnarios, which in fact has 100 litrae.

Also the oil metrētēs is double this; and the // other measures   *p. 27ͦ*

65 agree; for what proportion the litra weight has to / the mna, the

same the measured litra has to the kotylē or to the hemixeston.

      14. The Attic medimnos is equal to 6 Italian modii, and

the modius is called hekteus.   The modius has two hemiekta, the

hemiekta has 4 choinixes, the choinix has two xestai, so the modius

70 consists of 16 xestai. The / remaining measures of dry substances

are similar to the forementioned liquid.

      15. The Ptolemaic medimnos is one and one half of the Attic

and consists of two of the ancient artabai: for the artabē consisted

of 4 1/2 Italian modii, but now, because of the Roman usage, the

75 artabē provides 3 modii.

      16. The Phoenician koros is 30 sata; the saton is one and a

half modii; there are a few different kinds of sata.

      17. A three finger pinch is 2 drachmai of a dry composi-

tion.

      18. The chous is the six-xestai measure; the weight of wine

is 10 li., that of oil 9 litrae, and that of honey has 15 li.; and

80 there are / many differences in the weight of all measured substances.

      19. The onkia has 400 peppercorns; the litra has 5000 corns.

      20. But in order that we should not err in the whole, finding

something signified by a symbol in the discoveries of drugs, which of the things which have been enumerated is manifested through each one,

85 we will subjoin.

      21. The talent must be indicated by the letter ξ having a

line through the // middle (⟊), and the mna by the μ having a   *p. 275*

ν placed over it ($\overset{\nu}{\mu}$) (a ν΄ $\overset{\nu}{\mu}$ is fifty mnas, but sometimes ρ having

a mark through the middle signifies the same ⍴), and the litra

by the lambda having the iota inserted or adjacent (λ; λι) and the

90 onkia by the gamma having the o placed over or under it / ($\overset{o}{Γ}$; Γο);[1]

and a lambda placed sideways having the horns to the right makes a

drachmē (<), and half of a drachmē also has entirely the same ap-

pearance, having been turned to the left (>); and the μ having the

ε placed over it signifies a metron ($\overset{\varepsilon}{\mu}$); and the obol, the sixth of

the drachmē, a sort of longish sigma ($\int$)[2] or an iota placed sideways

(−), and two obols the same lying opposite (each other) (=); and

95 the / three-obol piece the Γ having the top horn tilted upward (ϲ);

and it is called by some cheramis.

---

    [1]Or: $\overset{o}{γ}$, γο.

    [2]Or: ~? I have not found the former attested for this use in
published texts.

Listed by Duchesne paragraph numbers (symbols included from paragraph 21):

WEIGHTS:

2. talent (ϟ) = 60 mnas = 1500 stat(ers) = 60 drach(mas)

    mna (ℵ) = 25 stat.

    stat. = 4 drach. (= holkai)

    drachma (∨) = 6 obols = 48 coppers   (1/2 drach.: ⟩)

    obol (∫, or —) = 8 coppers

8. mna = 25 stat.

    litra (λ, λι) = 24 stat.

9. litra = 12 onkiai = 1728 keratia   [= 5000 peppercorns (par. 19)]

    onkia (℞, ℞ο) = 8 drachmas   [= 400 peppercorns (" ")]

    drachma = 3 grammata (scruples)

    gramma = 2 obols (2 obols: =)   (3 obols: ⟨)

            = 3 thermoi

    thermos = 2 keratia (carats)

10. denarius = 2 tropaïka = 4 nummi = 16 assaria

    nummus = onkia (uncia) in weight

    assarion divided into: 1/2 1/3 1/4 1/6 1/8 1/9 1/10 1/12 1/16 1/24 1/36 1/48 1/72

LIQUID MEASURE:

11. Wine: amphoreus (metretes: ε, μ) = 2 hemiamphoria ("kadoi"/"urnas")

        = 4 prouchoi (jugs) = 8 choes ("kongia"/"kaboi") = 48 xestai   [= 96 kotylai]

    chous = 6 xestai (xestes = "hinion")

12. Antiochian metretes = 2 Italian

13. xestes = 2 kotylai ("hemina") = 96 kochliaria

    kotyle = 2 oxybapha

    oxybaphon = 3 kyathoi

    kyathos = 4 mystra (listria)

    1/2 mystron = kochliarion [mystron = 2 kochliaria]

    <u>Oil</u>: kentenarios = 100 litras

    oil metretes = 2 kentenarioi

RELATION OF WEIGHTS AND MEASURES: litra : mna :: litra : kotyle (hemixeston)
                     [i.e., 24 stat. : 25 stat. :: 1/100 kent. : 1/96 amphor.]

DRY MEASURE:

 14. Attic medimnos = 6 Italian modii (hekteus)

    modius = 2 hemiekta = 16 xestai

    hemiekton = 4 choinices

    choinix = 2 xestai

    other dry measures = liquid measures previously discussed

 15. Ptolmaic medimnos = 1 1/2 Attic medimnoi = 2 "old" artabai

    "old" artabe = 4 1/2 Italian modii

    artabe = 3 modii

 16. Phoenician koros = 30 sata

    saton = 1 1/2 modii

WEIGHTS OF VARIOUS LIQUIDS:

 18. chous = 6 xestai: of wine = 10 li.; of oil = 9 li.; of honey = 15 li.

    all other measured substances have many different weights

Fig. 2. Summary of Africanus's "Weights and Measures"

The Kestoi Fragments, V:

Papyrus Oxyrhynchus 412[1]

[Col. i / λε]

[[But when by vow]s and prayers [to the]] host of the dead,

[[I had prayed,] and, taking [the]] sheep, slaughtered it

[[into the pit,] and the dark blood [flowed]]: and gathering the

[[souls from beneath Ere]]bos, of corpses having died,

5 [[maids and you]]ths and the much enduring aged

tender [[virgins]] late-mourned while in the prime of life;

[[and many w]ounde[d by b]]razen pointed spears,

[[Ma]rs-slain [me]]n in gore-stained arms,

[[the multi]]tude beside the pit wandering about from place to place

10 [[with awf]]ul cries; but me, pale fear seized on.

[[But]] I, d[[r]]awing the sharp sword from by my thigh,

[[sat, n]]ot allowing that any fleeting shade near to

[[the bloo]]d might come; and replying, the song I sang:

(That which it was necessary to perform, he has said)

---

[1]Grenfell and Hunt, Oxyrhynchus Papyri, III (1903), pp. 36-41,
and plate 5.
      I have followed Vieillefond's convention in using double
brackets to indicate missing portions of the papyrus text, but where
these are broken up due to changes of word order in the translation,
I have used only single brackets within the double sets. In the
prose portion at the end (col. ii), I have continued to give Vieillefond's line numbers in the margin, but have added, in angle brackets,
the numbers of the lines in the papyrus as given by Grenfell and Hunt.

15 "[[O Rive]]rs and Earth and Those Beneath who suffering

   [[me]]n repay, who are of oath forsworn,

   [[you]] are witnesses, fulfill our song;

   [[I came]] enquiring how I may come unto the land //

   [[of Telem]]achus, whom I left on nurse's lap,   *p. 287*

20 my [[so]]n." For of suchlike was the most useful spell.

              (That which it was necessary to sing he uttered)

   "[[Hear]] me, propitious and watchful, rich see[[ded An]]ubis

   † . . . (<u>illegible line</u>)   †

   [[Come Her]]mes, thief; Hither, fair-haired subterranean Zeus,

25 granting [[to be success]]ful, fulfill this spell;

   [[hither Had]]es and Earth; immortal Fire, Titan Helios,

   [[come also]] Yaa and Phtha and law-sustaining Phrē,

   [[both Neph]]tho much-revered and Ablanathō rich in blessings;

   [[fier]]y-serpent-girded, earth-turning, ibis-headed,

30 [[Abrax]]as, far-famed god of cosmic name,

   dispensing [[axis]] and revolution and cold light of northern Bears;

   [[come a]]lso, for self-control most excellent of all to me, Phrēn, //

   † . . . o̅ri̯eu and <u>phasie</u> and <u>sisyon</u> †   *p. 289*

   [[and Bi]]rth and Death and beauteous burning Fire,

35 [[come Isi]]s earthly and heavenly and dreams'

   [[guardian]]ess, and Sirius who . . . ."

   [[And thes]]e things, standing beside the pit, I sang;

   [[for well]] I remembered Circe's stern admonishings,

   [[who so many d]]rugs knows, as broad Earth rears;

40 [[and there came]] a great wave of lion-fighting Acheron,

[[Kokytus]] and Lēthē and mightiest Polyphlegethōn,

[[and a gh]]ost army standing round about and 'side the pit;

a[[nd first]] came the soul of our comrade Elpēnor"

[Col. ii / λϛ]

(and so on)

\<45\>   Whether then, thus having the overwrought part, the Poet him-

45 self suppressed the rest of the invoca/tion for the sake of the dig-

nity of the work, or the Peisistratides, putting together the other

\<50\>verses, detached these, considering them foreign to the progression

of the work, † over much I knew †[1] which as a very valuable conception

\<55\>of epic, I myself have inserted here; // you will find this whole   P

50 passage deposited both in the archives / of the ancient fatherland,

\<60\>Colonia Aelia Capitolina of Palestine, and in Nysa of Caria, and up

to the thirteenth in Rome near the baths of Alexander in the beauti-

\<65\>ful library in the Pantheon which I myself designed for the Emperor.

55   Of Julius Africanus

\<70\>   Kestos

18

---

[1]Grenfell and Hunt read ep[i] pollo[i]s egnō-, and translate,
"I should much like to know" (Oxyrhynchus Papyri, III, pp. 39 and 40,
respectively). Vieillefond, following a suggestion of Desrousseaux,
in his notes on line 49 (Les Cestes, p. 289 mg), suggests reading
. . . egō on . . . . ("since I am occupied in many things, I . . .").
He omits the passage from his translation on p. 288.

The Kestoi Fragments, VI:

Kestos 13, Chapter 22

From the Kestoi of Africanus   *p. 297*

that is, of Kestos 13, chapter 22: Simple purgatives[1]

43

a

Cyclamen juice smeared on the navel is an active purgative.
But a summer purge is this: having brayed gourds in a mortar and
having strained the juice with linen, drinking with a little blended
honey for purging. That more suitable for winter: having boiled
the white beet, <depositing> into another, new vessel, make a broth   **b**
5 from the water itself with a little salt also, boil/ing it; and
these, the beets, eat beforehand without bread, then stirring the
broth, drink. A painless evacuation for spring similarly, the juice
of safflower seed being mixed with whey from milk and drunk.

---

[1]First published by Müller, "Zu Julius Africanus" (1881).
Also published by Max Wellmann, "Die ΦΥΣΙΚΑ des Bolos Demokritos
und der Magier Anaxilaos aus Larissa: Teil I," Abhandlungen der
preussischen Akademie der Wissenschaften, Philosophisch-historische
Klasse, no. 7 (1928), p. 70.

The Kestoi Fragments, VII:

Concerning Cinnamon

From the _Kestoi_ of Africanus: Concerning Cinnamon[1]   _p. 3_

But Herodotus indeed says that no one knows how cinnamon is
produced; but that birds build nests of cinnamon on the tops of inaccessible rocks. The natives are not able to go up to the peaks,
but those near us sa[[crifice]] many [[ca]]ttle and dismember them, if
they believe these particular birds to be carnivorous, [[leaving them]]
5 out in sight./ The birds carry the carcasses up to their own dwellings
and fill them until they are borne down by the weight; and they take
away the cinnamon to sell. Herodotus prides himself on knowing this
fable; but by experience, I assert the cinnamon plant to be similar
to a bush and [<multi-branching>], and the tree appears [<most>]
sim[<ilar, on the one hand>] to the agnus; but the height as much as
10 thri[<ce. It is stripped off>], on the one hand, entirely;/ but it is
divided into [<five parts. The>] first of it, that [<cut off toward>]
its top, [<then the second, the>]n the rest in order.

---

[1]Originally published by Vieillefond as "Un fragment inédit de
Julius Africanus." That publication gave the text in 19 lines, following the lines of the manuscript (the defects are generally at the left
edge of the original column). It was accompanied by the text and a
translation of Herodotus 3. 111. Besides other differences in details,
Africanus changed Herodotus's "Arabians," to "those by us."
     In _Les Cestes_ (p. 303 mg, re lines 9-12), Vieillefond gives
the text of Theophrastus _Hist. pl._ 9. 5, to which the latter part of
Africanus's account is very similar. Based on this parallel, I have
conjecturally completed the text at several points (marked by the use
of angle brackets within the square brackets) which Vieillefond leaves
open.

The Kestoi Fragments, VIII:

Concerning Dyeing[1]

1. Of Africianus's Book: Production of
            Bright Purple   *p. 309*
[P. Holm. κα. 1-6; Lagercrantz, pp. 32-33]

Taking the mordanted wool, soak in 1 cho(inix) of crimnos,
4 cho of seaweed--after having boiled it--, soak the wool and leave
for a long time, and taking it out, wash it off in brine, then in
(fresh) water.

2. Of Africianus, from Book 3
[P. Holm. κδ. 19-27; Lagercrantz, p. 37]

A mordant for every dye is this: first the animal or also
the fleece is washed well; for thus it may admit the (action) of the
mordant. Then one must dissolve the alum in vinegar and anoint whatever may need to be dyed. Having dried in the sun, it is washed well
and when entirely freed of the moisture, it admits dye. But it is
5 necessary to keep the / thing being mordanted in the mordant a day
and a night.

---

[1]Otto Lagercrantz, Papyrus Graecus Holmiensis (Uppsala: Akademiska Bokhandeln, 1913, and Leipzig: Otto Harrassowitz, 1913).   I
have followed Lagercrantz and the MS in retaining the form Africianus
in the heading, rather than correcting to Africanus with Vieillefond.

The Kestoi <u>Fragments, IX:</u> Citations   *p.31*

1. Michael Psellus, <u>Concerning Curious Readings</u>
[Westermann, ed., ΠΑΡΑΔΟΞΟΓΡΑΦΟΙ, pp. 143-46]

(God and Nature produce conception, as I indeed believe, but)
Africanus says that generation is a kind of craft, and he will beget
in a craftsmanlike manner, if the man, being about to enter into intercourse, should anoint the member with hare's blood or with goose
fat; but by the former means a male, and by the latter a female.
This man both draws milk from breasts by a craftsmanlike method; and,
5 they / being swollen after delivery, he dries up with a salve of
copper. He also makes a woman sterile, a contraceptive having been
appended to her; and it is a frog's brain[1] enclosed in a linen rag.
For those having difficult delivery, a jet stone being put into the
left hand, he causes them to deliver quickly. There is also made by
10 him other conception promoting compounds and artifices, and child-/
begetting plasters. There is by him a certain styptic compounded of
boughs of mulberry, appended while the stars are under the earth;
and he would give the power to it by a certain secret spell. He also
dyes hair white with powdered litharge. He also makes a preparation
for improving the voice from iris and tragacanth; and he corrodes
15 even gold with saliva of a maddened dog. / He makes a remedy for
stings of venomous beasts with the "two-faced" plaster; and he

---

[1]Or, "navel." See the discussion in Chapter III, below.

speaks a certain wonder relating to scorpions. He produces a certain   **g**

test for secret thieves, of tadpoles' tongues cut off and preserved,   **h**

then at need mixed up with groats and given in advance to the ones

under suspicion of the pur//loining of the things being sought. He   *p. 319*

20 claims that the one who took the thing stolen, / as if being in a

trance, clearly makes himself public; and he calls the food "thief-

convicter." Concerning agriculture also this man speaks marvels.

For a mulberry, he says, will bear white mulberries having received

a white poplar implant; and a white poplar in which there should be

grafted a mulberry is also supposed to bear the same. Peaches will

25 be inscribed the reddest, if one inscribes / the kernel lying in the

stone. He stops even pestilence, either by juice of balsam, or by   **i**

joining the evil smell of tanning in opposition. He prepares also

wine of every sort, one with heads of spikenard, another with flower

of mastic, and another with another drug. He forms also hyacynthine

30 stones and smaragdys, and sardonyx. He cures bites of asps and mist / **j**

of eyes, not by the known drugs, but by certain amulets and charms.

From droppings and the urine of cattle that have mated, he makes a   **k**

man to eliminate and a woman to urinate and to laugh heartily, when-

ever he wishes. A craftsmanlike, or rather sorcerous, fertility he   **l**

produces in fields, and the opposite barrenness by antipathies. He

35 gathers the moon/stone from the dew of plants and the beams of the   **m**

moon. He maintains undrunken those passing the night with wine. He
                                                                        n
talks marvels of certain helps from tortoises, from bear pudenda,

and of other animals and beasts. There is made by him also a reduc-

ing drug for excessive flesh. He destroys the insects in the

40 vegetables, setting forth certain new ways /. He speaks also concern-

ing the <u>gorgonium</u>. This is a plant, underground usually, but he

says, indeed, that if a girl should be involved near it according

to Aphrodite's rule, the plant raises up at the sight and curiously

watches the goings on. He makes both eye shadow and esoteric prepara-

tions. Most easily, by him, even the woman who has been involved   o

45 with many men is made a virgin again /. He also puts a parasite to   p

sleep, and the sequel is a source of mirth to him. He also stops   q

the having of dreams, and most easily he causes the after birth // to   p.

be expelled and he darkens grey eyes. There is by him also a bar to   r

varicose veins and some other night-shining thing. He both kindles

and quenches loves. He makes white hair black, and makes the black   s

50 white. And certain other / such things as these this man tells as   t

marvels and details in his <u>Kestoi</u>.

          2. Zosimus in "Concerning What the Art Has
          Spoken Everywhere concerning a Single Dye"
     [Berthelot-Ruelle, <u>Coll. des anc. alch. gr.</u> 2:169]

For instance, indeed, Africanus also says, "The Things util-

ized for dye are metals and liquids and earths and plants."

          3. Olympiodorus in "On the 'Concerning
              Energy' of Zosimus"
     [Berthelot-Ruelle, <u>Coll. des anc. alch. gr.</u> 2:75]

But salt was intended by the ancients that the arsenic would

not adhere to the glass cup, which glass cup Africanus called

<u>asympoton</u>.

4. Anonymous in MS <u>Parisinus graecus</u> 2286
[<u>Catal. des mss alc. gr.</u>, vol. 1: <u>Les Parisini</u>,
ed. Henr. Lebéque, pp. 185-86]

As Africanus the Babylonian says that if one wishes to pro-   **45**
duce a child, before coming together with the woman, that is to say,
when he is about to enter into intercourse, let him anoint his member with hare's blood and he will produce a male child, but if he
anoints with goose fat he will produce a female. //

5. (Pseudo-)Diophanes in <u>Geoponica</u>   *p. 323*
[5. 45. 2; ed. H. Beckh, p. 163, lines 13-15]

For the followers of Democritus and Africanus say the grape
remains altogether perfect only six days, and not more; if, therefore, the stone is no longer transparent green, but dark, it is a
sign that it is ripe.

6. Fulgentius <u>Mythology</u>
[F. P. Fulgentius, <u>Mitologiarum</u>, bk. 3, chap. 7;
in <u>Opera</u>, ed. R. Helm, p. 71, lines 17-19]

The stimulating plaster which Africanus the medical professor
called "<u>stisidem</u>"[1] he prescribed applying to the big toe and heel.

_____

[1]In the apparatus, Helm suggests that this may relate to the
Greek <u>styō</u> (to erect), a suggestion further developed by Vieillefond
(<u>Les Cestes</u>, pp. 322-23, note <u>a</u>), who suggests an original Greek
<u>stysida</u>, from a postulated noun <u>stysis</u>.

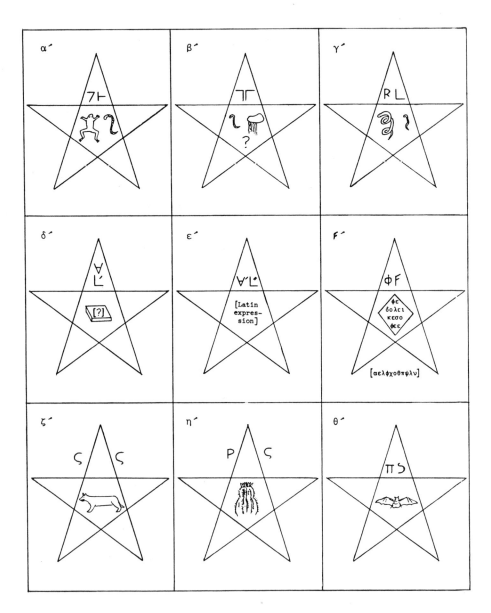

Figure 3. Hypothetical Reconstruction of the Pentagons in the _Kestoi_.

Appendix: Selected Fragments of the
Chronography

46/1. Routh, Fragment VII (first part), (Rel. sacr. 2:241-42)
       = Syncellus Chronographia (ed., Dindorf 1:34. 11-35. 6)
       [= ANF 6:131, fragment 2.]

      Of Africanus: Concerning the "Watchers"   **46/chr 1**

Multitudes of men having become upon the earth, angels of
heaven came together with daughters of men. In some copies we find,
"the sons of God." But it is being recounted, as I consider, from
Seth, the sons of God being so called because those being traced from
him are both righteous and patriarchs until the Savior. But he
labels those from Cain "men's seed," as having nothing divine, on
account of evil of race, and on account of the lawlessness of their
nature; they being mixed together, the vexation to God was produced.
But if he is considered to hold this concerning the angels, (it is)
of those concerned with magic and sorcery, and more, of power of
numbers, who delivered over to women the knowledge of celestial phenomena; from whom they produced children, the giants, through whom
the evil having come into being, God determined to obliterate every
faithless kind of beings in a flood.[1]

_____

    [1]The rest of the fragment in Routh (= a later passage in
Syncellus [ed. Dindorf 1:38. 9-39. 5], which begins with the last
line of the preceding) recounts also the landing of the ark. It
notes both the traditional landing site, Ararat, "which we know to
be in Parthia," and the suggested alternate, Kelainai of Phrygia, both
of which Africanus says he has seen.

47/2. Routh, Fragment XI, Dyn. IV, β. (Rel. sacr. 2:249-50),
        = Syncellus (ed. Dindorf 1:105. 8-11)

47/chr 2

   2nd - Souphis, 63 years: Who raised the greatest pyramid;

which Herodotus says was produced by Cheops. But this man also be-

came haughty toward the gods and composed the sacred book, which, as

a great value, being in Egypt, I procured for myself.[1]

48/3.   Routh, Fragment XL (Rel. sacr. 2:288; cited from: "Joannes
        Monachus in Sacr. Parallel. lit. ε᾽. tit. 7. p. 463. ed.
        Lequien Op. S. Joan Damasc.")

48/chr 3

   It is recorded by Africanus, that while Manasseh was saying

the ode, the bonds, being iron, were shattered, and he fled.[2]

---

   [1]Cf. Eusebius's account, as reported by Syncellus (Dindorf,
1:107. 1-3): "who also had become supercilious toward the gods, so
that, having repented, he composed the sacred book, which the Egyptians treat as a great treasure." (This passage is not found in
either the Latin or Armenian versions of the Chronicon, which seems
to have begun its account several dynasties later.)

   [2]Compare the slightly longer form given by Pitra, Analecta
sacra, 2:292 (from codex Coislianus 276, fol. 162, as from John, an
unknown seventh century monk): "It is recorded by way of Africanus
that while Manasseh was confessing, and saying the ode spoken by him,
his bonds, being iron, were shattered, and he escaped from the prison
of the Assyrians."

CHAPTER III

AFRICANUS'S VIEW OF MAGIC

In Africanus's writings, especially the Kestoi, we find a considerably different world from that in the other early Christian writings. The Kestoi is written from a different perspective; it has a secular, literary approach and contents,[1] and is addressed to a pagan audience (or at least, a non-Christian one).[2] Also, whatever his attitude toward them, Africanus presents a number of procedures which can only be regarded by moderns as magical. The passages manifesting such knowledge and interest must be studied in order to define more precisely the nature of their contents and the viewpoint and purposes of the author in presenting them.

Passages to be Considered

In the discussion of Africanus's knowledge of magic, a number of passages must be considered. It is questionable whether some of

---

[1] It could also be characterized as "scientific" in interests. This characterization, however, refers to the nature of much of the contents and the writer's attitudes toward them, not to the organization of the work. The latter is anecdotal rather than systematic. This viewpoint, however, does not distinguish the Kestoi from Africanus's other writings. The Chronography and the letters, while written for a Christian audience and dealing with largely Christian questions, still manifest a basically "objective," "scientific" approach to the questions addressed.

[2] This is true even if Vieillefond is correct that the author is writing for Diaspora Jews (Les Cestes, pp. 17, 41-42); even so, the audience would be one living in a largely pagan environment. (Note also, ibid., pp. 41, 56-58.)

them really relate to magic, but they present at least a surface appearance of doing so; others are clearly magical.

In the following pages, a brief list of the suspect passages is presented, to give an overview of their natures, and of the order of their appearance in the text of Africanus.[1] This is followed by a topically organized discussion[2] of these passages of possible magical import.[3]

---

[1] The passages from the Kestoi will be presented first (in the order of Vieillefond's Les Cestes), then those from Africanus's other major writing, the Chronography. (The letters have no such passages.)

[2] In the discussion, two modern studies besides Vieillefond's are especially used: Björck, "Apsyrtus"; and Riess, "Aberglaube," PW, 1, part 1 (1893): cols. 29-93. Björck, next to Vieillefond, has devoted the most attention to Africanus among modern studies; Riess's survey was the only complete one up to his time, and, as a broad scale study, has not been superceded. (Though a very large proportion of Riess's examples come from Pliny, this really makes it more valuable for comparison with the type of materials Africanus presents.)

[3] The dividing line between the two categories of magic and superstition is admittedly vague, but an attempt has been made to distinguish those items which are actively magical from those which are only passively superstitious, even if proven guilty of being irrational. Note Riess's distinction between superstition as folk-beliefs, and magic as the (mis)use of such beliefs in attempts to gain power over things ("Aberglaube," cols. 31-32); he further distinguishes false beliefs, ideas based on erroneous observations of nature, from superstition (ibid., cols. 32-33). This last area does, however, provide another source for magical practices.
    While such a distinction is proper, superstition is not only the bedrock on which magic is founded, but it also provides the quarry from which many of its building blocks are drawn. For this reason some superstitious items (and "false beliefs") must be included in the discussion, even though there may be no overt procedures prescribed for their use.

From the <u>Kestoi</u>

1.   I. 2. 57-69[1]   – Imitating the gods; poisoning food: animals –
                                  pentagon 1 with musical signs

2.   Ibid., 86-98   – Poison drink: animals – pentagon 2 with signs

3.   Ibid., 117-35   – Poison air: snakes – pentagon 3 with signs

4.   I. 3. 1-21   – Stones and cocks

5.   I. 4. 8-11   – Plaque (?): pentagon 4 with signs

6.   I. 5. 1-9   – "Hoplocrisma": spells

7.   I. 6. 23-30   – Horse-taming: inscription – pentagon 6 with signs

8.   I. 8. 6-18   – Divining from horses (seeing daemons; color of
                                  eyes)

9.   I. 9. 1-4   – Horses not to be frightened: wolf's tail –
                                  pentagon 7 with signs

10.   I. 10. 1-12   – Horses' swiftness: wolf's feet, astragali, and
                                  teeth

11. a.   I. 11. 17-20 – Horse-troubler: (drug in) pentagon 8 with signs

    b.   41-43   – " : smoke from menstrual cloth

12. a.   I. 12. 20-28 – Preventive veterinary medicine: smoked wolf
                                  flesh, rotted dog's head

    (?   41   – " : [mixture] infused into left nostril)

    b.   53-55   – " : lice or bedbugs

13. a.   I. 13. 1-3   – Unmanageable mules: cf. above (pentagon 6)

    b.   3-5   – " : box seed and water chestnuts (?)

14. a.   I. 17. 7-11   – Insomniac preparations: Hypnos

---

[1]Cited by part (in Roman numerals), chapter, and line of
Vieillefond's edition of the text in <u>Les Cestes</u>.

```
    b.          22-32  - Insomniac preparations: mythological back-
                          grounds (cf. lines 45-49)
15. a.  I. 17. 33-43, -  " : bat's head and wings -
               50-53         pentagon 9 with signs
    b.          44-49  -  " : spell and mythological support (?)
- - - - - -
16.  II. 1. 7          - Sleep producing compound: includes wax from
                          ass's right ear
17.  II. 3. 1-6        - Destroying trees: sea-ray sting, bean shells
18.  II. 4. 1-7        - Stopping horses: wolf's astragalus (cf.
                          no. 10, above)
19.  II. 5. 5          - Anointing of arrows: heat in new-made pot  (?)
20.  II. 8. 1-4        - Closing a wound: bulb plaster  (?)
21.  II. 10. 1-2       - Preventive for horses: deer antler pendant
- - - - - -
22.  III. 1. 1-2       - For elephantiasis: sun-dried hedgehog liver
23. a.  III. 2. 11-14 - Ophthalmics: stones in nestlings' gizzards
    b.          15-19 -    : the same, for epilepsy
    c.          20-27 -  " : partridge gall, vulture's eyes and gall
    d.          28-32 -  " : frog's eyes and gall
    e.          32-37 -  " : salve of ivy root, infant urine, copper
24.  III. 3. 1-7       - Horse breeding: pre-determining sexes
25.  III. 4. 1-11      - Restoratives of power
26.  III. 5. 1         - Frequent, easy intercourse: skink's flesh in
                          wine
27.  III. 6. 1-7       - Aid for birth, determining sexes
28.  III. 7. 1-4       - For much milk: milk stone
29.  III. 8. 1-6       - Against miscarriage: remora fish
```

30. III. 11. 1-3   - Dysurea: virgin's girdle

30A. III. 12. 1-2   - For dropsy: crow fat, hedgehog ashes

31. III. 15. 1-2   - Mange: sea-urchin body

32. III. 16. 1-2   - Fracture: dog's brain in bandage

33. a. III. 17. 1-6 - Tumors and warts: dog urine clay

    b.   6-9 - " : plants

34. III. 18. 1-2   - Acrocordons: serpent slough

35. III. 19. 1-5   - Maggots: pure water with "physician's" finger

36. III. 22. 1-8   - Asp bites: bedbugs, tortoise urine, etc.

37. III. 23. 3-5   - Apotropaic against scorpions: "abbas" on tin

                                  sheet

38. a. III. 32. 10-11 - Various bites and stings: brains of a living

                                  hen

    b.   11-12 - " : urine of a child

    c.   18-19 - " : frogs boiled with wine (against beasts

                                    and toads)

    d.   30-32 - " : head of biting animal (fresh or ashes)

    e.   34-36 - " : wild vine root appended

39. III. 34. 1   - Soothing feet: seven figs

40. III. 35. 1   - Colonic: right testicle of swan

41. III. 36. 4-6   - Horse markings: pulse, in hexagon 7, at first

                                  moon, third hour

- - - - - -

42. V   - Oxyrhynchus papyrus 412: nekyomanteia

- - - - - -

43. a. VI, line 1   - Purgatives: cyclamen juice over navel

    b.   4   - " : . . . a new vessel . . .

- - - - - -

44. IX. 1, lines: -   Psellus, <u>Peri paradoxōn anagnōsmatōn</u>

    a.   1-4   - Generation of sexes: hare's blood or goose

                           fat

    b.   5-6   - Breasts: producing milk or reducing

    c.   6-11 - Contraceptive pendant: frog's navel in

                           linen; birth and conception aids

    d.   11-13 - Styptic: sycamine branches appended, secret

                           spell

    e.   15   - Rusts gold with mad dog saliva

    f.   15-16 - Antipathy to beast bites: "two-faced"

                           plaster

    g.   16-17 - Scorpion paradox

    h.   17-22 - <u>Kleptelenchon</u>: tadpole tongues

    i.   26-27 - Stops pestilence: balsam juice, or smell of

                           tanning

    j.   30-32 - Cures . . .: amulets and charms

    k.   32-34 - Causes elimination as a joke: cattle excre-

                           tions

    l.   34-35 - Fertility and barrenness in fields: antip-

                           athies (?)

    m.   35-36 - Moonstone

    n.   37-39 - Aids from tortoises, etc.

    o.   44-46 - Restores virginity

    p.   46-47 - Puts parasites to sleep

    q.   47-48 - Stops dreams, brings down afterbirth, darkens

                         eyes

r.   48-49 - . . . and some other night shining thing

s.   49   - Kindles and quenches loves

t.   50-51 - Many other such things this man *teratologei*

                         and expounds

45. IX. 4. 1-4   - Generation of sexes [cf. Psellus, above,

                         no. 44a]

From the Chronography

46/chr 1. Routh, frag. VII <a> - "Concerning the 'Watchers'"

47/chr 2.   " , frag. XI, Dyn. IV, β - Souphis's sacred book

48/chr 3.   " , frag. XL - Manasseh's ode, and broken chains

Knowledge of Magic

Pentagon Passages

A number of the subject passages (or "magical passages"),
those listed above as numbers 1, 2, 3, 5, 6, 7, 9, 11, and 15a, are
linked together by references to pentagons. Certain information relating to the respective procedures is said to be found at the end
in successively numbered pentagons, or, in the case of another, mp
41,[1] as being found in hexagon seven. Besides the references to the
number of the figure, and to the information found in it, the pentagon series is also marked by a pair of musical signs in each figure.
(This feature is not mentioned in the sole surviving hexagon example.)

---

[1]Throughout the discussion, these passages will be designated
by their numbers in the preceding list, usually preceded by the abbreviation "mp" (plural "mpp"), for "magical passage," "magical procedure,"
and/or "main passage."

The figures

Purposes

The foremost characteristic of these passages is the reference to the pentagon (or hexagon) itself.[1] These figures are located "at the end,"[2] but without specification of whether of the whole work or of the individual Kestoi (e.g., of Kestos 7 for the pentagons). In 1932, Vieillefond noted the absence of pentagons from ancient literary, and even magical, texts.[3] He continued, "Pour la première fois, on le voit nettement décrit et utilisé dans les Cestes. A neuf reprises . . . , Jules Africain fait appel à ses vertues occultes, et d'une manière bien étrange."[4] Further study apparently convinced him that this statement was too broad, for, in 1960, it was reduced to "Africanus fait un abondant usage de ces figures géométriques. A neuf reprises . . . il en appelle au pentagone."[5] This reduction in the introductory statement was accompanied, however, by an attempt to show a specific magical connection in their use:

---

[1] The numbers assigned to each are sequential and seem to have no significance other than serving to distinguish the successive figures. Besides this they have value to us as providing the information that references to (at least) six other hexagons are apparently missing from our sources.

[2] Specifically stated in passages 1, 11, 15a, and 41, regarding pentagons 1, 8, and 9, and hexagon 7.

[3] Jules Africain, p. lvi; this absolute assertion was modified somewhat in 1960, by provision of a few examples of their occurrence (Les Cestes, p. 46, n. 63).

[4] Jules Africain, p. lvi. In a "Communication," "Sur deux signes magiques" (Revue des études grecques 43 [1930]: lix-lx), Vieillefond had asserted that Africanus "a recours aux pentagones pour donner plus de force à ses recettes magiques." Cf. also, Bardy, "Un encyclopediste chrétien," pp. 266-67.

[5] Les Cestes, p. 46.

Obéissant à la grande loi magique sur 'l'interdiction le vocabu-
laire,' et afin de ne pas détruire par avance la vertu de la
recette, Africanus ne désigne point par leur nom les êtres ou
les choses représentés. . . .[1]

A little later, he assumes that the pentagons and hexagons serve as

prophylactic amulets, and then speaks of their co-operating for the

achievement of the most diverse acts (military uses, horse training,

etc.); but he provides no real evidence for either function.[2] In the

background discussion, Vieillefond has provided instances of the pop-

ularity of pentagons and hexagons in the magic and superstition (and

simple decoration) of numerous peoples from ancient to modern times,[3]

but there is nothing really comparable to Africanus's use of them.

Indeed, they can hardly be said to be used at all by Africanus, they

just sit there.[4] Key ingredients or phrases are listed in them, but

only as a place to put them; the pentagons themselves are not other-

wise used or even referred to (prophylactically or in any other man-

ner).[5] The use of the figures does not seem to be for purposes of

---

[1]Ibid., pp. 46-47.

[2]Ibid., p. 49. The only specific example (for the former,
prophylactic amulets) is "l'usage habituel du sceau de Salomon."

[3]Ibid., pp. 42-45.

[4]Contrast with this the figures referred to in the London
Magical Papyri which had some close connection with the procedures being given (PLond. 121. 249, 918; 122. 109 note; the first was to have
been found "at the beginning of the book"; the last occurs at the end
of the book, but immediately following a reference to it; F. G.
Kenyon [and H. I. Bell], Greek Papyri in the British Museum, 5 vols.
[London: British Museum, 1893-1917], vol. 1 [ed. Kenyon, 1893]: 92,
113, 120; see also p. 116).

[5]Unless their prophylactic function is seen as that of safe-
guarding these items, either in respect to their secrecy (?) or their
potency; but Vieillefond's discussion does not seem to be that specific as to its meaning. Further, in the single instance where a

real secrecy. In one instance, noted by Vieillefond,[1] the significant

information is given in the text, before the reference is made to its

inclusion in the pentagon (no. 3). In another case, the bat,[2] the

identification is so self-evident that small credit adheres to guess-

ing it (lines 50-51). Since Africanus still proceeds to record the

information in the pentagons in these cases, there must be some other

purpose for doing so, but what? It does not really seem to be to

avoid dissipation of power by speaking them in advance, as Vieillefond

suggests,[3] since most of the situations involving the pentagons do

not involve any type of charm and only one involves a spoken spell

(pentagon five).[4] What else is possible?[5] Some sort of magical con-

vention? This could be assumed, but there are no parallels to sup-

port it; that is part of what makes these figures so puzzling. It

would appear that there is no blanket, magical explanation that seems

to fit; but to argue for a different reason in each case would be to

---

cross-reference to one of these passages is extant (I. 13. 3, p. 149;
referring to I. 6. 27-28, p. 133 [=pentagon six]), there is no mention
of the pentagon; reference is made only to "the Latin expression . . .
given above (prokeitai)."

[1] Les Cestes, p. 47, n. 64, re the serpent thrissos (I. 2. 117-
21, p. 121).

[2] I. 17. 33-34 and 50-53, pp. 165 and 167.

[3] Les Cestes, p. 46.

[4] Spoken spell, I. 5. 3-4, p. 129; also one written charm (in
pentagon 6), I. 6. 26-28, p. 133.

[5] Vincent seemed to assume that they functioned as some sort of
"talisman," with the musical signs serving to distinguish them, "en
même temps qu'à compléter leurs vertus occultes" ("Notice sur trois
manuscrits," p. 345), but he gives no proof or elaboration.

resort to special pleading. Thus, perhaps the reason should be sought
in another realm. Is it perhaps a literary device, a "conceit" of
the writer? We will have occasion to repeat this suggestion later.

Musical signs

In each pentagon was a pair of musical signs. These signs,
the "vocal" and "instrumental" signs for the same note, are described
in the text both by their function in the theoretical scale, and by
their form (variously positioned and/or modified letters of the alphabet). Their positions in the pentagons are variously described,[1] but
seem not to be significant. The musical values of the notes seem not
to be significant either, they are simply the first nine notes in a
theoretician's list of the notes of the "Lydian mode." They are generally those of the diatonic scale, but they include also two notes
of the enharmonic scale and one from the chromatic, a mixture that
would not take place in actual performance.[2]

Over a century ago, this musical series had attracted the
scholarly attention of Vincent, but as part of a broader notice concerning the realm of ancient music.[3] Unfortunately, this, no more
than the more passing references by later writers,[4] does not shed any

---

[1] Grammoeides enkeitai (pentagon 1); pyramoeides enkeitai (pentagon 4); engegraptai (pentagon 6); hyperkeitai (pentagons 7 and 8).

[2] Further, as Vieillefond points out (Les Cestes, pp. 47-48),
they involve duplications: each of the two enharmonic notes is
musically the same as the diatonic note that precedes it in the list.

[3] Vincent, "Notice sur trois manuscrits," pp. 344-59, 40-41,
73-74, 100-9, and table facing p. 128; also, briefly, Letter to the
President of the Academie, p. 174.

[4] E.g., Kroll, in his generally excellent discussion in Pauly-

significant light on these passages, serving only to set the notes
into their context in ancient music theory.

But perhaps this lack of progress (or even attention to finding any specific magical significance of the notes) is itself significant. Here again, as with the pentagons themselves, there is no active use made of, or suggested for, the notes. They seem to serve
only to further identify the figures. This conclusion was also arrived at by H.-I. Marrou, Vieillefond's mentor in this area, who saw
them (in Vieillefond's words) as "une manière de numérotation re-
cherchée et savante."[1]

Other features

Biological depictions

The animals and plants depicted will be discussed individually,
below. Here it may simply be noted that those which can be identified are all such as have association in human thought with malevo-
lent things, or at least are objects of aversion. Among animals

---

Wissowa, devotes four lines to it, and his comments seem to suggest that
he had interpreted these passages in Africanus as thoroughly as he discussed them ("S. Julius Africanus," col. 120, line 67-col. 121, line
2). Despite Kroll's assertions, in chap. 6 (of Thevenot, Vet. math.;
=Vieillefond, I. 4), the "musikalisch mystische Zeichen" is not used
by the surgeon to steady his hand, and in chap. 23 (Vieillefond, I.
17), it is not the musical sign (either alone or in association with
the pentagon) which is the supposed means of causing sleeplessness.
Unfortunately this type of hasty generalization is as typical in interpretations of Africanus as it is a-typical in Kroll's discussion.

[1]Les Cestes, p. 48. Vieillefond adds his own suggestion, that
since this is a second numeration, the notes were chosen chiefly because of "leur forme extraordinaire le lettres," connecting this with
the cabalistic uses of the alphabet (ibid.; and see also p. 49). (But
this seems to come close to "begging the question" again, assuming
that they must have some occult significance.)

there are toads, snakes of various types, medusae (?), wolves and
bats; from the plant realm, euphorbia (and an unknown pulse, in the
hexagon).[1] Despite their generally suspect associations, these
items are not all used in a magical manner. It is necessary to consider the procedures in which they are used to determine this.

Operations involved

Three sets of animals, those in the first three pentagons, are
used for poisoning (of food, water, and air). The first and third of
these procedures (Cestes I. 2. 60-69, p. 117, and 2. 117-32, pp. 121
and 123) involve sealing the animals together in jars, until they
kill each other, or die otherwise. In the second (I. 2. 86-98, p.
119), the animals (supposedly three in this case) are simply chopped
up together and boiled.

The sealing of the animals into jars to either kill each
other (I. 2. 65 and 125) or to die from heat (lines 125-26; and "from
time," line 126) or lack of air (lines 64-65) would seem to be to
maximize the baleful effects of the remains (sort of bestial biaio-
thanatoi?). This is probably part of some originally magical procedure, but is here presented as a rather matter-of-fact (though not
quite "scientific") one. In the first case, the vessel is sealed
with clay, hōs diapnoian mē genesthai tois thērois (lines 64-65).

---

[1]There was also an unknown substance (perhaps of vegetable
origin?) in pentagon four. Vieillefond concludes it is some sort of
(metallic?) plaque (p. 337, n. 47; cf. his translation on p. 126).
But whatever its identity, it would appear to have been some benevolent
substance (if of biological origin something such as Comfrey, or one of
the All-heals? [or even onion, etc.? cf. II. 8. 4; or, on the contrary,
dog brains? cf. III. 16. 1-2]).

The dative might conceivably be taken as instrumental or causative,
"So that there is no exhalation by/from the beasts . . .", i.e., so
that none of their spirit or virtue will be lost,[1] but it would seem
better to take it as a dative of advantage ("no air vent _for_ the
beasts"), as taken above.[2] Linguistically, the former approach would
be rather tenuous; if that were the meaning, it would be less ambiguously expressed by a genitive (perhaps with _apo_ also; and with an
apo- or _ek-_ compound instead of the _dia-_ form?).[3] Procedurally, the
sealing seems designed to insure the quicker[4] death of the captives,
and the operative element sought for use is the _liquified_ remains,
not the pneumatic. Then, in the third procedure (lines 117-32), for
poisoning air, where the _pneuma_ might be thought important, while

---

[1]As, for example, in the somewhat similar procedure cited by
Björck from Oder-Hoppe, _C.H._ 2:98. 12ff, where the jar is sealed _hyper_
tou mē diapneisthai tēn energeian ("Apsyrtus," p. 60). Africanus
was apparently so understood by the redactor of the variant of this
procedure in the "Sylloge," appendix 1 of Vieillefond, _Jules Africain_:
hōs diexodon mē echein tina tēn tōn thēriōn anapnoēn (chap. 3, lines
3-4; p. 68). (The "Ecloge" [appendix 2 of _Jules Africain_], _pros to mē_
ginesthai anapnoēn [chap. 2, lines 3-4; p. 78] agrees more closely
with the text given above from I. 2.)

[2]Vieillefond so understands it, translating: "pour que l'air
ne parvienne pas aux bêtes" (_Les Cestes_, p. 116).

[3]Björck's example might argue against this; but the "Sylloge"
variant does provide an _ek_ in the preceding _diexodon_. In any case,
is clarity a necessary consideration in evaluating Africanus?

[4]And the death of both equally? Whatever the ancient reputation of the toad (of whatever species), it would appear to be at a
distinct disadvantage in a _guerre à outrance_ with a viper. (Or is
the sealing so the viper will have no relief from the [poisonous]
breath of the toad?) Besides this, the pot was presumably not to be
opened for quite some time, so who would know which had survived the
longest?
See Hugo Plomteux, "Le crapaud, magie et maléfice: à propos
de quelques zoonymes italiens," _Revue de linguistique romaine_ 29 (1965):
132-40, concerning the ancient reputation of the toad, and its continuation into recent times.

close sealing is emphasized (lines 123-24) (and is absolutely required
by the nature of the "product"), the main term used, stegnon (line
124), technically suggests water-tight, rather than air-tight. Also,
the term used to describe the airy product (line 127) is none of the
pne(u)- forms, but rather apophora, "effluvium," "foul smell."[1]

The manners of usage of the products of these three procedures seem fairly straightforward,[2] though the results promised sound
rather overblown. These results--a spreading plague that will wipe
out a whole camp, or city, or nation of enemies; a slow poisoning
causing extreme swelling, pain, and desire for death; or a smell
that will kill a running horse or knock a bird from the

---

[1]In the contra-procedure (Vieillefond, Les Cestes, p. 123 mg.,
re line 134) provided by MSS V and D (presumably from the earlier
passage mentioned in lines 134-35), the threat is referred to both as
to loimikon pneuma (or simply tou pneumatos), and as tou aeros notheuomenou. The countering barrier (hōs antimachesthai) is ta hyph' hēmōn
genomena, i.e., from the thymiatēras. This was to be aided by locat-
ing tanning pits upwind of the camp to intercept the "corrupted air."

[2]In the first, the liquid remains are used in making bread
and for coating the baking vessels; in the second, a "broth" made
from the chopped up ("liquified") whole animals is poured into the
enemy's water supply; in the third, the vessel is opened upwind of
the enemy camp.
If there is any empirical basis for the first two procedures,
it must involve some sort of animal toxins and not a germ-caused
plague (nor a bacterial poison such as botulism). Bacterial organisms
would be destroyed by the heat in the cooking processes, but some animal toxins (such as that of certain puffers [used in the Japanese fugu
stew], geographically distant relatives of one candidate for the physa
in mp 2) do survive it. The sand viper, a possible candidate for the
Thrissos-Bathanerathan of mp 3, kills by a hematoxin which causes symp-
toms somewhat like those described in mp 2 (cf. section discussing
"Land Animals," below). On the other hand, the spread of the plague
described in mp 1 (lines 74-77, and 81-84, Vi., pp. 117 and 118) re-
quires a communicable or contagious disease organism. (But we should
not expect too much in the way of "scientific" accuracy and consistency
from this sort of source, even if the intent should be non-magical.)
(And does even seeking a rational explanation for such items put the
seeker in the same class as their author?)

sky[1]--are not especially magical, though when they, and the counter-
procedure for the third, are connected with a critical study of the
details[2] of the means proposed to achieve them, they tend to make one
sympathetic to Björck's theory.

A fourth procedure in this series appears in connection with
pentagon nine (mp 15a, above; Vi., I. 17. 33-43, 50-53, pp. 165 and
167). The animal involved there is the bat. Though not named, it is
indicated in such unmistakable terms that small praise comes from
recognizing it (lines 50-51). The procedures involved are also un-
mistakable--they are various types of sympathetic magical procedures:
using the head in an amulet (or secreted in someone's pillow as a
prank), or using the wing(s) for consuming liquids, as a means to
sleeplessness. Though Sleep, personified, is featured in the con-
tiguous account, in passages that could be taken as a magical "mythological narrative" (mp 14 a and b; and cf. the latter part of 15b),

---

[1] A sort of magical commonplace? Cf., Pfister, "Epode," PW,
supp. 4 (1924): col. 343, lines 40-44--bringing down a flying eagle
with a spell (cited from Philostorgios, Artem. Passio, ed. Academ.,
1913, p. 161); but as a variation on the legend of Pythagoras compelling a flying eagle to come to him (Pfister, ibid., lines 32-36).

[2] For example, the tanning pits upwind of the camp in the anti-
procedure to number three. There is also the question, unanswerable
now because of the incomplete nature of this item (if indeed, it were
ever answerable), as to how much warning the camp had that an ox-eating
binge could be ordered, tanning pits set up, etc. (Or was this supposed to be standard camp procedure in suspect areas? The "Ecloge"
clarifies this somewhat, specifying that lamps and censers were to be
used when near the enemy with an adverse wind blowing toward "us"
[Jules Africain, app. 2, chap. 1, lines 24-26, p. 78]. The tanning
pits, positioned some distance [apo makrothen, line 33] from the camp
appear to be established as a precaution against "blowback" when the
formula is used and the pot opened [lines 30-31]. But this still does
not clarify the original context in which the preventive had "previously" been given by Africanus.)

and as an incantation against Sleep (mp 15b, especially the first part),[1] they are not presented as such;[2] they seem more like the classical and other allusions and references with which Africanus, the litterateur, loved to embellish his accounts.[3] If this view is correct, then the actual magical procedures involved are a type of "direct," impersonal magic, not an "indirect" use, working through personal (daemonic) forces.[4] As a matter of fact, where Africanus

---

[1] They may have so functioned at some stage in their life history (assuming that they had a previous history, and are not Africanus's production entirely). According to Vieillefond's view of the meaning of Kestoi, at least lines 47-49, with the reference to Aphrodite's Kestoi in line 48, must be an Africanian original (cf. Les Cestes, p. 39).

[2] This is a significant point. If Africanus intends these items to be used magically, he must be assuming that his readers will so recognize them and know the proper procedures (and safeguards) for making use of them; but would his book be of any use to such adepts? An excerpter can hardly be blamed for this gap: (1) why would he keep the allusions while leaving out only the magical directions for them? (2) this is in one of the more fully preserved accounts; if there are such omissions here, can we have confidence in the integrity of any passage? Indeed, this involves reading more into the work than even Björck's contrary view.

[3] Note, for example, the list of sources, from Homer on, given by Vieillefond, Les Cestes, p. 59.

[4] Though Sleep is spoken of in these personal terms: as subject to being taken (labein . . . zētō, I. 17. 27, p. 165), enslaved and 'monopolized' (tēs emēs empeirias hētonna, . . . par' emoi monō . . . oikē., lines 28-29), and warred against (antitattomai . . . stratēgēsō, lines 30-32). But the following procedures deal with sleep, not Sleep, with no indication of any attempt to conquer or control the latter, unless possibly such appears in lines 44-45 ("Night's son you are, O Sleep; night's bird conquers you; . . ."). But this again appears to be rhetorical embellishment, with no explicit directions for, or other suggestions of, real magical use; boasting rather than incantation (though possibly using, or patterned after, incantation forms). It may be noted that in the Oxy. Pap. fragment, such explicit notations of magical procedure are included, even when they interfere with the progress of the narrative and the poetic form (Les Cestes, part V, lines 14 and 21, pp. 285, 287). (Wünsch makes passing mention

does refer to such daemonic forces, it is to oppose (or exalt himself over) them, not to invoke or otherwise use them (this applies
even in his statements to and about Sleep).

The procedures involved in the other pentagons are rather
mixed. In connection with pentagon four (I. 4. 8, p. 127), there
occurs the utilizing of an unknown substance or object (identified
only in the [missing] pentagon) in the treatment of a wound. Vieillefond's text is epipasatō tē plinthō hēper . . . , which he translates as "fasse une application de la plaquette qui. . . ."[1] He suggests, but does not adopt, the possibility that it might involve
sprinkling with the substance of some powdered brick.[2] If Vieillefond's preferred interpretation is correct, this might suggest a
magical procedure, depending on the nature of the plaque: of what
material is it? is it uninscribed or inscribed? if the latter,
with what inscription? But even if he is correct, it still might be
a "medical" procedure.[3] Conversely, if one of the other views is

of these lines as evidence of knowledge, on the part of their author,
of the twofold division of most magical procedures ["Deisidaimoniaka,"
p. 3].)

[1] Les Cestes, pp. 127, and 126; the MSS read hoper.

[2] Ibid., n. 47 on p. 337. Alternately, if plinthos could be
taken in the sense of plinthion, it could refer to the bandage for the
wound, to be sprinkled with the designated substance (cf. Henry George
Liddell and Robert Scott, comps., Greek-English Lexicon, rev.
and augm. Henry Stuart Jones and Roderick McKenzie, 9th ed., with a
supplement [Oxford: Clarendon Press, 1968], s.v. "πλίνθιον," sense II,
3, "a bandage, =ἡμιρρόμβιον, Gal. 18[1]. 798, cf. Heraclas ap. Orib.
48. 13. 1." [Cited hereafter as LSJ.]).

[3] Note, e.g., Pliny N.H. 34. 166 (cited by Vieillefond [Les
Cestes, p. 337, n. 47]) concerning the medical use of laminae plum-
beae, though the uses listed there (and in the following sections)
are for other purposes (but, in sec. 169, calcined lead is used for

correct, it might still be magical, though a medical intent would be
more likely.

A time-honored treatment, "hoplocrisma," the anointing of the
injuring weapon,[1] is combined with the use of two "spells" (discussed
below), along with a prophylactic or apotropaic use of spitting, in
connection with pentagon five (mp 6; I. 5). (But this is to relieve
the suffering; it is followed by a directive to give the usual medical treatment to the wound.)

Pentagon seven held the key element in a procedure with several points of contact with magic. An object to prevent a horse from
being frightened is to be fastened to his right ear, the object to
be used is the tail of a wolf,[2] and this is to be cut off the living
animal.[3] The basic operation is a fairly simple act, the tying of a
suitable, and suitably prepared, prophylactic charm to the subject in
a suitable location. The ear would provide a handy, even obvious,
point of attachment, as well as putting it near the eye, thus having
some possible connection with the causing of fright (the causes

---

hemorrhage and to promote cicatrization). In 33. 84, he also recommends gold as an amulet for people suffering from wounds.

[1] Cf. Keith Thomas, Religion and the Decline of Magic (New York:
Charles Scribner's Sons, 1971), p. 190 and p. 191 with n. 1; also p. 229.

[2] Unidentified in the main manuscript tradition, but specified
in a repetition of the chapter in the two British Hippiatrica MSS,
Londinensis and Cantabrigiensis, Vieillefond's Λ and Γ (Les Cestes,
p. 139 mg., on line 2; Oder-Hoppe, C.H. 2:249-50, Hipp. Cant. 108. 5).

[3] These four factors ("right," "tail," "wolf," "living") will
be discussed below, under the "Land Animals" and "Miscellaneous"
headings. (On the last three factors, in various combinations, see
Vieillefond, Les Cestes, p. 340, n. 61).

mentioned are sights and shadows, rather than sounds). Suitable prep-

aration here consists of cutting it off the living animal, which is

not quite so simple a procedure, but no other conditions (or cautions)

are prescribed. Thus it could be viewed as more passive, "supersti-

tious," than actively magical in underlying beliefs.

With pentagon eight (mp 11; I. 11. 17-31) the only readily

observable magical element is the pentagon itself. The drug involved

(euphorbia, according to MSS V and D) could easily have the effect

ascribed to it, and the manner of usage (squirting [or, "puffing"]

at horses' nostrils from pus-extractors), whatever its practicality

in actual battle conditions, is not magical.

Pentagon nine (mp 15; I. 17. 33-53), involving the bat, has

already been discussed above. Here it may simply be noted further

that two of the procedures involve a part (a wing [lines 36-37], or

the head [lines 40-41]) taken from the living animal. Again there

are no other circumstances, conditions, or precautions[1] specified.

The final figure, "hexagon seven" (mp 41; III. 36. 4-6, p.

255), is somewhat typical of the Africanian procedures (and the prob-

lems in studying them). The substance represented, a legume (osprion),

is unknown; even an early copyist, who apparently had the figure,

misunderstood it and glossed the passage as "blackberry" (baton).

The substance is to be used at a specific time, "at the first [=new?]

moon, at the third hour" (line 5). This would seem to have a magical

basis, but an attempt is made at providing a physical rationale for

---

[1]This despite the fact that he is challenging the daemon who
"holds sway over all," seeking to enslave and domesticate him.

the operation of the substance (lines 6-7). Further, the procedure
is designated a techne ("art," "craft"), a term used both by magic
and by everyday technology (line 8).

Associated spells and charms

Two pentagons, numbers five and six (mpp 6 and 7; I. 5, and
6. 23-30), involve the use of spells or inscriptions along with other
procedures. In the former, Africanus prescribes a sort of double
"double-whammy": "hoplocrisma" with spitting, and two spells.[1] The
first "spell" appears rather simple, "ta ta" repeated three times,
but the "ta ta" is similar to forms known from other magical sources,[2]
and repetition (double, triple, or even more; but especially triple)
is a recognized means of reinforcing or multiplying the effect of a
spell.[3] The other spell is lost along with the rest of the pentagon
sheet, but is identified in the text as a Latin expression (Rhomaian
tina rhesin, lines 3-4, p. 129). This feature is in keeping with the
tendency in magical circles to make use of the foreign, exotic; but it
adds a new variation in that it is not the ancient and mysterious,
but the modern and powerful which is selected.[4]

---

[1] Make that a triple; he also adds medical treatment and co-operation of the patient (lines 7-8).

[2] See the discussion under "Spells," below.

[3] See the discussion of "Numbers," under "Charms and Rites," below.

[4] This factor (shared with pentagon six) would seem to be more of an argument for Björck's view, questioning the seriousness of the author in these items, than for Vieillefond's view of their production by a contemporary (though foreign [specifically, Jewish]) of the Romans. But Rome had had a long history already, and some of their early kings or adversaries (e.g., Romulus, Numa, Tarquinius) were "names to conjure with" almost literally.

Zoological Passages

The importance of animals in Africanus's procedures is obvious, even from the limited sample provided above in the pentagon
passages. This impression is borne out by the range of animals, from
land, sea, and air, presented in the other parts of Africanus's work.
For purposes of organization, the discussion of the specific specimens
is separated into land animals (including amphibians), aquatic animals, and birds. In the procedures, these are not kept strictly separate, items from these different groupings being either combinable
or substitutable in some procedures.[1]

Types of usage

Whole or living animals

Generally these usages involve some part of the animal, but
in several cases the use of the whole animal is specified or implied--
in pentagon one, the "remains" of the two serpents are used (I. 2.
65-66); in pentagon two, the three animals are to be chopped up whole;
and in pentagon nine (mp 15a), while parts of the bat are specified for
use, this is followed by a comparison to the results if it were worn
whole (living?) (I. 17. 42-43); in mp 29, the remora fish, preserved
or living, is used, apparently whole (III. 8. 1-2, 4); in mp 30A,

---

[1]For a possible example of the former, note pentagon two,
which uses "a snake, a _physalos_ or aquatic _physa_" (whatever that may
be), and a third, unknown animal (mp 2; I. 2. 86-90, with p. 119 mg).
The latter is illustrated by mpp 23 (b,c,d) and 38 with their various
cures for eye troubles (stones from nestlings' gizzards, in fawn or
calf skin [for epilepsy], vulture eyes in dog skin; frog's eyes--
III. 2. 15-18, 21-25, 28-31) and for bites and wounds (brains from a
living hen in wine; frogs boiled with wine--III. 32. 10-11, 18-19).

the ashes of a hedgehog, presumably whole, can be used (III. 12. 1-2);

and, in mp 31, the "body" of the sea urchin is specified (III. 15).[1]

A large number of procedures specify that the part is to be

taken from the living animal: mp 9, I. 9. 1-4--wolf's tail, to pre-

vent horses from being frightened; mp 10, I. 10. 5-12--wolf's canine

teeth for swiftness of horses; mp 15a, I. 17. 36-42--bat's wing(s)

or head for sleeplessness; mp 23d, III. 2. 28-31--frog's eyes for

protecting or curing eyes;[2] mp 38a, III. 32. 10-11--brains of a hen

soaked in wine, for relief from (poisonous) bites.[3] Three other,

---

[1]Besides these, mpp 12b and 36 prescribe the administering
of lice and/or bedbugs--these would presumably be used entire (I. 12.
53-55, and III. 22. 1-2).

[2]In this case it is additionally specified that the frog be
released where it was taken (line 31). This would seem to have the
effect of leaving nature "undisturbed," and of "sealing off" the "living" eyes from any possible loss of power consequent on the donor's
death ("When last seen the frog was alive and well in his native hab-
itat"), or at least of knowledge of it ("Out of sight, out of mind";
"What you don't know won't hurt you"; etc.). (Compare the stingray
whose sting was to be used as an amulet by a pregnant woman, which
was to be returned to the water [Pliny N.H. 32. 133]. See further
under the discussion of "Rituals," below.)
    This same principle could also apply in the case of the
wolf's tail or teeth, or the bat's wings. On the other hand, in the
case of the bat's head, or of the hen's brains in the next item (mp
38a; if it is really intended magically), death would be an unavoidable part of the procedure (and could thus be viewed as proving the
signal potency of the part taken?). (The purpose of the release
might be a "scape-goat" idea, but such an idea would seem to require
some direct contact between the sufferer and the animal [as, for example, in the use of the fish rhombus against disease of the spleen
(Riess, "Aberglaube," col. 76, citing Pliny N.H. 32. 102)].)

[3]The major possibly-magical element here is the specification
of the living hen; the basic remedy, and those surrounding it (including possibly those designated as mp 38 b, c, d, e) are well within
the realm of "home remedies" or various types of empiric or sympathetic
medications (including one [mp 38d] of the "hair of the dog" type, the
application of the biting head). (This last [Vi. III. 32. 30-32]
would also presumably be cut immediately from the living animal; but
this is more incidental/practical than prescriptive.)

special, cases are presented by mpp 29, 1, and 3. In the first (mp
29; III. 8. 4-6), the whole animal (the remora fish), living, is held
to the belly of a mare to prevent miscarriage, rather than some part
being used. In the last two (pentagons one and three; I. 2. 61-65,
117-25), the pairs of animals involved are confined alive in pots,
to kill each other or die otherwise.

Parts of animals

As noted above, most of these passages involve the use of
some specified part of an animal. Closely related to these are the
uses of certain animal substances, and/or the applying of the procedure to some specified part. The reason for the choice of a particular part is fairly obvious in most cases, and can be reasonably
second-guessed in others. Three main categories seem to cover the
greater number of these cases, the parts specified being either:
(1) the same as the part affected (for good or ill) by the proposed
procedure; (2) representative, in some way, of the "essence" of the
specified animal (for whatever reason it was chosen); and/or (3) in
some way associated in concept with the end desired. These categories
are, of course, not mutually exclusive.[1]

Under the heading of the part affected, the following may be

_____

[1]It must also be kept in mind that they are essentially post
facto rationalizations; in most cases the ancient rationale has not
been transmitted.

Riess, in a more general discussion ("Aberglaube," cols. 29-
93), suggests seven types of superstitious Vorstellungen: (a) "Binden,
Bannen und Verbannen"; (b) avoidance (close to "tabu"); (c) transfer
and substitution; (d) sympathy and antipathy; (e) "ὃ τρώσας καὶ ἰά-
σεται"; (f) the unnatural; and, (g) "Hinderungsaberglaube" (preven-
tion, or reversal, of an adverse omen or act) (cols. 33-38).

noted: a foot or astragalus, of a wolf (mpp 10 and 18; I. 10. 1-5;
II. 4. 1-7), either to stop or to increase the speed of horses[1]
(but these may rather be examples of the next category, representative of the "essence" of the animal); eyes, of a vulture or of a frog
(mp 23 c and d; III. 2. 21-25, 28-31), to cure or prevent various eye
problems; afterbirth of a dog (mp 27; III. 6. 2-3), used to promote
conception by horses; and tadpole tongues (mp 44h; IX. 1. 17-22) in
the kleptelenchon preparation (to "loosen the tongue" of a thief).

Many more procedures specify parts which seem to represent in
some way the "essence" of the animal used. Some of these are fairly
clear examples: the tail or canine-teeth[2] (i.e., the fangs) of a
wolf (mpp 9 and 10; I. 9. 1-4 and I. 10. 5-11, to prevent fright and
to increase speed, respectively); the head or wings of a bat (mp 15a;
I. 17. 33-43, to cause sleeplessness); the flesh (fat?)[3] from the ribs
of a wolf (mp 12a; I. 12. 20-25, as a veterinary preventive medicine);
the liver[4] of a hedgehog (mp 22; III. 1. 1-2, for elephantiasis of

---

[1]Cf. Riess who refers (col. 81) to the great antipathy of
horse and wolf, and also to the effects on horses of wolf tracks and
the throwing of an astragalus at a four-horse team; on these points he
can cite the ancient testimony of Aelian (N.A. 1. 36) and Pliny (N.H.
28. 157).

[2]Riess (cols. 81-82 [cf. also, Will Richter, "Wolf," PW,
supp. 15 (1978): col. 970]) includes this procedure, citing Pliny
N.H. 28. 257. The wolf-tail is also mentioned, but for a different,
though still protective, end (Richter, ibid., citing Geop. 17. 13. 2).

[3]Richter, "Wolf," col. 970: both fat and flesh (with different manner and purpose use for either, but still apotropaic).

[4]I originally excluded this from the mp list, since the liver,
with its various enzymes, might conceivably be of some actual medical
benefit, but Riess's survey of animal materials in superstition shows
so many uses of various livers, that this no longer seems possible.
This is especially true in view of the wide variety of usages which

horses); the ashes[1] of a hedgehog (mp 30A; III. 12. 1-2, for dropsy

of horses); and possibly the foot, or astragalus, of a wolf (in the

preceding paragraph). Other items might fit here also, though in

some of them it may be the nature of the substance itself which is

the controlling feature, and the specification of the animal a sec-

ondary, qualifying feature. These include: pig marrow (mp 25),

brains (mpp 32, 38a,44c), skin (mp 23 b and c), blood (mpp 44a and 45),

fat (mpp 30A, 44a and 45), urine (of a tortoise, mp 36; of a dog, mp

33), ear-wax (from a donkey, mp 16), and saliva (of a mad dog, mp 44e).

The third category, concept association with the end desired,

may be the explanation of some of the items in the immediately pre-

ceding list. The following would seem to be so explainable: gall

(of partridge or vulture, with honey, etc., mp 23 c and d), against

cataract or similar eye problems;[2] serpent slough (mp 34), to remove

warts (causing them to "slough off"?); the head of the biting

---

seem easier to link (usually by "antipathy," or "ho trōsas ...") with
the natures of the animals involved than with the liver as such
("Aberglaube," 70. 7; 71. 20; 73. 3; 75. 1, 30; 78. 22; 82. 56 [here,
and in similar lists of examples later, citation is by Pauly-Wissowa
column and line numbers]).

[1]With this can be compared mp 38d. In that case the ashes are
equivalent to the fresh biting head (thus representing its "essence").
But in that case it is the biting head and not the whole animal (and
especially not another, even of the same type) which is needed. (Pliny,
however, illustrates the point that some of these other variations were
possible; e.g., either a different head may be used, or the whole of-
fending serpent may be "steamed" [N.H. 29. 69].)

[2]Because its bitter taste and/or smarting sensation in the
eyes would suggest potency (unless this is of some actual medical
value)? Galen prescribes a preparation which includes partridge bile
(among other kinds), honey, etc., for sharpness of sight and dispersal
of beginning cataracts (Claudii Galeni opera omnia, ed. C. G. Kühn,
Medicorum Graecorum opera quae exstant, vols. 1-20, 20 vols. [Leip-
zig, 1821-33; repr. ed., Hildesheim: Georg Olms Verlagsbuchhandlung,

animal[1] (either fresh or its ashes: mp 38d); cattle excretions (mp
44k), to cause elimination.

Certain items do not present enough evidence to support even
a reasonable guess at the rationale behind them: the right testicle
of a swan (for diseases of the colon; mp 40); bear pudenda (use un-
specified;[2] mp 44n). The hare's blood and goose fat in procedures
44a and 45 (listed above as possibly representing the essences of the
animals involved) perhaps belong here also. The leather or skin of
the amulets in procedures 15a and 23 b and c would have a practical
basis, but the specification of the types of skins in the last pair
suggest some additional reason besides this.

Besides the derivation of one of the materials (wax) in procedure 16 _from_ the right ear of an ass, three procedures specify that
they are to be applied _to_ a particular part of the animal involved.
In mp 7 (I. 6. 23-30), the horse-taming inscription is to be engraved
in the hollow of the left front hoof. This part is closely related
both to the essence of the animal and to its problem, the hoof being
one of the items with which it could manifest its unruliness (a front
one as being closer to either the head or the heart of the

1964-65], 12:279). Among Pliny's prescriptions for eye complaints are
numerous examples involving gall (e.g., N.H. 28. 167-72; 29. 117-25);
note especially 29. 123   concerning vulture gall and 29. 125
which   includes partridge gall.

[1]This is an example of Riess's fifth type of superstitious
Vorstellung: "ho trosas kai iasetai" ("Aberglaube," col. 36) (see
also p. 215, n. 3, above).

[2]It could easily be presumed that this would have some repro-
ductive or other sexual use, in which case this would fit into the
third category above. But, however reasonable this may be, it is
still a conjecture based on a conjecture.

animals?).[1] On the other hand, the cure for fright in mp 9 (I. 9;
pentagon seven) is to be attached to the horse's right ear.[2] The
ear, while not the part affected, would be a handy point of attachment very near the target area, the eye.[3] Slightly farther away, and
back on the left side, the frog's eyes as an ophthalmic (mp 23d;
III. 2. 28-31) are to be appended to the horse's left shoulder or
neck. The left, as the dangerous side, would also be an appropriate
place to put the defense, while the shoulder or neck would perhaps
be vulnerable points of attack in general.[4]

Land animals

    As noted above, this term is used here to cover both land ani-
mals and amphibians, with separate discussion of aquatic animals and
fowls following. The present section is divided in terms of modern
zoological categories and presented in the order of prominence in the
magical references. The presentation contains the following three

---

[1]Left (on which see below) would be most appropriate for a
"threat" (apeilē, I. 6. 28).

[2]Again, the right side (see below also) would be quite appropriate for a beneficial operation.

[3]Whatever the theoretical intent and rationale, the procedure
might work: a short time with anything flopping around and bobbing in
and out of the edge of the field of vision should inure the horse to
most unexpected movements and shadows.

[4]This would be especially true if this is an example of transferred human medical lore. Björck notes such transfer as a characteristic of the added materials in the British hippiatrica manuscripts
("Zum Corpus Hippiatricorum," pp. 31-44, and "Apsyrtus," p. 13, with
n. 1), but this seems to be a distinct series, separate from the Af-
rician additions. That, however, would agree with Björck's failure
to accept this excerpt as Africanian ("Apsyrtus," pp. 15-16).

divisions: reptiles (including turtles) and amphibians; canines

(wolves and dogs); and other land animals (generally presented in the

order of their first appearance in the Kestoi texts).

Reptiles and amphibians

   Snakes. Not only is this rather conglomerate classification

the largest group of references, but, within it, snakes are one of

the first, and the most, mentioned type of animal in the magical pro-

cedures of the surviving portions of the Kestoi.[1] The discussion here

will be restricted to those in which these animals are themselves used

in the various procedures; any used against them will be discussed be-

low in the presentations of the particular types of procedures involved.

   The first three pentagon passages involve at least one snake

each (one in the first, at least one in the second, two in the third).

But "snake" is a rather general term which takes in numerous types;[2]

this makes the identification of specific individual kinds rather

tenuous, even when Africanus provides some descriptive detail (assum-

ing that the identifications in Vieillefond's manuscripts V and D are

---

   [1]In general references, it might be surpassed by the horse,
especially in view of the prominence of the horse in the military sections, as well as in the hippiatrica; but such a consideration of non-
magical contexts would then also add numerous references to snakes, in
snakebite treatments, etc., of a non-magical sort.

   [2]Heini Hediger ("Introduction to Snakes," Grzimek's Animal Life
Encyclopedia, editor-in-chief, Bernhard Grzimek; vol. 1: Lower Animals;
vol. 2: Insects; vol. 3: Mollusks and Echinoderms; vol. 4: Fishes I;
vol. 5: Fishes II and Amphibians; vol. 6: Reptiles; vols. 7-9: Birds I-
III; vols. 10-13: Mammals I-IV; 13 vols. [English edition]; [New York
et al.: Van Nostrand Reinhold Company, 1968-72]; 6:346) gives the
figure as 2500 species; Roger Caras (Venomous Animals of the World
[Englewood Cliffs, N.J.: Prentice-Hall, Inc., 1974], p. 157) suggests
2700.

Africanian, at least in essence). In pentagon one, the second animal

is identified as a viper (echis; Vi., I. 2, p. 117 mg, re line 61).

The term "viper" in modern zoological usage covers several species in

Europe and Asia,[1] the most widespread and familiar European types

being the adder (Vipera berus) and the asp viper (Vipera aspis).[2] In

pentagon two, the first animal is simply "a snake" (ophis).[3] The

third pentagon presented two snakes of which we have somewhat more

description, but still not enough to clearly identify them. The

first, called Thrissos, was identified as a Thessalian snake, red (?)[4]

colored, about as long as a dracontis. An added note, regarded by

Vieillefond, probably correctly, as a later gloss, indicates that it

was also common in Asia, and was called Bathanērathan by the Syrians.

---

[1]Hubert Saint Girons, "Adder and Asp Viper," Grzimek's, 6:441
(in chap. 21, "Vipers and Pit Vipers," 6:439-84); cf. also, Gossen
and Steier, "Schlange," PW, IIA, part 1 [=second series, vol. 2, part
1 (or, "Zweite Reihe, dritte Halbband")] (1921): cols. 494-557, esp.
cols. 537-38, 556-57.

[2]The genus name Echis is used only of the "Saw-scaled Viper"
(Echis carinatus and E. coloratus), but while very widely spread in
Africa and Asia, it is a desert snake whose range seems to touch the
Mediterranean only in Egypt and Libya (H.-G. Petzold, "Family: Vipera,"
Grzimek's, 6:453, with fig. 21-12, a distribution map for Echis cari-
natus). Gossen and Steier ("Schlange," col. 538) identify the Echis
in Greek, or Greek-based, sources as the Sand viper (Vipera ammodytes).

[3]The second is a physalos ("puff-toad"?) or an aquatic physa
(thus either amphibian or aquatic, both discussed below); the third
is not identified (MSS V and D, in Vi., p. 119 mg, re I. 2. 88).

[4]The specific color, pyrrhos, comes from the paraphrase in the
"Tactics" of pseudo-Constantine (Vieillefond's Ecloge [Vi., p. 121 mg,
re line 117; Jules Africain, app. 2, p. 77, chap. 1, line 10]). (In
Les Cestes, p. 335, n. 35, Vieillefond, apparently relying on his mem-
ory, adds the "Sylloge" to the "Ecloge," but this seems to be incorrect; this passage does not appear in the "Sylloge," though the companion passages concerning food and drink poisons do [Jules Africain,
app. 1, pp. 65-74].)

The second snake, Leōn, appeared in both large and small types, with
the small preferred; again, an added note indicates that it was abundant in Syria. Unfortunately, all these added descriptions are not
much help.

Thrissos is unknown and the attempts to explain it are not
certain. Roulin suggested a scribal corruption of drissos, for
dryïssos or dyrissos = dryïnos/-as.[1] Both Roulin and Vieillefond call
attention to a type of serpent called Trissos by Hesychius, but since
the full text of the entry is "Trissos eidos opheōs," little more can
be done with it.[2] The identification as Thessalian is probably conditioned by the ancient magical notoriety of Thessaly, since the range
of a serpent would hardly be confined to so restricted an area (and
the gloss, if correct, proves otherwise). Rather, it indicates that
the range included southeastern Europe (or the Hellespontine area).
The length comparison is equally imprecise, since the dracontis is
also unidentifiable.[3] The Syrian name, Bathanērathan, was analyzed by

_____

[1] In Vincent, "Notice sur trois manuscrits," p. 563. (The
dryïnas does appear in Africanus, in III. 31, but in a non-magical
account. Gossen and Steier identify it as the Vipera berus ["Schlange,"
col. 537]).

[2] Roulin, in Vincent, "Notice sur trois manuscrits," p. 563;
Vieillefond, Les Cestes, p. 335, n. 35.

[3] This form, which seems to be required by the genitive drakon-
tidos in the text, is not found in the lexicons of a species of serpent, and its base form, drakōn, is as non-specific as ophis. Gossen
and Steier identify the drakōn, when used of an individual species,
as referring either to the Indian python or to the Aesculapius snake
("Schlange," col. 532). Of the two, only the latter would be even
remotely possible here. (Is the -id- suffix a diminuative suggesting
this? or does it suggest a similar but still smaller snake?) Roulin
suggests an aural error (which he had also suggested as lying behind
the form thrissos) for akontidos, akontis (an unattested form) being

Julianus Puchardus as from the Hebrew or Syriac <u>Pethen raten</u>, <u>pethen</u>

("serpent," or "asp") being the source of the Greek and Latin <u>Python</u>,

and <u>raten</u> signifying <u>incantator</u>; thus <u>Bathanērathan</u> meant the same as

"serpens incantator."[1] This would seem to indicate a serpent which

charms (and not a serpent which is charmed), or which is distin-

guished by the sound it makes.[2] Either idea might be suited to the

cobra (actually many snakes are popularly credited with the power of

"charming" or hypnotizing their prey--birds, frogs, etc.).[3] The

---

employed in place of the usual <u>akontias</u>. In favor of this view he can
cite Aetius (13. 29) as giving the length of both the <u>akontias</u> (or
<u>kenchritēs</u>) and the <u>dryīnus</u> as being two cubits (in Vincent, "Notice sur
trois manuscrits," pp. 563-64). On the latter page, he further cites
Lacépède's Histoire des reptiles (= <u>Histoire naturelle des serpents</u>,
1789?) as equating <u>druinus</u>, cenchrite, and ammodyte, and identifies it
as "la vipère à museau cornu," which has both the indicated length and
color.

In a survey of the pertinent chapters of <u>Grzimek's</u>, vol. 6, assuming that what was indicated was a venomous serpent, of moderate
size, and searching for one of reddish color, with a distribution range
which included both Thessaly and Syria, I concluded that the Sand viper
(<u>Vipera ammodytes</u>) seemed to best fit these specifications (see Petzold,
"Family: Vipera," pp. 449-51, with fig. 21-6, on p. 450, a distribution
map for the Sand viper). This seems to be the same as Roulin's "vipère
à museau cornu." This feature is something of a problem, however; if
this was the intended serpent, why was this distinctive item not included in the description? Or is that the "hair" which might lie behind
the form <u>thrissos</u>, if it is retained? (If Gossen and Steier are correct about the <u>Echis</u>, this would be the same as the snake in pentagon
one [see p. 222, n. 2, above].)

[1]In Boivin's "Appendix" to his "In Julium Africanum Notae"
(Thevenot, <u>Math. vet.</u>, p. 360 [note to p. 290, col. 2, line 26]). The
Abbé Chaine, consulted by Vieillefond on this point, validates the
possibility of Puchard's analysis; but this still leaves the serpent
unidentified (<u>Les Cestes</u>, p. 335, n. 36).

[2]The latter idea, that of a distinctive sound, might suggest
some snake such as the Saw-scaled viper (<u>Echis carinatus</u>), but its
southerly and easterly range seems to eliminate it (see p. 222, n. 2,
above), as do its smaller size and its more brownish color range
(Petzold, "Family: Vipera," p. 453).

[3]On this idea in the ancient world, note Clemens Zintzen,

reddish color, if correct, and the range may be somewhat more reveal-

ing. These, together with a presumably venomous character and mod-

erately large size, would be met by the Sand viper (<u>Vipera ammodytes</u>).[1]

The second of the two serpents in pentagon three, the le$\bar{o}$n, is

even less certain. Roulin suggested reading the somewhat more common

form [h]ele$\bar{o}$n, which is identical with the <u>skytal$\bar{e}$</u> in Hesychius.

This in turn would be identified with "l'eryx turc,"[2] which could be

one of the Sand boas (perhaps the Javelin sand boa, <u>Eryx jaculus</u>).[3]

"Zauberei, Zauberer," <u>Der Kleine Pauly: Lexikon der Antike</u>, rev. and
ed. Konrat Ziegler and Walther Sontheimer, 5 vols. (Stuttgart: Alfred
Druckenmüller Verlag, 1964-75), 5 (1975): 1461; LSJ, s.v. "δράκων,"
(probably derived from δέρκομαι, δρακεῖν); and Gossen and Steier,
"Schlange," col. 533, lines 26-28.

[1]Pp. 223-24, n. 3, above. According to Petzold, this is
Europe's most dangerous snake (though its venom is not nearly as potent as that of cobras or rattlesnakes) (like other vipers and pit
vipers [rattlesnakes, etc.], its venom is hematoxic, in contrast to
the neurotoxic venom of cobras and related species). It is up to 90
cm. in length, color variations range from gray to brown to <u>brick-red</u>
and black-brown, and it has a range from southeastern Europe, across
Asia Minor, into northern Syria and the upper Mesopotamian area
("Family: Vipera," pp. 449-50, with fig. 21-6).

[2]In Vincent, "Notice sur trois manuscrits," p. 564. A description he cites as from "<u>Thes.</u>" (read "<u>Ther.</u>," i.e., Nicander,
463, 474-77) seems to support this, since the ancients supposed the
pythons to suck the blood from their victims (or at least, their ele-
phantine opponents)(cf. Pliny <u>N.H.</u> 8. 32-34; Aelian <u>N.A.</u> 6. 21; the
description in Gossen and Steier ["Schlange," col. 533, cf. 536];
and H. H. Scullard, <u>The Elephant in the Greek and Roman World</u> [Aspects
of Greek and Roman Life, gen. ed. H. H. Scullard; n.p.: Thames and
Hudson, 1974], pp. 216-17).

[3]Cf. Bernard Grzimek, Zdenek Vogel, and Herbert Wendt,
"Boids," <u>Grzimek's</u>, 6:374. The <u>Eryx jaculus</u> has an appropriate range
(southeastern Europe, Asia Minor, and northern Africa), and possible
length (up to 80 cm.) (ibid.). It is, however, not poisonous; but a
snake which crushed its prey would, perhaps, be sufficiently awesome.
(Indeed, for a procedure designed to "choke" its victims, it might be
a positive advantage.) The reference to large and small types (Vi., I.
2. 121-22, p. 121) might be a problem for this identification, however; but Africanus may be assuming a rather wide knowledge of snakes,

The <u>results promised</u> from these procedures are rather extrav-
agant, though it is not absolutely clear, given the imprecision of
ancient biological knowledge, that they were not expected to follow
from natural, rather than magical, causes. From a modern viewpoint,
such natural causation appears impossible in at least two of the
cases. The procedure involving pentagon one might be considered possible, if it were a case of simple poisoning, but Africanus promises
an epidemic of plague (I. 2. 74-77, and 84). As noted above, this
would require a bacterial infection. Thus its success is ruled out
by the baking process which would effectively sterilize the product.
Conversely, since procedure two is a case of poisoning, it might work,
though the description of the results is rather strong (I. 2. 91-98).
The swelling, pain, etc., might be a generalization from the effects
of the bite or sting of the animals prescribed; for example, if the
snake were a viper (as suggested above for procedure <u>three</u>), this
would involve a hematoxin, producing blood poisoning.[1] The third procedure seems to require the assumption of some unnatural causation.
While at least one of the snakes was poisonous (even on the identification theorized above), and while certain smells can "take one's

----

including the large Asian or African <u>boids</u> (see preceding note).
(Strabo has a similar reference to Egyptian asps: they are of two
kinds, a larger and a smaller, with the bite of the latter more quickly
fatal [<u>Geogr</u>. 17. 2. 4].)

[1]Note Petzold's description of viper hematoxic poisoning in
<u>Grzimek's</u> ("Family: Vipera," p. 440). The symptoms sound much the same
as those promised by Africanus, though confined more to the local area
of the bite. Internal consumption of an "amplified" (use of the entire
animal) poison might have been expected to generalize and increase the
effect. If this is the true rationale, this expectation would apply
also to the effect of the other ingredients, the second of which, the
<u>physalos</u>/aquatic <u>physa</u> is yet to be discussed.

breath away" almost literally (and/or be said to be "strong enough to
kill a horse"), such a poison could not be transmitted in such a manner. In addition, Africanus seems to be unclear about the precise
nature of the results, despite his graphic examples (killing a running horse, a nearby man, or a flying bird, I. 2. 129-32).   These
examples suggest that it is like some sort of poisonous gas, killing
instantly; but in the next paragraph (and the antidote preserved from
an earlier passage) it is presented as a "pestilence" (loimos, I. 2.
134; to loimikon pneuma' . . . tou aeros notheuomenou, Vi., p. 123 mg,
re line 134), which might also arise from "one of the elements" (tinos
tōn stoicheiōn, I. 2. 134), and the onset of which apparently allowed
time for countermeasures. All in all, the picture that emerges is
one of very jumbled attempts at finding more potent empirical means
of exploiting "known" malignant agents. One of the sources of such
"knowledge" (both of the agents and of their manipulation) would
likely be magic, but the procedures themselves seem to be an attempt
to operate[1] with such agents--whatever the ancestry of their use--by
natural, "rational" means.

By-passing another reptilian reference (mp 26) for the moment,
we find further possible magical uses of snakes in procedures 34 and

---

[1]I deliberately avoid an expression such as "to transcend this
background and operate . . .", since that would imply that Africanus,
unlike his contemporaries, had a fairly clear conception of magic as
distinct from natural science, and was self-consciously trying to dis-
entangle them. He does, however, have some appreciation for empirical
procedure ([experimental would be too strong] cf. the various peir-
forms, e.g., I. 11. 34 [but sometimes with implied reservations, e.g.,
II. 7. 6; III. 17. 4; and esp. III. 32. 9]). He also recognizes the
existence of such a category as deisidaimonia (cf. III. 17. 3), though
he has difficulty recognizing actual examples of it, except in its more
extreme forms.

36 (III. 18 and 22, pp. 239 and 241). In the former, a shed serpent's
skin is hidden in a date and fed to an ailing animal against acrocor-
don, a type of wart.[1] In the latter, a physician, Phobios, following
a tradition of Inaron the Libyan,[2] prescribed the serpent Hemorrhoïs
for asp bites, and vice versa. While this might involve the magical
idea of antipathy, Africanus seems to emphasize the medical nature
and ancestry of this prescription.[3] Thus, while allowing for possible magical elements in its origin and/or uses (the origins of ancient magic and medicine are, after all, very closely intertwined),
it appears more like a type of ancient "allopathic" medicine.[4]

---

[1]For a suggested rationale for these, see the discussion of
"Animal Parts," above. Snakeskin had a regular place in veterinary
medicine (cf. Gossen and Steier, "Schlange," cols. 506, 527, 542-43,
555); Vieillefond calls attention to Pliny N.H. 30. 69, as paralleling
its usage against warts (Les Cestes, p. 358, n. 211) (it is not clear,
however, that any but the last item in Pliny's list here applies to
wart removal, but such a usage is given in 30. 81).

[2]Vieillefond indicates that these two personages are unknown,
though there are some references to a noted fifth century B.C. Libyan
prince, Inaron (Les Cestes, p. 359, n. 220) (cf. Thucydides 1. 104,
110; Herodotus, 7. 7).

[3]One could almost say he goes out of his way to do so, except
that, for a literary name-dropper and embellisher such as Africanus,
it is not really out of his way.

[4]Assuming the "asp" was an Egyptian cobra (Naja [formerly
Coluber] haje: LSJ, s.v. "ἀσπίς," def. II; and Gossen and Steier,
"Schlange," col. 524) its venom would be basically a neurotoxin (but
note Caras's caveat about the use of such terms [Venomous Animals, p.
198]), but was credited by the ancients with thickening the blood in
the arteries (Gossen and Steier, col. 526, line 41). The "hemorrhois,"
conversely, was named for its reputed causing of hemorrhage in its
victims. Caras's description of the effects of the bite of the Saw-
scaled, or carpet, viper (Echis carinatus)(hemorrhagic factors resulting in severe [sometimes fatal] bleeding from gums, nose, and in kid-
neys [p. 251]), would suggest it as a candidate for the "hemorrhois"
(it is so identified by Gossen and Steier, col. 521). Thus a deduc-
tive approach to medication would suggest that they should oppose each
other's poison.

Other reptiles. Earlier in the passage just discussed (mp 36; III. 22. 2-4), Africanus also prescribes tortoise urine, soaked up and dropped on the bite, either alone or with bedbugs. The turtle, unlike other reptiles, evokes a consistently positive response from humans,[1] so, not surprisingly, it has a corresponding type of usage in magic.[2] Urine also had a regular place in remedies to counter magic,[3] thus the combination of the two seems quite a logical step in medical magic theory.[4] This is the only extant example of the use of the tortoise by Africanus, but Psellus seems to indicate that there were others ("certain helps [ōpheleias] from tortoises, . . .": mp 44n; IX. 1. 38, p. 319).

Procedure 26, by-passed above, introduced a final type of rep-tiles in a different type of usage: an infusion of skink's flesh in mixed wine as an aid for studs (III. 5, p. 229). The skinks, like

---

[1]Note, e.g., the introductory remarks by Marian Mlynarski and Heinz Wermuth, "Order: Testudines," Grzimek's, 6:75 (in chap. 3, "The Turtles," pp. 75-123).

[2]Riess, "Aberglaube," col. 77; Gossen and Steier, "Schild-kröte," PW, IIA, part 1 (1921): col. 432. Numerous influences may combine in producing this reputation and the usage of the turtle here for snakebite: e.g., its non-aggressive behavior toward man; its similarities to, but yet obvious differences from, the snake; its relative personal safety from attack; etc.

[3]Riess, "Aberglaube," cols. 85, 86. The (bed?)bug also had a reputation for countering snakebite (ibid., 80-81; and Will Richter, "Wanze," PW, supp. 14 [1974]: col. 824; citing, esp., Pliny N.H. 29. 61).

[4]Note Richter, "Wanze," col. 824. True, snakebite is not explicitly magical, but any type of danger could be so regarded, and thus the same principles can be applied without distinguishing between "natural" and "magical" evils.

lizards in general, were anciently reputed as aphrodisiac.[1]

Amphibians. The ancient Greeks, like speakers of English and other modern European languages, distinguished between frogs (batrachoi) and toads (phrynoi). Yet they also recognized a relationship between them, whether it be regarded as sympathy or antipathy. Africanus illustrates both of these features.

In the first instance of the appearance of toads or frogs, pentagon one, the scribe who transferred the contents of the pentagon into the text of the ancestor of manuscripts V and D apparently could not distinguish which was intended. These manuscripts present the first animal as "a forest frog or toad . . ." (I. 2, p. 117 mg, re line 61). In view of the generally evil reputation of the toad, Roulin is probably correct in arguing for it, rather than the tree-frog, as the creature intended.[2] Sealed in a pot with a viper, it was

---

[1] Skinks: Ion E. Fuhn, "The Skinks," Grzimek's, 6:249; lizards: Riess, "Aberglaube," col. 69 (citing Theocritus 2. 58). Vieillefond calls attention to the occurrence of another use of the skink as aphrodisiac which appears in a paragraph preceding this prescription of Africanus in the corpus hippiatricorum (Les Cestes, p. 228, n. b). In that case it involves skink urine along with several other ingredients (Oder-Hoppe, C.H., 2:144. 25-28). Pliny says the skink is an aphrodisiac for males (N.H. 8. 91; 28. 119; see also Diosc. M.M. 2. 66 [Pedanii Dioscoridis Anazarbei de materia medica libri quinque, ed. Max Wellmann, Editio altera ex editione anni MCMVII lucis ope expressa, 3 vols. (Berlin: Apud Weidmannos, 1958)], al., 2. 71; in the first reference in Pliny this use is secondary to its value as an antidote to poisons).

[2] In Vincent, "Notice sur trois manuscrits," pp. 561-62; cf. Plomteux, "Le Crapaud," pp. 132-33, on the ancient reputation of the toad. Frogs shared somewhat in this reputation though (M. Wellmann, "Frosch," PW, 7, part 1 [1910]: cols. 113-19, esp. 115).

expected to be as fatal to the viper as the viper was to it.[1]

Pentagon two had as the second of its three animals the physa-los or aquatic (literally, "river") physa (I. 2, p. 119 mg, re line 88).

The physalos (mentioned by Lucian Philopseudes 12, and Dipsades 3)

was supposedly a type of toad which puffed itself up, even to the

bursting point, and had poisonous breath. This serves to illustrate

something of the ancient reputation of the toad; but these references

in Lucian are the only support given by Liddell and Scott's Lexicon

for such a usage of this term.[2] Aelian used the word of a type of

---

[1] Compare the discussion above in connection with the penta-gons, esp. p. 206, n. 4. This dangerous reputation is emphasized within the Africanian corpus itself in a non-magical passage: the hippiatrica fragments include the provision to protect cattle from being blown on by toads (Vi., III. 33, p. 253: keeping a fire always burning in the stable), since this was expected to produce "diseases most pestilen-tial to animals and tumors most difficult to treat, so as to render useless every aid for the suffering" (lines 2-4). Note also mp 38c (discussed below) in which toads are grouped with iobola as the ob-jects of an antidote using frogs.
    This reputation might arise from two sources (besides the toads generally repulsive appearance [cf. Plomteux, "Le crapaud," p. 133]). Some frogs puff themselves up to appear larger to try to discourage snakes from trying to swallow them (cf. Walter Reinhard and Zdenek Vogel, "Family: Colubrid Snakes," Grzimek's, 6:390; also Günther E. Freytag, "Modern Amphibians," Grzimek's, 5:298, and color plate, p. 456) (Reinhard and Vogel suggest that this behavior on the part of a toad may also lie behind the belief in snakes' hypnotic powers [ibid.]). This is coupled with the fact that many types of toads do secrete a type of poison from their skins which renders them unappetizing (or even deadly) to some potential enemies (Plomteux, p. 133, n. 7; Caras, Venomous Animals, 134-37; Hans Rudolf Heusser, "Higher Anurans," Grzimek's, 5:419, 422). Either from this or other causes, they are sometimes regurgitated by snakes (Reinhard and Vogel, p. 382; Hans Rudolf Heusser, "Frogs and Toads," Grzimek's, 5:369), which would certainly not lessen their noxious reputation. Wellmann, on the other hand, explains the toad's reputation by the tradition of its underworld origin, confirmed by its pale color and the supposed toad-like appearance of Hekate ("Frosch," col. 117).

[2] LSJ, s.v. "φύσαλος."

poisonous fish (N.A. 3. 18), and this seems to be in accord with the
second designation of the creature in the manuscripts.[1]

In another series of passages, various frog substances are
used for curative or protective purposes. In one (mp 23d), noted
above in the discussion of "Living Animals," the eyes from a living
frog are used, tied in linen as a pendant, to protect or cure the
eyes of horses (III. 2. 28–31).[2] Frog bile is also used as an ointment against eye irritation[3] and cataract (III. 2. 31–33).[4] Frogs
boiled in wine are an antidote for venomous beasts in general and toads
specifically (mp 38c; III. 32. 18–19, p. 251).[5] Psellus also reports

---

[1]On this suggestion, see "Aquatic Animals," below.

[2]A pair of similar usages is reported by Pliny N.H. 32. 74.

[3]Following Vieillefond's suggestion concerning the meaning of
oxyopia, rather than the usual "sharpsightedness" (Les Cestes, p. 356,
n. 191). But Jacques André, in a review of Vieillefond's Les Cestes,
defends the former idea, "for clearness of sight," etc. (Bulletin de
l'Association Guillaume Budé, 4th ser., no. 2 [1971]: 283).

[4]Bile seems to have been a popular substance, both medicinally
and generally. Note the use of partridge and vulture bile in the preceding paragraph (mp 23c; III. 2. 20 and 25). Riess cites uses of
the gall of several different animals (from Pliny, Palladius, and the
Geoponica), but for various purposes, generally agricultural rather
than medicinal ("Aberglaube," cols. 69. 30; 73. 26, 32; 76. 42, 44;
81. 29; 82. 62; two [73. 32, and 82. 62] are veterinary medicinal:
Vegetius prescribes dog bile for swollen testes of a horse [5. 7. 1],
and a mixture of goat bile and goat milk for a ruptured vein in the
eye [6. 23. 10]).

[5]For the first, as a natural prey of snakes, etc., might it
be thought to "absorb" the poison? And, in the case of toads, rather
than as a prey, as a sort of "positive" antithesis?
    Pliny refers to the use of frogs boiled in various substances
(N.H. 32) including boiling in old wine (32. 118, for dropsy), and
using for snake poisons (in a broth, 32. 48; also, prepared with wine,
against scorpion sting, ibid.), but he does not combine the two ideas.
Nicander also prescribes the flesh of a frog, boiled or roasted, for
toad poisoning (Alex. 573–74), or boiled in vinegar for snake poison

two usages of the frog. In one, frog's navel (?)[1] in a linen rag is
used as a contraceptive pendant (mp 44c; IX. 1. 7-8).[2] The other
preparation is somewhat different, and presented at more length,
Psellus apparently reflecting something more of the Africanian style
here (perhaps Psellus himself was intrigued by this one). Preserved
frog's tadpole tongue was used (surreptitiously?) in groats, as a
"thief-convicter" (kleptelenchon), to get a sneak-thief to confess
"as if in a trance" (mp 44h; IX. 1. 17-22, pp. 317, 319). The reason
for the use of the tongue is fairly obvious,[3] but the choice of the

----

(Ther. 621-22). See Wellmann, "Frosch," cols. 117-19, and Riess,
"Aberglaube," cols. 70-71, 74-75, for various superstitious uses of
toads and frogs.

[1]Westermann's text (ΠΑΡΑΔΟΞΟΓΡΑΦΟΙ, p. 144, lines 9-10) is
omphalos, "navel," which Wellmann, "Frosch" (col. 118, line 51) understands as "eye" (ophthalmos), but Vieillefond, following a reading of
a reported Paris manuscript (cf. Les Cestes, p. 313), reads enkephalos,
"brains." "Navel" could have obvious relevance in a usage such as
this, but frogs' navels are scarce items ("vive Björck"?).
     Brains also do seem to have had a rather wide reputation.
Africanus reports two other uses, mpp 32 (dog's brains for a fracture)
and 38a (brains of a living hen for poisonous bites). Riess also
notes two examples (from Pliny) in his summary, but of protective
rather than medical natures ("Aberglaube," cols. 81. 36, and 82. 31);
the differences suggest it is the animal involved, rather than the
nature of the brain, which is the controlling factor. (How this would
apply in the case of mp 44c, if it is brains that are involved, is uncertain.)

[2]Judging from the examples cited by Riess, animal preparations
were not as popular for contraceptive purposes as they were for promoting conception and assuring a safe pregnancy and easy birth. He
gives only three preparations as preventing conception or making im-
potent ("Aberglaube," cols. 71. 46; 75. 39; 81. 41-43. (The situation
in regard to plant preparations [discussed below] is somewhat different.)

[3]Riess presents a similar use of "houndstongue," though uncertain as to whether it was a zoological or botanical reference
(ibid., col. 73. 17-20); and Wellmann ("Frosch," col. 119, lines 3-9)
notes the application of the tongue torn from a living frog to assure
that a wife speaks the truth (citing Democritus, in Pliny N.H. 32. 49).
PLond 46 gives a lengthy procedure for cathing a thief which involves

tadpole is less obvious. Perhaps it is an example of the use of the
unnatural or the rare. While tadpole tongues are not quite in the
same class as "hen's teeth" (or, frog's navel), they are considerably less obvious than those of mature frogs.[1]

Canines

   Wolves. Wolves, also, appear first in the pentagon passages,
in pentagon seven (mp 9; I. 9. 1-4). This passage, involving the appending of a wolf's tail to prevent a horse being "spooked," has been
discussed previously, both in connection with those passages and in
the consideration of the different animal parts.[2] Two of the remaining three references overlap to a considerable extent. They both
prescribe the use of certain wolf parts (especially the astragalus)
to affect the movements of horses. In mp 10 (I. 10. 1-3, p. 139), in
a corrupt passage, Africanus notes something about the effect of
wolves in staying horses, but also in making them quicker.[3] For the

---

an invocation as well as the giving of a preparation including frog's
tongue (lines 172-201, 293-303; Kenyon, Greek Papyri, 1:70-71, 74).

   [1]Samuel J. Holmes, The Biology of the Frog, 4th rev. ed. (New
York: Macmillan Company, 1938), p. 123, refers to the tongue increasing greatly in size, as one of the changes in the metamorphosis of
the tadpole. Other than this, references to the tongue are absent in
descriptions of tadpoles, even in those making special reference to
their mouth formations (e.g., Albert Hazen Wright and Anna Allen
Wright, Handbook of Frogs and Toads of the United States and Canada,
3d ed. [Ithaca, N.Y.: Comstock Publishing Associates, a Division of
Cornell University Press, 1949], pp. 46-79, with Plates XII-XIV).

   [2]Above, pp. 211 and 217.

   [3]The text given by Vieillefond from the MSS reads: lykos
antipathes hekastē istatai kai narka tō pode thatton de autou chthoni
hypo lykou gignetai. Follet, review of Les Cestes, pp. 318-19) suggests transposing and correcting to: lyko(u) antipa(tēsas) <chthoni>
hekast(os) istatai kai narka, tō pode, thatt(ō)n d' heautou [chthoni]

latter he then gives a regular use of the wolf foot or astragalus
(lines 3-5), but recommends rather the use of the canine teeth taken
from a living wolf (lines 5-9).[1] Africanus deals with the other
possibility, staying horses, in mp 18 (II. 4, pp. 203, 205). There
he cites the Physica of Neptunianus as authority for the assertion
that casting the astragalus from a wolf's right forefoot before a
four-horse team will bring it to a stand (lines 1-3).[2] From this he
generalizes a military application: giving them to some of the front-
line slingers. In both passages, the items cited seem to have been
fairly widely held views (at least in the circles with which Africanus
was familiar), his contribution being their "practical" adaptations.
In the former, he counsels working the tooth into the bridle, as a
decoration; in the other, he turns the astragalus (from a horse-

---

hypo lykou gignetai. This is possible and does provide a meaning for
the passage which appears to be not too far from its intent.
        The latter part (only) of the passage might be construed more
simply by reading thattonte for thatton de (if we could assume an
Atticizing form thattō for the somewhat rare thassō [this is not en-
couraged by LSJ, s.v. "θάσσω"]), and ichnesi for chthoni (cf. the
passage from "Nepualios" cited by Vieillefond, Les Cestes, p. 352, n.
165, concerning II. 4; note also Pliny N.H. 28. 157 [and 263];
Aelian N.A. 1. 36). But besides leaving the first part still un-
clarified, this has the additional disadvantage of not providing any
reference to increasing of speed, which is the main point of this
chapter.

[1]Cf. Pliny N.H. 28. 257, in somewhat similar terms.

[2]Cf. Aelian N.A. 1. 36, immediately following the reference
to wolf tracks noted above (second note preceding), but without reference to a foot. Indeed, A. F. Scholfield translates it "vertebra"
(Aelian: On the Characteristics of Animals, Loeb Classical Library,
3 vols. [Cambridge: Harvard University Press, 1958-59; London:
William Heinemann, Ltd., 1958-59], 1:55).

racing trick?[1]) into a front-line weapon for doing damage to the
enemy on a large scale.[2]

The other reference to wolves (mp 12a; I. 12. 20-25, pp. 145,
147) is of a different nature. The flesh from wolf ribs, preserved
by drying and smoking, is made into a broth and, mixed with wine and
oil, is used as a yearly veterinary preventive medicine.[3] Presumably
the purpose of this was to transmit the endurance (here interpreted as
"disease resistance") of the wolf to the pack-animal. Thus it is
based on a magical idea, but the procedure is more of a home-remedy
than a magical operation.

Dogs. In the passage just discussed (mp 12a; I. 12), the
next lines (26-28) suggest an alternative, the smoking of the head
taken from a dead, already rotting, dog. The cure was to be produced
by "the continuous effluvium of the odor" (tē tēs odmēs apophorą syn-
echei) during the smoking process. Thus the dog may not have been
chosen for any intrinsic reason,[4] but simply as being a relatively

---

[1] Without the earlier context, the original application is uncertain, but the use of the term tetraoros (= quadrigae) suggests
racing rather than war as the more likely.

[2] In the introduction to the latter, he also calls attention to
his effort (philoponon) in "researching" his work. Thus, while the
organization of the Kestoi is loose, it was intended as something
more than just a notebook of randomly acquired miscellanies.

[3] The use of wolf flesh for this purpose seems not to be otherwise attested. But wolf flesh was used for other purposes (cf.
Riess, "Aberglaube," cols. 81-82; Richter, "Wolf," col. 970), and
Riess calls attention to the preserving of a boiled suckling pup for
veterinary use (col. 73, lines 53-56, citing Vegetius 1. 18. 16).

[4] But Vieillefond calls attention to another use of a dog's
head in the hippiatrica ([Oder-Hoppe, C.H., 1:136. 14] Les Cestes, p.
342, n. 78). Pliny also presents a use for a burned dog's head, but
it is the end product, the ashes, which he prescribes (used internally
or externally against a maddog bite, N.H. 29. 98).

common, moderate-sized animal. It may also be noted that it is not

the smoke, but the smell, which is supposed to be efficacious.[1] The

relative commonness of the dog may also account for the prescription

of mud made from fresh dog (probably bitch) urine in mp 33 (III. 17.

4-6, p. 239), for "shutting up the cause" (to aition . . . synape-

kleisan, line 6) of warts.[2] The reasons for the choice of dog skin

for carrying the vulture eyes to prevent ophthalmia (mp 23c; III. 2.

24-25, p. 227), and of putting dog's brains on a bandage to speed

knitting of a fracture (mp 32; III. 16. 1-2, p. 237),[3] and the use of

mad dog saliva to rust gold (mp 44e; IX. 1. 15, p. 317) are not clear.

On the other hand, the reasons for the remaining canine references are

equally transparent. In procedure 27 (III. 6. 1-3, p. 231), dog's

---

[1]Compare the plague in mp 3 and its antidote (I. 2. 126-32,
and p. 123 mg, on line 134; see above, p. 207, with n. 1, and p. 208).
The exact nature of the malady is not specified here. In line 27, it
is "dire" (deinos), while earlier in the passage reference is made to
deadly (thanatēsion, line 16), and pestilential (loimikon, line 3)
ailments (this last provides another verbal contact with mp 3).

[2]The animal is not given in the text; Vieillefond supplies it
from Dioscorides Eup. 1. 177 [= 168, ed. Wellmann], and Marcellus 19.
65 (Les Cestes, p. 239 mg, and, especially, p. 238, note a). In note
a, Vieillefond calls attention to Pliny (N.H. 28. 223) who prescribes
the use of ass's urine (with its mud) against warts. Pliny N.H. 30.
81 is more directly parallel: fresh dog urine with its mud cures all
kinds of warts.
     Urine of all types seems to have had a widespread reputation
in ancient medical practice, as well as in more superstitious beliefs
(note, for example, Pliny 28. 65-67 on its reported natural and supernatural uses).

[3]The common reputation of dogs as "watch-dogs" might have some
significance in relation to the former, a basically apotropaic function. The latter might be related to the dog's ability to survive apparently serious injuries. See also the use of brains noted above in
the discussion of frogs (p. 233, esp. n. 1). These two ideas would
make the connection (and the supposed virtue of the substance) doubly
strong.

afterbirth, suitably anointed and cleaned, is used as a container

for the plant <u>polygonon</u>, as an amulet to promote easy birth.[1] After-

birth would be a natural choice for such a use, and that of a dog

would be appropriate from more than one standpoint. The dog is rela-

tively prolific, and this idea could be strengthened by a connection

of the name <u>kyōn</u> with the verb <u>kyō</u>.

Other land animals

Several other animals appear once or twice in Africanus's

prescriptions. Most are mammals, the others arthropods.

Arthropods. Among the arthropods, lice or bedbugs, levigated

in wine, are prescribed for exhaustion or <u>orthopnoia</u> of pack animals

(mp 12b; I. 12. 53-54, p. 149), or many bedbugs are to be taken for

asp bite (mp 36; III. 22. 1-2, p. 241), or may be used with tortoise

urine in an external application (ibid., lines 3-4). These prescrip-

tions, especially the last, have close parallels in ancient sympathetic

medical ideas. Richter cites several passages supporting the reputa-

tion of bugs as an antidote for poison, especially that of the "asp,"

including the use of the bedbug with tortoise blood or urine.[2] None

of Richter's examples quite matches the use for exhaustion or <u>orthop-

noia</u>, but several of them have various points of similarity.[3]

---

[1]Pliny also prescribes a use of dog afterbirth for the same
purpose (<u>N.H.</u> 30. 123).

[2]"Wanze," col. 824; Pliny cites the Magi as authority that
tortoise urine was specific for asp bites, made more efficacious if
bugs (<u>cimicibus</u>) were added (<u>N.H.</u> 32. 34).

[3]Ibid.; note the use in human medicine for <u>lethargia</u> (taken
with water); or their use (drunk in a variety of liquids; smoke in-
haled; rubbed around the nostrils) against leeches in the throats of

Zoological Passages   239

Psellus says that Africanus relates a certain wonder (paradoxa) relating to scorpions (mp 44g; IX. 1. 16-17, p. 317), but there
is no further evidence to indicate even what type of passage it was.[1]

Mammals. Numerous mammals besides the canines appear in Africanus's procedures. Bats, the only ones extensively discussed, have
been mentioned already, in the pentagon passages (pentagon nine, mp
15a). The other mammals appear only briefly, most in only one procedure each. They are: wax from the right ear of an ass[2] (mp 16;
II. 1. 7; one ingredient of a sleeping potion in wine); a deer antler
pendant (mp 21; II. 10. 1-2, p. 211; a veterinary apotropaic);[3] fawn
or calf skin (mp 23b; III. 2. 17, p. 227; to hold the swallow stone
prophylactic against epilepsy);[4] hedgehog liver or ashes (mpp 22 and

---

animals. Richter traces the rationale for this procedure to the repulsive smell of the bugs (ibid., lines 62-66) (with this compare the
rotted dog's head in mp 12a [Vi. I. 12. 26-28]).

[1]This could cover anything from a procedure against scorpions
(such as Africanus gives in mp 37) to tales about scorpions (such as
that of their communication and mutual help recounted by some of the
fathers [e.g., Clem. Al. Strom. 1. 21/143], as well as secular writers).
(See Chapter IV for a presentation of Clement and the system of citation of his works.)

[2]Hopfner characterizes the ass as being regularly regarded
as an animal of "unheilvoller Mächte" in ancient superstition and
magic ("Mageia," PW, 14, part 1 (1928): col. 318, lines 43-44).

[3]Cf. Geoponica 16. 1. 17 and 16. 3. 6, both as from "Apsyrtus."

[4]Deer and cattle substances were used in various apotropaic or
preventive procedures (cf. Riess, "Aberglaube," cols. 72 and 76). The
specification of the young animal might be in sympathy with the probable youthfulness of the victim at the first appearance of the disease
(or of the source of the stones: nestlings); though it might not be
especially significant. Dioscorides (M. M. 2. 56), a possible source
of this passage, does not specify this element (see the discussion
under "Fowls," below, noting that this passage is not regarded as
certainly authentic by Björck).

30A; III. 1 and 12, pp. 225 and 235; for elephantiasis and dropsy);[1]
pig marrow, especially the spinal (mp 25; III. 4. 9-11, p. 229; an
alternative substance to restore the virility of a horse); hare's
blood (mpp 44a and 45; IX. 1. 4 and 4.3, pp. 317 and 321; to produce
a male);[2] cattle excretions (mp 44k; IX. 1. 32-34; to cause human
elimination[3] as a practical joke); and bear pudenda, and other ani-
mals('[?]) (mp 44n; IX. 1. 37-38; "marvelous helps").

Aquatic animals

Four procedures utilize what are probably aquatic animals,
or more specifically in at least three of them marine animals.

The second of the three animals said to be in pentagon two
(mp 2; I. 2, p. 119 mg) was the physa or "river" physalos. This
might be a toad of some sort as discussed above ("Amphibians"), or
it might be an aquatic of some sort. If it is the latter, it might
be either a "puffer" or some type of medusa. Various types of "puffers" (Tetraodontidae), most poisonous to some extent, are found
around the globe.[4] One species, the Tetraodon fahaka, inhabits the

---

[1]Aelian N.A. 14. 4 (liver for elephantiasis); Pliny N.H.
30. 105 (dried flesh for dropsy).

[2]The natural prolificness of the hare would suggest its use to
promote conception (as, e.g., Galen 14:476; per contra, Dioscorides
[M. M. 2. 19] prescribes its rennet as a contraceptive). Why it would
be specifically connected to the production of a male is unclear, but
Pliny prescribes the eating of significant parts of it by the woman
for this purpose (N.H. 28. 248).

[3]Presumably by some type of "sympathetic" connection.

[4]Aelian (N.A. 3. 18) describes a poisonous fish, physalos,
found in the Red Sea, which puffs itself up. A "puffer" might be
intended, but many of the details seem unreliable.

Nile and thus would fit Africanus's adjective, potamios, literally.[1]
Several, apparently more poisonous, species on the other side of the
globe are utilized in Japan for the preparation of fugu stew, a highly
regarded, but dangerous, dish, if the fish are improperly prepared:
the poison involved, tetradoxin, surviving the cooking process.[2] Alternately, some type of medusa may be the animal intended. Roulin
suggests this, specifically the Physalia, or Portuguese man-of-war.[3]
The results portrayed by Africanus (I. 2. 91-98) have some similarities to the results of an attack by this organism (and thus might have
been assumed for its properly prepared remains, administered internally).[4] Whatever the correct identification of the creature, the results promised from the procedure seem to be based on an exaggerated
view of its naturally poisonous nature, and an expectation that they
could be "captured" and transmitted, in an augmented form, by their
proper utilization. As noted in the previous discussions of this procedure, this is not necessarily magical or even superstitious, but

---

[1]Physa is used of a Nile fish according to LSJ, s.v. "φῦσα"
(citing Strabo 17. 2. 4, and Athenaeus 7. 312b).

[2]Franz Krapp, "Puffers," Grzimek's, 5:252. This poison, however, is very potent and relatively quick acting, killing by respiratory paralysis through depression of the respiratory center of the
brain (ibid.).

[3]In Vincent, "Notices sur trois manuscrits," p. 562. He also
regards them as the creature described by Aelian (3. 18), but this
identification seems harder to harmonize with the description than a
puffer. (Or is Aelian perhaps conflating a description of the
physalia with the effects of eating the puffer? Who would attempt to
eat a physalia? Also, Aelian describes them as a Red Sea fish, but
the physalia occurs also in the Mediterranean.)

[4]Conversely, the description of the swelling of the body
could be connected to the puffing up of the body of the puffer when
disturbed.

more misdirected ingenuity in the physical ("scientific"?) realm.

The other three creatures are all marine types and can be identified fairly confidently, at least by zoological order (or suborder). The first is the sting-ray, which was anciently credited with the power Africanus attributes to it, the use of its sting in killing trees ([except apple] mp 17; II. 3. 2-4, p. 203; cf. Aelian N.A. 2. 36; 8. 26; and Pliny N.H. 9. 155; 32. 25). The fish, echeneïs, or remora, so called because it supposedly held ships fast, hindering them,[1] thereby acquired a repute for holding other things. This includes its uses for preventing miscarriage and promoting conception as reported by Africanus in the veterinary fragments (mp 29; III. 8, pp. 231, 233).[2] The final item is the rubbing of an animal with mange with the body of a sea urchin (probably some species of Echinidae) to produce soundness (mp 31; III. 15, p. 237).[3]

All these items, if magical at all, would seem to fall into the category of nature magic (magia naturalis), not the indirect, daemonic, type.

Fowls

Some procedures involving fowls have already been discussed or noted above: mp 23c, partridge gall, and vulture gall and eyes[4]

---

[1] Arist. H.A. 505[b] 19 (2. 14); Aelian N.A. 1. 36 and 2. 17; Pliny N.H. 32. 2.

[2] Cf. Pliny N.H. 9. 79; 32. 6 (or, easing childbirth, ibid.).

[3] Cf. Aelian N.A. 14. 4 (also Pliny N.H. 32. 67: its ash, "cum carnibus suis cremati . . .").

[4] See above, p. 218, n. 2, re partridge and vulture gall. The use of appropriate vulture parts in such procedures would seem

as ophthalmics; mp 38a, hen's brains for poisonous bites;[1] mp 40,
swan testicle, as a colonic.

Africanus proposes two methods for capitalizing on the virtue, and victory, of champion game-cocks (mp 4; I. 3, pp. 125, 127).
The one supposes the power to lie in certain stones found in the gizzards of the cocks when sacrificed, rather than in the cock itself.
These stones were customarily worn, by soldiers and contestants, in
amulets[2] or under the tongue; Africanus's own contribution is the
suggestion of a more secure method of carrying the stone--apparently
by swallowing it (line 11). The other method seems to operate on an
opposite assumption, that the virtue did lie in the cock itself. The
cock, suitably prepared, is eaten by the contestant, keeping the
skeleton whole, and then burning it.[3] This ritual, which would seem
to be intended to keep the virtue intact, results in the transfer of
the bird's invincibility to the man, into whom he has moved, virtue-
wise (lines 12-17). These two procedures, while inconsistent with

---

natural in view of its repute for distance and sharpness of sight.
Pliny seems to imply such a rationale for the use of eagle gall at
the beginning of N.H. 29. 123.

[1]Both Hopfner ("Mageia," col. 317) and Orth ("Huhn," PW, 8, part 2,
col. 2533) call attention to the significance of the chicken, or at
least the cock, in protective magic (esp. in healing, col. 2533).
For chicken brain, note Nicander Ther. 557-58, 562-63 (outer membranes
in wine), and Pliny N.H. 29. 78 (in wine; or hen brain on wound).

[2]Pliny cites this as the practice of one notable champion,
Milo of Crotona (N.H. 37. 144).

[3]Cf. the partial parallels in other ritual contexts: e.g.,
the burning of the remains of Jewish sacrificial feasts, especially
the Passover lamb (Exo. 12:10), and the maintenance of wholeness of
the bones (though individually, not as a whole skeleton) (Exo. 12:46,
as well as in the Norse tales of Thor's goats).

each other in their views of wherein the virtue lay, operate on a

similar, "contagious magic" principle. They assume some sort of

"physical" transfer of the virtue to the one who uses the power

source in an appropriate manner.[1]

Stones from bird's gizzards also appear in another pair of

procedures, mp 23 a and b (III. 2. 11-19). They follow a paragraph

describing the supposed origin and power of the "Swallow-plant"

(chelidonion), and thus presumably refer to swallows also, though

the sources are referred to only as "nestlings" (line 11) and

"spring nestlings" (line 15). In the first procedure, two stones,

identified as being white and black,[2] found when the birds are opened

with a sharp reed,[3] are used as an ophthalmic pendant. This use re-

quires the sacrifice of a white dove, and the invocation of Aphrodite,[4]

then the enclosure of the stone in a gold necklace. These all suggest

---

[1]This passage allows Africanus several rhetorical flights, especially that concerning the cock as messenger, not only of day, but of coming victory (line 15). It is also augmented by a suitable "historical" precedent for both procedures: Themistocles' victory over the Persians (lines 18-21). This last is also presented in a suitably rhetorical manner.

[2]Following Vieillefond's interpretation; the references could conceivably be to their being found in both color swallows (see Gossen, "Schwalben und Segler," PW, IIA, part 1 (1921): col. 769, concerning white as well as the usual black [and white] swallows; Aelian reports, second-hand, the existence of the former [N.A. 10. 34 and 17. 20]).

[3]An example of the avoidance of the use of iron? Cf. Björck, "Apsyrtus," pp. 58-59, and Delatte (Herbarius [2d ed., 1938], pp. 133-34) there cited; also Riess, "Aberglaube," cols. 50-51 (iron neutral-izes magic), and col. 73, line 11 (an example from Pliny N.H. 24. 171).

[4]The swallow being dedicated to her (along with other house-hold gods) (Aelian N.A. 10. 34; this and other references in Gossen, "Schwalben und Segler," col. 775). On the relation of the dove and

a magical (and otherwise non-Christian) procedure. The power still
seems to arise from the nature of the stone and its source, but the
invocation of a spirit (Aphrodite) keeps it from being purely nature
magic.[1] The next paragraph (mp 23b; III. 2. 15-19) comes apparently
from another source,[2] and the procedure fits in only by virtue of the
reference to the stones. The source of the stones here is more specific, the _spring_ nestlings,[3] the stones are identified as variegated
and clear in color, and the use is different, to cure or lessen
epilepsy[4] (the preceding and following paragraphs, and the chapter

---

Aphrodite, see H. Hubert, "Magia," in Dictionnaire des antiquités
grecques et romaines, ed. Ch. Daremberg and Edm. Saglio, 5 vols. in
10 (Paris: Librairie Hachette et Cie., 1877-1919), vol. 3, part 2, p.
1520 (first col.), citing Pap. Paris. 2891, and Pap. V. I. 91; VII. 2.

[1]It should be noted that this is one of the hippiatrica passages which Björck does not include in his probably Africanian list
("Apsyrtus," pp. 15-16). The references to the sacrifice and to
Aphrodite might support this (but note the reference to sacrificing
[though not a part of the procedure] in the last passage discussed,
mp 4, Vi. I. 3. 7 [but with some textual uncertainty]). (Compare
also his mention of sacrifice to Poseidon-Taraxippos, which is superceded by his own procedure in mp 11 [I. 11. 16-18, p. 141].) While
Africanus's literary embellishments also include mythological items,
his avoidance of religious references (cf. Les Cestes, pp. 56-58)
also applies largely to pagan religious acts.
    This passage would appear to be one of those that had its
origins in human medicine (few horses, or similar animals, would rate
a gold necklace). This also would argue against the accuracy of the
Africanian attribution (see above, p. 220, n. 4). (See the further
discussions under "Rites," and "Gods and Daemons," below.)

[2]In this case, possibly Dioscorides M.M. 2. 56 (ed. Wellmann),
or a source lying behind it, used also by Pliny (N.H. 30. 91), and
others. Vieillefond (Les Cestes, p. 356, n. 186 [giving the Dioscorides
reference as 2. 60]) and Gossen ("Schwalben und Segler," cols. 773-74,
and 769) cite these and other references.

[3]Dioscorides says, "the first hatching," i.e., of the two broods
which swallows produce in a year (Gossen, "Schwalben und Segler," col.
769).

[4]This passage also would seem to derive from human medicine

title, concern the eyes). The procedure for using them is also different: the stones are not to touch the earth (a common magical or
superstitious proscription),[1] they are to be bound in fawn or calf-
skin (Dioscorides: heifer or deer), and this must be done during the
beginning and increasing phase of the moon.[2]

Crow fat in heated wine (with hedgehog ashes as an alternative) is prescribed for dropsy of an animal (mp 30A; III. 12, p. 235).
Goose fat is to be used as an ointment to secure the conception of a
female (mpp 44a and 45; IX. 1. 4, and 4. 4; the counterpart of the
hare's blood for production of a male noted above). Goose fat had
many uses in Greek and Roman writers, especially in the treatment of
female problems.[3] These fit well with the goose's generally closer
association with women, and its aphrodisiac connections,[4] but not its
specific use in Africanus. Indeed, Galen includes goose fat as one
element in a preparation for the conception of a male.[5]

(and thus may be non-Africanian). The same may be true of the rest of
the chapter; note, e.g., the use of partridge bile in Galen (see above).

[1]Cf., e.g., Riess, "Aberglaube," col. 44, lines 32-37, with numerous examples following, cols. 61, 63, 64, 73, 75, 79, 80, 82 (all from
Pliny); Lynn Thorndike, History of Magic and Experimental Science, 8
vols. (New York and London: Columbia University Press, 1923-58), 1:79.

[2]I.e., apparently at the new moon, or in the first, waxing,
phase of the moon (whether quarter, third, or half); cf. Follet, review
of Les Cestes, p. 319, n. 2, contra Vieillefond, Les Cestes, p. 356, n.
187. The significance of the moon phase would likely be because of the
supposed moon related or caused nature of the malady being opposed.

[3]Olck, "Gans," PW, 7, part 1 (1910): cols. 719-20.

[4]Ibid., cols. 729-30.

[5]Ed. Kühn, 14:476: to be used by the female? (cf. the veterinary conception-promoting pessary, which contains both goose fat and

On the whole, these references have a distinct magical connection. This connection is generally to "nature magic," with the exception of the invocation of Aphrodite. This latter, however, is somewhat out of character with Africanus's other "magical" procedures,
and further, is one of a number of passages whose Africanian authenticity is suspect.[1]

Human Substances

The number of occurrences of use of human substances in Africanus's procedures is extremely limited, and even some of them are of
questionable authenticity.

According to Riess, spit and urine are among the most magically powerful of human substances.[2] The former occurs in mp 6 (I. 5.
3; an accompaniment of the spells in the "hoplocrisma" ritual),

---

hare rennet [among other things] in Hipp. Cant. 10. 14 [Oder-Hoppe,
C.H. 2:144-45]). But the goose fat might simply be the "vehicle" in
Galen's recipe, with the other ingredient, turpentine, the active one.

[1]This is not a case of ruling out disruptive evidence, since
the passage is suspect on other grounds: lack of positive Africanian
characteristics (see Björck, "Apsyrtus," pp. 14-18), and transfer of
a (series of) prescription(s) (i.e., most of the items in III. 2)
from human medicine (esp. Galen), to hippiatrica (cf. Björck, "Zum
Corpus Hippiatricorum," pp. 31, 40-44). It might be argued that Africanus was the medical source so converted, but this is unlikely
since Björck's analyses show that the redactor here used a source
which had used the major medical writers of the time (Aetius, Paullos,
Oribasius, etc.) directly (ibid., pp. 32-40).

[2]Riess, "Aberglaube," cols. 85. 22-26; 86. 25-49; 87. 67-88.
41; also, Björck, "Apsyrtus," pp. 57-58. On the use of animal urine,
see above concerning mpp 33 and 36 (use of dog and tortoise urine).
The use of human urine as a medical substance continues down to modern
times; note the use of it in a mud plaster for a wound by Tom Joad in
John Steinbeck's Grapes of Wrath (New York: The Viking Press, 1939
[reprinted 1966]), chap. 16 (p. 235).

though it is the act of spitting rather than the spittle that appears
to be significant there. Urine of a specially potent kind, that of
an infant,[1] occurs in a questioned passage, mp 23e (III. 2. 32-37,
the greatest eye-salve). Similarly, urine of a child is administered
in wine against poisonous bites (mp 38b [also questioned]; III. 32.
11-12, p. 251).

Another potent material was menstrual blood, generally for
negative or destructive uses.[2] According to mp 11b(I. 11. 42-43),
the smoke[3] from a menstrual rag injures horses. On the positive side,
a virgin could use her girdle to cure a horse suffering from dysurea
(mp 30; III. 11). This usage, which is also of disputed authenticity,
is discussed further below, under "Other Factors" (loosing) of "Rites."

Plant Passages

The number of plants mentioned by Africanus in his various
procedures far exceeds the number of animals named. The number of
passages classed as magical, however, is much smaller than in the
former case.[4] This may be somewhat the result of a double standard,

---

[1]Björck, "Apsyrtus," p. 58; see also Pliny N.H. 28. 65-67,
especially 65.

[2]Riess, "Aberglaube," cols. 85. 41-86. 20.

[3]For other uses of smoke see the discussion above (p. 207,
with n. 1, and p. 208, with n. 2) of mp 3 mg., with its apparent reflection in mp 44i (smoke and incense vs. plague), and of mp 12a
(rotted dog's head, to relieve a suffering horse) (above, p. 237, n.
1). These uses are basically apotropaic; but apotropaics by their nature are somewhat negative, protecting by countering some threat.

[4]A similar disproportion is noted in Pliny by W. H. S. Jones,
"Popular Medicine in Ancient Italy," in Pliny, Natural History, trans.
H. Rackham, et al., Loeb Classical Library, 10 vols. (Cambridge:
Harvard University Press, 1938-63), 8 (1963): 573.

but if so, it results from an attempt to restrict the discussion to
those passages which are fairly clearly magical. In the case of the
zoological passages, almost all the procedures were included as potentially magical; significant medical products from animal sources
are not as abundant as botanical ones, and are usually the product of
rather complex development and/or extraction procedures.[1] In contrast,
numerous chemical substances of medical significance are found in
readily usable form in various plants. This is evidenced not only by
their popularity in ancient times, but by their continuation in use
down to modern times,[2] not only in the "herbals" (which are experienc-
ing something of a revival of popularity in recent years), but also
in their scientific, medicinal derivatives.[3] For this reason, only
those procedures which use plants whose supposed virtue seems clearly
based on some association of its name or external appearance, or the
use of which manifests other magical characteristics, are considered
here.

----

[1]As, for example, the extraction of insulin from animal pan-
creases, and the production and extraction of various vaccines and
antivenins. This is not a universal truth, of course, some treatments,
such as the use of milk to soothe ulcers, require no special preparation, only the recognition of their value (cf. also the second note
following).

[2]Perhaps also partially because the misinformation in the area
of plant culture and use was better organized and preserved (and thus
more "respectable"?).

[3]Note, for example, Heber W. Youngken, Text Book of Pharmacognosy (4th ed., rev. and enl.; Philadelphia: P. Blakiston's Son & Co.,
1936). This work devotes one chapter each to drugs of vegetable and
of animal origins. Chapter one, "Drugs of Vegetable Origin," covers
pages 51-811, with chapter two, "Drugs of Animal Origin," occupying
only pages 812-57. In both chapters, however, the manner of use is
largely expressed in terms of derived preparations rather than of the
crude drugs. This shift in manner of use correlates with the medical
terminological shift from "materia medica" to "pharmacology."

Polygons and ancient medicaments

Two of the passages referring to the geometric figures, pentagon eight (mp 11a;   I. 11. 17-36, pp. 141, 143) and the surviving
hexagon reference (hexagon seven, mp 41; III. 36. 4-6, p. 255), involve plants.[1] In the former passage, any magical connection is in
the use of the pentagon, the drug specified, euphorbium[2] (Euphorbia
resinifera), being capable of producing the results promised.[3] In
the latter, the case is not so clear. Since the plant (osprion,
"pulse," "a legume") cannot be identified, its actual effectiveness
cannot be judged; but Africanus, at least, seems to regard it as a
natural, physical result, since he presents a rationale for its operation.[4]

------

[1]In addition, pentagon four (mp 5; I. 4. 8-11) involves some
unknown substance which could be botanical.

[2]So identified by MSS V and D, Vi., p. 143 mg, re I. 11. 27;
cf. also, "Sylloge," chap. 9, line 3 in Jules Africain (app. 1), p.
71.

[3]See D'Arcy Wentworth Thompson, "Ancient Chemical Warfare,"
Classical Review 47 (1933): 171-72. Thompson suggests that as a
practical measure the drug must have been puffed in powdered form,
rather than squirted in liquid form. (He illustrates its usage in
this form by certain lines from Rabelais, concerning one, Monsieur
Panurge.)

[4]Vieillefond, Les Cestes, p. 255, lines 6-7: "For scarring/
ulcerating by the burning, it yields white hair." Whether this is
supposed to occur from the residual heat (the pulse was to be well
boiled and plastered on), or from something (perhaps an acid?) in
the plant is not specified. It is difficult to imagine a plant substance with a high enough specific heat to effect a result similar to
a red-hot branding iron; but if the plant is a legume, in the modern
sense, none of them would seem to have a sufficiently active nature,
acid or otherwise, to effect such a result.
     In a passage appearing earlier in the hippiatrica excerpts
(Vi., III. 13. 5-6, p. 235), Africanus prescribed boiled squill
(with vinegar and pumice? [line 5]) to produce a white coat. If this
could be the plant intended, it might produce something like the

Even among those passages picked out as most magical appearing, a number seem to be at worst examples of, or variations on, irrational connections in ancient medical practice.[1] The two clearest
are: mp 23e (III. 2. 32-37, p. 227), the "greatest" (ouden de meizon,
line 32) eye-salve, composed of ivy root and infant urine, combined
with verdigris from the exterior of its copper container after it had
been buried in horse manure for 40 days;[2] and mp 25 (III. 4, p. 229),

stated result. According to Grieve, the juice of the squill, which
contains a significant calcium oxalate component, is highly irritant
to human skin (Mrs. M[aud] Grieve, A Modern Herbal, ed. Mrs. C. F.
[Hilda] Leyel, 2 vols. [New York: Dover Publications, Inc., 1971
(reprinted from the edition of Harcourt, Brace, & Company, 1931)],
2:767, second column; cf. also, Youngken, Pharmacognosy, p. 148).
(There may be some question of its efficacy, however, since, unboiled,
it produced the opposite result, a black color [Vi., III. 13. 5].
But in the one case it functions as a dye, in the other as a bleach.)
    Another possibility might be some variety of oxalis (wood
sorrel), the eponym of oxalic acid (produced synthetically, it is
used as a bleach, metal cleaner, etc., in modern times). The family
is similar in many ways to the leguminosae, with seed pods of somewhat
similar appearance, and a sketch of the hairy stems of some of its
varieties (especially those sometimes separated into the subspecies
xanthoxalis) could be mistaken for the briars of a blackberry (as in
the misplaced gloss, Vi., III. 36. 6). In the medieval herbal called
"Agnus Castus," this herb "rostyd on colys" is credited with the
power to "frete awey ded flesch." (Gösta Brodin, ed., Agnus Castus:
A Middle English Herbal, Reconstructed from Various Manuscripts, The
English Institute in the University of Upsala: Essays and Studies on
English Language and Literature, ed. S. B. Liljegren, no. 6 [Upsala:
A.-B. Lundequistka Bokhandeln, 1950; Copenhagen: Ejnar Munksgaard,
1950; Cambridge: Harvard University Press, 1950], p. 127 [s.v. "Al-
leluya"; p. 164, lines 1-6, of Stockholm MS X 90, the publication
base]).

[1]Or perhaps weak or unreliable substances abandoned by modern
medicine as useless (or at least not worth further study to see if,
or how, they did fulfill any of the ancient claims).

[2]Though this particular procedure is not attested elsewhere,
the key elements in it are not unusual in ancient medicine. Ivy,
whether common ivy (Hedera helix) or ground ivy (Glechoma hederacea),
had an ancient and continuing reputation as a medical herb (cf. Agnus
Castus, p. 153; MS X, p. 184, lines 4 and 15), including use as an eye
medication (Grieve, Modern Herbal, 2:442, 443). Galen prescribes for

sweet cicely (<u>Myrrhis odorata</u>) as a restorative of virility to

horses.[1] Another might fall into this category except for its pe-

culiar manner of use: mp 43a (VI, line 1, p. 297; discussed below

as a "Sympathetic" operation), the prescribed substance, cyclamen,

having a recognized purgative effect, and ancient (and/or folk) med-

icine sometimes using external application to produce internal opera-

tions.[2]

Some other of the prescriptions may possibly be of value, but

even if so, the results promised seem exaggerated (such that if really

accomplished, it could hardly be regarded as other than magical). In

mp 12b (I. 12. 53-55), the wine in which the lice or bedbugs were ad-

ministered might have some stimulating effect, while in the alterna-

tive prescription, the barley groats should help restore the strength

of an exhausted animal, eventually, and the raw pitch (crude resin)

---

sores which are resistant to treatment a preparation produced from
urine of a child and copper filings produced by working it, over a
period of days, in a copper mortar with a copper pestle, until both
mortar and pestle are worn away and the urine becomes honeylike (ed.
Kühn, 12:286-87). (Gerard reports what may be a related prescription,
ground ivy juice and verdigris, for fistulas and hollow ulcers [The
Herbal], cited by Grieve, 2:443).) Thus, however weird or repulsive
such prescriptions may be to scientific, hygienic moderns, they are
not therefore magical.
      It may be noted that this passage (Vi., III. 2; mp 23 a-e)
is one of the <u>hippiatrica</u> passages whose Africanian status was not regarded as proven by Björck (see the discussion above, p. 245, n. 1).
The whole passage, with its various prescriptions, seems to be derived
from human medicine.

[1]Vieillefond reports a similar description of the plant in
Dioscorides (<u>M.M.</u> 4. 114 [= 115, ed. Wellmann]) and Pliny (24. 154
and 26. 108), but giving the virtue of the plant as against <u>phthisis</u>
(<u>Les Cestes</u>, p. 356, n. 193). Grieve indicates the reputation of the
plant as an aphrodisiac, as well as a general tonic for old people
and adolescent girls (<u>Modern Herbal</u>, 1:201-2).

[2]Cf. Pliny <u>N.H.</u> 28. 203: wolf's fat with elaterium applied to
the navel.

could be of help in certain respiratory problems.[1] In the treatment

for a kicking mule, mp 13b (I. 13. 3-5), the prescription may be some

sort of tranquilizer,[2] but, even if so, the results could hardly be

expected to last six months. In procedure 20 (II. 8, p. 209), closing

a wound without sutures, Africanus appears at first sight to have gone

too far, even using one of the "code" words for magic, physikos (line

3). But this appearance is probably deceiving; physikos is seemingly

used here in the sense of "natural,"[3] and the suggested remedy, "a

bulb of the edible type," may have had value, even if it did not pro-

duce a miraculous (or magical) closing of the wound.[4] The bulb is

identified by André as Muscari comosum ("purse tassel," a near relative

---

[1]Pitch from various pines, or its derivatives, apparently has
some value as a stimulating expectorant (Grieve, Modern Herbal, 2:635
[col. 1], and 636 [col. 2]., s.v. "Pine," and "Pine [Larch]." See
also Youngken, Pharmacognosy, pp. 95 and 103, s.v. "Pix pini U.S.P.
[Pine Tar]" and "Oleum pini pumilionis U.S.P. [Oil of Drawf Pine
Needles].")

[2]Boxwood at least (Africanus prescribes the seed) is said to
be narcotic and sedative (Grieve, Modern Herbal, 1:121). The other
plant, tribolos, caltrop, cannot be certainly identified. Both the
land (tribulus terrestris) and the water (trapa natans) caltrop were
well known to the ancients; the term tribolos could be applied to
other plants as well (see, LSJ, s.v. "τρίβολοs").
     It is possible that the plants were chosen for their names,
as implying enclosure (boxing in) or damage to the foot (cf. the
military caltrop), but the manner of use does not suggest such a connection. In view of Africanus's rhetorical proclivities, one might
expect such a verbal connection, even if none existed in the original
intent of the prescription, rather than the reverse.

[3]As Vieillefond argues (Les Cestes, p. 354, n. 172).

[4]What is promised is "healing by first intention"; this could
be made possible, but not caused, by a good antiseptic material.

of "grape hyacinth"),[1] by Vieillefond as the onion,[2] and garlic is

near related to both.[3] If the "wild vine" of mp 38e (III. 32. 34-35,

p. 253) is bryony (Bryonia alba),[4] and if the appending (periaptomenē)

is here taken as referring to binding around the wound, this could be

viewed as a medical prescription, being intended as a counter-

irritant.[5] But that involves a somewhat extended series of conjec-

tures, with the suggested use of periaptō rather unlikely.

Polygonums and other "sympathetics"

In several procedures, the basis for the prescription is

fairly clear, and clearly based on the principle of "sympathy."

The most striking of them, mp 27 (III. 6. 1-7, p. 231), begins

with an etymological connection. Polygonum ("many-joints"; knotgrass),

---

[1]Review of Les Cestes, p. 283. See also LSJ, s.v. "βολβός."

[2]Les Cestes, p. 208, and p. 354, n. 173.

[3]In addition to the onion's ancient reputation as a near pan-
acea (ibid.), both it and garlic (Allium cepa and A. sativum) have a
significant antiseptic action which made them of value even in modern
wars (e.g., as recently as World War I) (Grieve, Modern Herbal, 2:599,
and 600, n. 1; 1:342-44; David Conway, The Magic of Herbs [New York:
E. P. Dutton & Co., 1973], p. 109).
   See also Pliny's descriptions of the value of various bulbs
(onions, leeks, "red bulbs," and bulbine) in N.H. 20. 39, 47, 103,
and 107, as well as animal products valuable for similarly closing
wounds (earthworms, and horned owl brains with goose grease) in N.H.
30. 115 and 118.

[4]Cf. LSJ, s.v. "σταφυλή, 2," "μηλωθρον, I," and "ἄμπελος,
2, 3."

[5]See Grieve, Modern Herbal, 1:133 (col. 2), for use of the
root of a closely related species, Bryonia dioica, as a skin irritant. The berries also are emetic and possibly poisonous (ibid.
[col. 1]), and thus could have been viewed as a counter-poison to
animal toxins.

with the name apparently interpreted as meaning "prolific,"[1] and

strengthened by a nickname, drōsa ("doer"), is prescribed as a pend-

ant to promote conception (lines 1-3).[2] To ensure the production of

an animal of the desired sex, the appropriate gender of mercury (Mer-

curialis annua and/or perennis?), or of vervain (Verbena officinalis

and supina?) should be added to the pendant (lines 3-7).[3]

Africanus attributes to the Quintilii,[4] the view that bean

shells, put on the roots of trees, dry them up (mp 17; II. 3. 5-6,

---

[1] It is described as being "abundant everywhere" (line 1; cf.
the similar opening of Grieve's description of it, "The Knotgrass is
abundant everywhere, . . ." [Modern Herbal, 2:457]. This similarity
is probably not entirely coincidental; note the description in Agnus
Castus, "[th]is herbe growy[th] ny oueral" [p. 144; s.v. "Centenodium,"
MS X, p. 177, line 5]).

[2] It is to be appended in dog's afterbirth, discussed above.

[3] Cf. LSJ, s.v. "λινόζωστις," "περιστερεών , II," and
"περιστέριον, II." On mercury, see also: Riess, "Aberglaube," col.
60, lines 8-12, and, esp., cols. 63. 68-64. 5; Grieve, Modern Herbal,
2:529-30 ("Mercury, Dog's," and "Mercury, Annual"). Mercury may be
dioecious or monoecious (Gray's Manual of Botany, illus., largely rewr.
and exp. by Merritt Lyndon Fernald, 8th [centennial] ed. [New York:
American Book Company, 1950], p. 960), usually the former, but the
differences are not such as to be noted except by a very careful observer (Nathaniel Lord Britton and Addison Brown, An Illustrated Flora
of the Northern United States and Canada, 2d ed., rev. and enl., 3
vols. [New York: Dover Publications, 1970 (repr. ed. of An Illustrated
Flora of the Northern United States, Canada and the British Possessions,
Charles Scribner's Sons, 1913)], 2:460), and they certainly seem not
to be those intended by Africanus's description. The distinction
here, as with the vervain, would seem to be between two different species of each of the named genera (cf. Diosc. M.M. 4. 59, 60, 189
[Wellmann] concerning the varieties of these plants, esp. 189. 2 concerning the female and male varieties of linozōstis and their corresponding uses).

[4] Vieillefond traces this view to Theophrastus C. Pl. 5. 15. 1
(Les Cestes, p. 352, n. 164; see also n. 163, re the Quintilii). The
Quintilii appear after Africanus among the stated sources of the Geo-
ponica (book 1, pref.).

p. 203).[1] This could be connected with the general association of the bean with death and funerary rites (cf. Pliny N.H. 18. 118).[2] (Africanus's own preferred method is much more utilitarian, though in its own way as unrealistic as the methods it replaces: cut everything down [lines 6-9, concluding, "this indeed is a perfect destruction"].)[3]

In the procedures against warts (myrmēkiai), Africanus presents two which involve plants (mp 33b; III. 17. 7, 8). These may be based on a "sympathetic" connection, although their basis could be empirical. In the first (line 7), crushed squirting cucumber (Elaterium) is put on, overcoming the wart. The habit of this plant of ejecting its ripe seeds might cause it to be regarded as having an expulsive power which could be turned to good use (or the apparently irritating substances in the plant[4] might have caused it to be used as a counter-irritant). In the second botanic item here, the plant may be of some actual value, whether it is chicory (Cichorium intybus) or, possibly, pimpernel (Anagallis arvensis).[5] Both plants have been used

---

[1]This follows the suggested use of the sting of sting-rays (II. 3. 4-5), discussed above.

[2]Riess, "Aberglaube," col. 53; note also its use, cited there, against nut trees (Geop. 10. 67. 3 [actually the whole of chap. 67 is devoted to the subject, but sec. 3 involves the burial of the bean]), or to prevent untimely loss among olives (Geop. 9. 12) (both these items are cited by Geoponica as from "Democritus").

[3]This particular bit of advice, which relates specifically to fruit trees, would seem to argue against a Jewish background for Africanus (cf. Deut. 20:19, 20). (The aberration could, of course, be attributed to his "Christianization.")

[4]Cf. Grieve, Modern Herbal, 1:241.

[5]According to LSJ, s.v. "κιχόριον," it is so used in Diosc. M.M. 2. 178.

against inflammation, freckles, and other skin conditions.[1] On the

other hand, if the plant intended is really the heliotrope (genus

Heliotropium; cf. line 8), it has explicit ancient use against warts.[2]

The precise identification of the plant may be pointless, however,

since the procedure appears to be more magical than therapeutic.[3]

The flower is to be picked before sunrise[4] (so its contracted, or

sun-avoiding, powers will be at maximum, to be transferred to the

wart?), and the affected spot (topos) is to be thrice circumscribed

(tris perigraphe); this will "quiet" (pausetai) the wart. Both the

circumscription and a threefold repetition are recognized magical

procedures.[5]

     In procedure 43a (VI, line 1, p. 297),   cyclamen juice is

prescribed as a purgative. Cyclamen has a long history of use for

----

[1]Grieve, Modern Herbal, 1:198-99, and 2:633; also, re pimpernel, Conway, Magic, p. 131. Both also have a "heliotropic" character
(Grieve, 1:197, and 2:632; Conway, p. 131).

[2]Vieillefond, Les Cestes, p. 358, n. 208 (citing Pliny 22. 61;
Marcellus 19. 64; and Dioscorides Eup. 1. 176 [= 167, Wellmann; note
esp. 167. 2]). (But in Pliny it is the root, and in Dioscorides the
fruit, rather than the flower, which is specified.)

[3]Unless the circumscription actually involved more than a token,
light contact with the skin. If it involved some pressure so that the
juice from the flower (augmented by dew from the pre-dawn picking?) was
expressed on the skin around the wart in the process, it could conceivably have value, if the plant prescribed was really efficacious
(in the case of the chicory it was material from the flower or leaves
which was used [Grieve, Modern Herbal, 1:198-99]).

[4]Cf. Pliny N.H. 25. 145: anagallis has a special power if
dug up and expressed before sunrise.

[5]Cf. Björck, "Apsyrtus," pp. 58-59 and 65. See also the discussion of these features in the related sections below.

this purpose,[1] but Africanus prescribes that it be applied externally, to the navel. This seems a singularly inept way of using it, except by some sympathetic rationale,[2] but this was the method also used by late European herbalists, not only for purging the bowels, but also, applied over the bladder, for increasing urination.[3]

The use of mulberry boughs as a styptic pendant in procedure 44d (IX. 1. 11-13, p. 317) has ancient precedent (Pliny N.H. 23. 137 [unripe berries], 138 [twigs with unripe berries]).[4] This use as a styptic might be based on an analogy with the milky nature of mulberry sap.[5] Africanus reportedly directed that they be appended while the stars were under the earth.[6] This feature, as well as Psellus's reference to the secret spell, will be considered in the pertinent sections below.

In procedure 44i (IX. 1. 26-27, p. 319), balsam juice is an

----

[1]Note Vieillefond, Les Cestes, p. 296, n. a (Diosc. M.M. 2. 193 [194]; =2. 164, 165, Wellmann); Grieve, Modern Herbal, 1:245.

[2]Cf. Riess, "Aberglaube," col. 65, lines 23-26, for its magical reputation. But the examples given there are as counters to harmful magic which is not the use here.

[3]Grieve, Modern Herbal, 1:245. See also Pliny N.H. 28. 203, the use of wolf's fat with elaterium noted above.

[4]Cited by Riess, "Aberglaube," col. 61. According to Pliny, they must not touch the ground, and for the latter use, they must be picked at the full moon.

[5]Or because the unripe fruit (as in Pliny's uses) are still "restraining" the bloody juice of the ripe fruit? Or, the lateness of its budding suggests its "restraint"?

[6]Line 12. Vieillefond treats this as a separate statement, "an amulet of the stars found under the earth" (cf. Les Cestes, p. 316), but gives no explanation of rationale, or of connection with the preceding reference to the mulberries (from which it is separated only by a comma).

alternative to the "foul smell of tanning" (probably an allusion to
the counter-procedure to mp 3, discussed above) for the stopping of
pestilence. The rationale for it would presumably be much the same,
except that it overcame by the good odor rather than the evil one.
Due to the nature and value of the substance,[1] its use must have been
on a small (almost individual) scale.[2]

Numerics and other suspicious proceedings

As noted above, in procedure 33b (III. 17. 9, p. 239), the
wart is to be thrice circumscribed with the specified flower. "Thrice"
alone is not enough evidence to convict of magic, but together with the
other elements in the procedure, and other uses of significant numbers,
it raises the suspicion of magical intent. The use of number, in
another, otherwise rather prosaic, largely botanical prescription, mp
39 (III. 34. 1, p. 253),[3] also may suggest some magical connection:

---

[1] Apparently Balm of Gilead/Mecca Balsam, the resinous juice,
or oil from the juice, of the Commiphora opobalsamum (al., meccanensis)
(cf. Grieve, Modern Herbal, 1:78).

[2] Since the first part of the counter-procedure involved the use
of censers (thymiateres; Vi., I. 2, p. 123 mg, re line 134), it is con-
ceivable that this is Psellus's counterpart to that part of the procedure. Opposed to that is the question of the practicality of fumi-
gating a whole military camp with such a substance, and the testimony
of the "Ecloge," which refers to the smoke also as being dysodias
(Jules Africain, app. 2, chap. 1, line 28; p. 78). (The "Ecloge" is
not too clear here, the smoke is to be produced by many great torches,
with incense [thymiamata] provided in addition, to provide smoke to
fight against [antimachesthai] the smoke coming from [par'] us [ibid.,
lines 28-30]. The redactor perhaps thought of the incense as providing relief from the smell of the protective smoke screen, having misunderstood the original ta hyph' hemon genomena as the object of the
infinitive antimachesthai rather than as its "subject.")

[3] The genuineness of this and the next two items discussed
(Vi., III. 2 and 32) is not regarded as determinable by Björck
("Apsyrtus," pp. 15-16).

the main ingredient of a formula for soothing inflammation of horses'

feet is <u>seven</u> figs. This is really the only suspicious part of the

passage, and apart from other such numerological references in Afri-

canus, would be unexceptionable.[1]

Another somewhat suspicious item is the use of a sharp reed

(<u>kalamos</u>) to open the gizzard of the swallow nestling in mp 23a (III.

2. 12, p. 225).[2] This might be simply a conventional directive, but

in view of the inefficiency of such an implement for such a task, it

suggests a ritual avoidance of the use of a metallic instrument.[3]

The appending of the root of the wild vine (or bryony, see

above) in mp 38e (III. 32. 34-35) is quite likely magical in origin.[4]

While this item comes at the end of a long passage of miscellaneous

remedies, most of which seem <u>intended</u> medically (whatever their ac-

tual virtues), there are a number of probably magical item mixed in

(i.e., mp 38 a, b, c, and d, hen brains, infant urine, frogs, and

reptile heads, all discussed above).

Psellus includes three other items that may be mentioned

here, though the first is not really botanical, the second is not

---

[1]See the discussion of "Numbers," below, for ancient examples.

[2]As noted above, this passage is questioned by Björck.

[3]On the ritual non-use of iron, note Björck, "Apsyrtus,"
pp. 58-59; and re both iron and bronze, Riess, "Aberglaube," cols.
50-51; cf. 54. 64; 60. 58 (use wood hoe, then no iron near); 61. 62;
65. 10 (no metal); 73. 11. See also Pliny <u>N.H.</u> 20. 3; 24. 171; 29.
114, for the use of a reed for cutting or opening; also 30. 102, cutting out without iron.

[4]Cf. Riess, "Aberglaube," col. 66, lines 58-60, re the vine as
counter-magical, and, more specifically, 67. 13, for the use of the
wild vine as an amulet (citing Pliny <u>N.H.</u> 23. 20).

strictly magical, and the third is not certainly identifiable.[1] Africanus is said to gather the moonstone (aphroselēnon) from plant dew and moonbeams (mp 44m; IX. 1. 35-36, p. 319).[2] A few lines later (lines 41-44), he is said to have spoken of the gorgonium.[3] No usage is mentioned, but the account given by Psellus would fit well as an Africanian anecdotal embroidery of an aphrodisiac prescription, since eryngo had a reputation in such usages.[4] A little later, among the miscellaneous items at the end of Psellus's summary, a remedy for varicose veins is paired with a reference to "some other night-shining thing (ti allo nyktiphaes)" (ibid., line 49, p. 321). This item cannot be identified even probably; it might refer to something like the night-lantern credited to Africanus by Casaubon,[5] but it could conceivably be a reference to the paeony, which had such a reputation.[6]

---

[1]Besides these references in Psellus, Zosimus quotes Africanus as listing plants as a fourth item, along with metals, liquids, and earths, among the substances used as dyes (in alchemy?) (Vi., IX., 2, p. 321; Berthelot and Ruelle, Collection, 2:169).

[2]Cf. Hopfner, "Mageia," col. 312, lines 43-48.

[3]Eryngium creticum/campestre: LSJ, s.v. "γοργόνιον", "ἤρύγγος."

[4]Grieve, Modern Herbal, 1:408 (s.v. "Holly, Sea") (this passage also notes the large size of the roots, esp. of E. maritimum); Riess, "Aberglaube," col. 54, lines 32-39 (lines 36-39 note its use in love magic, citing Pliny 22. 20). Pliny's description connects this usage with the supposed shape of the roots of some specimens.

[5]C. Suetonii Tranquilli Opera, ed. Wolfius, 3:141 ("In Iulium Caesarem," cap. 31). (But the item cited is chap. 69 in Thevenot's edition of Africanus in Math. vet., one of the chapters not now commonly regarded as authentic.)
    This general approach is favored by Vieillefond's translation (Les Cestes, p. 320).

[6]Visible only by night, by moonlight: Hopfner, "Mageia," col. 324, lines 42-48 (the following quarter column of text describes precautions for digging, and uses of, the plant; note, e.g., Aelian N.A. 14. 27).

The uses of wine, oil, and linen have been excluded from considera-

tion above, since, despite their use in superstitious and magical

practices, and the "anti-magical" reputation of the first,[1] they do

not appear to be generally so used by Africanus. Africanus's uses

of oil and wine are as vehicles for other substances, not primarily

as active agents in themselves. Linen, while specified as the ma-

terial for several pendants (e.g., mpp 23 c, d, and 44c), seems to be

the usual material for such a use, and it is specification of some

other material which is noteworthy.

Mineral and Similar Substances

Stones and "stones"

All of the operations involving stones seem to be based on

types of sympathetic principles, possibly contagion, based on their

source (mpp 4, and 23 a and b), or formal, based on their appearance

(mpp 28 and 44c). In mp 4 (I. 3. 1-11, p. 127), the stones found in

the gizzards of cocks are probably true minerals, small stones or

gravel picked up in their feeding and retained in the gizzard. It

can easily be seen why different descriptions would be given of their

texture and color (lines 5-6); but according to Africanus, they (the

potent ones?) are black. Also, in his view, the virtue of the stone

is from its own nature;[2] the victory of the cock only demonstrates,

---

[1]Riess, "Aberglaube," col. 66, line 58; note also col. 62,
lines 59-67, concerning oil.

[2]See "Fowls," above, for a contrary theory in Africanus's
next paragraph.

it does not give, the virtue to the stone (lines 8-9). The stone,
thus identified, transmits its virtue to man also, if properly carried (lines 2-5, 9-11).

Similarly, "stones" found in the gizzards of swallow nestlings,[1] properly obtained and used, have transferrable power (mp 23
a and b; III. 2. 11-14, 15-19). Probably because of the reputation
of swallows (especially associated with the plant chelidonia, described in the preceding paragraph of the passage), the stones in the
first instance (23a; lines 11-14) are used to protect from ophthalmia.
In the second instance (23b; lines 15-19), spring nestlings, the product of the first of the swallows two yearly broods, are specified.
In this case they are to be used as a cure for epilepsy. For this
use they must be procured at the proper phase of the moon, and must
not touch the ground. The former requirement (as well as the specification of the spring nestlings?) would seem to be associated with
their use against a moon related malady; the latter is a common su-
perstitious/magical precaution against the loss of "power."[2]

In the other two passages which specify uses, the uses seem
to be based on the appearance of the stone. In mp 28 (III. 7, p.
231), the milk stone, apparently so called because it gives a milky

---

[1]In this case, since the birds are nestlings, the "stones"
would seem to be some type of stony concretion, a bezoar, rather than
a true mineral. If so, this might provide a more prosaic reason for
the use of a reed to open the bird--a metal knife, due to its hard-
ness, could damage the "stones." (Thus proving the deleterious effects of iron for such use?)
    But Pliny regards them as true stones; he says that swallows
were reported to give a bit of stone to each chick at hatching (N.H.
30. 91).
    [2]See further the discussion and examples above, under "Fowls."

color to water,[1] is to be used to increase production of milk. Two
different ways of use are given, fastening around the udder, or pow-
dering and administering in a wine and water mixture. In the other
passage, in Psellus (mp 44c; IX. 1. 8-9, p. 317), a gagatēs "stone"
(jet, or possibly lignite)[2] is to be used to ease and quicken a difficult birth. If the material is jet, its slick appearance and feel
could suggest such a use. The stone is to be put into the left hand
of the subject, otherwise no special procedures are directed.

Besides these passages, Psellus also refers, as noted above,
to Africanus's gathering the moonstone (aphroselēnon [selenite?])
from the dew of plants and the beams of the moon (IX. 1. 39-40).[3] He
does not give further indication of method or of purpose (though it
would be easy to suspect some magical intent).[4]

Metals

Africanus has possibly three references to bronze or copper
(chalkos, kyprinos). The first is the clearest and is clearly magical, not just superstitious. In the sixth "pentagon passage" (mp

---

[1]Vieillefond, Les Cestes, p. 357, n. 196; LSJ, s.v. "γαλακτίτηs."

[2]Both are types of coal, and thus of organic origin, not true
minerals.

[3]Dioscorides says selenite is found in moonbeams, by night
(M.M. 5. 141, Wellmann).

[4]Psellus also tells us that Africanus formed various stones,
hyacynthine, smaragdys, and sardonyx (Vi., IX. 1. 29-30, p. 319). This
sounds like some alchemical feat, but we are not provided with any
further details. Pliny reports that there were various works which
told how to simulate these very stones from crystals, etc. (N.H. 37.
79, 197). Note also Pap. Holm. 6.27-16.29 (ed. Lagercrantz, pp. 8-24;
see also pp. 92 and 100-3).

7; I. 6. 23-30, p. 133), Africanus prescribed "a threat of Roman prescription," to be engraved in the proper hoof of a stubborn horse,
under proper conditions, with a bronze pen (line 27). The use of
bronze[1] for the pen is fully in keeping with the other magical elements of the passage (which will be more fully dealt with below in
the discussion of "Charms and Rites"). The other references to copper, both of which involve a salve, are less clear. In the one, the
eye salve of ivy root, etc. (mp 23e; III. 2. 32-37), besides the
question of Africanian origin, there is the question of the nature
of the remedy, magical or medical. On this question, it is the use
of copper filings, with infant or child urine, which is most closely
similar to the Galenic parallel presented above. In the case of the
other salve (mp 44b; IX. 1. 5-6), Psellus notes that in addition to
producing milk by a craftsmanlike method (technikḗ methodǭ, i.e.,
magic, at least in Psellus's view[2]), Africanus dries up breasts
swollen after childbirth by a "copper cerate" (kērotḗ kyprinḗ).[3]

_____

[1]On the magical significance of copper and/or bronze, note
Riess, "Aberglaube," col. 51, and Hopfner, "Mageia," col. 326; also,
Vieillefond, Les Cestes, p. 132, note b.

[2]In line 34, at least, he equated Africanus's technikḗ with
goētikḗ.

[3]The active ingredient might be the plant kypros, henna,
rather than copper; but while henna was used in some skin conditioning
salves (cf. Grieve, Modern Herbal, 1:405), its real reputation lay in
other directions. (But according to a modern presentation of astrological herbalism, perhaps it should work. As a member of the loosestrife family [Lythraceae], it might be, with loosestrife itself, a
moon herb, and thus effective for breast complaints [Conway, Magic,
pp. 22-23].)

The context seems to indicate that Psellus regarded the procedure as sorcerous.[1]

Two passages involve gold. The first, part of the suspect passage 23a (III. 2. 11-14, p. 225), specifies the use of a gold necklace for wearing the "swallow-stones" against ophthalmia. The second, again from Psellus (mp 44e; IX. 1. 15, p. 317), notes enigmatically that Africanus corrodes gold with mad dog saliva. The intended use is not specified.[2]

In two final passages, each questionable for its own reasons, Africanus may specify the use of some type of plaques. Passage 37 (III. 23. 3-5, p. 243) directs the use of an inscribed tin sheet, tied around the throat of an animal, to protect it from scorpion stings. This passage is not accepted by Björck as being proven Africanian,[3] and, as noted below, the inscription itself further supports this doubt. In the other passage (mp 5, pentagon four; I. 4. 8, p. 127), the doubt attaches to the nature of the thing applied. Was it a plaque of some sort, perhaps of metal (Vieillefond compares it to Pliny's reference to the use of lead plaques),[4] applied to the surgical incision, or was it some other substance "sprinkled on"

---

[1] It could, however, have been originally intended as a medical procedure, the dryness of the copper (presumably powdered) being supposed to produce the desired effect.

[2] Perhaps as a dye or tinting substance? Cf. Berthelot and Ruelle, Collection, 2:170 (Zosimus 3. 18. 2, quoting Marie the Jewess, "Concerning the oxidized material from silver, lead and iron").

[3] "Apsyrtus," pp. 15-16.

[4] Les Cestes, p. 337, n. 47 (citing Pliny N.H. 34. 166).

(epipasatō) the wound or the bandage?[1]

Charms and Rites

This topic is probably the most significant as far as the magical views of Africanus are concerned. While the group of passages here considered is perhaps not as spectacular, over-all, as the pentagon series (with which it overlaps in several procedures), most of the passages involved here can only be regarded as magical in intent and form. The only real question is what type of magic: of what is Africanus guilty? and is it something completely inconsistent with the views of his Christian colleagues?

Spells and inscriptions

Spells

Along with the manipulation of the wounding iron in mp 6 (I. 5, p. 129), two verbal pronouncements are to be used. One is the triple repetition (see below on this element) of the sounds "ta ta"; the other is the use of a Latin expression[2] which was to be found in pentagon five. The latter is now lost; the former cannot be exactly paralleled[3] but is quite similar to various magical manipulations of sound involving combinations of vowels, or of vowels and

---

[1] See the discussions above under "Pentagon Passages" and under "Plant Passages": "Polygons and Ancient Medicaments."

[2] The next chapter in Kestos 7 is closely linked to this example, in involving a Latin prescription, as well as being the next pentagon passage (pentagon six, mp 7; I. 6. 23-30, p. 133). But it involves an inscription rather than a spoken spell, and so is considered below.

[3] Cf. Vieillefond, Les Cestes, p. 337, first par. of n. 48.

consonants.[1] Mp 15b (I. 17. 44-49, pp. 165, 167) contains a rather

rhetorical address to Sleep, followed by a brief mythological ac-

count. This might be a spell, but Africanus gives no directions to

use it as such, so it is more likely simply another of Africanus's

literary embellishments, beginning here with an apostrophe to Sleep.

The most extensive example of a spell[2] is in mp 42 (V, pp.

285-89; Oxy. Pap. 412). This is the amplified version of Odysseus's

nekyomanteia which Africanus reports having found in Homeric manu-

scripts in three widely separated libraries. Numerous studies have

contributed to the clarification of individual points in the text,[3]

and have indicated the spiritual ancestry and mechanical aspects of

the interpolation process,[4] but have largely left the question of

Africanus's relation to it unsolved. The opinions which were ex-

pressed on this point were regularly derogatory to Africanus. He was

_____

[1]Note the various "-a" forms in the magical papyri, e.g.,
PLond 47. 45 (Kenyon, Greek Papyri, 1:83).
    Various possibilities for its origin could be suggested. It
could be a variation (or corruption) of "tatai" as an expression of
pain (LSJ, Supplement, s.v. "ταταῖ"), the performer "absorbing" the
pain of the sufferer and then spitting it out (cf. line 3) or counteracting it with the Latin formula. It might be a corruption or development of the triply repeated name, "Tat, Tat, Tat" which appears, for
example, in DMP xvii.1ff; v. 15ff; vii. 11ff (cited by Morton Smith,
Jesus the Magician [San Francisco: Harper & Row, Publishers, 1978], p.
132, with note on p. 206). It might be, functionally, a sort of soothing or distracting sound while the weapon is "driven into (epikrousai)
the wound."

[2]Explicitly identified as such in lines 20 and 21 (epaoidē,
and epasai, respectively).

[3]See the discussion, "Oxyrhynchus and Beyond," in Chapter I,
above; and the discussion by Vieillefond, Les Cestes, pp. 280-83.

[4]Notably Wünsch, "Deisidaimoniaka," pp. 2-19.

charged with either forgery, or, even worse, being taken in by <u>such</u>
a forgery.[1] There is no question about the magical nature of the
composition reported by Africanus, an amalgam of Egyptian, Greek, and
Hebrew elements;[2] but how and why he reports it are less clear. Its
location, however, suggests that it is a sort of grand finale for the
eighteenth <u>Kestos</u>, a rhetorical literary flourish similar to the archery tales which conclude <u>Kestos</u> 7. His stated reason for including
it is that it is a very valuable conception of epic (<u>kyēma [pollу-</u>
<u>te[l]esteron epik[e]s</u>, line 49, p. 289). This appears not to be be-
cause he is under any illusions as to its literary quality; he has
just described it as "overwrought" (<u>periergon</u>, line 45), not in accord
with the dignity (<u>axiōma</u>, line 46) of the work, "foreign" (<u>allotria</u>,
line 47) to its progression. But despite this, he seems to entertain
no question about its authenticity; the only two theories suggested
to account for its absence are omissions by the Poet himself or by
the Peisistratides in their supposed revision (lines 45-48). There is
no hint of the possibility of a later interpolation. Such a lapse on
the part of the critic who attacked the authenticity of Susanna is
hardly credible. It is almost enough to drive one to the alternatives,

---

[1]Cf. Ludwich, cols. 1502-3 (not a forger, but a poor critic);
Kroll, "S. Julius Africanus," col. 122 (if not a forger, a very poor
critic).
        It may be noted, in defense of Africanus against Ludwich's
characterization of him as "dem Durchstöberer alter Papierkorbfetzen"
(col. 1503), that it was not Africanus but modern scholars who found
this scrap while going through waste paper. Africanus tells us that
he found it on the shelves in respectable libraries.

[2]See Vieillefond, <u>Les Cestes</u>, p. 281 (and the studies cited
there, as well as the others cited above), and p. 288, note <u>b</u> (cont.
on p. 290).

either a forgery or a joke.[1] There are, however, at least two other

possibilities, though neither of them necessarily excludes either of

the preceding two. It is possible that in designating the passage as

"very valuable" Africanus is thinking of its magic contents, either

historically or for current practice, or both. This is not impossible,

and could coincide with either of the preceding two views. The other

possibility is that, perhaps as being aware of numerous aberrations in

the Homeric text, Africanus has come to regard them as variant lines

from a common source, and thus, finding this passage attested in sev-

eral widely distributed manuscripts, had no reason to suspect their

authenticity.[2] This view would not be inconsistent with an ironic

intent is his evaluation of the lines. I am rather inclined toward

this last view, including the ironic twist, but a historical regard,

at least, for the magical contents of the lines is not hard to imagine

of the writer of some of the other passages preserved under Africanus's

---

[1]Cf. Kroll, "S. Julius Africanus," col. 122, lines 37-41;
and Björck, "Apsyrtus," pp. 24-25.

[2]Grant ("Historical Criticism," p. 191) criticizes Africanus's
failure to take sufficient cognizance of the differences between the
Roman manuscript and the others. On the other hand, Louis Robert ("La
bibliothèque de Nysa de Carie," Hellenica 1 [1940]: 144-48), followed
tentatively by Vieillefond (Les Cestes, pp. 281-82), suggests that the
three manuscripts were related (thus, despite their geographical distribution, they represented only one witness, a factor not suspected
by Africanus). (Vieillefond's major reservation is concerned with the
question of how a copy of the work would have gotten to Jerusalem [p.
282]. Might it be that a transcript was made from the Roman examplar
for the library of [or some individual in, or, who went to] the new
colony of Aelia? Or even that an existing copy of the "deviant" manuscript was declared surplus and disposed of in this manner? [How were
libraries established and stocked in Roman colonies?].)

name.[1] But a more positive, active evaluation of the magic is not im-

possible. Since we do not have Africanus's introduction to the passage

to indicate his purpose in using it and his attitude toward it, our

final decision can only be a subjective judgment based on consistency

with the reading of the other passages.

Passages 44 d and j (IX. 1. 11-13 and 30-32, pp. 317 and 319)

give Psellus's answer on two such items. In the former, the mulberry

bough styptic was given its power by a secret spell (epōdē tini

aporrhētō, line 13). The latter attributes certain healings of poison

bites and eye problems to certain pendants and "enchantments"

(epasmasin, line 32).

The third passage cited from the Chronography (mp 48/chr 3;

Routh, frag. XL), considered simply in itself, might be regarded as

referring to a magical spell (ōdē). Since, however, the item referred

to is known, the so-called Prayer of Manasseh,[2] this conception of the

incident seems to be ruled out. Its designation as a "song" is a re-

flex of its poetic form, not really a synonym for epōdē, "spell" or

"charm." The only argument for the latter would be an automatic

classification of its "miraculous" result as evidence of "magical" in-

tent.

---

[1]This would be especially true of such items as mpp 14, 23a,
and 35 (I. 17; III. 2. 11-14; and III. 19).

[2]This identification is strengthened by the reference to the
fetters being iron (ta desma . . . sidēra onta). They are so identified in Pr. Man. 10 (desmō sidērou), while the Hebrew text of the Old
Testament reference, 2 Chr. 33:11, suggests that they were bronze
(nĕḥuštayim). (Pitra suggests that this passage provides our earliest
testimonium to the Prayer [Analecta sacra, 2:292].)

Inscriptions

The first, and most significant, use of an inscription in the preserved fragments is closely associated with the first spell example as noted above in connection with the discussion of it. Both involve clearly magical procedures, indeed, the present passage, mp 7, penta-gon six (I. 6. 23-30, p. 133), is introduced as an "art of nature" (technē physeōs, line 24).[1] The inscription, to tame an unmanageable horse, is to be inscribed with a bronze pen, in a particular manner, at a particular time, in the bottom of the left front foot of the horse.[2] It has a "necessity of obedience" (anankēn echei peitharchias, line 28). This inscription, "a threat of Roman prescription," which was to be found in the sixth pentagon, may be preserved for us in a cryptogram in the Cambridge hippiatrica codex. Arranged in four un-equal lines within a lozenge or diamond form, it reads "φε/δολει/ κεσο/φεε"; under it is the line "αελφχοθπψλν."[3] Using a system de-scribed by Gardthausen, Vieillefond deciphers the last line as

---

[1] Either element of this expression could be used as a "code" word for magic.

[2] Compare and contrast the hypotaktikon charm given in PLond 121. 926-39. It was to be engraved with a bronze pen on a leaden flake from a mule yoke and placed under the sole of the left foot of the person desiring the power. The inscription, surrounded by a square and various symbols, occupies lines 931-39 (Kenyon, Greek Papyri, 1:113-14). Note also another charm of the same type to be worn in the right sandal (PLond 124. 29-34, followed by approximately 10 lines containing four columns of names; ibid., pp. 122-23).

[3] Oder-Hoppe, C.H., 2:225; Vieillefond, Les Cestes, p. 133 mg (re line 28), and p. 132, note c (cont. on pp. 134, 136, 138). Oder-Hoppe read the last letter as o or u, rather than n.

"θεοφύλακτον."[1] The letters in the figure have not yet been satis-

factorily explained.[2]

Another inscription occurs in mp 37 (III. 23. 3-5, p. 243),

the prescription of a tin sheet pendant as a protection of an animal

from scorpion attack. The inscription is the word "abbas." Vieille-

fond points out the Aramaic background of this word,[3] which could

support his view of Africanus's Jewish origin (though he does not so

---

[1]Les Cestes, p. 138 (cont. of n. c). The system in Gardthausen is a numerical variation of athbash. It uses the Greek alphabet
including the three older letters retained as numerical symbols, divided into three shorter series of nine letters each, α-θ, ι-ς, and
ρ-ϡ (units, tens, hundreds), with the center letter of each series,
ε, ν, and φ, remaining unchanged in the cipher (V. Gardthausen,
Griechische Palaeographie, 2d ed., 2 vols. [Leipzig: Verlag von Veit
& Comp., 1911-13], 2:311).

[2]Vieillefond suggests that it is a translation of Africanus's
Latin formula (ibid.). In addition, we can perhaps regard the theophylakton as a scribal cue to the procedure rather than as an original
part of the formula (such a reference would seem to run counter to
the non-theological strain in the Kestoi noted above). With certain
other assumptions, this might furnish a solution to the cipher. The
inscription can be transliterated into the Roman alphabet as "FE/
DOLEI/KESO/FEE." An ad hoc cipher can then be set up using the 24
letters of the Roman alphabet, having two groups of 9 each, as in the
original, and then using the remaining 6 as a final group: A-I, K-S,
and T-Z, with E and O central and unchangeable in the first two
groups. Using this cipher, the letters decode as "DEFOREASEKODEE."
Could this have been intended to represent something such as "defore
aseco de e(quo)," interpreted as "to be about to be wanting/fail,
cut off from (being?) a horse"? The solution does not necessarily
have to be good Latin, only such as a tyro might have produced. This
would be true whether Africanus got the "prescription" from someone
else or concocted it himself. The latter is not outside the realm of
possibility; if Africanus can be suspected (even if innocent) of composing the nekyomanteia interpolations, such an item as this is even
more likely (especially if the possibility of regarding such items as
practical jokes is kept as an open option).

[3]Les Cestes, p. 359, n. 222. The same note attributes to
A.-M. Desrousseaux the observation that this is, in effect, a palindrome (though the term is not used); specifically, one involving the
first two letters of the alphabet.

use it). This passage is not accepted by Björck as of proven authenticity, however. The precise form of the inscription, "abba_s," unless it has suffered in the transmission,[1] would suggest this latter
suspicion; a person from a Semitic background would presumably not
have used such a form. Perhaps even more to the point, the very religious background of the word cited by Vieillefond, emphasized by the
New Testament passages which he gives, would also seem to argue
against the Africanian origin of the prescription.[2] Also, the use of
an Aramaic phrase as a magical charm, by someone from an area where
this was one of the common languages, would be unusual,[3] though probably not unprecedented.[4]

Amulets

A number of Africanus's procedures fall under the heading of
amulets, a type of protective item kept on or near the body. One or
two of them are charms (i.e., their power comes from a written spell
engraved on them), the others involve some type of sympathetic or apotropaic principle.

---

[1]This is not unlikely since the added s does destroy the symmetry of the palindrome, and is likely to have been added in the Greek
tradition once its original Aramaic significance was lost from sight.
(Or is it possibly not an expansion of abba, but a truncated form of a
corruption of Abrasax?)

[2]Note again Vieillefond, Les Cestes, pp. 56-58.

[3]See the discussion of "Foreign and Strange Elements," below.
The use of such an item in a charm would be in a different category
from the use of Aramaic (or other native) names in common prescriptions or narratives.

[4]But such a use in a charm would seem to require some sort of
"numinous" quality in its background. In Africanus's case this would
come from its Christian use, which would strengthen the objection above.

Amulets and charms

Africanus is said to cure asp bites and mists of eyes by amulets (periaptois) and incantations (Psellus; Vi., IX. 1. 30-32, p.
319), and two of the items he prescribes, the stone found in a cock,
mp 4, and the withered bat's head, mp 15a,[1] may be worn in a skytis,
a leather amulet (I. 3. 3, p. 125, and I. 17. 35, p. 165).[2] Two
other passages prescribe a charm to be borne on the body: mp 7, the
Roman prescription for an unmanageable horse, and mp 37, the questionable tin charm against scorpion stings. The former may not be
strictly an amulet, but it is borne on the body (in the hoof) as a
"protective" device.

Other pendants

A number of Africanus's other procedures involve attaching
the prescribed items to (literally "around," usually involving a form
of periaptō)[3] the subject, usually on or near the specific part of the
body involved, if any. These procedures are[4] mpp: 10, wolf tail and

---

[1]In place of the bat's head, apparently the whole bat might be
worn (I. 17. 42).

[2]Though Africanus suggests a more secure container (apparently
the contestant's body) for the former (I. 3. 11, p. 127). (The stone
might also be carried in the mouth, under the tongue [lines 3-4 and 9].)

[3]This also applies to mp 15a, above (I. 17. 36 and 42). The
exceptions are mp 10, where Africanus refers to "necklaces" (peri-
deraiois, and perithema, I. 10. 8 and 11); mp 23 a and b, which involve
a gold necklace (hormō, III. 2. 14) and a skin container (with no specific order to wear the latter [or the former, for that matter]); and
mp 37, in which the tin sheet is to be "tied around" (peridesmei,
III. 23. 5) the animal's throat. Note also mp 4, peri brachioni
phoroumenos (I. 3. 9-10).

[4]Items in parentheses are hippiatrica passages questioned by
Björck.

teeth; 21, deer antler ornament; (23 a and b, swallow stones in a
gold necklace and in fawn or calf skin); (23 c and d, vulture eyes in
dog skin[1] or frog eyes in linen); 27, polygonum in dog's afterbirth;
25, milk stone; (38d, the biting head); (40, swan testicle); 44 c,
frog's navel (brains?), and d, the mulberry bough styptic.

Foreign or strange elements

One of the fairly constant elements in most systems or examples of magic is the foreign or exotic strain in the various procedures. This feature is somewhat minor in Africanus's magical references despite the fact that he is something of a "name-dropper" and
retailer of exotic (and/or esoteric) information in his general narratives.

Famous magical areas

Three passages involve names or places noted in ancient magic:
mp 3, a Thessalian snake (with a Syrian name also given, though perhaps a gloss); mp 42, the nekyomanteia with its numerous magical names;
and mp 47/chr 2, the book by an ancient Egyptian king, Souphis. In
addition, another passage involves a near neighbor of the Egyptians,
the Libyan Inaron in mp 36.

Roman prescriptions

Three passages, mpp 6, 7, and the cross-reference to the latter in 13a, involve prescriptions attributed to the Romans (cf. also

---

[1]In addition, vulture eyes in linen may be applied to the eyes
daily, though apparently not worn continuously (mp 23c; III. 2. 21-24,
p. 227).

the reference to the Quintilii in mp 17). This is something of a surprise, since the Romans were not a distant[1] or especially ancient race in the days of their empire. But the fact of their dominance, together with their relative distance from Palestine, and their relative antiquity (approaching a millennium), might account for their inclusion here. On the other hand, as noted above at the end of the discussion of the "Pentagon Passages,"[2] these references do not contribute greatly to belief in Africanus's seriousness, at least at these points.[3]

Magical classes?

"Those by whom wolves are caught most easily" (mp 12a), and sailors (mp 29) may be named only because they are those who would have access to and possess knowledge of the remedies named (wolf flesh, and the remora). There might be some tendency, however, to regard them as having special knowledge of magic in general. The former, as inhabitants of more remote (inaccessible) or distant (uncivilized) areas (i.e., pagani or barbarians) might be so regarded. Sailors, regarded as a superstitious lot, might, by reflex, be regarded as having special knowledge or powers in such areas; or they might be so regarded as having contact with distant, exotic, places.

---

[1]This same disability would also apply to the Aramaic abbas in mp 37, if it is regarded as coming from either a Palestinian resident (a common view of Africanus), or a Jew writing for Jews, even in the Diaspora (as in Vieillefond's view).

[2]Above, p. 213, with n. 4.

[3]Note the other questions about mp 7 (above, pp. 272-73, with n. 2 on the latter page).

Rites

A number of the procedures involve the performance of certain actions, or the observance of certain restrictions (limitations)
or requirements of behavior, in which the actions seem to be of significance in themselves; they are not simply acts necessary to use or
manipulate the substances prescribed. These involve the use of a
certain side (right or left) for some function, the observance of
proper times, the use of certain numbers, or other requirements or
"tabus." These factors will be considered below, climaxed by a consideration of certain passages which present combinations of them in
more extended rituals.

Right or left

Several passages specify that a particular procedure uses or
involves a part from a certain side, or is performed with a certain
hand.

Four passages involve the right side: the wolf tail to prevent fright in horses is attached to the subject's right ear (mp 9);
the sleeping potion for use in wine included wax from the right ear
of a donkey (mp 16); it was the right astragalus of a wolf which was
supposed to stop a four-horse team (mp 18); and the right testicle of
a swan was to be applied to aid colon distress in horses (mp 40).[1]
These seem to be explainable by the idea of the right as the more

---

[1]This last procedure was not accepted by Björck, "Apsyrtus,"
pp. 15-16. The report of the procedure in the hippiatrica is simply
too short to provide any stylistic criteria to support its claim.
There seem to be no particular reasons based on content to either
oppose or support it.

potent[1] and/or the positive side. There seems to be no significant
difference, however, between the wolf tail to prevent fright, which is
attached to the right side, and the frog eyes to protect from ophthalmia (mp 23d) which are attached to the left shoulder, or the lignite stone to aid birth (mp 44c) which is put in the left hand. The
choice of side seems to be rather arbitrary, at the unconscious whim
or fortuitous rationale of the originator.

Operations involving the _left_ side occur a little more frequently. In mp 7 there are two such references: the taming inscription
is to be engraved in the left front foot, and it is to be done with
the left hand. A veterinary prescription given between items a and b
of mp 12 is to be infused into the left nostril of the ailing beast
(I. 12. 41, p. 147). As noted in the preceding paragraph, the frog's
eyes as an ophthalmic (mp 23d) and the lignite stone to aid birth
(mp 44c) are to be used on the left side. Also, in the sprinkling
against worms (mp 35), the left hand is used. These cases of attachment (or placement) on the left side can perhaps be explained as an
apotropaic function, since the left was regarded as the side of ill-
omen (compare the reverse rationale for the designation of it as
euōnymos). The uses of the left hand, in the first and last procedures above, are probably to be explained by Riess's suggestion that
it is the unusualness of its use which conveys the supposed power.[2]
This might also carry over to such a "passive" use as that in mp 44c
(lignite stone). The fact that the frog's eyes in mp 23d could be

[1]Riess, "Aberglaube," cols. 83-84.

[2]Ibid., col. 84, lines 46-50.

worn on the left shoulder or neck (III. 2. 29) seems to confirm the
somewhat arbitrary nature of the specification of a side.

Times

        Five passages specify times at which the procedures must be
performed. Three of these specify days in relation to the moon, and
three specify a time of day. In the former group, the taming inscription (mp 7) is to be engraved at the sixteenth day of the moon, perhaps because this marks the beginning of the moon's waning, and thus
could carry an implied threat to the animal. The spring nestlings in
mp 23b are not to be cut open until the new or waxing phase of the
moon,[1] the performer waiting (epidechomenon, III. 2. 19, p. 227) for
this time to do so. The color-changing plaster for horses in mp 41
(hexagon seven; III. 36, p. 255) specifies both a day and time for
its use: the first day of the moon,[2] at the third hour (line 5).[3]

_____

        [1]See above, p. 246, with n. 2.

        [2]Following Vieillefond's translation, Les Cestes, p. 254.
The text as given by Vieillefond (following Oder-Hoppe, C.H. 2:250.
15) reads prōtē selēnē . . . . This could mean the "first month,"
but the specification of the hour favors Vieillefond's interpretation.
A reference to the day might have dropped out, or be assumed, but this
would restrict its use to once a year. (Such a restriction would, of
course, help to counteract any encouragement the formula might give
to horse thievery, but that does not seem to concern the author.)
        Alternately, following the London manuscript's pros tē
selēnē (Oder-Hoppe, C.H., 2:250 mg, re line 15 [MS C reads pr with
a superscript o]), the time might be conceived to be "before the
moon [i.e., on a moonlit night] at the third hour" (of the night, or
after moonrise).

        [3]On the phases of the moon in superstition see Riess, "Aber-
glaube," cols. 39-41. On various times, ibid., cols. 38, 44-46;
Thorndike, History, 1:91. Riess provides numerous other examples of
both factors, especially in his discussion of superstitions involving
plants (cols. 51-68).

The hour of <u>what</u> is not specified, but in view of the reference to
the moon, and the type of operation which might be involved (horse
theft), it might be the third hour of the night. Night (or at least,
non-day) is clearly specified in another operation: the chicory/
"heliotrope" to be used against warts is to be picked before sunrise.
The final operation of this sort is also unclear in its specification
of time. The mulberry styptic (mp 44d) is to be appended while the
phōstērs are under the earth (IX. 1. 12, p. 317).[1] If this is interpreted simply as "stars," it would apparently have to mean the day-
light hours, but would seem to be a rather cumbersome way of express-
ing the idea (unless it is taken as a definite parody of such magical
prescriptions). Perhaps, especially in view of his Semitic and/or
Biblical background, Africanus is using the term to mean the two
major "stars" (the "two great lights" of Genesis), the sun and the
moon.[2] If so, this would then mean a moonless night, specifically,
"the dark of the moon."

Numbers

        Africanus includes the "power of numbers" (arithmōn kinēseōs)
as, along with magic and sorcery (mageias kai goēteias), among the
things taught to women by certain angels (mp 46/chr 1).[3] Such a

---

[1]Vieillefond makes a separate clause of this, "amulette des
astres qui se trouvent sous la terre" (p. 316), but gives no explanation of how the "star" amulet relates to the mulberry styptic.

[2]Cf. LSJ, s.v. "φωστήρ," re "οἱ δύο φ.".

[3]Routh, Rel. sacr. 2:241-42 (Fragment VII, first part; Syncellus 1:34-35, ed. Dindorf). The preceding context indicates some
uncertainty on Africanus's part concerning these angels. The uncertainty seems, however, not to be about their existence or acts, this

tainted origin of the knowledge concerning these things would not

undercut belief in their objective reality.[1] Thus it is not surpris-

ing to find several passages from the Kestoi which reflect this idea

of the power of numbers.

Several passages involve the multiple repetition of some pro-

cedure; in all the Africanian examples they are triple.[2] Thus the

"ta ta" in mp 6 is to be thrice repeated, the wart in mp 33b is

thrice circumscribed, and the maggoty sore in mp 35 is sprinkled

three times.

Three other passages involve numbers which may have been

specified for their supposed power, rather than established on a

---

he seems to assume as established (cf. I Enoch 6-10). The uncertainty is whether they should be identified with the "sons of God" of
Gen. 6:2, 4. Africanus rather doubts this (ei . . . nooito . . .,
in contrast to the earlier hōs oimai . . .: Routh 2:242. 3 and 241.
19-20; Syncellus 1:35. 1 and 34. 14) in contrast to most early Christian and contemporary Jewish opinion (and I Enoch). (Among the early
church fathers [see Chapter IV, below] these fallen angels were commonly identified as the source of magic, pagan worship, etc., and,
identified as the "sons of God," as the progenitors of the daemons.)
If this identification is made, Africanus still sees the progeny only
as giants (Routh 2:242. 7; Syncellus 1:35. 4), not as demons.

[1]Nor, necessarily, of their morality. Many of the other
fathers included various practical arts (e.g., cosmetics, metallurgy,
mining) among those taught by the angels. To them, this made most of
these things suspect ethically, but did not affect belief in their
effectiveness.
    If one were looking for any available proof of Africanus's
philosophical acumen, he could say that Africanus here refuses to fall
into the trap of the "genetic fallacy." (But credulity is really difficult to transmute into philosophic insight.)

[2]The use of multiple (especially triple) items or repetition
of performances is widespread in magic, cf. Riess, "Aberglaube," cols.
49. 38-50. 10, with numerous illustrations in the following discussion
of plants, cols. 51-68; Björck, "Apsyrtus," p. 65 (citing a text from
Heim, "Incantamenta," p. 557); Thorndike, History, 1:91-92; Hubert,
"Magia," p. 1519 (col. 2).

practical basis. The eye salve preparation is to be buried in horse dung for <u>forty</u> days (mp 23e), the dog brain "plaster" on the bandage will heal a fracture in <u>fourteen</u> days (mp 32), and the foot treatment in procedure 39 starts with <u>seven</u> figs. Otherwise, as noted above in the discussion of each, these procedures, though bizarre, are not too far removed from ancient medical (folk-medical, at least) practices.

Other elements

Several other features noted in the various procedures discussed in the preceding pages could come under the heading of rites, i.e., actions significant in themselves.

The victorious cock from which victory-giving stones are to be used is to be eaten so as to leave the skeleton whole, and then the bones are to be "purified" by fire (mp 4, see the discussion above, p. 243). Three of the "ophthalmic" procedures in mp 23 involve rituals of greater or lesser extent. In the first (23a), which is the most elaborate, and involves a feature (sacrifice to Aphrodite) which seems to confirm Björck's omission of this passage from his authentic list,[1] the swallow stones are found and used in an elaborate manner: the nestling is opened with a sharp reed, a white dove is sacrificed and Aphrodite is invoked, and then the stones are put into a gold necklace. In the other two items, the stone from the swallow nestling in 23b must not touch earth before use,[2] and the frog from which the eyes

---

[1]"Apsyrtus," pp. 15-16; see above, p. 245, with n. 1.

[2]See above, p. 246, n. 1.

are taken in 23d must be released where it was taken.[1] The passage

designated as mp 30 (III. 11, p. 233), if it is really Africanian,[2]

would probably fit into this category. To cure a horse of dysurea,

a virgin, having loosed (lysasa) her girdle, should strike him about

the face with it. The key element here would appear to be loosing, a

virgin probably being specified because of a common magical belief in

their "potency,"[3] and the striking a means of transferring the power

----

[1]See above, p. 215, n. 2. Thorndike suggests that this type of
procedure may come under the head of "magic transfer" of disease
(History,   1:88-89). This interpretation was avoided in the previous
discussion, since there is no actual contact between the diseased person and the released animal. Perhaps a "magic transfer of health,"
might be a better description, the release of the frog serving only as
a way of disposing of an "unsightly" by-product of the operation. The
specification that it be released "where it was taken" would seem an
unnecessary detail if the animal need only carry the disease away; it
seems to imply a re-integration of the creature into nature, a maintenance, as much as possible, of the "wholeness" that its eyes symbol-
ize. (It could, however, be a precaution that the animal does not
remain in or return to the vicinity of the sufferer, thus threatening
to return the disease to him, or to die leaving the disease where it
could return to him, or where he might "run across" it again.) Jones
("Popular Medicine," p. 574) suggests that such an amulet "absorbs"
the illness and "transfers it to the mutilated animal," its death taking along the illness. This sounds reasonable, but would restrict the
usefulness of the amulet temporally.

[2]Björck specifically rejects the authenticity of this piece
because of the great extent of its verbal coincidence with Aelian N.A.
11. 18; it is more likely to be a scribal or redactional adaptation
directly from Aelian than a passage coming through a writer such as
Africanus ("Apsyrtus," pp. 17-18). This is the same type of evidence
used by other students of Africanus in rejecting many of the other
chapters credited to Africanus in the manuscripts and the printed
editions of Thevenot and Lami, because of their close repetition or
adaptation of the texts of Aeneas Tacticus, et al. Vieillefond apparently does not accept Björck's reasoning on this passage, since he
included it in his 1970 edition, but he did not answer the objection
on this point.

[3]E.g., Riess, "Aberglaube," cols. 58. 61; 72. 39; 85. 5; 86. 5,
9; cf. also, 80. 9 and 86. 44 (an innocent boy). All of these passages
except 86. 5 involve some type of healing or apotropaic procedure.

of the loosed girdle to the animal which is in need of a sort of loosing. The striking could, however, be viewed as a means of driving
out or subduing some hostile force; such a force could most naturally
be viewed as "personal," but need not be.

Two further passages involve ritual prescriptions. Circumscription of the affected place (a wart) is one procedure prescribed
in mp 33 (III. 17. 7-9, p. 239). As suggested above in the discussion of plants, if the substance prescribed, flowers of chicory/"heliotrope," had some medicinal value, this might be a practical way of
applying it. Such a value is not clear, however, and the other features of the procedure, picking before sunrise and the threefold action, suggest that the circumscription itself is a ritual act.[1] The
sprinkling with water against maggots (mp 35) was to be done with the
"physician's finger" (III. 19. 2, p. 239). Whatever the precise finger
involved,[2] its designation suggests that it has come to have some
special use in connection with healing, and thus the simple use of
that finger provides such a virtue to an act performed with it.

(Two other items, if they are magical, or even superstitious,

----

[1]Vieillefond, Les Cestes, p. 358, n. 209; Björck, "Apsyrtus,"
p. 59; cf. examples in Riess, "Aberglaube," cols. 61. 20-21; 62. 16.

[2]Either the index finger (as translated by Vieillefond, Les
Cestes, p. 238; but with reservations, see his note 213, p. 358), or
the ring finger (ibid.; see also Björck, "Apsyrtus," p. 20, cf. also
p. 60; both cite the brief note by R. Ganszyniec, "Welches ist der
ἰατρικὸς δάκτυλος?", Byzantinisch-neugriechische Jahrbücher 1 [1920]:
342). Ganszyniec shows that the latter is its reference, at least in
some writers and passages. Riess suggests that the term was applied
sometimes to the middle finger, sometimes to the ring finger ("Aberglaube," col. 84, lines 62-65).

at all, would probably come under this heading. They are the specification of the use of a <u>new</u> pot in mpp 19 [neourges] and 43b [kainon]
[II . 5. 5, p. 205, and VI, line 4, p. 297], and the specification of
a <u>black</u> mortar for mixing the <u>automaton pyr</u> [II. 11. 3, p. 211]. But
a new pot may mean no more than one that is clean, or uncontaminated in
the literal sense,[1] and the color of the mortar might have practical
significance[2] in a delicate procedure which must be performed under a
noon-day sun [mesouranountos hēliou, ibid.; repeated, with the added
warning: "guard the face, for it kindles suddenly," lines 6-8].)

Extended rituals

　　Several of the procedures involve the performance of a connected series of significant acts.

　　One of the most impressive of these series is the "hoplocrisma"
passage (mp 6, pentagon five; I. 5. 1-9, p. 129), the anointing of the
wounding weapon.[3] In this procedure, the wounding iron is to be
anointed and then struck onto (or, driven into? [epikrousai, line 2])
the wound. This is to be accompanied by a triple repetition of "ta
ta," and, while spitting,[4] the use of the Latin expression (Rhōmaian

---

[1]Cf. Björck, "Apsyrtus," pp. 60-61.

[2]Note Vieillefond's parenthetic comment, Les Cestes, p. 355,
n. 177.

[3]See the discussion above, p. 211, with n. 1 and the
references in Thomas, Decline of Magic, cited there.

[4]On spitting as an apotropaic (or medical) procedure, note
Björck, "Apsyrtus," pp. 57-58; Riess, "Aberglaube," cols. 87-88, with
other examples 65. 1, 11; 85. 22-24; Vieillefond, Les Cestes, p. 337,
n. 48 (citing Pliny N.H. 28. 35 as providing numerous examples of its
use in medicine); Thorndike, History, 1:82-83, 92-93 (spitting thrice)
(all re Pliny); 174 (Galen); note especially Pliny N.H. 28. 36,

. . . rhēsin, lines 3-4) in pentagon five. This elaborate procedure
is to alleviate the suffering from the wound, it must still be treated
by the medical aides (iatrōn paides, line 7).

The following procedure (mp 7, pentagon six; I. 6. 23-30, p.
133) is perhaps even more elaborate. It is introduced by the rhetorically[1] stated magical programme: "let evil of nature by art of nature be corrected" (kakia physeōs technē physeōs diorthousthō, line
24).[2] A taming inscription, of Roman origin, is to be engraved in the
left front hoof, with the left hand, with a bronze stylus, under a
sixteen-day-old moon (lines 24, 26-27). With such an array of powerful elements, it is not hard to see how the inscription could be described as "having a necessity of obedience" (anankēn echei peitharchias . . ., line 28), apart from the question of whether its preser-
vation in a pentagon (see the discussion of the "Pentagon Passages"
above) was of real magical significance.

Considerably less elaborate, but still quite striking, is a

---

spitting on the ground three times as a customary ritual in using any
remedy, and 30. 108, triple action (circumscription) accompanied by
triple spitting by both parties.

[1]See Vieillefond, Les Cestes, p. 130, note a, on the rhetorical character of the first paragraph of this chapter (lines 1-13,
pp. 129, 131).
    The lines describing the inscription provide opportunity for
further rhetorical display: hēn ou phob- . . . hēn ouch hypopt- . . .
hēn phorōn . . . (line 25); cheiri e- encharatte graphiō chalkō, . . .
(lines 26-27).

[2]On "nature by nature," see Lagercrantz, Pap. holm., pp. 90-91,
with n. 3 (re Berthelot and Ruelle, Collection, 2:57. 3-15), and pp.
109-10 (re Berthelot and Ruelle, 2:43. 22-53. 15); on the "art of nature" (= alchemy), see Berthelot and Ruelle, 2:272. 3-4. See also,
Vieillefond, Les Cestes, p. 132, note a (physikos in the sense of
"magique"), and the title of IX. 2, p. 321 (again, = alchemy).

procedure for driving maggots from a sore, given in mp 35 (III. 19,
p. 239). Clear water, taken up with the thumb and curled back "physician's" finger of the left hand, is sprinkled three times on the
infected place. While no spell is prescribed, the water is described by a poetic line: "by a stream of pure water."[1] The result
is that the maggots emerge, following one another out, not one being
left behind (lines 4-5). It is difficult to see how such a procedure
could be presented seriously, unless something crucial has been left
out in the condensation or transmission. A more elaborate procedure
could be protected from apparent failure by charging failure in some
detail of its performance, but such a simple procedure, involving
what would not be a rare condition, seems too vulnerable to empiric
disproof.[2]

Gods and Daemons

A number of passages in Africanus refer to pagan gods and/or
daemons. Most of these references occur in connection with the
various magical procedures, yet few if any of them are directly involved in the procedures themselves. In this way, Africanus's magical procedures, including the incantations and charms, are somewhat
atypical.

---

[1] Vieillefond, Les Cestes, pp. 358-59, n. 214; Björck,
"Apsyrtus," p. 16.

[2] This argument could apply, of course, to its transmission in
the manuscript tradition, but once an item entered the tradition, under
the auspices of some "authority," it seems to have been passed on by
the successive scribes with little real thought of its rationale. But
the original authority, presumably, would show a little more common
sense.

Invocations

    This atypical character is illustrated by the references to

invocation of the gods in Africanus. There are possibly four such

references, of which one (prelude to mp 11, prayer to Poseidon Horse-

troubler; I. 11. 16-17, p. 141) is only that, a (passing) reference to

pagan practice in that regard.[1] The relation of the other three to

Africanus's beliefs is each uncertain in a different way. The first,

the address to Sleep in mp 15b (I. 17. 44-45, p. 165), even if it

should be more than a rhetorical apostrophe, is rather a challenge

than an invocation (cf. also mp 14b; ibid., lines 30-32), and will

thus be considered in the next section below. The second, an invoca-

tion of Aphrodite in connection with the use of stones from swallow

nestlings (mp 23a; III. 2. 11-14), occurs in a passage of suspect

authenticity, and is itself so out of keeping with Africanus's usual

practice as to provide support for that suspicion.[2] The third, mp

42, the Oxyrhynchus fragment of the end of Kestos 18, is definitely

part of the Africanian corpus, but there is question as to the intent

of its inclusion: is Africanus recommending it as a magical

_____

    [1]There is a reference to the sacrifice of a victorious cock
in mp 4 (I. 3. 7-8, p. 125), but only in describing the finding of
the stones. There is no reference to the invocation of a god, nor
any indication that the sacrifice plays any part in the virtue of the
stone. In the second procedure (lines 12-17, p. 127), there appears
to be some sort of ritual, including the burning of the bones, but
here there is not even a specific reference to the procedure as sacrifice.
    In mp 7 (I. 6. 23-30, p. 133, with marginal note on line 28),
if the theophylakton should be part of the original "Latin expression,"
it still would not exactly be an invocation (and need not be in reference to a pagan god [though originally so, if from Africanus's
time?].)

    [2]See above, p. 245, and n. 1.

procedure, or simply including it only as a literary embellishment, a

Homeric novelty rediscovered by his own sharp eye?[1]

Rivaling the gods

The goal of many ancient magical rites seems to have been the

attainment of divine or semi-divine power by union with a god, or by

identifying or associating oneself with a god (or the gods) in some

way.[2] This is an ambitious procedure, related in some ways to the

acquiring of a "familiar," a paredros. Two lines in Africanus might

be read as reflecting this latter goal--"I desire Sleep to become

subservient to my practice, that with me alone this master and all-

subduer may dwell" (mp 14b; I. 17. 27-29, p. 165)[3]--but Africanus's

basic attitude towards the gods and spirits seems to be entirely other-

wise. Rather than seeking union with such spirits (or even their

servile subservience), he sets himself against them; he seeks nothing

less than equality (self-achieved) with them, or even hostile

---

[1]See above, pp. 268-71.

[2]Note, e.g.: Morton Smith, Clement of Alexandria and a Secret Gospel of Mark (Cambridge: Harvard University Press, 1973), pp. 220-23 (including PGM IV. 154-221, on p. 221), note esp. p. 222, "Many magical operations were designed to produce such incarnate deities; . . .", and p. 226, "Claiming to be a god or a son of a god, or united with some god or supernatural entity. . . ."; also his arguments and examples in Jesus the Magician, pp. 96-106, especially the rites which claim or are designed to achieve identity or union with a god, pp. 98-99 (PGM I. 54ff), and p. 103 (PGM IV. 170-221). Note also, Björck, "Apsyrtus," p. 64 (this occurs in the discussion of his passage no. 7, and cites passage no. 9, on pp. 67-68); and compare the various "egō eimi" forms in PLond 46, e.g., lines 108-9, 113, 145-46 (with note), 151, 154-55, 156, 236 (with note), 240, 472, 476-77 (Kenyon, Greek Papyri, 1:68-80).

[3]But such an interpretation of these lines is probably exces-sive; these seem to be only rhetorical exaggeration of a personifica-tion of sleep (cf. the related lines from 15b and 14b discussed just above).

dominance of them. This attitude is shown in the introductory lines
of the first of our magical passages: "The victorious attribute the
wars of such kind to their peculiar gods. These gods also we will
imitate; spontaneous fortune by our arts will be produced" (I. 2. 57-
59, p. 117). This attitude of defiance toward the gods is further
manifested in regard to the horse-troubler drug (mp 11; I. 11. 17-20,
p. 141) which is sharper than prayer, a replacement for the sacrifice
many make to Poseidon (lines 16-17). It is also shown in the "sleeplessness" passage referred to just above. There (mp 14b) the element
of emulation--"I do not deem myself unworthy of the equality of privilege with them" (I. 17. 25-26, p. 165)--is directed toward men, but
men who had gained advantage over daimonia/-es, earthbound and humble
to be sure (line 26), but daimones none the less. Further, his real
challenge is not to the men who conquered them, but to the one who had
really bound them, Sleep, the all-conquering one (anax kai pandamatōr,
lines 28-29). This is the setting for the apostrophes to Sleep in
the following lines (30-32) and in mp 15b (lines 44-45). These lines
are probably a literary device, but if it is held that Africanus
really conceives of Sleep as a daemonic being, his attitude of defiance and conceit (outright hybris, in fact) is even more striking.[1]

---

[1]This is not really paralleled by the desired power to command
various gods in the passages cited by Smith (e.g., Clement of Alexandria, p. 221), or the attitude of fearlessness toward the gods gained
during the "Mithras Liturgy," lines 555-73 (Marvin W. Meyer, ed. and
trans., The "Mithras Liturgy," The Society of Biblical Literature Texts
and Translations [no. 10], Graeco-Roman Religions Series [no. 2],
edited by Hans Dieter Betz and Edward N. O'Neil [Missoula, Montana:
Scholars Press, for the Society of Biblical Literature, 1976], pp.
8-9). In those passages the status is gained by the protection and
"sponsorship" of a higher power (Typho, God of gods, king; and King

This theme of imitation of or contempt for the gods appears
in two other references. In a later chapter, which, despite its
title, Geōrgias paradoxa, is not magical, Africanus proposes to imitate Dionysus--who had given wine and vines to the Greeks--by providing alternative friendship cups from other produce (I. 19. 21-25,
p. 173). From another source, mp 47/chr 2, we learn that Souphis's
book, prized by Africanus, resulted from Souphis's hauteur or super-
ciliousness (hyperoptēs; Routh 2:250. 2; Syncellus 1:105. 9, ed.
Dindorf) toward the gods.

Mythological narratives

Another characteristic of magical procedures of various ages
and areas is the use of a narrative presenting a "mythological" background, a sort of preternatural precedent, for the result proposed.[1]
Here also, Africanus has passages that appear close to this, but yet
are not really the same. Mpp 14 a, and b, and 15b, already noted in
the preceding two discussions, present such items. In the former
pair, Africanus gives a rhetorical description of the influence or
associates of Sleep, and then cites the cases of the Phrygian king
who bound Silanos, and another hero who found a satyr asleep (I. 17.
7-11, and 24-25). In the latter, 15b, besides the apostrophe to
Sleep already discussed, he adds a comparison to an enigmatic event
relating to the nuptials of Pasithea and Sleep (I. 17. 45-47, p. 165).

---

of gods, in Smith; Helios Mithras, in the "Mithras Liturgy" [cf. lines
480-84, pp. 2-3; or some even higher power? lines 639-43, pp. 14-15])
while Africanus is armed only with a dead bat.

[1]See, e.g.: Björck, "Apsyrtus," pp. 64-65, 69; Hubert,
"Magia," p. 1507 (col. 1).

None of these items is presented as being used in any way in the actual magical operation in 15a (lines 33-43), and fit into the chapter
simply as literary embellishments such as those found throughout these
chapters.[1] This seems especially true in the one of these passages
which has the greatest magical appearance (lines 45-47, in 15b).
Despite their obvious strengthening of the potentially sympathetic
or associational elements in the preceding apostrophe (Night's son-
Night's bird [line 44]; winged-a wing [lines 44-45]), they are given
a literary turn by the reference to Hera, leading rather to an author-
ial "conceit," the reference to "the Kestoi" (line 48, p. 167), than
to a magical application. A reference to the birth of Dionysus, with
Fire as midwife (I. 19. 15-16, p. 173), is not used, for example, to
enhance the power of fire and/or wine in some ritual, but appears to
be a literary embellishment. It is presented as an ancient idea which
Africanus asserts is explained by the improvement of wines by boiling.[2]
In mp 24 (III. 3, pp. 227, 229), also, the mythological references
provide a "natural" rationale for the procedure. The universally
reported fact that the Sun/the Flame is drawn by stallions, and
Night/the Moon by mares[3] explains why facing horses to the east or

---

[1]E.g., in this very chapter, lines 1-5, 12-15; also, I. 2. 6-
16; I. 3. 18-21; I. 7. 6-9; I. 11. 1-15; I. 20; II. 4. 1-2, 4-5; III.
22; IV. (5). 24-30; VII. The other passages discussed in this section
(esp. I. 9. 15-16) also illustrate the point, insofar as the evidence
concerning them is convincing, and is independent of the conclusions
concerning this passage.

[2]But despite the rationalistic explanation given to the myth,
there does seem to be some "superstitious" physics involved in the
procedure, as if the flame imparted some of its quality to the wine
(lines 14-15).

[3]It is not clear that this reference indicates that Africanus

west while breeding produces male or female offspring, respectively.

It is a sympathetic type operation,[1] not a verbal one. The drench

against maggots (mp 35; III. 19, p. 239) seems to require something

more, and the poetic line, "by a stream of pure water," could be

part of such a narrative to provide it potency. But there is, again,

nothing in the text as it stands to support such a use, and its in-

clusion simply as a literary ornamentation would be consistent with

Africanus's style as shown in the preceding passages. The Oxyrhynchus

fragment (mp 42; Vi., V) might be considered an extensive example of

such a narrative, intermixed with supporting incantations, but we do

not really know why Africanus was citing it. What we do have of his

statements about it suggest purely literary(?) and antiquarian in-

terests.

Daemons

Besides the occurrence of the designation daimōn for the gods

or similar personages in some of the passages discussed above (mp

1, I. 2. 6; mp 14b, I. 17. 26; mp 42, V. 30), they appear in one

---

believes in this personification of the Sun and Night, it may be
simply an ad hominem argument to show that the maleness of the sun and
the femaleness of the moon is common knowledge.

Is this rationale also given because Africanus is consciously
giving a system which differs from the commonly accepted ones? The
usual pattern for male-female determination was a distinction of
right or left (e.g., Pliny N.H. 30. 149; Lactantius, De op. dei 12. 3),
or of north and south (e.g., Aelian N.A. 7. 27; Pliny N.H. 10. 180).
Was Africanus's system (attributed to an unknown "Maurousios, the
horse-breeder") just different (perhaps another attempt at improvement?) or was it a parody of the common system?

[1]Cf. the "male" and "female" plants in mp 27 (III. 6. 4-5,
p. 231).

other passage, mp 8 (I. 8. 12, p. 137; cf. also line 3, p. 135). In

this passage it is used of creatures more like the Christian concept

of demons, invisible, malignant beings, but beings which are es-

pecially associated, in accord with popular belief, with road junc-

tures (triodos, line 13).[1] Horses, especially those with different-

colored eyes (heterommatos, line 15),[2] can see them and give warning

of the danger (apeilēn, line 14), by various acts and sounds. Of

this Africanus is certain (pisteuson legonti, . . . kai oida pollous

. . ., line 12), though he is uncertain of the precise reason for the

ability. It may be a product of the soul, or it may be due to the

nature of the eyes (eite oun psychēs ergon, eite physis ommatōn, . . .,

lines 16-17). Whichever it is, he seems to regard it as a natural

phenomenon, one which can be further developed (askēteon, line 17),

either by teaching and skill or by attention, respectively (ta men

didaskalia kai technē, ta de phrontidi, lines 17-18) (cf. also lines

4-5: "those now commanding clearly need to learn divining from

horses, but they are inexperienced" [asynētheis]).[3]

---

[1]E.g., the evocation of "the old serving woman of Apollonius
of Tyana" was to be performed at a spot beside a river or a lake or a
triodos (PLond 125. 1-4; Kenyon, Greek Papyri, 1:123-24). Compare
also the custom of erecting "herms" and other shrines at crossroads.

[2]Perhaps regarded as significant because of their "unnatural"
character (cf. Riess's sixth category of superstitious beliefs ["Aberglaube," col. 37]).

[3]Numerous things which horses "divine" are given in lines 6-
11, probably derived from folk beliefs; but they are at most superstitious, not actively magical. Some of them are purely natural re-
actions to sounds or smells inaccessible to human senses, but they
are intermixed with the superstitious beliefs without distinction.

Other Features

Designations of the "art"

Africanus, on at least one occasion, refers to the procedure
he presents as an "art," techne (mp 7; I. 6. 24, p. 133: "by art of
nature" [cf. also mp 8; I. 8. 18: divination developed by teaching
and techne]), quite probably in the sense of "magical art."[1] The word
techne may be used in this sense in mp 41 (III. 36. 8, p. 255 [cf.
III. 13.3--technoo?]; though it may simply be used in the general
sense there); and in several lines in his summary, Psellus used the
adjectival form, technike, to describe some of the procedures, perhaps reflecting Africanus's own terminology[2] (IX. 1. 2, 5, 34; also,
technikos, line 3; and technasma, line 10, though this last perhaps
in a general sense, "device," "artifice"). (Elsewhere, however, Africanus uses the term simply in the general sense of "craft" or
"skill."[3])

Africanus also used the term empeiria to describe his procedure for overcoming sleep (mp 14b; I. 17. 28, p. 165).

----

[1]See above, p. 287, with n. 2; also p. 265, with n. 2, and
p. 272, n. 1.

[2]Since Africanus uses the form techthenai of generation (of
desired sexes) in III. 3. 1, p. 227, it may be that this and/or related forms should be assumed as lying behind Psellus's gennesis
and gennethesetai in IX. 1. 2. This would provide a neat rhetorical
counterpoint, of the type favored by Africanus, to the technike.

[3]E.g., Vi., I. 2. 19, 25; I. 6. 23 (the line preceding the
first "magical" usage cited above); I. 7. 5 (technetos); III. 13. 3
(technoo).

Antipathies

Various forms of the term "antipathy" are used by Africanus
in several passages.[1] The adjective form, antipathēs, appears in
one manuscript[2] in the textually uncertain line in mp 10 (I. 10. 1;
concerning the wolf and the horse), in the title of III. 23 (mp 37,
the apotropaic against scorpions),[3] and in mp 44f (IX. 1. 15). In
this last passage, Psellus uses it to describe Africanus's use of
the "two-faced plaster" (tē diprosōpō emplastrō [ibid., line 16][4]
against wounds from poisonous beasts. In this case the antipathy may
well be in the general (or medical) rather than the magical sense
(though Psellus does not seem to regard it so). In a later line
(35; mp 44l), Psellus also uses the noun form, antipatheiōn, of Africanus's means of producing barrenness in fields. This is in contrast to the technikēn, or rather, goētikēn, productivity he was
said to produce, so presumably Psellus regards this operation as
being in the same category.[5] (The verb form is also used in two

---

[1]On the other hand, while several passages seem to involve
"sympathetic" procedures, the term is not used by Africanus to describe any of them.

[2]Laurentianus   V, 4 ;   Vieillefond's L (Les Cestes, p.
139 mg).

[3]The title presumably was supplied by the compiler, but could
well come from the introductory lines of the abstracted text. The
passage, however, is one of uncertain authenticity.

[4]A plaster of such a name is described by Galen (11:127,
Kühn), but may not be the same. Galen's plaster (also called di-
chromous) was so-named because the material used in it (some type of
iron compound?) appeared gray on the surface, but was orange within
when it was crushed.

[5]Vieillefond (Les Cestes, p. 363, n. 270), however, compares
this barrenness to II. 2 (p. 203), which, though partly enigmatic, is

passages, III. 30. 8, and III. 32. 34, but apparently in the general
sense of a counter-remedy [but the latter is part of mp 38e]).

Ancient books

The Egyptian book attributed to Souphis, the contemner of the
gods (mp 47/chr 2), which Africanus purchased in Egypt, is quite
likely to have been a work of occult lore, but the identification of
it as one of the Hermetic works[1] is probably too specific for the
evidence available. Africanus apparently had no suspicion about the
authenticity of this work, for he also attributed books, an anatomical
work, to an even earlier king, Athothis, the second king of the First
Dynasty of Egypt, apparently regarding them as being still extant.[2]
This provides an additional datum to be taken into consideration in
evaluations of Africanus's critical abilities (and respect for tradition?) and the likelihood and/or "reasonability" of his acceptance of
the nekyomanteia interpolations as really Homeric.

Purposes of Uses

The ends proposed for achievement by these means cover the

---

not especially magical. Africanus there prescribes the cultivation of
hellebore (citing Alexander and the Alans as historical precedent [cf.
also, I. 2. 16]), or the sowing of fields with salt. The latter is a
traditional destructive technique long practiced by both the Romans
(cf. the treatment of Carthage) and the Jews (Judges 9:45), though more
as symbolic (perpetual desolation on the sites of enemy cities) than on
a large scale as a strategic device in an ongoing campaign.

[1]E.g., by Scaliger (Animadv., p. 251, cited and rejected by
Goar in his "Emendationes et Annotationes" as reprinted by Dindorf,
Syncellus, 2:385), and Routh (Rel. sacr. 2:386, note to 250. 2 [cit-
ing also Scaliger, Not. in Gr. Eus., p. 412]).

[2]Routh, frag XI (Rel. sacr. 2:247. 3-5); Syncellus 1:101,
ed. Dindorf.

areas of special concern in magical operations, i.e., pretty much the
full range of human concerns. They deal with procedures for both
harming and helping, and, in the latter area, with both passive
(protective) and active means (healing, empowering, etc.).

The procedures for harming are only a small minority of the
passages, mainly occurring in the military section. They include
poisoning of man and beast (mpp 1, 2, 3), killing of vegetation (mpp
17 and 44l), stopping or maddening horses (mpp 10, 18, and 11), causing sleeplessness or sleep, either for serious harm or as a joke (mpp
15a, 16, and 44p), causing elimination (mp 44k), changing the color
of horses as a fraud (mp 41), possibly some cases of kindling or
quenching love (mp 44s), and causing a thief to convict himself (mp
44h [harmful to the thief!]).

The protective procedures include countering plague (mpp 3
mg, and 44i); and protecting from fright (mp 9), from scorpions (mp
37 [cf. 44g?]), from conception (mp 44c) or miscarriage (mp 29), from
sickness or weakness (mp 21), specifically, from eye trouble or epilepsy (mp 23 a-e [or, to heal one already suffering]) or varicose
veins (44r [or is this healing?]).

Some of the procedures gave power, either to achieve something or to control events. These include: giving aid/victory in
battle or contests (mp 4), controlling unmanageable animals (7 and
13 a and b), giving easy birth (44c), controlling dreams (44q),
kindling or quenching loves (44s), determining of sex conceived (24,
27, 44a, and 45), and taking advantage of a horse's natural divinatory
powers (8).

The largest number of procedures are concerned with the <u>cure</u>
of illnesses, wounds, or other physical problems:[1] wounds, frac-
tures, bites, and stings (mpp 5, 6, 32, 36, 37, 44 f, g, and i);
cure or help, in general (12 a, b; 21; 44n); eye trouble (23 a, c, d,
e; 44j); generation, conception, birth, etc. (27, 29, 44 b and q; cf.
also 44c, above); dysurea (30 [if Africanian]); mange, warts, and
maggots (31; 33, 34; 35); soothing feet of horses (39); bowel problems, actual or potential (40, 43); bleeding, and varicose veins
(44 d and r); and restoring virginity (44<u>o</u>).[2]

Summary of Africanus's Knowledge of Magic

While the preceding studies have left some items undetermined,
several aspects of Africanus's magical procedures have been brought
into rather clear focus. These include items related to the areas
of magical operation, the types of procedures prescribed, and also
the general type of magical theory which lies behind the procedures
given by Africanus.

Areas of Magic

The areas of human endeavor and concern for which Africanus
provides prescriptions cover many of those presented in the various
sources concerned with magic, whether those making charges of magic,

---

[1]Compare these with Björck's list of conditions most suscep-
tible of attempted magical treatment: bleeding, venomous bites,
childbirth, and choking ("Apsyrtus," p. 66). All except the last are
fairly well represented in Africanus's procedures. Cf. also the list
given by Hubert, "Magia," p. 1495 (col. 2).

[2]Pliny refers to a procedure (using fumes of jet) to detect
attempts to simulate virginity (<u>N.H.</u> 36. 141).

or those giving magical prescriptions.

Magic was mainly of concern to the ancient legal systems only as it involved charges of harmful acts, maleficii, and/or as they involved subversion of affection, especially in the erotic realm. In other areas of private life, medicine, agriculture, etc., it was generally ignored as being a practical question, not a legal one.

Harming/helping

Several of Africanus's procedures are of the type that could well be classed as maleficii if they were practiced on an individual basis. Most of them, however, are prescribed for military use against opposing armies, and thus perhaps can escape that label. These include procedures 1-3, 11, 16-19, and possibly 44l. Some others are passed off as practical jokes (e.g., 15a and 44k [and p?]), or harm only indirectly, by providing an extra (unfair) advantage to the user (4 and 10).

Only another step removed from this last is the apotropaic function, helping by averting some threatening evil. Most of these are medical; possible examples of non- or only semi-medical apotropaic procedures are: the counter-procedure to poison air (mp 3 mg), and mpp 7, 9, 13a, 29, 37, and 44 c and i.

Love magic

Psellus says that Africanus kindles and quenches love (mp 44s; IX. 1. 49). His reference to Africanus's restoring of virginity (mp 44o) is somewhat related to this area, but the nearest examples of this type of procedure are a few "aphrodisiac" prescriptions in the

veterinary fragments, e.g., mpp 25 and 26. (The other prescriptions
relating to generation and birth are medical rather than erotic procedures.)

Medical (and veterinary) magic

The largest single type of Africanian procedures is the medical one (and within that, the veterinary). Besides the whole group
of fragments from the hippiatrica (most of the procedures from 22 to
41), there are several in the other chapters that relate to either
human (mpp 5, 6, 20, 43, 44 a-d, f, j, q, and 45) or veterinary medicine (mpp 12 and 21).

Agricultural magic

Psellus also tells us that Africanus produces a sorcerous
fertility in fields (mp 44l), as well as various other marvels and
recipes about agricultural matters (IX. 1. 22-26, 27-29 [cf. I. 19],
and 40). There are probably examples of them preserved in the Geoponica, but they can no longer be certainly identified. On the other
side, the "agricultural" references in the preserved portions from
the other sources do not fit this category--they are only magical
uses of botanical items for other purposes (especially medical), or
are not magical at all (e.g., I. 19, the chapter of "Agricultural
Paradoxes").

Other areas

Several procedures do not fall exactly into any of the categories named above, though they are closely related to them. Most of

them are examples of "harming," "protecting," or "giving power" (cf.
those given in the preceding section "Purposes of Uses") which are
not precisely examples of maleficii or apotropaics.

Types of Procedures

Magical operations can, in general, be performed by direct
manipulation of the "subject" to be affected, by vocalizations (incantations, etc.), by graphic representations of powerful words,
items, etc., and/or by the use of special substances. These last may
receive their reputation by sympathy or antipathy, or by some other
sort of association with the subject or the condition to be achieved
or removed.[1]

Africanus's procedures present examples of all these types:
direct manipulation--mpp 6, 20(?), 35; incantations--6, 15b(?), 42,
44 d and j; inscriptions--7 and 37. The use of special substances
is illustrated in most of the procedures, including several of those
just listed.

Besides these factors, Africanus's procedures also involve
other considerations, such as right/left, times, and numbers (see
the discussions of these areas in the preceding pages, under "Charms
and Rites").

Types of Magic

Magic is frequently divided into direct (or impersonal) and

---

[1] Compare the discussion by Hubert ("Magia," pp. 1507 [col. 2]-
1509 [col. 1]), though he presents the items in an order somewhat the
reverse of this, and derives the others, in essence, from the sympathetic principle.

indirect (or personal, demonic) types.[1] There are some situations

to which this distinction might not apply,[2] or in which a decision

as to the type represented might not be possible, but, in general,

it appears to be a valid distinction and one that is productive when

applied to the Africanian examples.

In these terms, Africanus's magical procedures are essen-

tially, if not exclusively, of the impersonal type. While a number

of procedures are ambiguous, of such a nature that they cannot be

definitely assigned to either category, others are clearly of the

impersonal type (and the very ambiguity tends to favor a direct, im-

personal interpretation of most of the others; if demons or other

personal beings were involved, some explicit reference to them would

be expected). Only in a few cases does an indirect, personal ap-

proach seem to be presented, and, as noted in the discussions above,

there are questions that arise about each of these cases.

Direct magic

At the very beginning of Africanus's "magical" passages, in

lines which form the prelude not only to mp 1, but also to 2 and 3,

---

[1]E.g., Kirby Flower Smith, "Magic (Greek and Roman)," p.
279; Hubert, "Magia," p. 1506 (col. 2).

[2]Either because both factors might be mixed together in a
particular system, or because the situation proved to be even more
complex. Norbeck, for example, in discussing the distinction of
Religion and Magic, suggests that besides the Personal power-Imper-
sonal power pair (with the Impersonal approximating the concept of
mana), there could also be added a concept of Automatic, or Mechanical, efficiency. This concept he regarded as approximating to the
concept of cause and effect sequences in science (Religion, pp. 48-
51). If such a further distinction is justified, Africanus's position might be closer to the third category.

Africanus proposes to imitate the gods, producing "automatic fortune"
by his "arts" (<u>automatos tychē hypo tēs hēmeteras technēs ginetai</u>,
Vi., I. 2. 59, p. 117). The poisoning procedures which follow confirm
this impression of an impersonal, automatic operation, not involving
personal, spiritual mediation.[1]

In mp 4, despite the reference to sacrifice in the first
paragraph, and the ritual burning of the cock skeleton in the second,
the rationale presented for the operation of the stones is, in the
one case, the nature of the stone (<u>tēs physeōs tou lithou</u>, I. 3. 8,
p. 125), and in the other the cock's "virtue" of "invincibility"
(<u>aretē</u>, <u>aēttēsias</u>, ibid., lines 17 and 16, p. 127). The inscription
in mp 7 has a necessity of obedience (<u>anankēn echei peitharchias</u>, I.
6. 28, p. 133). This could fit into the "personal" type operation,
but it is not spoken to a spirit, but written in the animal's hoof,
and there is no hint of any other parties to the action than the in-
scriber and the animal whose hoof is inscribed. The preceding lines
also refer only to "him," the recalcitrant horse, with the sole control instrumentality being the inscription. Similarly, in mp 10, it
is the <u>wolf</u> which contributes to the horse's swiftness (I. 10. 6, p.
139: by the use of his teeth) (cf. also mp 18 [II. 4, p. 205]:
the wolf's astragalus to stop a team).

Again in mp 11, despite an opening reference to prayer and
sacrifice, Africanus's procedure is presented as in contrast (and

---

[1]Even the counter-action to procedure 3 is presented, not in
terms of spirits in conflict, but in terms of fumes counteracting
"pestilential wind" (<u>pneuma</u>), or rather "corrupted air" (Vi., p.
123 mg).

superior) to such means. The procedure presented, use of euphorbium
juice (or dust), is clearly "direct" in operation, so much so that its
only connection with magic is the placement of its identification in
one of the pentagons (pentagon eight; I. 11. 16-20, p. 141). Mp 20
(II. 8, p. 209), if it is magical at all,[1] is of a similar nature.

The active principle in the sleeplessness paragraphs (mpp 14
and 15) is the "sympathetic" operation of parts of the bat (mp 15a;
I. 17. 33-43, p. 165), the surrounding references to Sleep being apparently rhetorical embellishments (see the discussion of these passages above, and further, below). (Note also the mp 23 series [23
b-e], which, even if Africanian, are basically sympathetic procedures,
only the opening item, 23a, having any indirect connection.)

The "sympathetic" principle, based on etymology or similarity
of appearance, etc., on an earthly plane, not involving any mediation
through a higher realm, appears in mp 27, polygonum in dog's afterbirth, with the possible addition of "male" or "female" plants (III.
6, p. 231); mp 28, milk stone (III. 7, p. 231); and mp 29, the fish
echeneïs or remora (III. 8, pp. 231, 233). Its counterpart, antipathy, may be involved in the latter part of mp 36, the use of asp and
hemorrhoïs as counters to each other's poison (III. 22. 4-7, p. 241).

In passage 41, Africanus attempts to provide a physical explanation of the procedure, "ulceration by the burning" (III. 36. 6,
p. 255), and in an earlier passage, mp 8, speculated about such a
basis, the "nature of the eyes," for a horse's ability to see demons

---

[1]Note Vieillefond, Les Cestes, p. 354, n. 172: physikos here
probably does not mean magic.

(I. 8. 17, p. 137).[1] In Psellus's summary (mp 44; IX. 1, pp. 317-21),
about half of the items are "curiosities" or "paradoxes," several of
them similar to items in the Geoponica, rather than strictly magical.
Even in the magical items, nothing suggests the use of "spiritual"
intermediaries.[2]

Indirect (daemonic) magic?

The various passages in which Africanus's procedures are connected in one way or another with spiritual beings have been discussed above in the section headed "Gods and Daemons," and thus need
only be recapitulated and summarized here.

Africanus believed in the existence of spiritual beings, some
of whom, at least, were evil, and with some, at least, of these evil
spirits called daemons (mp 46/chr 1, and mp 8). These same passages
indicate that these beings could (or, in the past, had) come into contact with mankind, but that the results of those contacts were evil
(in mp 46, evil resulting in the cataclysm; in mp 8, "the threat"
[I. 8. 13-14, p. 137]). At the same time, the former passage presents these beings, there described as "angels," as related to magic
and sorcery.

Despite these beliefs, however, there are no examples of the

---

[1]Even the alternative suggested, a "work of the soul" (psychēs ergon, lines 16-17), is not necessarily different, and he regarded it as capable of development by teaching and craft (lines 17-
18).

[2]Unless the reference to incantations (epōdē, line 13;
epasmasin, line 32) is held to necessarily involve that idea, but that
is an untenable position.

involvement of such beings in the accomplishment of Africanus's procedures. Although such beings are named rather prominently in a number of the passages (mpp 14 a and b, 15b, 24, and 42), they are not
called upon in any actual procedure presented by Africanus, nor are
any directions given to utilize them in any way. They appear rather
as rhetorical or literary embroidery of the accounts. This applies
also to mp 42 despite its clear character as a magical invocation.
Though Africanus presents it at rather great length, he presents no
programme for putting it to magical use. His only surviving references to it are concerned with its literary and manuscript ancestry.

This leaves only mp 23a, the invocation and sacrifice to
Aphrodite, as a possible example of daemonic magic. But, as noted
above, this passage is not accepted as of proven authenticity by
Björck,[1] and the very reference to Aphrodite and the sacrifice seem
out of character with the Africanian outlook as revealed in the Kestoi itself: it presents a generally "secular" approach. This
point is strengthened by the fact that this passage stands essentially alone as an example of direct daemonic involvement in Africanus's magical procedures; the ambiguity, or lack, of evidence for
its appearance elsewhere weakens the case for its appearance here.
On the other hand, if this passage should be authentic, it does not
thereby increase the likelihood that such daemonic involvement should
be seen in some of the other passages above. An invocation of

---

[1] "Apsyrtus," pp. 15-16. The factor under discussion may,
however, have influenced Björck's evaluation here. Except in one
instance, he provides a rationale only for those passages which he
accepts.

Aphrodite would be hard to correlate with Africanus's Christian reputation, but it would be, on the surface at least, idolatrous, not
magical.[1] (Whatever else Psellus may think or say about Africanus,
he does not charge him with that.[2])

Attitudes toward These Procedures

Africanus's programme, at least for Kestos 7, as sketched in
the "Proem" to that book, is an amalgam of the utilitarian, the esoteric, and the aesthetic: "gathering . . . fruitful helps; (either)
treatment of ills, or secret accounts, or beautiful expressions . . ."
(I. proem. 3-4, p. 103). This mixture appears throughout his work,
sometimes in incongruous forms: medical prescriptions and military
accounts are decorated with rhetorical flourishes and augmented with
ideas carefully searched out or fortunately acquired; and fond mem-
ories of marvelous sights are generously shared, or a "long lost"
(magical) passage is presented as an epic prize.

But overarching all this is the practical intent: "manifold
fruitful helps." These helps are presented as natural, "technical"
processes, of a secular nature.

Natural Processes

Africanus's general attitude toward his procedures is shown

---

[1] Whatever its origin, it appears to be more closely paralleled
by the sacrifices to Poseidon (in the prelude to mp 11), or to the
customary sacrifice of the victorious cock (referred to in mp 4),
than to the invocation in the nekyomanteia (mp 42).

[2] Aphrodite does appear in Psellus, but only in the euphemism
in the account of the gorgonion (Vi., IX. 1. 41-44, p. 319). This reference itself provides a parallel to Africanus's "literary" use of
pagan religious terminology.

by the terminology used to describe them. He uses various <u>techn-</u>
forms and also describes them as "natural" (<u>phys-</u>). These usages
have been presented above (under "Designations of the 'Art'") and
need not be repeated here. It is sufficient simply to note again
that he uses the same terminology for magical and non-magical items[1]
(sometimes in the same passages, e.g., I. 6. 23, cf. line 24; note
also I. 2. 19, cf. line 59). Thus he appears not to draw any real
distinction between the procedures he presents (to have done so would
have been to manifest a "modern" distinction between magic and sci-
ence/technology).

Not only in the use of the terms, but also in presentation
of procedures, Africanus alternates, or intermixes, the magical and
non-magical. Thus the three poisoning procedures in I. 2 alternate
with definitely non-magical suggestions, and sound (though not necessarily profound) medical or surgical advice precedes mp 5 and follows mp 6 in I. 4 and 5.

The type of "physical" explanation that Africanus provides
for some of his magical procedures is also provided for non-magical
ones (e.g., I. 16. 18-20, p. 161--the attempt to explain why his
"theft of sound" procedure should work). Further, in III. 33. 6 (p.
253), he provides an "ethical" explanation of the toad's avoidance of
the light, and in part VII (Vi., p. 303), he presents a botanical account of the origin of cinnamon. The only thing that separates this
last explanation from the others, whether magical or non-magical, is

---

[1]Note also the same variation in the use of the term "antipathy" (above).

the fact that in this instance he happens to be correct.

Non-religious (Secular) Outlook

Pagan references

Africanus makes a number of references to pagan gods or
heroes, but they are mainly, if not entirely, of a literary, not a
religious, nature, much like those of a modern student of the clas-
sics. A number of them have been discussed above from various viewpoints; these are: the reference to prayer and sacrifice to Poseidon
Horse-troubler before races (to which Africanus presents mp 11 as a
better alternative); the references to Hypnos, as well as various
associates, and to legendary figures (the Phrygian king and Silanos;
another chieftain and a satyr) in mp 14 a and b, and to Night, Hypnos,
Pasithea, Eros, Hera, and Aphrodite in mp 15b; an appeal to the male
and female gender and use of corresponding horses by Sun/Flame and
Night/Moon in mp 24; and, especially, the lengthy roll-call of dieties
and powers from assorted backgrounds in the Nekyomanteia (mp 42).
There are also references to Pan and a possible reference to Erinys
in the context of mp 1 (I. 2. 6, 12, p. 113, and line 78, p. 119). The
references to these figures illustrate especially clearly the literary nature of this type of reference in Africanus; they are simply
personifications of the corresponding concepts. Besides these, there
is also the reference to Dionysus as giving vine and wine to no
peoples but the Greeks (I. 19. 17-25, p. 173). Vieillefond points
this out as an example of the pagan inspiration of Africanus.[1] While

---

[1]Les Cestes, p. 57.

this is true, it is just as true that it is a pagan literary, not a pagan religious, reference.

Anti-pagan references

Some of these same passages, along with others, contain references which in one way or another are actually derogatory of the pagan gods and beliefs.[1] In mp 1, Africanus will "imitate these gods" who are credited with giving victories (I. 2. 58-59, p. 117), and in mp 11 (I. 11. 17, p. 141), considers the drug he presents as sharper than prayer (to Poseidon, specifically), or greater than whatever they may have. The reference to the poets lulling Zeus to sleep (I. 17. 1, p. 163) is nothing that any pagan literary man could not have said, but would probably find its closest parallels among the Christian apologetic writers. To these examples may also be added the functionalistic explanation of the midwife at Dionysus's birth, in I. 19. 15-16 (p. 173).[2] Souphis's book, which Africanus prized, was written as a "contemner of the gods" (mp 47/chr 2).

World-view Vector Summary

While Africanus's complete world view cannot be deduced from the surviving fragments, at least the main outlines of those areas

---

[1] Most of these passages have been noted above under the heading "Rivaling the Gods."

[2] Africanus's challenge to Sleep (mp 14b; I. 17. 30-32, p. 165), as discussed previously, is probably rhetorical personification. If it is held to be more than this, it would still be more hybris than representative of an anti-pagan attitude. (If it is such, this attitude [hybris] might be based on confidence in the magical procedure, but a procedure relying solely on the material involved, not on some other spirit, for control of and defense against the one challenged.)

which border on magic can be sketched.

Spiritual realm

Africanus believed in the existence of a spiritual realm,
inhabited by at least a God (the Judaeo-Christian God), and by lesser
spiritual beings, angels (good and bad), and daemons. God is concerned with good and evil (mp 46/chr 1). There are numerous references to other gods, but it is uncertain whether they are viewed as
having more than a literary existence (and if so, what their relation
to other spiritual entities might be). The evil angels were related
in some way to magic and sorcery, and taught women other occult arts;
from their liaison with women, giants were born, resulting in wickedness bringing God's judgment in the flood (ibid.). It is not indicated if their spirits survived and/or if they have connection with
the daemons. Daemons do evil, however, and are a danger to man; in
accord with ancient views, they have some special connection with
crossroads (mp 8).

Physical realm

Besides the normal amount of information and misinformation
about nature, animals, etc., which Africanus shared with the ancient
world, there are aspects of his belief which are especially connected
with occult or magical beliefs. He believed in the power of sympathy
and antipathy, though not necessarily in an exclusively magical
sense; this principle was viewed by the ancients as operating in many
areas (medicine, physics, etc.), and is even utilized by some of the
church fathers in explanations of physical or biological phenomena.

Insofar as "contagion" can be distinguished from "sympathy," Africanus

apparently believed in it also: power could be acquired by certain

stones from the birds in which they were found (or, had already trans-

mitted power to them); and the power of these stones, and of other

substances, could in turn be imparted to other beings by binding them

to persons or animals. Such power could be increased by observation

of certain appropriate times in their acquisition and/or use. Also,

certain words (or sounds), either spoken or written, had power to

compel results if used in proper ways. At least as far as any ex-

plicit indications are concerned, this result was expected to follow

automatically, without intervention of a spirit intermediary.

Civil and social aspects

Since the main body of Africanian materials are military strat-

agems, and many of the others are medical (veterinary or human) in

nature, they would be relatively immune to legal enquiry, even at a

period when magic might be regarded as actively criminal (which was

not true in Africanus's day). Perhaps only in the cases of horse-

thievery (mp 41) and tampering with affections (mp 44s) might such a

charge lie. Africanus does not appear to be in any disadvantaged

political group, at least insofar as this work (the Kestoi) is con-

cerned.[1]

Socially, also, Africanus does not appear to be of a disad-

vantaged status, so his interest in magic cannot be explained by such

a sociological factor. Not only are there the various personal

---

[1]Except, perhaps, under Vieillefond's view of him as a Jew
writing for Diaspora Jews; but that view is questionable.

references suggesting circulation in the higher social circles, even

having personal contact with the emperor, but the nature of some of

his procedures suggest this also. Two of them are applicable not only

to war but to sporting events also: the stone from cocks (mp 4), and

the aids for horses swiftness (mp 10; cf. also mp 41).[1] Further, the

reference to parasites (putting to sleep: mp 44p) would suggest a

moderately high social level.[2]

About the only viewpoint from which Africanus can be regarded

as a member of a disadvantaged or powerless class (and thus in need

of magical aid to redress the balance) would be from that of his human

condition,[3] powerless before the forces of nature (or supernature)--

subject to poor crops, disease, wild beasts, the uncertainties of

generation and heredity, etc. In these areas, his procedures could

be seen as an attempt to take up some of the slack in the nebulous

reins of man's control of his own fate.

---

[1]Does the latter passage suggest that he moved in circles
where making away with a good horse was viewed more as a "dirty trick"
than a crime?

[2]Thus indicating that he was on a level compatible with the
"hosts" (unless it is viewed as a procedure for embarrassing rivals,
but there is nothing to suggest this).

[3]Or, possibly, as a provincial, subservient to Rome. But he
seems to have had (or made) adequate personal compensations for any
pressures from that area. (Or was he possibly a nouveau homme whose
relation to the emperor was an ultimate compensation for early disadvantage? His references to places seen, relation to the court of
Abgar, etc., seem to suggest not.)

CHAPTER IV

THE EARLY CHRISTIAN VIEW OF MAGIC

Introduction

In order to establish an early Christian background with which
to compare and assess the magical ideas in Africanus, it is necessary
to consider the nature and extent of the knowledge of magic, and the
attitudes toward it, among the early Christian writers. That is the
purpose of the present chapter.

In the consideration of magic in the early fathers, the following general order of discussion is observed. The major part is a
consideration of the knowledge of magic shown by the various fathers,
individually or by groups. This area is introduced by a survey of
their references to magic, to suggest the general attitude and range
of knowledge of the particular writer(s); this is followed by a consideration of any passages in which magic or related areas are discussed; then follows a consideration of additional references and allusions to items or areas which are probably related to magic.[1]
Within the discussions, the order of items and the emphasis varies

_____

[1]References to passages in the fathers are given in in-text
citations. Titles of Greek works are usually given, and abbreviated,
in English translation; in the cases of a few especially well known
works the traditional Latin forms of the title and their abbreviations
are retained (e.g., Irenaeus Adv. haer.; Origen C.C. and De pr.).
Titles of Latin works are regularly used in their Latin forms (exceptions are those with obvious English counterparts, such as Apology).

somewhat, according to the emphasis of the particular writer. Some
summaries are included at significant points in the presentations,
and the section is concluded with an over-all summary of the basic
knowledge of magic on the part of the early fathers. The chapter itself then concludes with a summary of the attitude(s) of the fathers
toward these items, and a consideration of its relation to their belief system(s).

In deciding what items to include in the presentation, a broad
interpretation of magic is used. This includes the various areas defined or listed in the Introduction, modified and amplified in accord
with the emphases of the various writers discussed. In general, anything called magic by the fathers, and any items closely related to it
in their discussion, are included.

Apostolic Fathers and Apologists

Apostolic Fathers

Passing references to magic

Direct reference to magic by the writers of this period is
rather limited. Most such references are of an incidental nature,
occurring either alone or in lists, supplemented by some mentions or
discussions of related areas.

Single references

In the area of isolated references, Ignatius asserts that
from the birth of Christ "every sorcery and every spell [pasa mageia

kai pas desmos] was dissolved"[1] (Eph. 19. 3). This is a minor, and

somewhat idealized, anticipation of a theme developed by the later

apologists: the superiority of Christ/Christians to magical/demonic[2]

power.

Ignatius also exhorts Polycarp to "Flee evil arts, or rather

hold thou discourse about these" (Pol. 5. 1). The term used here,

kakotechnia, may be a reference to magical practices,[3] though Light-

foot concludes that it is probably the designs of false teachers as in

Philadelphians 6. 2,[4] and the context (to which it is only loosely

connected on either of these two views) might suggest that it has ref-

erence to adultery or its allied wiles (which, of course, would

------

[1]Passages from the Apostolic Fathers are quoted (with occasional modifications) from the translation of J. B. Lightfoot, The
Apostolic Fathers, edited and completed by J. R. Harmer (London: Macmillan and Company, 1891; reprint ed., Grand Rapids: Baker Book House,
1956).

[2]In this chapter I revert to the usual spelling, demon, in
contrast to daemon which was used in connection with the Greek view
in which it is at least partially synonymous with theos.

[3]See, e.g., Robert M. Grant, ed., The Apostolic Fathers: A New
Translation and Commentary, vol. 1: An Introduction, by Robert M.
Grant; vol. 2: First and Second Clement, by Robert M. Grant and Holt H.
Graham; vol. 3: Barnabas and the Didache, by Robert A. Kraft; vol. 4:
Ignatius of Antioch, by Robert M. Grant; vol. 5: Polycarp, Martyrdom
of Polycarp, Fragments of Papias, by William R. Schoedel; vol. 6: The
Shepherd of Hermas, by Graydon F. Snyder; 6 vols. (New York [before
1966], and Camden, N.J.: Thomas Nelson & Sons, 1964-68), 4:133; and
Gerald G. Walsh, "The Letters of St. Ignatius of Antioch," The Apos-
tolic Fathers, trans. Francis X. Glimm, et al., The Fathers of the
Church, ed. Ludwig Schopp [vol. 1] (New York: CIMA Publishing Co.,
Inc., 1947), p. 126.

[4]J. B. Lightfoot, The Apostolic Fathers, 2 parts in 5 vols.
(London and New York: Macmillan and Co., 1889-90), part 2: S. Ignatius,
S. Polycarp, 2:346-47.

not completely exclude magic).[1]

Listings

The Didache has three passages in which magic and related practices appear as parts of longer lists of various evils: "thou shalt not deal in magic, thou shalt do no sorcery [ou mageuseis, ou pharmakeuseis], thou shalt not murder a child by abortion nor kill them when born . . ." (2. 2); "My child, be no dealer in omens [oiōnoskopos], since it leads to idolatry, nor an enchanter nor an astrologer nor a magician [mēde epaoidos mēde mathēmatikos mēde perikathairōn[2]], neither be willing to look at them; for from all these things idolatry is engendered" (3. 4); "But the way of death is this. . . . idolatries, magical arts, witchcrafts [mageiai, phar- makeiai], plunderings . . ." (5. 1). In the first of these passages, the reference to abortion might be based on a connection of it with magic/sorcery as its most likely means (though it may be simply an amplification of references to murder and adultery, which have pre- ceded these items in the list; the whole passage is an interpolation and expansion of the Ten Commandments[3]). The latter two passages

---

[1]Compare the somewhat more general view of P. Th. Camelot, Ignace d'Antioche, Polycarpe de Smyrne, Lettres, Martyre de Polycarpe, Sources chrétiennes, ed. C. Mondesert, no. 10; 4th ed., rev. and corr. (Paris: Les Editions du Cerf, 1969), p. 150, n. 2, "plutôt de métiers interdits aux Chrétiens, specialement de ceux qui étaient plus ou moins entachés de magie. . . ."

[2]Compare Wilfred L. Knox, "ΠΕΡΙΚΑΘΑΙΡΩΝ (Didache iii 4)," Journal of Theological Studies 40 (1939): 146-49.

[3]Grant considers the reference to magic to be an expansion of the commands not to commit adultery or steal (Apostolic Fathers, 1:101).

cited illustrate a common theme extensively developed by later writers, the close connection, or even identity, of magic and pagan worship (idolatry).

The Epistle of Barnabas has a close parallel to the last passage above in his version of the "two ways" document: "But the way of the Black One . . . wherein are . . . idolatry . . . witchcraft, magic, covetousness . . ." (Barn. 20. 1). While he gives idolatry greater prominence, putting it at the head of his list, he thereby plays down the connection with it of magic, etc., which come near the end of the list of vices.

In contrast to these two writings, Hermas, though he has several lists of evils similar to the preceding (e.g., 36. 5 and 38. 3, 5 [Man. 6. 2. 5 and 8. 3, 5], and 65. 5. 5 [Sim. 6. 5. 5]), does not include magic or related items in any of them. Apart from references to soothsaying/-ers in a discussion of true and false prophecy (discussed below), Hermas has no interest in magic; apparently it presented no perceived danger to him or his church.

Discussions of magic and related areas

There are no real discussions of magic in the Apostolic Fathers, the closest thing being the assertion of the connection of magic and idolatry in Didache 3 and 5, referred to above. There are, of course, various other references to idolatry (as, for example, 2 Clem. 1. 6 and 3. 1), but none of them make any explicit connection of it with magic: it is rejected simply as irrational.

There is, however, a fairly extensive discussion of a related area, sooth-saying, in Hermas (43 [Man. 11]).[1] Four points may be

noted in this passage. There is, here also, an emphasis on the tie

between such (magical) practices and pagan worship ("idolatry," sec.

4). Second, there is an attempt to find objective criteria for dis-

tinguishing false from true. The answer to this is presented as two-

fold, with the first part itself double. There is first the personal

conduct of the prophet, but incorporated into this is the question of

submission to the divine sovereignty in contrast to a "specific,"

---

[1]The discussion there concerns false-prophets, but is a sort
of sequel to the discussion of double-mindedness in Man. 9 (39). The
false-prophet corrupts the minds of the servants of God, but only of
the double-minded, not of the faithful (43. 1 [Man. 11. 1). They come
to him as to a soothsayer (mantin) and ask concerning their future;
he, not having the power of the Divine Spirit, speaks according to
their requests and wicked desires (sec. 2). He is empty and speaks
empty answers to empty men, but some true words, for the devil fills
him with his spirit, to try to break the righteous (3). The strong
in faith refrain from such spirits, "but as many as are doubters and
frequently change their minds, practice soothsaying [manteuontai] like
the Gentiles, and bring upon themselves greater sin by their idolatries.
For he that consulteth a false prophet on any matter is an idolater
and emptied of the truth and senseless" (4). This is so because the
Spirit from above is not consulted, but speaks by the Divine initiative
(5), while the spirit which replies to questions, according to men's
desires, is earthly and light (6).
    But how does one tell the difference? By their lives (7 and
16). The true prophet is meek, etc., not speaking by himself, but
when God wishes (8), especially in meetings of righteous men where the
"angel of the prophetic spirit, who is attached to him, filleth the
man, and the man . . . speaketh . . . as the Lord willeth" (9). The
one with the earthly spirit, on the other hand, exalts himself, etc.,
lives in luxury, accepts rewards, and does not prophesy without them
(11 & 12). He also shuns the assembly of righteous men, but "cleav-
eth to the doubtful-minded and empty, and prophesieth to them in cor-
ners" (13). When he comes to an assembly of righteous men who have
the Spirit of deity, and intercession is made from them, the man is
emptied and the earthly spirit flees from him in fear (14). "But do
thou trust the Spirit that cometh from God, and hath power; but in the
earthly and empty spirit put no trust at all; for in it there is no
power, for it cometh from the devil" (17).

"goal-directed," "individual," "instrumental" approach to prophecy
(or divination).[1] Then, there is also the religious conduct of the
prophet: does he attend and join in, or shun, the meetings of
righteous men? This question leads to the third noteworthy point:
the one who shuns does so for good reason, the earthly spirit will be
driven out by such men. Though Hermas does not use the word, this is
the idea of the exorcism of evil spirits which is much relied on by
later writers as a proof of the power (and truth) of Christianity.
Finally, this spirit is not just earthly, it is devilish (secs. 3 &
17), and therefore especially dangerous, for it thus presents some
true words (3).

The idea of exorcism among the Christian practices finds something of an anticipation in the passage cited above from Ignatius that
all sorcery was dissolved at Christ's birth (Eph. 19. 3).[2]

References and allusions to related areas

Theory and praxis

Drugs. Hermas provides one possible allusion to this area,

---

[1]Cf. the eleven point polar distinction of religion and magic
given by William J. Goode, Religion among the Primitives (Glencoe,
Ill.: The Free Press, 1951), pp. 53-54, especially points 1-5, 8, 9,
and 11.

[2]Though the connection is rather remote, it is possible to
see the opposite of this (i.e., a curse or binding, instead of a deliverance) in Clements's warning to his readers: "But if certain . . .
be disobedient . . ., let them understand that they will entangle
themselves in no slight transgression and danger; but we should be
guiltless of this sin" (1 Clem. 59. 1, 2). The concluding line and
the following prayer seem to indicate, however, that this is simply
a warning of potential divine judgment, not a curse (cf. 14. 2).

admonishing the church rulers to "be not ye like unto the sorcerers.
The sorcerers [pharmakoi] indeed carry their drugs [pharmaka] in
boxes, but ye carry your drug and your poison [pharmakon kai . . . ion]
in your heart" (17. 7 [Vis. 3. 9. 7]).

Ignatius compares those who poison Christian truth with heresy
to those who "administer a deadly drug in sweet wine" (Trall. 6. 2).
This could refer to common poisoning and is not specifically magical,
though the lexicons support the close connection of the ideas of sorcery and drugs which is reflected in the translation of the preceding
passage in Hermas.

Spiritual beings and powers. As might be expected in view of
the limited references to magic, none of the writers in this group
explicitly connect magic and the spirit world. They do, however,
present a view of that world which, in other hands, could easily be
so connected, either as a basis for magic, or in a polemic against it.

Ignatius presents an informal hierarchical list of powers on
the positive side. He names "the arrays of angels and the musterings
of the principalities, things visible and things invisible" as among
the "heavenly things" he comprehends (Trall. 5. 2), and says concerning
"heavenly beings and glory of angels and rulers visible and invisible,
if they believe not in the blood of Christ . . ., judgment awaiteth
them also" (Smyrn. 6. 1).

The early homilist to the Corinthians(?) is not really concerned with such abstruse, occult matters, but he does speak of a basic
polarity, "this world and the next are two enemies" (2 Clem. 6. 3), and
then later refers to the spiritual opponent, the devil (18. 2; with

this compare Ign. Trall. 4. 2).

Barnabas presents a glimpse of a wider field of negative powers, speaking of the heart, "before we believed on God," as being "a temple truly built by hands; for it was full of idolatry and was a house of demons . . ." (16. 7). He further refers to their leader as "the Black One" in introducing the second of the "two ways" (20. 1), a way which, as noted above, includes idolatry, witchcraft, and magic.

Hermas, in a pair of references which seem to go beyond simple personification,[1] presents anger and sorrow each as being (or being the result of?) the most evil spirit, which chokes or crushes the Holy Spirit if allowed entrance into the heart (33, 34 [Man. 5. 1, 2], and 40. 2 [10. 1. 2], respectively). He further presents the devil as continually tempting every man, but not able to overcome those aided by the "angel of repentance" (47-49, especially 47. 6 [Man. 12. 4-6, especially 4. 6]). This latter figure is, of course, a prominent one in the Shepherd, and also seems to go beyond a mere personification or literary device.

In short, the views in this area are simply an extension of those presented in the New Testament writings, with only slight, speculative development. Most of them would not be noteworthy in a discussion of magic were it not for development of these areas by later Christian writers.

---

[1]But note Man. 6. 2. 1ff (36. 1ff) and 9. 11 (39. 11) and the comments on them by Snyder, Hermas (=Apostolic Fathers, ed. Grant, 6), pp. 78, 79, and 83. Snyder presents this as anthropology rather than demonology.

Related field

Astrology. The only specific reference in this area is that
of Didache 3, cited above, where "astrology" is included in the list
of evil practices leading to idolatry. Other references to the heavenly bodies are of a strictly rhetorical nature. Clement speaks of
the order of creation, "the sun and the moon and the dancing stars according to His appointment circle in harmony within the bounds assigned
to them, without any swerving aside" (1 Clem. 20. 3). Ignatius waxes
eloquent in describing the nativity of Christ and speaks of "all the
rest of the constellations with the sun and moon form[ing] themselves
into a chorus about the star" (Eph. 19. 2; he then follows this with
his assertion concerning the dissolving of sorcery and spells [19. 3]).

Attitudes revealed

The discussion here is especially concerned with evidence of
excessive credulity, or of its absence. All such examples must be
judged, of course, in terms of ancient knowledge and world-views, not
of modern ones.

Superstitions, etc. The Martyrdom of Polycarp reveals the
beginnings of some such attitudes. Chapter 13 refers to the desire
on the part of the faithful to touch Polycarp's flesh even before his
martyrdom (13. 2), and this continues following his death (17. 1).
Though thwarted in obtaining his body (17. 2; 18. 1), the Christians
"afterwards took up his bones which are more valuable than precious
stones and finer than refined gold . . ." (18. 2). Although this was
probably done from worthy motives and was given an edificatory

explanation (17. 3; 18. 3), it was from such roots that the cults of
saints, martyrs, and relics, with their magical overtones and usages,
grew. (This attitude later extended even to the account of the martyrdom itself [22. 3].)

Some of Hermas's statements concerning baptism (93. 3-7, [Sim.
9. 16. 3-7]) could easily lead to a magical view of its operation and
effect, though that was not his meaning.

Old Testament and New Testament miracles. These areas became,
in the later apologists and polemicists, sort of test cases in the re-
buttal of charges of magic levelled at Christianity. In this period,
however, they were simply assumed with little explicit citation of
examples.

In the Old Testament area, Clement cites at length the case
of Aaron's budding rod (1 Clem. 43), but to reinforce the idea of
unity around God-appointed leaders, not as a polemic against magical
connotations. He further utilizes the signs and wonders worked by
Moses (the primary O. T. example used by later writers), but only to
prove the danger of recalcitrance (51. 3-5).

Papias (in a fragment preserved by Philip of Side) makes the
somewhat enigmatic comment that "those who were raised from the dead
by Christ . . . survived till the time of Hadrian."[1] This is possibly
to be explained by the sole surviving fragment from the Apology of
Quadratus (who lived under Hadrian) which appeals to the abiding

---

[1]Included by Lightfoot, Apostolic Fathers, in his "Fragments
of Papias," no. 5, and as fragment XI. 2 by Schoedel, Polycarp, . . .
Papias (=Apostolic Fathers, ed. Grant, 5), p. 119.

character of Christ's works to prove their reality, asserting that
those healed or resurrected not only survived while Christ lived, but
a considerable time after, some even down to his own times (preserved
in Eusebius H.E. 4. 3. 2).[1]

Summary

The evidence we have suggests a world view not materially
different from that of later Christian writers, so that, if the writers
in this period had been forced by circumstances, they would probably
have arrived at much the same positions as their successors, or, if
presented with such views, would have accepted them. But they were
not so confronted. The small number of references to magic and related areas, and the rhetorical use of them when they do appear,
leaves the impression that magic was basically an alien factor which
was regarded as presenting some danger to the church members (as having some attraction to them), but was far from being the church's
greatest worry, and was of no other interest to them (except to provide an occasional rhetorical flourish, either positive or negative).
Also, the more specific passages occur in what are probably among the
latest works in this group, Hermas and the Didache.[2] In addition, as
noted above, Hermas, especially, has little real concern about magic.

---

[1] Schoedel (Polycarp, . . . Papias, p. 119) suggests that it is
simply a misattribution to Papias (who appears in Eus. H.E. 3. 39. 9)
of (notes on?) the statement of Quadratus given in H.E. 4. 3. 2.

[2] Assuming a mid-second century date for the Didache in its
present form. This dating is supported by Kraft, Barnabas and the
Didache (=Apostolic Fathers, ed. Grant, 3), p. 76. Others would date
at least parts of it up to a half century earlier.

The Apologists

In the period of the apologists we find more conscious attempts to "explain" magic, but most of the passages are still relatively brief.

Passing references to magic

The apologists see a close and variously manifested connection between magic and pagan worship. This is illustrated clearly even by those who do not discuss the matter. In three passages in his discussion of Greek religion, in his *Apology*, Aristides connects the Greek gods with magic. In 8. 3 and 13. 7, he includes pharmakoi and pharmakeia in a list of actions or characteristics which the Greeks represent their gods as displaying. In a later, individual listing of gods, Hermes is presented as, among other things, a magos (10. 3). Similarly, the Syriac pseudo-Melito asserts (as part of a Euhemeristic explanation of idolatry) that the images of Nebo and Hadran at Mabug actually represent (as the priests know) Orpheus and Zaradusht, Thracian and Persian magoi, respectively, who had practiced in the area (*Apology*;[1] this passage is discussed further, below).

Tatian, in the opening rebuke of his *Discourse against the Greeks*, lists various things as among the institutions of the Greeks which

---

[1] B. P. Pratten, trans., "Remains of the Second and Third Centuries," *Ante-Nicene Fathers: Translations of the Writings of the Fathers Down to A.D. 325*, ed. Alexander Roberts and James Donaldson, rev. A. Cleveland Coxe, American ed., 10 vols. (New York: Christian Literature Company, 1885-87; reprint ed., Grand Rapids: Wm. B. Eerdmans Publishing Company, 1951), 8:752-53. (Cited hereafter as *ANF*. Translators of various portions are identified in first references [insofar as this information is provided by the editors]; subsequent references are included in the documentation in the text, cited as *ANF* with volume and page numbers.)

they have derived from the Barbarians. The first listing is:

> The most trustworthy of the Telmessians discovered divination
> (mantikēn) through dreams; Carians, prognostication by stars;
> by flights of birds, Phrygians and the most ancient Isaurians;
> sacrificial, Cyprians; to astronomize, Babylonians; to use magic,
> Persians; geometry, Egyptians; the instruction through letters,
> Phoenicians (Disc. 1, p. 1, lines 4-8).[1]

All except the last two of these have definite magical connotations,
though Tatian, for the moment, treats them neutrally, simply listing
them as among the "institutions" (epitēdeuma) of the Greeks.

Another use of the term "magic," as a simple pejorative, is
illustrated in the Epistle to Diognetus. The author sums up the theories of various philosophers as to the nature of God (fire, water,
etc.) by saying, "But these things are only the quackeries and deceits
of the magicians" (terateia kai planē tōn goētōn) (8. 4).

Discussions of magic and related areas

Two writers in this group, Justin and Tatian, discuss magic
(and related areas) at some length. Other related areas come in for
less extensive consideration by some of the other apologists.

Justin

Magic. Justin seems to accept the reality of magic and related
practices without question. He even appears to class himself with
those who formerly used magical arts (Apol. I 14. 2). But, though he
accepts its reality, he does not approve of it: its operations, as

---

[1]Cited according to page and line of Eduard Schwartz, ed.,
Tatiani oratio ad Graecos, TU 4, part 1 (1888). The translations of
the apologists are my own.

well as its origins, are thoroughly demonic.[1] Demons attempt to gain

control of men, sometimes by appearances in dreams, sometimes by mag-

ical impostures (dia magikōn strophōn) (14. 1); it is demons who have

put forward various heretics, especially Simon and Menander, support-

ing their teaching by great marvels worked by magic art (magikē technē)

(26. 2, 4; 56. 1); the devil and his angels work in imitation of mir-

acles, especially in Egypt at the time of the Exodus (Trypho 69. 1;

79. 4); and the Magi had been "held as spoil for the doing of all evil

deeds by the energizing of that demon" (but they revolted from his do-

main by coming to worship Christ) (78. 9). Strictly speaking, magic

did not originate with the demons, but with the fallen angels who

fathered them (Apol. II 5[4]. 2-4), as one of their means of enslaving

mankind (5. 4),[2] but the following lines indicate their close connec-

tion--the fallen angels and the demons become the gods and their off-

spring of the poets and mythologists (5. 5)--and elsewhere Justin does

not maintain this terminological distinction.[3]

---

[1]But in one passage he does present several means of divination, along with demoniacs or madness, as witness to the immortality
of the human soul (Apol. I 18. 2-5).

[2]Another of their means was teaching man to offer sacrifices,
incense, and libations (5. 4). (Passages in Apology II are cited by
traditional chapters following the manuscript order, but the alternate
chapter numeration resulting from Grabe's transfer of chap. 3 to a
position after chap. 8 are included after them in parentheses/square
brackets at the first reference to each.)

[3]Note especially Trypho 79, in which Old Testament texts referring to angels, the devil, and demons are all used to show that some
angels sinned and revolted; and 85, in which the demons of sec. 3 are
emphatically identified as the angels and powers in sec. 4.

Related areas. Justin does not discuss the theory of magic,
other than attributing it to the operations or energizings (strophōn,
Apol. I 14. 1; energein, e.g., 26. 2, 4)[1] of spiritual powers. These
powers are usually presented as demonic, but in Apology I 18, they are
apparently the souls of dead men. He does, however, give some information regarding divination in the passage just mentioned, and regarding exorcism in two later passages, Apology II 6 and Trypho 85.

The passage relating to divination (which is introduced as
testimony to the immortality of the soul) names its major divisions,
which serve as a sort of catalog of its procedures: necromancy
(nekyomanteia), divination (epopteusis) by uncorrupted children, invoking (klēsis) of human souls, those called dream-senders and assistants (oneiropompoi kai paredroi) by the Magi (para tois magois), and
whatever is done by those who know these things (Apol. I 18. 3; see
also Trypho 105. 4, 5). The following lines add "those who are
seized and flung about by the souls of those who have died, whom all
call demon-possessed and madmen" (daimonioleptous kai mainomenous)
(Apol. I 18. 4). Justin then concludes his examples by referring by
name to classic Greek oracles (manteia) and authors, especially
Homer's description of Odysseus's trench and descent to inspect
(eis . . . episkepsin) these things (18. 4, 5; and see Odyssey 11.
23 – 50, etc.).

---

[1]In addition, he regularly uses technē and dynameis (modified
by magikē/ai), but this is standard terminology and reveals nothing
about the actual procedures and results. The one minor exception is
in regard to Christ's miracles which the opponents asserted to be
phantasian magikēn, according to one passage (Trypho 69. 7).

In the continuation of his discussion, Justin also includes
a passing, rather non-committal, reference to the Sybil and Hystaspes
(Apol. I 20. 1).

Justin is also aware of various procedures used in exorcism.
In Apology II 6(5), he refers to successful Christian exorcism, simply
in the name of Jesus Christ, in contrast to the unsuccessful efforts
of "all the other exorcists and enchanters and sorcerers" (eporkistōn
kai epaston kai pharmakeutōn) (Apol. II 6. 6). This listing is amplified in Trypho 85 where Justin is arguing the superiority of Christ
to Judaism. The Christians exorcise successfully in his name (85. 2);
but the Jews' success is questionable. Exorcism by any of their great
names, whether kings, righteous men, prophets, or patriarchs, will
fail; but if any of them should exorcise in the name of the God of
Abraham, of Isaac, and of Jacob, he might perhaps (isōs) succeed.
But, in general, the Jewish exorcists (eporkistai) use the same craft
(technē) as the Gentiles when they exorcise, employing both fumiga-
tions and incantations (kai thumiamasi kai katadesmois chrōntai)
(85. 3).

Magic is regarded by Justin as an integral part of pagan religion and of the heresies, especially since all three are demon inspired and empowered. The references to magic in Apology I 14 are
part of the preceding argument against idolatry (chaps. 9-14). This
connection is further emphasized in Apology II 5 where the fallen
angels introduce not only magic, but also sacrifice, incense, and
libations, in order to subdue the human race to themselves (5. 4);
and they and their demon offspring are directly identified with the

pagan gods (5. 5, 6).[1] The various heresies result from men put forward by demons and gaining recognition by magic, even to the extent
of being worshipped, even by the pagans (Apol. I 26. 1-4; 56. 1, 2;
Trypho 120. 6).

Miracles. If magic does produce mighty works, albeit by demonic power, what is the status of Christian miracles? Justin raises
and answers this question, directly, in relation to Christ's works,
and indirectly (and perhaps more significantly), in regard to contemporary Christian activities. The question was raised specifically
in Apology I 30, "What prevents that the one who is called Christ by
us, being a man from men, did what we call his miracles by magic art
(magikē technē) and appeared from this to be Son of God?" He recognizes that mere assertion is inadequate, and proposes a proof (tēn
apodeixin) which he thinks will appear even to his readers as the
greatest and truest proof, the so-called "proof from prophecy":[2]
things have happened and are happening as foretold. The following
chapters elaborate this assertion.

The devil has also apparently profited from prophecy, counterfeiting the things predicted, though the very counterfeiting is a
testimony to the underlying truth(s) (Trypho 69. 1). The nations

---

[1] Note also Apol. I 9. 1--names and forms of idols; 66. 4--
bread and cup in Mithraic initiation a demonic imitation of the Eu-
charist; Trypho 69, 70--various fables and the Mithraic mysteries
diabolic imitations of prophecies.

[2] Whatever the common modern assessment of this proof, it was
apparently decisive for Justin personally (Trypho 3-8), and he here
expects it to be highly regarded even by his pagan readers. It was
also used extensively by other apologists and later Christian
writers.

will ultimately believe; but as to the Jews who had the prophecies
when they were fulfilled, "those seeing these things being done asserted it to be magical art (phantasian magikēn), for they even dared
to call him a magician (magon) . . ." (69. 7). In this passage Justin simply amplifies his previous answer to the charge: the "proof
from prophecy" still stands despite the counterfeiting, and is even
enhanced by it. Also, by the nature and the greatness of his works,
Christ importuned (edysōpei) those who saw them (69. 6; these works
are presented here as a fulfillment of Isaiah 35:1-7, quoted in the
preceding section). But this "proof" applies also to the future;
Christ's works stand as a persuasion to those who will later believe
(tous ep' auton pisteuein mellontas): even if maimed in body, they
will also be raised up whole at the second coming (69. 7).[1]

Justin does not present a discussion or defense of Christian
miracles (i.e., exorcisms[2]); rather, he assumes them as well known,
both to pagans and Jews, and argues from them for the power of the
name of Jesus and the validity of the Christian faith (Apol. II 6. 6;
Trypho 85. 1, 2; see also Trypho 30. 3; 76. 6). In the two main

---

[1]While hope is not proof, it can be highly persuasive. Note
also, in connection with the next topic, that he envisages their
restoration as taking place at the resurrection, not in the present.

[2]Though Justin refers to "mighty works (dynameis) even now being done through His name" (Trypho 35. 8), exorcisms (and the world-
wide spread of the Gospel, e.g., Trypho 117. 5; 121. 2, 3) are the
only specific examples he gives. The reference to healing in Trypho
39. 2 is not necessarily an exception to this since Justin uses this
term in relation to exorcisms in Apol. II 6. 6. On the spread of the
Gospel, Apol. I 50. 9 connects the giving of power to the apostles to
their being sent and teaching the nations (cf. also 31. 7, "to pub-
lish these things").

references, he implies that his readers will themselves have been able
to observe such, and further contrasts the Christians' success, simply
by the use of the name of Jesus,[1] to the failure of the pagan and
Jewish exorcists using the various traditional techniques (Apol. II
6. 5, 6; Trypho 85. 1, 3, on which see the discussion above under
"Related Areas"). Justin's emphasis on Christian activity in this
area is not accidental, it lies at the heart of his soteriology:
Christ's coming was "in behalf of believing men, and for destruction
of the demons" (Apol. II 6. 5). Further, from his perspective, such
acts need no defense against charges of magic since they are directed
at the demon forces which lie behind magic. This point is emphasized
by the case of the Magi, who, by coming to Christ, showed that they
had revolted from the power which held them captive, captive to every
evil deed by the energizing of "that demon" (Trypho 78. 9; cf. also
88. 1).

The status of the Old Testament miracles is unintentionally
presented rather ambiguously. In line with the rest of his teaching,
Justin represents them as imitated by the demons (e.g., Trypho 69. 1
and 79. 4, the Egyptian magicians), but as ultimately non-probative.
He represents the old man who had been instrumental in converting him

---

[1]While this could be regarded as the use of a "name of power,"
such use differs from that represented by Justin and other Christian
writers. The "name of power" functions either from simple knowledge
and use of the name or (and) by previously gaining influence over the
"power" by proper rites, etc. In Justin it is only Christians who can
use the name (though Justin does not mention it, he would probably
agree with the transmitter of the "sons of Sceva" story, Acts 19:14-
16). Further, to Justin, its use represents not power over the One
who bears the Name, but submission and obedience to Him.

as arguing that the prophets did not use demonstration (Trypho 7. 2);
yet they were worthy of belief because of the miracles (dynameis)
which they did. But this was because their miracles glorified the
Creator and proclaimed Christ, in contrast to certain ones worked by
false prophets (filled with deceptive and unclean spirits) for the
amazement of men and the glorification of deceptive spirits and demons. This presentation was followed by a prayer for his enlighten-
ment, without which no one can understand these things (7. 3). The
end result of this seems to be that miracles are a witness to the
truth, but this witness cannot be understood without an enlighten-
ment as to the truth. This is one manifestation of the general
dilemma confronting all apologetics: basic-belief systems are not
amenable to rational proof or attack.[1] Justin tries to escape this
dilemma by the appeal to prophecy, but this also confronts difficul-
ties as he shows in Trypho 76. 6: the prophecies could not be understood until clarified by Christ.

Tatian

        The views of Tatian are essentially the same as those of his
master Justin, but more intense, and less broad in presentation.

        Magic. It is not easy to delineate Tatian's idea of magic,
since, for him, it is all of one piece with the almost total demonic
domination of all things earthly and material (note especially Disc.

---

[1]On belief-systems as closed systems note: Thomas, Religion,
p. 641; and John M. Frame, "God and Biblical Language: Transcendence
and Immanence," in God's Inerrant Word: An International Symposium on
the Trustworthiness of Scripture, ed. John Warwick Montgomery (Minne-
apolis: Bethany Fellowship, 1974), pp. 166-71 ("Basic Commitment Language").

7, 9, 11, 15 [p. 17. 2-4], and 16 [p. 18. 2-4][1]), including medicine (especially chap. 18, but also, *inter alia*, the end of chap.
16, and the opening of chap. 17 [p. 18. 6-12, 23-24]). Chapter 17,
however, is the essence of his attack on magic, especially as represented by the system of sympathies and antipathies of Democritus (p.
18. 13-14). Apart from its content, this chapter is connected with
magic by a reference to Democritus as "the one who boasted in the
Magian Ostanes" (line 17) and by a threat that Tatian's auditors, if
they continue mocking, "will enjoy the same vengeance as the jug-
glers/sorcerers" (*goētes*) (lines 18-20). In the matter of a few
lines of chapter 17, Tatian reflects a broad spectrum of magical concerns: goals (healing, pp. 18. 23-24, 25, and 19. 10-11; love, pp.
18. 25, and 19. 8-9; hate, pp. 18. 25, and 19. 9-10; vengeance, pp.
18. 26 and 19. 21-22), materiel ("antipathies," p. 18. 23; leather
amulets, p. 18. 24; roots, p. 19. 2, 12; sinews and bones,[2] p. 19. 3;
herbs, p. 19. 12; human remains, especially of one who died a most
pitiable death, p. 19. 19, 21-22), and, above all, not so much its
theory, as a counter-theory—demonic conspiracy (pp. 18. 26-19. 5).
The various materials do not have any effect of themselves (p. 19. 3-
4), but the demons have determined a purpose for each (p. 19. 4-5),
just as men invented the alphabet (pp. 18. 27-19. 2). The demonic
goal of magic, as of all their operations, is the enslavement of

---

[1]As noted above, more precise references are cited by page
and line(s) of Schwartz, in addition to traditional chapters.

[2]*Neurōn te kai osteōn paralēpseis*; either "application of
. . ." or "the juncture of. . . ."

mankind (p. 19. 6-7; cf. chap. 18, p. 20. 15, re medicine; chap. 15,

p. 17. 1-5, and chap. 16, pp. 17. 11-12 and 18. 2-3, re the soul and

matter), and the turning of man from God (p. 19. 11-12).

Related areas. Though he cannot completely deny the efficacy

of medicine (chap. 20, p. 22. 9, and chap. 18, p. 19. 26-28),[1]

Tatian regards it as essentially the same as magic. Chapter 18

opens,

> But medicine (pharmakeia) and everything in it is a contrivance
> (epitechneseōs) of the same form. . . . As harmful compounds are
> material, in the same manner those which heal are of the same
> substance. (P. 19. 25-26, 28-30)

The chapter concludes with a presentation of the demonic operations:

they possess a man, causing sickness, and then, when satisfied, leave

the man, appearing to cure the sickness (p. 20. 15, 19-24; cf. also,

chap. 16, p. 18. 6-10).

Similarly, oracles and divination are the work of demons

(chap. 12, p. 14. 6-7, "the trickeries of frenzied demons"; and es-

pecially chap. 19, p. 21. 14-p. 22. 2). The discussion in chapter 19

is part of the same discussion of the work of demons as the discussion

of magic in chapter 17, and divination is presented as catering to

basically the same human desires as does magic: war (p. 21. 15; p.

22. 1), lust (p. 21. 16-17), and cure of illness (p. 21. 18), as well

as greed (p. 21. 25-26). The means of divination known to Tatian are

dreams, stars, flights of birds, and sacrifices (chap. 1); from the

---

[1]He also associates it with a bit of ancient animal lore:
Why ignore God and "seek to cure yourself, like the dog by grass,
and the stag by a viper, and the pig by the river crabs, and the lion
by the ape?" (chap. 18, p. 20. 8-12).

Babylonians and oracular oaks (chap. 12); by some woman frenzied by
drinking water and by fumes of frankincense, and again, by an oak,
and birds (chap. 19, p. 21. 19-20, 22-23).

Astrology, especially, is rejected by Tatian as being a key
part of a major demonic scheme, the introduction of the doctrine of
Fate to ensnare man by giving him an excuse for his (evil) acts--
i.e., that he is not responsible for them--(chaps. 8 and 9, especially
the opening lines of each[1]), and to lead him into further sins (chap.
8, p. 8. 15-18).

As such, astrology's connection with prognostication is min-
imal in Tatian's presentation, appearing only briefly (and obliquely)
in the previously discussed references in chapters 1 ("prognostication
by the stars," "astronomy") and 12 ("the Babylonian prognostication").
Similarly, while Tatian was impressed by the Scripture prophets (chap.
20, pp. 22. 29-23. 3; chap. 29, p. 30. 4-16), his major interests
were elsewhere than the argument from prophecy (note especially the immediate context of the passage in chap. 29).

Religion and magic. In regard to the relation of magic and
religion, Tatian does not directly identify pagan practices and
magic; both, rather, are subsumed under the greater system of demonic
domination. He does, however, present magic as specifically designed
to turn men from the true God, and as a perversion of His good creation (chap. 17, p. 19. 11-17). He also lists the pagan gods with the
divinatory practices presented in chapter 19 (p. 21. 16, 17, 18, 21,

---

[1]Chapter 8, in line with Tatian's doctrine of free-will, shows
that man himself bears responsibility for this result, but chapter 9
goes on to indicate its underlying demonic foundation.

26; p. 22. 1), regarding these practices, as they were, as an integral part of pagan religion.

Conversely, while he has much to say about the contrast between pagan (demonic) religion and Christian beliefs, Tatian has little to say about Christian miracles. A single passage seems to refer
to exorcism,[1] but is not quite clear: sometimes when demons have disturbed a human body, "being stricken by the word of the power of God,
terrified, they depart, and the sufferer is healed" (chap. 16, p. 18.
10-12). Basically, the defeat of the demons is not by combat, but by
quiet disengagement, rejecting them and the material realm that they
have usurped (e.g., chap. 11, pp. 11. 25-12. 17; chap. 16, p. 18.
3-4--"should anyone wish to conquer them, let him deprecate matter";
chap. 20, p. 22. 18-19; chaps. 29 and 30, p. 30. 11-21).

Other apologists

Quadratus's reference to the continuing, real works of the
savior implies non-continuing, insubstantial works by some other per-
son(s); these might be magicians, or other wonder-workers, or they
might be the work of some recognized pagan deity such as Aesculapius.
In any case, the abiding nature of the works is acclaimed as a test
of genuineness in a contest of miracles.

Melito, in a highly rhetorical passage in his homily On
Baptism, pictures Iris as "fill[ing] the rivers, invoked by a water-

---

[1]There are also references to turning to God for healing in
chapter 18 (e.g., p. 19. 27-28; p. 20. 8-10, 14).

leading spirit."[1] Though this appears to be based on the traditional
(pagan) religious language, it is close to magical ideas.

Coincidentally, the clearest reference to magic in pseudo-
Melito's Apology also involves water, etc. It pictures Orpheus and
Zaradusht (respectively, a Thracian and a Persian magus) as practicing magic at a well in a wood near Mabug where there was an unclean spirit. This spirit interfered with those passing by, so

> these Magi, in accordance with what was a mystery in their Magian
> system bade Simi, the daughter of Hadad, to draw water from the
> sea and pour it into the well, so that the spirit should not come
> up and commit assault.(ANF 8:753)

While this is apparently traditional material, the apologist seems to
accept it as authentic, since it is part of his explanation of the
true origins of the pagan gods.

References and allusions to related matters

Athenagoras has nothing to say directly about magic, but he
does present elements of the standard Christian demonology. Some of
the angels created by God to exercise providential care over creation,
led by one special one, the spirit or ruler of matter, fell into impure love, became subjected to the flesh, and begat the giants (Plea
24. 2-6; cf. also Tatian Disc. 7, pp. 7. 19-8. 3, re this pre-
eminent, "first-born" angel). These angels and the souls of the
giants, the demons, confined to the air and/or earth, act according
to their appetites and natures; mankind is thus moved hither and

---

[1]Cited from Robert M. Grant, ed., Second-Century Christianity:
A Collection of Fragments, Translations of Christian Literature, series
6, Select Passages (London: SPCK, 1957), p. 73.

thither by their operation, caught between the tendency of matter and
the affinity for the divine, so that some have concluded the universe
has no order, being driven by irrational chance (Plea 25. 1-4).
Further, the demons, eager for the blood of sacrifices, draw men to
idols, using for the gods the names of historical men, but acting according to their own natures (chap. 26). These demons who "hover
about matter, greedy of sacrificial odours and the blood of victims, and ever ready to lead men into error" (27. 2)[1] take advantage
of unknowledgeable souls. They take possession of their thoughts to
pour in empty visions (phantasias), or take credit when the soul, of
itself, as being immortal and moving in conformity with reason,
either predicts (promēnyousa) the future or attends (therapeuousa)
the present (ibid.). This latter would appear to be a reference to
either oracles or (and) the Asclepieions.

 This connection of pagan worship with magic and/or demons is
also reflected by other apologists. Aristides, in the passages cited
above at the opening of the discussion of the apologists, rebuked
the Greeks for connecting the gods with magic, and pseudo-Melito not
only identified two noted idols as ancient Magi, as noted above, but
a little later in the Apology described the pagans, "severed from the
knowledge of the living God," as "wallow[ing] on the ground before demons and shadows" (ANF 8:754).

 Finally, in contrast to the demonic forces, there are also
references to an angelic hierarchy counterpoised and antecedent to it.

---

[1]Quoted from the translation of B. P. Pratten, "Writings of
Athenagoras," ANF 2:143.

But the angelic ranks, while exercising providential care for mankind
(e.g., Athenagoras <u>Plea</u> 10. 5, and the passage from 24. 2-6 cited
above), are not open to human contact and manipulation. Though the
angels function as God's messengers, basically He deals directly with
man. For example, when He wished to make His great revelation to
mankind, He sent not by "a subaltern, or angel, or ruler, or one of
those that direct the affairs of earth, or one of those . . . entrusted
with the dispensations in heaven, but the very Artificer and Creator
. . . Himself" (<u>Diognetus</u> 7. 2).[1] It is only the evil angels, who because of their fall are no longer able to rise to heavenly things, who
interact with mankind regularly (cf. <u>Plea</u> 25, etc.).

<u>Summary</u>

The attitudes toward magic among the apologists are much the
same as those in the previous period, but are expressed more explicitly, due to the outward orientation of the apologetic task, and in
more detail, because of the greater length of the works involved.
The proportion of space devoted to magic is not significantly greater
than in the Apostolic Fathers--magic is still one of their lesser
concerns.

Within the group, the views of the apologists are essentially
the same but with the individual emphases which characterize their
works in general such as Justin's emphasis on the "proof from prophecy" and Tatian's extreme rejection of the present material world.

---

[1]From Lightfoot's translation, in Lightfoot-Harmer, <u>Apostolic
Fathers</u>, p. 255.

The dominant terms for magic/magician are the various mag-
forms, with occurrences of pharmak- forms in the sense of "magic(ian),"
"sorcerer/-y" in Aristides, and goēt- in Tatian and Diognetus.
Various forms and compounds of mantik- also appear, along with some
general synonyms. The powers seen behind magic are usually referred
to as demons (commonly daimonia, but several times daimōn), but they
are also referred to as (unclean) spirits, or as powers (dynameis).
The last term is also used to refer to either their acts, or to
Christian miracles. The word technē occurs many times, both as a
general term and also as specifically connected with magical procedure.

In the areas of practices and materials, Justin provides
several indications of the procedures in two related areas, divination (Apol. I 18) and exorcism (Apol. II 6 and Trypho 85). Tatian
provides some examples of the materials used (Disc. 17). Pseudo-
Melito also provides a partial example of a magical procedure.

While all these are regarded as evil, they are also seemingly
regarded as actual effects (except for the non-Christian exorcisms
mentioned in Justin). The reason for this is the underlying theory
of demonic power behind such acts, which is most clearly outlined by
Tatian (especially in Disc. 17).

In the area of the overlap between magic and religion, two
problems are faced, the relation of magic to Christian miracles (including those of the Old Testament) and to pagan religion. In the
former area, no clearcut answer appears, though both Quadratus and
Justin address it. Quadratus suggests continuing results as a test

(a test which does suggest some question of the reality of the results
of non-Christian operations). Justin, apart from an empirical answer
(this exorcism works, that doesn't), is forced back to an unprovable
proof: revelation, i.e., the "proof from prophecy" and divine "en-
lightenment."

In the latter area, the apologists see no essential distinction; both magic and pagan religion are manifestations of the demonic
power and activity. Yet, in the demonic interactions with man, there
does seem to be some distinction maintained. In one type of action
the demons impose on men as dominant beings from behind the facade of
idols, directing the acts of men (including answering them) for their
own benefit; in the other type, they let men think that they are controlling events (cf. Tatian Disc. 17), though it is still all part of
the demonic plan. These two areas, which could be described in modern
terms as the "supplicative" and the "manipulative," are basically the
apologists' pictures of pagan religion and of magic (and, for Tatian,
of medicine).

In essence, magic did not "fit" in the Christian world-view
while it was a natural counterpart of the pagan religion. Those among
the pagans (e.g., some of the philosophers) who rejected one commonly
rejected the other also.

Greek Polemicists and Systematizers

Irenaeus

References to magic

An accusation of magic is a fairly standard item in Irenaeus's
identification of the various heretics and heretical systems which he
combats (against Marcus in Adv. haer. 1. 13. 1, etc.; Simon, 1. 23. 1;
Simon's followers, 1. 23. 4; Menander, 1. 23. 5; the followers of
Basilides, 1. 24. 5; Carpocrates and the Carpocratians, 1. 25. 3; but
not, expressly at least, indicated of Saturninus, 1. 24. 1, and of
various others, 1. 26-31).[1] It also appears as a regular appellation
added to the names of Marcus "the Magician" and Simon Magus in subsequent references to them (e.g., 2. praef. 1; 2. 9. 2), and is commonly
used as the sole designation for Marcus in the lengthened discussion
of his system (e.g., 1. 13. 5, and 1. 14. 3).

Discussion of magic and related areas

Such a charge of magic is probably to be expected in a religious conflict in which each side claims supernatural validation, but
in these cases in Irenaeus, it seems to go beyond conventional religious polemic. If Irenaeus correctly represents the practices of his
opponents, the charge of magic would seem to be sustained.

Magic

Marcus, who is presented first, is also described at greater

---

[1]The chapter and section references are given according to the
system of Massuet (and Stieren) as given in PG 7, and in ANF 1. (The
book numbers go back to Irenaeus himself.)

length, with the later systems compared to his. Marcus is first
introduced as "a perfect adept in magical impostures" (magikēs . . .
kybeias empeirotatos) (1. 13. 1, ANF 1:334),[1] as is Menander after
him (1. 23. 5), while Simon was especially named for his magical
powers (1. 23. 1). Behind Irenaeus's derogatory picture there appears
to be a showman of considerable ability (note especially 1. 13. 1-3),
but Irenaeus has nothing good to say of him explicitly. At least some
of Marcus's results (prophecy, specifically) are attributed to a demonic familiar (kai daimona tina paredron echein, 1. 13. 3), and his
motives are entirely base (1. 13. 3, 5), as are those of his disciples
(1. 13. 6) and later groups (Simonians, 1. 23, 4; Basilides, 1. 24, 5;
Carpocratians, 1. 25. 3, 4). To further his immoral ends, he compounds philters and love potions (philtra kai agōgima, 1. 13. 5), a
charge also made against the Simonians (1. 23. 4) and the Carpocratians (philtra . . . et charitesia, 1. 25. 3). Irenaeus's disparaging
picture of Marcus is summed up (and amplified) in some poetic lines
quoted from a certain "divine elder": he is a "maker of idols and
inspector of portents / Skilled in astrology and the magical arts"
(magikēs technēs), he uses tricks and signs, "undertakings of apostate
wonders" (apostatikēs dynameōs encheirēmata), enabled by Satan,
"through an angelic power, Azazel" (1. 15. 6).

   But Marcus's wonders were performed in sacramental or prophetic contexts, and were, of course, not regarded by his followers

---

[1]English translation from [Alexander Roberts, et al.,]
"Irenaeus," ANF 1:307-578; Greek and Latin texts are given according
to PG 7.

as magic, but as miracles (1. 13. 1; see also 2. 31. 2, re Simon and
Carpocrates), just as Simon's acts brought him honor, not as a magician, but as a god (1. 23. 1; cf. Justin Apol. I 26).

Simon, noted already as a magician, gave himself more zealously to studying the "whole magic art" (universam magicam) after his
contact with the apostles. Besides the philters and charms already
noted, his followers were charged with using exorcisms and incantations, "familiars" and "dream-senders" (paredri et oniropompi), and
whatever other curious arts (perierga) there are (1. 23. 4). Similarly, the Basilidians use images, incantations, invocations, and
every other kind of curious art (reliqua universa perierga) (1. 24. 5),
while the Carpocratians were accused of the whole composite list (1.
25. 3, 6).

Most commonly these things are mentioned in connection with
this-worldly activities (especially recruitment, reinforcement of
loyalty, and seduction of followers, e.g., 1. 13. 1-6), but, in at
least one case, Irenaeus also applies the term magic to their other-
worldly acts or teachings: Menander, for example, was said to affirm
that the magic (magiam) he taught enabled one to overcome the angels
who made the world (but even this has a this-worldly goal--evasion
of death) (1. 23. 5). Similar ideas were represented by the other
groups, though Irenaeus uses, at most, the term "invocation"
(epiklēsis) in describing them (e.g., Marcus, re prophesying, 1. 13.
3; Marcosians, re deliverance from "the judge" or various principalities and powers, 1. 13. 6 [simply tade eipoien] and 1. 21. 5).

Theory and praxis

Irenaeus basically regards magic as a demonic activity.
Marcus, at least in his "prophetic" activities, "probably" (eikos)
has a demonic familiar (daimona . . . paredron) (1. 13. 3, cf. also
secs. 4 and 6), and the Simonians and Carpocratians operate with the
"familiars" and "dream-sending" spirits noted above (1. 23. 4 and
25. 3; see also 2. 31. 2, 3 for other demonic associations of these
two groups). At the end time, the second beast of Revelation (13:11-
17) will also do wonders (signa) "by the working of magic [magica
operatione] . . . since the demons and apostate spirits are at his
service" (5. 28. 2, ANF 1:557).

But Irenaeus seems to be somewhat divided in mind regarding
these things. While he recognizes the effectiveness of Marcus's
propagandizing and seductive activities, and while allowing the likelihood of demonic workings, he seems to have some reservations about
the reality of these things. Marcus "join[s] the buffooneries [paignia]
of Anaxilaus to the craftiness [panourgia] of the Magi" (1. 13. 1,
ANF 1:334); Simon, Carpocrates, and others "are said to perform
miracles" (virtutes operari dicuntur), but they are "by means of
magical deceptions [magicas elusiones], and with universal deceit,"[1]
and they cannot free from any demons except from those they themselves
send, if even this much (2. 31. 2, see also 3; cf. also 2. 32. 3 "if
in fact they have accomplished anything by magic [per magicam]").

---

[1]ANF 1:407. The charge of fraud and deceit could arise from
the fact that these are demonic, rather than divine, acts, but
Irenaeus's meaning seems to go beyond this to the questioning of the
reality of the acts themselves.

In addition, the effects produced are illusory (phantasmata; phantasio-
dos) and transitory (statim cessantia), not real and permanent (et ne
quidem stillicidio temporis perseverantia) (2. 32. 3, 4).

    The references to incantations and charms would support the
demonic explanation of the magic acts, but the use also of physical
means, such as drugs, may be implied by Irenaeus's use of the terms
philters and love potions (?, charms?). Of the two specific procedures which Irenaeus describes, one, changing the color of a liquid,
seems to be chemically based (i.e., drugs, pharmaka), and Hippolytus,
at least, explains the other, filling a larger cup from a smaller,
in the same way (1. 13. 2; cf. Hipp. Ref. 6. 35).

Related areas

    Irenaeus does not discuss collateral occult areas, but, in
the lines quoted from "the elder," Marcus is accused of observing
portents (teratoskopos), i.e., divination, and astrology (astrologi-
kes . . . technes). This is perhaps a variant manifestation of Marcus's prophetic interests which Irenaeus does elaborate on (1. 13. 3,
4).

    The Basilidians are represented as following the ideas of
the mathematicians, i.e., astrologers (or is it some kind of numer-
ology?) (1. 24. 7). The speculation concerning the various "aeons,"
etc., with the prevalence of the numbers seven and twelve would also
support astrological interests in the various other systems, but
Irenaeus does not develop this area. Besides this, in the general
description of the heretical operations in his second book, Irenaeus

refers to what is some type of divinatory practice involving "mere
boys"[1] (pueros investes) whose sight is deceived by an exhibition of
phantasms (oculos deludentes . . . phantasmata ostendentes) (2. 32. 3;
cf. Hipp. Ref. 4. 28; also Justin Apol. I 18. 3; contrast Tertullian
Apology 23, and Eus. H.E. 7. 10. 4).

Magic and other religions

Due to his primarily polemic, rather than apologetic, purposes, Irenaeus had little to say about pagan religion. He thus has
no occasion to connect it with magic as do his predecessors and contemporaries, except for the assertion that Simon Magus was honored
as a god because of his activities (1. 23. 1). He does, however,
assert a strong connection of magic and heretical beliefs and practices. In addition, Marcus is identified as "the magician" in connection with his prophetic activities (1. 13. 4) and after the expo-
sition of some of his esoteric doctrine (the body of Aletheia) (1. 14.
3); the Marcosians use various "Hebrew" words and other invocations
(1. 21. 3, 5; also, 13. 6); the Basilidians, along with their magical
practices, coin names as if of the angels (1. 24. 5), follow the practices of the "mathematicians," and name their chief Abraxas (1. 24. 7).
Menander, also, is said to represent that by the magic he taught the
angels who made the world could be overcome (1. 23. 5).

The heretics are "said (dicuntur)" to perform miracles

---

[1]Compare on this passage (and Justin Apol. I 18. 3) the parallel ancient and (relatively) modern descriptions of divination by
boys in John M. Hull, Hellenistic Magic and the Synoptic Tradition
Studies in Biblical Theology, 2d ser., no. 28 (Naperville, Ill.:
Alec R. Allenson, Inc., 1974), pp. 21-24, esp. 21-22.

(virtutes), but Irenaeus challenges them on the basis of their reality
and their results. They are magical deception and deceit (magicas
elusiones, et universa fraude) (2. 31. 2), error, misleading influence
(seductio), magical illusions (magica phantasia), deceit, demonical
working (operatione demoniaca), phantasms of idolatry (phantasmate
idolatriae) (2. 31. 3), phantasms that instantly cease and do not
endure (phantasmata . . . statim cessantia, et ne . . . perseverantia)
(2. 32. 3). Those who work such things "strive deceitfully to lead
foolish people astray" (2. 32. 3, ANF, 1:408); these things are all
done for the benefit of those doing them, not for their followers.

The method(s) employed by the heretics had been presented at
length in book one; in 2. 32. 5, Irenaeus summarizes these methods,
denying that the church uses any of them. The church does not work
"by angelic invocations, or incantations, or by any other wicked
curious art" (nec reliqua prava curiositate); she works rather by
prayer in a "pure, sincere, and straightforward spirit [munde, et
pure, et manifeste orationes], calling upon the name of our Lord Jesus
Christ," and this name "even now confers benefits" (2. 32. 5, ANF
1:409). This seems close to the modern suggestions, based on Frazer,
of supplication in contrast to manipulation/compulsion as one possible
distinction between religion and magic.[1] Such a distinction had also

---

[1]James George Frazer, The Golden Bough: A Study in Magic and
Religion, 3d ed., Part I: The Magic Art and the Evolution of Kings,
2 vols. (New York: The Macmillan Company, 1951 [1910], 1:224, 225.
See also, Goode, Religion, p. 53, item 2; and Mischa Titiev, "A Fresh
Approach to the Problem of Magic and Religion," Southwestern Journal of
Anthropology 16 (1960): 292-98, reprinted in Reader in Comparative
Religion, ed. William A. Lessa and Evon Z. Vogt, 3d ed. (New York: Harper
& Row, Publishers, 1972), pp. 430-33 (see pp. 430 and 431).

been explicitly applied previously in Irenaeus's rejection of Marcus's
prophetic activity: "If . . . anyone . . . does command . . . it will
follow that he who commands is greater and of higher authority than
the prophetic spirit, though he is but a man, which is impossible.
But such spirits . . . are earthly and weak, audacious and impudent
. . ." (1. 13. 4).[1]

    Another idea of Frazer's, the connection of magic and "sci-
ence," is possibly illustrated by Irenaeus's treatment of a common
Old Testament example, Moses and the Exodus. Due to unbelief, Phar-
oah's heart was hardened, so "while seeing that it was the finger of
God," he still believed "the exit was accomplished by magical power
[per magicam operationem], . . . not by the operation of God that the
Red Sea afforded a passage . . . but . . . by merely natural causes"
(sed naturaliter sic se habere) (4. 29. 2, ANF 1:502). Unless Irenaeus
is distinguishing between the Exodus as a whole complex of events and
the specific event of the opening of the Red Sea, he would appear to
be equating operations by "magical power (magicam)" and "natural
causes (naturaliter)" in some way.[2]

Clement of Alexandria

    Clement's interests are considerably different from those of
Irenaeus. While the latter deals specifically with charges of magic
against various heresies, Clement has no direct discussion of magic;

---

[1] Compare Hermas's distinction of true and false prophets
(Shepherd 43 [Man. 11], esp. secs. 5 and 6), discussed above, pp.
321-22.

[2] Or is naturaliter a translation of physis in some magical
sense?

however, numerous allusions to related areas are scattered throughout his works.

References to magical items

Clement manifests no real worry about magic, using references
to magical items[1] rather freely for rhetorical purposes, even, on one
occasion, specifically of Christian prayers (Q.D.S. 41. 5, "the
magic of familiar litanies" [ANF 2:603]).[2] Though he begins his Exhortation to the Heathen with a running account of the fabulous things
worked by music and soon introduces such terms as "charmed" (thelges-
thai, 1/2. 1), "sorcery" and "songs and incantations" (goēteia;
ǭdais kai epǭdais; 1/3. 1), Clement is using these terms rhetorically;
his target here is pagan worship and the poetry which caters to it
(Exh. 1/1. 1-3. 1; note also pharmakon, of the "charm" of the countering strain in 2. 4).[3] He makes various uses of the idea of charms
both positively—God is the "holy charmer" of sick souls (Paed. 1.

---

[1]Mageia, etc., occur only a few times (magois, Exh. 2/22. 2,
among Eleusinian celebrants, and several times of the Magi, as instruc-
tors of the Greeks, etc., Exh. 5/65. 4); Clement generally prefers
the even more pejorative goēteia and related forms. He also makes
some use of epǭdē/epaoidē, but generally uses more common or rhetorical designations in preference to technical terms.

[2]English translation by William Wilson, et al., "Clement of
Alexandria," ANF 2:163-604.

[3]The Greek text and more precise references, where needed,
are given according to the edition of Otto Stählin, Clemens Alexandrinus,
Die Griechischen Christlichen Schriftsteller der ersten drei Jahrhunderte [vols. 12, 15, 17, 39]; 4 vols. (2d ed. of vol. 1) (Leipzig:
J. C. Hinrichs'sche Buchhandlung, 1906-36). They are cited as St.,
with volume, page, and line numbers; when so cited they follow the
(book,) chapter, and section numbers. Where the longer chapters of
the older editions have been broken up into shorter sections and paragraphs, both systems are given, separated by a virgule.

2/6. 1); the "love-charm" (philtra) which causes God to love man is
within man (1. 3/7. 3); man can only defeat the serpent of wealth
"by the charm of the Word" (3. 6/35. 1)--and negatively, of being bewitched ([(kata) goēteuesthai/-ein] not by philosophy, but by pleasure, by the sentences of the Sophists, Strom. 1. 2/20. 2; 8/42. 4;
10/47. 2, respectively; and again in 2. 20/120. 3, in dreams by Pleasure).[1] He further suggests that a number of the noted Greek philosophers learned from the Magi, and some also from the secret teachings of the Egyptians (Strom. 1. 15/66. 2; 69. 6), and that philosophy
itself first flourished among the barbarians and such groups as the
Egyptian "prophets," the Chaldeans, the Druids, the Magi, and others
(1. 15/71. 3-5; also, Exh. 5/65. 4).

He reverts to the idea of charms (epōdas) again in Paedagogus
3. 4/28. 3 (but this time in a literal sense) along with various other
practices ("sacrificing and practicing divination . . . fortune tellers . . . old wives whisperings . . ., bearing charms and incantations
[philtra . . . kai epōdas] from soothsayers [goētōn]" ANF 2:278) in
which many women improperly engage. Another list of methods of divination (with their barbarian origins; apparently related in some way to
Tatian's list [Disc. 1], but expanded and modified) appears in
Stromateis 1. 16/74. 1-5, while in 2. 1/2. 3, Clement identifies the
Greeks' boasted "highest sciences" as "astrology, and mathematics,
and magic, and sorcery."

---

[1]On one occasion, he also uses the term thaumatopoioi, but of
those who "tumble on swords with a certain dexterity" (Strom. 7. 11/
66. 3; ANF 2:541).

Discussion of magical theory and praxis

Incantations

Clement cites Plato to the effect that the gods have a dia-
lect, this idea being derived from dreams and oracles, and, especially,
from demoniacs, who speak the language of the possessing demon rather
than their own (Strom. 1. 21/143. 1). This has possible implications
for a theory of incantation, though Clement is not considering such a
topic; his interests here are historical and linguistic. He does,
however, assert in the next paragraph that the "first and generic
barbarous dialects have terms by nature, since also men confess that
prayers uttered in a barbarian tongue are more powerful" (1. 21/143. 6,
ANF 2:333). This is an idea with obvious potential connection to
magic, a connection which Origen makes explicit, as we shall see
later.

Incantations (epaoidais) are named as the means by which the
Magi compel the demons to serve them in Exhortation 4 (58. 3). In
two passages, Clement refers to the "so-called 'Ephesian Letters.'"
In the first, he attributes their invention, along with numbers in
music, to the Idaean Dactyli (Strom. 1. 15/73. 1), while the second
suggests that they have a symbolic import, and illustrates this by
certain examples (5. 8/45. 1-3). But they are, perhaps, better classed
as amulets rather than as incantations (i.e., as being written magic,
rather than spoken).

Charms and amulets

Besides the references in the previous discussions and the

references to the "Ephesian Letters," Clement mentions charms in
other connections. The first speaks of "charms of healing" (epōdas
tas hygieis) as being derived from the Thracians (Exh. 6/70. 1).
The second refers to "amulets and charms" (ta periapta kai tas
epaoidas), received from necromancers "to ward off evil" (hōs
sotērious), comparing these to "the heavenly Word, the Saviour, . . .
God's own charm" (epōdē) which men refuse (Exh. 11/115. 2, ANF 2:204).

Spirits

Some people, holding that "plague, and hail storms, and tempests, and the like, are wont to take place, not alone in consequence
of material disturbance, but also through anger of demons and bad
angels," asserted that the Magi could avert impending hail by incantations and sacrifices (Strom. 6. 3/31. 1-2, ANF 2:487). The Magi
also boasted that the demons were their ministers, reckoned among
their household servants, the Magi "by their charms [epaoidais] compelling them to be their slaves" (Exh. 4/58. 3, ANF 2:188).

This fits well into the larger pattern of Clement's view of
the spiritual realm. He held the common view, derived from Jewish
speculations (cf. 1 Enoch 7 and 8), that fallen angels revealed
secrets to women (Strom. 5. 1/10. 2; cf. 1. 16/80. 5; 1. 17/81. 4;
and 7. 2/6. 4 regarding the origin of philosophy). These angels had
originally been part of a greater hierarchy, which still existed,
ordered vertically, from God down to us (Strom. 7. 2/9. 3), and
horizontally, with various regiments over nations and cities, and,
perhaps, individuals (6. 17/157. 5), as well as some being set over

the planets (5. 6/37. 2).   The unfallen angels function as agents

of divine providence, having co-operated in the production of things

below (ibid.) and so continue, bestowing good things on the "Gnostic"

(6. 17/161. 2), being saved and saving (7. 2/9. 3).

        The evil spirits who receive sacrifices may be called gods or

angels (Strom. 6. 3/31. 4), but they are daemons, and may include

souls of the dead, empowered in consequence of the purity of their

life (in the view of their worshippers) to wander near the earth to

minister to men (6. 3/31. 5).   This opinion is held, "for they knew

that some souls were by nature kept in the body" (ibid., ANF 2:487).

While these beings are celebrated by the Greek poets, so far is their

worship from the truth that David not only did not celebrate them in

his songs, but actually drove them away by his music, curing Saul

when plagued by a demon (Exh. 1/5. 4).

        These spirits also operate in prediction (Strom. 1. 21/135. 2).

Discussion of related fields

Oracles and divination

        The abiding human interest in the future finds many official

and unofficial outlets, and Clement was aware of a very large variety

of them.   In Stromateis 1 (16/74. 2-5), he gave the list similar to

Tatian's already mentioned: astrology (credited to the Egyptians or

to the Chaldeans), followed by prognostication by the stars (from the

Carians), then attention to the flights of birds, haruspicy, augury,

and divination by dreams (each derived from some barbarian nation or

the other).   In the second chapter of the Exhortation, he lists the

noted pagan (mainly Greek) oracles (manteia; chrēstēria) of various
types and places,[1] followed by other more individual varieties: ex-
pounders of prodigies, augurs, dream interpreters (teratoskopoi,
oiōnoskopoi, oneirōn kritai), as well as those divining by flour or
by barley (aleuromanteis, krithomanteis), the ventriloquists (engastri-
mythous) yet honored by many;[2] besides the secret shrines (adyta) of the
Egyptians, and the Etruscan necromancies (nekyomanteiai) (ll. 1-2).
These are all insane devices (manika; the second use of this same
paronomasia in the passage), but they reach their climax (or anti-
climax) in the use of goats and crows (ll. 3; the latter, along with
the jackdaw, is also ridiculed in Exh. 10/104. 2).

This situation results from a superstitious dread of "irascible"
(euorgētous) gods that causes men to imagine all events as signs and
causes (sēmeia . . . kai . . . aitia) of evil (Strom. 7. 4/24. 1, ANF
2:529).   But it is not only the ignorant who observe such things.
Clement can present a long list of Greek philosophers, and their predecessors, who were involved in divination.   Noteworthy among them are
Pythagoras, who "always applied his mind to prognostication," Zoroaster the Mede, Empedocles of Agrigentum, and Socrates with his inner

---

[1]Besides these he also knows, apparently from Plutarch Caesar
19 (cited by Stählin, Clemens, 2:46, notes on lines 10-14), that among
the Germans whirlpools and eddies and the noises of streams were observed to predict the future (Strom. 1. 15/72. 3); and, from Aristotle
Polity of the Phocians (now lost), that Execestus, the Phocian tyrant,
wore two enchanted rings and judged propitious times by the sounds
they made against each other, but, despite their warning, was murdered
by treachery (Strom. 1. 21/133. 4).

[2]As noted above, idle women sacrifice and practice divination
and consort with fortune tellers (agyrtai) and goētes, from the latter
of whom they learn charms and incantations (philtra . . . kai epōdas)
(Paed. 3. 4/28. 3).

voice; Aristotle, however, apparently had reservations about such things (Strom. 1. 21/133. 1-4, ANF 2:330).[1]

These predictions are produced by various means. They come "for the most part from observations and probability, just as physicians and soothsayers judge from natural signs," but others come from demons, or from disturbances by water, or fumes or some sort of air (Strom. 1. 21/135. 2, ANF 2:331; all this in contrast to the Hebrew prophets who were moved solely by the power and inspiration of God); other practitioners judge people by their foreheads (metoposkopos) (Paed. 3. 3/15. 2).

The Sibyl(s) again receive special mention. The "host of Sibyls" are among the Greek diviners that Clement passes in review with only mention of the names (Strom. 1. 21/132. 3; nine are then specified by name [St. 2:82. 16-18]), once the Sibyl is mentioned in connection with Hystaspes (in an alleged quotation from the apostle Paul in Strom. 6. 5/43. 1), and once she is identified as "the prophetess of the Hebrews" (!) (Exh. 6/71. 4). But oracular powers apparently have a physical base of some sort: the original Sibyl, who sat beside the oracle of Delphi, still divines, at least according to Serapion the poet. At her death, he says, it was her vocal powers which proceeded into the air, but her body was changed to earth, the earth naturally produced grass, and the beasts which chanced to feed on it "'exhibited to men an accurate knowledge of futurity by their entrails.' . . . So much for the Sibyl" (Strom. 1. 15/70. 4, ANF 2:316).

---

[1]See the second note preceding.

Astrology

    This other means of knowing the future was also very prominent in the ancient world, and has left several impressions on Clement's works. A number of references attest to its widespread influence and ancient origination, two express its theory, and a few suggest its influence, at least rhetorical, on Christian thought. While astrology and magic are sometimes opposed in modern theoretical discussions, Clement presents astrology as closely related in places of origin and in theory to the traditional views of magic.

    With such a noteworthy art, various claims as to the honor of its origination are to be expected, and Clement obliges us. In one passage, apparently of compound origin, he attributes "astrology" to the Egyptians, and "similarly also the Chaldeans," while some said "prognostication by the stars" was invented by the Carians (Strom. 1. 16/74. 3). But observation of the heavenly bodies to predict future events was also practiced by the Indian holy men (3. 7/60. 4).[1] But, whatever its origins, it has been thoroughly taken over by the Greeks; they "prat[e] loftily of the heavenly bodies in the much vaunted science of astrology, not astronomy" (Exh. 6/67. 2, ANF 2:191), and boast of astrology, mathematics, magic, and sorcery, as the greatest sciences (megistais epistēmais) (Strom. 2. 1/2. 3).

    As to how it works, the mechanism is sympathy. Plato introduces two philosophers, one in the Epinomis who knew the course of all generation, which occurs by the instrumentality of the planets, and

---

[1] One or both of the first two claimants are supported by other references in Clement: the Chaldeans and the Egyptians, Strom. 1. 23/153. 3; the Egyptians, 6. 4/35. 4.

another, Timaeus, who, as an astronomer, knew the motion of the stars

and their sympathy and association (<u>sympatheias te kai koinōnias</u>) with

one another (<u>Strom</u>. 1. 25/166. 1). This "sympathy" also extends to

and affects earthly things, as Clement asserts in suggesting the sym-

bolism of the number seven (while discussing the fourth commandment).

According to the mathematicians, the planets are seven, and by them

the Chaldeans think "all which concerns mortal life is effected

through sympathy, in consequence of which they also undertake to tell

things respecting the future" (<u>Strom</u>. 6. 16/143. 1, <u>ANF</u> 2:513).[1]

Magic and religion

In the opening chapter of the <u>Exhortation</u>, Clement presents

the pagan religions as introduced and propagated by the poets, poets

famed in story and song for the magical powers of their music (1/1.

1-2. 1), men possessed by a spirit of artful sorcery (<u>entechnō tini</u>

<u>goēteia daimonōntes</u>), enticing mankind to idols, subjecting them to

the yoke by their songs and incantations (<u>ōdais kai epōdais</u>) (3. 1).

In chapter two, the official religious oracles are indistinguishable

from the popular ones (2/11. 1-3), and the mysteries contain hidden

sorcery (<u>goēteia</u>; 12. 1) and are full of deceptive wonders (<u>apatēs</u>

<u>kai terateias</u>; 14. 1). While <u>goēteia</u> is quite probably used here in

the figurative sense of trickery or fraud, the whole point is that

these beings and their arts are less than divine, and there is some-

thing strange about their being worshipped. Most of the rest of chap-

ter two (esp. secs. 24-39) is devoted to the demonstration of this

----

[1]On "sympathy," compare the discussion of "Biology and Medicine," below.

point in standard apologetic patterns. The concluding sections of the
chapter turn to those asserted to be in second rank to the gods, the
demons. These are gluttonous and impure (40. 1), and if they have
any concern for man, it is because "like flatterers, they approach
our livelihood, allured by the smoke" (41. 3). Chapter three develops
this further, emphasizing that superstition (deisidaimonia), preached
by men led astray by demons, became the source of wickedness and resulted in the multiplication of demons (3/44. 1-3).

The Magi, the eponyms of magic, whom the Greeks own as their
teachers in many areas (Exh. 5/65. 4; etc.), were originally a religious group, but now employ their charms to enslave demons as their
servants (Exh. 4/58. 3), or use incantations and sacrifices to avert
hail (Strom. 6. 3/31. 2). Astrology is of a piece with all these,
considering the universe, or the stars, as gods (Exh. 6/67. 1, 2).
Having originated with the Egyptians (or the Chaldeans) (Strom. 1.
16/74. 2), it continues to hold a place in their worship (Strom. 6.
4/35. 4).

The idle women in Paedagogus 3. 4 are pictured without distinction as sacrificing and practicing divination from temple to
temple, and spending time with fortune tellers and learning charms
and incantations (for immoral purposes) from soothsayers (3. 4/28. 3).
It makes no difference whether the spirits to whom sacrifices are of-
fered to avert evils are called gods or angels (Strom. 6. 3/31. 4;
and a few lines earlier they were identified as demons or evil angels,
31. 1). Further, "superstitious dread of those irascible [gods]"
leads to these other superstitious attitudes and acts: a constant

looking out for signs and portents, dread of inscriptions, and fear
of all sorts of things (wool, salt lumps, torches, squills, and sul-
phur) "bewitched by sorcerers, in certain impure rites of expiation"
(Strom. 7. 4/24. 1; 26. 1, 2, 4; ANF 2:529). Clement further illustrates this with lines from a comic poet, Diphilus, who repeats the
last three items of the list, and also adds asphalt (26. 4, St. 3:19.
16-18). Apparently such purifications were required by religious
scruples, but were performed by sorcerers (goētes, Strom. 7. 4/26.
2, 4, St. 3:19. 6, 12).

Thus, while he does not discuss it explicitly, it is quite
clear from these items that Clement sees no line of division between
the pagan religious and magical practices. (On the other hand, contrary to Irenaeus's views, he seems to regard the heretical sects as
deviating mainly in intellectual and ethical views, not as engaging
in magic.[1])

Indirectly related areas

Clement includes allusions to or discussions of other areas,
which, though not directly magical, manifest a somewhat analogous
attitude, or are related to items of significance for the study of
Africanus. The types of items vary from specimens of actual misinformation or superstition to what is simply poorly understood natural
science, and range from natural history to medical practice to music.

---

[1]Eusebius does report (H.E. 2. 15. 1) the extinguishing of
Simon's power and its destruction, along with him, possibly from
Clement's Hypotyposes, book 6 (St. 3:197. 32-198. 2); but this epi-
sode probably belongs to the conclusion of H.E. 2. 14, the story from
Clement being only that concerning the writing of the gospel of Mark.
Simon seems to be of no concern at all to Clement.

The misunderstandings, however, could leave one open to the acceptance of other, less trustworthy, ideas.

Physics and natural history

Clement knows of the touchstone (hē basanos lithos) or Lydian stone, but apparently is unaware of its nature or manner of use,[1] since, though using it as an illustration, he only reports its supposed power of distinguishing spurious from genuine gold (Strom. 1. 9/44. 2). He also knows of the power of magnetite to attract steel ("the much-touted stone," Strom. 2. 6/26. 2; "the Heraclean stone," 7. 2/9. 4), through affinity (dia syngeneian, 2. 6/26. 2) and its spirit (pneumati) even when diffused over many steel rings (7. 2/9. 4: this illustrates how the virtuous, attracted [helkomenoi] by the Holy Spirit, are added [oikeiountai] to the first abode [monē]; "influenced by an indefinable [arrhētos] spirit," 2. 6/26. 2). Along with magnetism, Clement is also aware of the power to influence (helkein) of static electricity as manifested by the power of the amber drop (dakryon soucheion), or of the piece of amber (ēlectron), to attract (epispaein) twigs and move (anakinein) chaff (ibid.). Naturally, he has no concept of the modern notions of such things, for him they are simply examples of the power of the spirit.

Biology and medicine

Clement has, apparently, strong interest in these areas, and according to the standards of that day, a fairly broad, accurate

---

[1]See LSJ, s.v. "βάσανος," "Λύδιος" (Lydia lithos), or "παρατρίβω."

knowledge. In the latter part of _Paedagogus_ 1. 6 (36. 1-51. 3), he
presents various biological items--milk and its relation to blood,
nutriment and digestion, and blood and its relation to other bodily
elements--all to prove that "children" (in various New Testament
passages, especially Pauline) does not mean "childish" and uninstructed.

Meanwhile, Clement is sure that soft beds are bad for digestion (_Paed_. 2. 9/77. 2), wine does terrible things to adolescents
(_Paed_. 2. 2/20. 3-4), beans cause barrenness, whether of mankind,
trees,[1] or birds (_Strom_. 3. 3/24. 2-3), and goat meat contributes to
epilepsy (_Strom_. 7. 6/33. 4). These items have to be taken more or
less on faith, and/or personal observation, but some others seem to be
based on the medical counterpart of the magical ideas of sympathy and
antipathy. Honey, being sweet, generates bile, but mustard lessens
it (_Paed_. 1. 11/96. 2), while bitter roots arrest eating sores (1.
9/83. 2). Clement is also aware of the properties, beneficial, injurious, or dangerous, of various flowers (some shown by the etymology of their names [connections based on associations of ideas]),
and of various unguents made from them (2. 8/64. 4; 68. 1-3; 70. 3;
71. 3-5; 76. 1-4).

Clement also refers several times to the different treatments
used by physicians (_Exh_. 1/8. 2; _Paed_. 1. 8/64. 4-65. 2; _Strom_. 1.
27/171. 2), and also to the different systems or schools of physicians (_Strom_. 7. 15/90. 3-4), especially the "empiric" (except that he
seems to know the name only by hearsay, and defines it as "the physician who has had large experience," _Strom_. 1. 9/ 44. 1, _ANF_ 2:310).

---

[1]Cf. Africanus, mp 17 (Vi., II. 3. 5-6, p. 203).

Other attitudes

Besides the "critical credulity" which Clement reveals in the
various areas presented above, he manifests, along with his contemporaries, both Christian[1] and pagan, a deep interest in number symbolism.
This is shown especially in Stromateis 6. 11 (84-88), dealing explicitly with proportion, ratios, and music, and 6. 16 (133-148), dealing
with the Ten Commandments. In the latter discussion, note especially
the introductory paragraph on the number ten (133. 1), and the discussion of the number seven (and other numbers) in his consideration of
the fourth commandment (138. 5-141. 6).

Origen[2]

Origen believed in magic: not just as fraud or sleight of
hand, or as a system of demonic responses, but as something that really
existed, based in the nature of things. But it was, equally, something that Christians (at least real ones) did not practice, did not
need. There was fraud in its purpose (to deceive and lead from the
truth), but not necessarily in its means (in the true cases); it involved demonic workings, but this was grounded in the nature of things,
not in a pre-determined system of signs which the demons themselves
had established (as Tatian had argued).

---

[1]Note, e.g., Barn. 15, on the days of creation and the ages of
the world, and Irenaeus Adv. haer. 5. 28. 3, on the same topic, and
the end of 5. 28. 2, on the number 666. (Cf., also, Africanus, mp
46/chr 1, "power of numbers"?)

[2]See also, Bardy, "Origène et la magie." A review of Bardy's
article was deliberately avoided while this study was in progress, so
the two studies differ in organization and emphases, but the conclusions are essentially the same.

In most details, Origen's views are quite similar to those of
Clement, but expressed more systematically and on a grander scale.

Discussions of magic

What is magic?

In general, Origen assumes a knowledge of the meaning of the
terms for magic (mageia and related terms, especially the goē- and
mangan- groups), and an understanding of what they involve; but in a
few passages, he lists some such items or corrects misunderstandings
of what he conceives to be their true meaning.

Near the end of Contra Celsum 8, Origen reacts to Celsus's
favoring of Egyptian beliefs regarding the demons over Christianity,
asserting that this is tantamount to recommending magic and sorcery
(manganeuein . . . kai goēteuein . . .; C.C. 8. 59, K. 2:276. 2; also,
mageia in line 9, the opening of chap. 60).[1] Celsus, however, recognizes this also, and cautions that it should not be overdone; at most
the demons can only heal the body, or foretell fortunes, or other
things relating to this life (8. 60, K. 2:276. 11-14, 18-20). Origen
is not fully convinced that they can do even this (lines 33-35), but
in the next chapter details the whole complex (which he has named
"magic and sorcery" just above) as being "curiously inquisitive about

---

[1] Origenes Werke, erster Band: Die Schrift vom Martyrium; Buch
I-IV gegen Celsus; zweiter Band: Buch V-VIII gegen Celsus; Die Schrift
vom Gebet; fünfter Band: De Principiis [ΠΕΡΙ ΑΡΧΩΝ]; ed. Paul Koetschau,
Die Griechischen Christlichen Schriftsteller der ersten drei Jahrhunderte [vols. 2, 3, and 22] (Leipzig: J. C. Hinrichs'sche Buchhandlung,
1899, 1913). (Cited as K., followed by volume, page, and line numbers,
where more precise references than the traditional books and chapters
are desirable.)

the <u>names</u> of demons, their <u>powers</u> and <u>agency</u>, the <u>incantations</u>, the

<u>herbs</u> proper to them, and the stones with inscriptions graven on them

corresponding symbolically or otherwise to their traditional shapes . . ."

(8. 61, <u>ANF</u> 5:662-63 [italics added], K. 2:277. 7-10).[1] Some time

prior to this, after correcting Celsus on the matter of demonic names

and, further, obliquely blaming him for confusing matters concerning

magic and sorcery (<u>phyrōn ta apo tēs magikēs goēteias</u>, 6. 39, K. 2:108.

25).[2] Origen quotes from him another list of magical operations (ap-

parently attributed by Celsus to Christians, an attribution which Ori-

gen emphatically denies).[3] These procedures include "methods of purifi-

cation, or expiatory hymns [<u>lytērious ōdas</u>], or spells for averting

evil [<u>apopompimous phōnas</u>], or (the making of) images, or resemblances

of demons, or the various sorts of antidotes against poison (to be

found) in clothes, or in numbers, or stones, or plants, or roots, or

generally in all kinds of things" (6. 39, <u>ANF</u> 4:591, K. 2:108. 29-109.

3). Elsewhere, however, Origen has objected to considering many of

these things as sorcery. Even granting that serpents and eagles are

acquainted with prophylactics for poisons and diseases, and the virtues

---

[1]English translation from Frederick Crombie, "Origen," <u>ANF</u> 4: 221-669.

[2]He is similarly taxed in <u>C.C.</u> 1. 58 (K. 1:109. 22-25) for not being able to keep the <u>magoi</u> and the <u>Chaldaioi</u> correctly distin- guished. Origen himself presents this distinction in 6. 80 (K. 2:151. 20-25), but he does not do the same for his understanding of <u>mageia</u> and <u>goēteia</u>.

[3]The denial is reinforced by a refusal to treat the matter fur- ther. Since Origen does not dodge hard issues elsewhere, there would appear to be no reason to question his ingenuousness here; he is not pleading ignorance to avoid an embarrassing question. See Origen's disclaimers at the end of 6. 26, and in 6. 28, 32, etc.

of various stones to preserve the young, these are not evidence of sor-

cery (goēteia) as it is commonly understood (4. 86, K. 1:357. 7-10).

Those from whom Celsus derived his accusations against the Christians

(Ophites, etc.), are themselves confused, "neither understanding magic

[ta mageias], nor discriminating the meaning of holy Scripture," and

have "thrown everything into confusion [pant' ephyran]," having "bor-

rowed from magic the names of Ialdabaoth, and Astaphaeus, and Horaeus,

and from the Hebrew Scriptures" various other names (6. 32, ANF 4:588,

K. 2:102. 17-21).[1]

The value of Celsus's arguments are ambiguous (and their refu-

tation more difficult), since Celsus does not make his own view clear:

does he believe his examples of supernatural power or not?[2] If not,

then he should admit it, and argue openly as an Epicurean, opposed to

the dominant Greek view (which would put the Greeks on Origen's side

in the question regarding supernaturalism, an apologetic coup); or, if

so, then he has admitted at least the basis of the Christian view of

Christ (C.C. 3. 35, K. 1:231. 12-29). Origen, on the other hand, is in

no danger from an attempt to reverse the dilemma; he already admits the

---

[1]Earlier in the chapter Origen speaks of them as "sorcerers"
(goētes) who "delude those who are easily carried away by the glitter
of names" (tēs tōn onomatōn phantasias (ANF 4:588, K. 2:102. 11, 12).
The whole passage serves to suggest that Origen regarded magic as a
distinct body of knowledge and practice (going back to the Persian
magoi?), not as itself being a confused amalgam of remnants of older religions, as frequently regarded today. That this is Origen's view seems
to be confirmed by the totality of his references to magic. (Note especially 3. 35, which follows in the text above.)

[2]Cf. also C.C. 1. 68 (K. 1:122. 17-20), where Origen scores
against Celsus's ad hominem argument which seems to allow the existence
of magic, while he, as apparently an Epicurean, did not really believe
in it. (Modern scholars reverse Origen's verdict on Celsus's Epicurean
views.)

existence of demons, only denying them a high status.

How does it work (in general)?

Names. Origen views magic as a consistent system, not an uncertain thing, for the names of the demons in various languages are
those appropriate to the demons of those countries. He expands this
view at some length in discussing the nature of names. It is important to distinguish these names properly, as the various nations ex-
pert in magic know; these names, pronounced in the right set of circumstances, naming the right demon for a particular task, in the proper
language of his area, have great power[1] (C.C. 1. 24, K. 1:74. 18-75.
12; cf. also, C.C. 5. 45 and 6. 39).[2] He develops this idea further,
in the next chapter, by arguing that incantations are vitiated by
translation, it is "not the things signified, but the qualities and
peculiarities of words which possess a certain power . . ." (C.C. 1.
25, ANF 4:406-7, K. 1:76. 16-22; repeated in C.C. 5. 45).[3] The same
view is presented in the Exhortation to Martyrdom: the demons, or
other powers summoned, would not respond to an arbitrary, conventionally

---

[1]Origen's explicit point here is an argument from the lesser
to the greater (if it is so of demons, how much more care should be
used in the names of God); but he accepts the reality of the lesser
from which he argues. Note also De pr. 3. 3. 2, 3, where the "wisdom
of the rulers of this world" (occult wisdom) is not something they impose on mankind deceptively, but something they themselves believe,
and believe as beings appointed to rule the various nations (K. 5:257-
60, esp. 258. 15-21).

[2]In addition to C.C. 1. 24, Bardy cites Selecta in Genes. 17.
5; In Num., hom. 25. 5; In Iesu Nave, hom. 23. 4 ("Origène et la magie,"
p. 134, continuation of n. 27); also, In Iesu Nave, hom. 20. 1 (ibid.,
p. 135, with n. 34).

[3]Again, this seems not to be an ad hominem argument, but Origen's real idea of the nature of things.

assigned (thesei/tethenta) name, but they do come quickly at the prop-

erly pronounced sounds, as by some unobservable natural force (physei

atheōretǭ) (Exh. Mar. 46, K. 1:42. 10-17). Those who know the appro-

priate names may thus use them effectively, without a true knowledge

of the being which is named. This is shown by the widespread use of

expressions such as "the God of Abraham," or "of Abraham, Isaac, and

Jacob," in the conjuration or exorcism of demons and in other incanta-

tions and magical rites by the Egyptians, and in treatises on magic

found in many places (C.C. 1. 22, K. 1:72. 27-73. 1; C.C. 4. 33, 34,

K. 1:303. 31-304. 4, and 304. 22-30).[1]

Augury and divination. A similar situation exists in augury

and divination: the demons responsible for it have entered into the

several species of animals, "each species of demon . . . [seeming] to

possess a certain affinity with a certain species of animal" (C.C. 4.

92, 93 [quotation from chap. 93, ANF 4:539, K. 1:366. 14-15]).

Further, in an argument to support the representative nature

of Christ's death by the use of the various Greek and barbarian ac-

counts of self-sacrifice for public advantage, Origen suggests that it

is "probable" (eikos) that "in the nature of things [en tē physei tōn

pragmatōn], for certain mysterious reasons [kata tinas aporrhētous . . .

logous] which are difficult to be understood by the multitude, [there

is] such a virtue [physin toiautēn] that one just man, dying a volun-

tary death for the common good, might be the means of removing wicked

---

[1]Note also C.C. 5. 45, and the use of Scripture names and expressions by the nations in their magic in In Jesu Nave, hom. 20. 1.

spirits, which are the cause of plagues, or . . ." (C.C. 1. 31, ANF
4:409, K. 1:82. 26-30).

How does it work (spells, incantations, and spirits)?

While the specific mechanics of magic are in some mysterious
force, the operative means are incantations[1] which in some way control
the demons who are the operative power behind it. The Magi, on familiar terms with evil spirits, worked such things as the supernatural
strength of the spirits could accomplish by using spells (epōdē) which
invoked the spirits (C.C. 1. 60, K. 1:110. 23-26). Magic and sorcery
"derive their power from evil demons, who are spell-bound by elaborate
incantations, and become subject to sorcerers" (kataklēsesi periergois
thelgomenōn kai anthrōpois goēsin hypakouontōn) (C.C. 2. 51, ANF 4:451,
K. 1:174. 13). Similarly the demons are led by invocations, or their
own inclinations, in certain operations (C.C. 7. 67, K. 2:216. 20-21),
or, more specifically, they are called upon by "charms" (philtrois ē
misethrois), by incantations and magical arts (epōdōn kai manganeiōn),
to induce them to do the wishes of the one invoking them (C.C. 7. 69,
K. 2:218. 22-26). This includes the dedication of famous temples accomplished by "curious magical incantations" (katakliseis periergous)
by those who zealously served the demon with magical arts (manganeiōn)
(ibid.; lines 30, 32). Elsewhere, Origen similarly speaks of the demons being attached to, or removed to, specific places "by a sort of
magical force" (or rites and incantations, teletōn . . . kai manganeiōn)

---

[1]Bardy calls special attention to In Iesu Nave, hom. 20. 1,
which lists various things the pagans accomplish by charms, incantations, and use of names ("Origène et la magie," p. 132, and n. 23).

or by their own evil preferences (C.C. 7. 5, K. 2:157. 1-3; and 3. 34,
K. 1:231. 3; also 7. 64, K. 2:214.10).

Who does it?

The Magi are the prototype practitioners of magic, but to Origen they are only historical figures (C.C. 1. 58 and 60). For him, and
for Celsus also, the main contemporary adepts seem to be the Egyptians
(C.C. 1. 22, 28, 38, and 68), but some barbarians are admired for
their marvellous powers of incantation (tais paradoxois ex epōdōn
dynamesi) (1. 30, K. 1:81. 19-20), and the books of magic which include the names of Abraham, Isaac, and Jacob, are found in "many
places" (4. 33, K. 1:304. 2). The picture which Celsus gives further
suggests that many of those who have learned from the Egyptians then
travelled about giving public demonstrations and teaching their knowledge to anyone for a few coins (1. 68, K. 1:122. 5-13).

Is it "true"?

As noted above (page 367), Origen believed in the reality of
magic, and he even scored Celsus for seemingly doubting it, yet he
spoke also of the refuting (or convicting, elenchtheisēs)[1] of the sorcery of the demons done for the Magi (C.C. 1. 60, K. 1:111. 4-5). In
one chapter alone he refers to "doing tricks" (terateuesthai) three
times (2. 55, K. 1:178. 10, 179. 8 and 11; plus one occurrence of
terateia in the same chapter [179. 1-2] and one occurrence each of the

---

[1] But paired with katalytheisēs, and so perhaps simply a factual
statement rather than a moral judgment. Henry Chadwick translates
"confuted" (Origen: Contra Celsum [Cambridge: University Press, 1953],
p. 54).

noun and the verb in the next chapter [179. 30 and 180. 23]). He uses

the pejorative terms goēs, goēteia, goēteuein, regularly, along with a

liberal sprinkling of manganeia, manganeuein. The specific examples

which appear, however, show that it is not simple fakery that is in-

volved. In some cases, that might be the explanation, though Origen

seems not to think so. Examples of this would be the production of

banquets with no real existence but only an appearance, and the caus-

ing of non-living things to move, having only an appearance of life

(1. 68, K. 1:122. 10-13; these are quoted from Celsus, but Origen ap-

pears to accept them as true accounts).

While Origen would seem to agree with the "Jew" of Celsus that

many "who practice such juggling tricks" (terateuesthai) do so to de-

ceive and make gain (2. 55; ANF 4:453-54, K. 1:179. 7-12), he dis-

agrees as to the nature of the deception. The specific "trick" re-

ferred to is the prediction and manifestation of a resurrection. In

the discussion immediately following, Origen basically utilizes an ad

hominem argument against the "Jew" (2. 55-58, K. 1:179. 5-182. 5), but

he returns to the question later (3. 26) using a more revealing line

of argument. Such reports must be either terateia or invention

(plasmata) (3. 27, K. 1:224. 16); assuming that they are not inven-

tion, they must have actually happened through the cooperation of some

demon (3. 31, K. 1:228. 13-15, re Abaris the Hyperborean), or a demon

contrived that the report should be committed to writing (3. 32, re

"the Clazomenian"; in this case Origen does not believe the demon

could actually contrive for such things to happen [K. 1:228. 26-28]),

or the demon caused people to think they saw it by a deception (apatē) of the eyes like the "show-off" jugglers (<u>tois epideiknymenois goēsin</u>)

(3. 33, K. 1:230. 12-14, re Cleomedes of Astypalaea), or effects were

produced by the "magical arts and rites of the Egyptians" (<u>manganeias</u>

<u>an Aigyptiōn kai teletas</u>) who set up a demon to impersonate the deified

person, prophesying and healing or punishing (3. 36, <u>ANF</u> 4:478, K.

1:232. 13-20, re Antinous). In the last case, some testimony is lying

(<u>katapseudontai</u>) by those who may gain, some witnesses are deceived

(<u>apatōmenoi</u>) by demons, and others are misled by their own guilty (or

"weak," <u>asthenous</u>) consciences (3. 36, K. 1:232. 20-24).

Thus, while there is human fraud involved, at least some is

demonic, consisting of the production of deceptive appearances, etc.[1]

The major duplicity, however, is in the purpose: to deceive men and

turn them from God(7. 5, K. 2:157. 5-6 [in context this refers to de-

monic use of powers of prophecy, but it is applicable to all their

acts]; 8. 54, K. 2:270. 1-271. 17). This constitutes the whole system

as "deceptive" irrespective of the question of possible frauds among

human practitioners. It ends in the corruption and destruction of all

who use it (6. 80. K. 2:151. 22-25).

Discussions of theory and praxis

There is, inevitably, a great deal of overlap between the pre-

ceding discussion and that which follows, but the preceding was in-

tended to identify Origen's basic ideas of magic and the magicians,

---

[1]Note <u>C.C.</u> 6. 45—the devil himself aids Antichrist to simulate
good, do lying miracles, etc., aid far surpassing that which the demons
give the sorcerers (<u>tous goētas</u>) who deceive men for the lowest purposes (<u>ta phaulotata</u>) (K. 2:116. 27-30).

while that which follows concentrates on its methodology, both theoretical and practical.

Names and incantations

The key to magic in Origen's view is demonic action (which will
be discussed below), and the key to demonic action is the proper use of
names and associated incantations.[1]

Nature of names. Names are derived, like language in general,
not from human convention or invention, but from nature itself (agree-
ing more closely with the Stoic, and, somewhat, the Epicurean, views of
names, than with the Aristotelian, but not quite bound to them either;
C.C. 1. 24). Each nation names it own gods (6. 39), and each language
expresses most accurately the nature of the demons known to those who
speak it (C.C. 1. 24; 5. 45). The same applies to the names and functions of angels (who are called by various names, appropriately to the
duties they perform according to God's will), and also to Christ whose
name has pre-eminent power over demons (C.C. 1. 25, K. 1:76. 8-15).[2]
The demons respond quickly (tacha) to their properly pronounced names
as though led by a certain unseen natural power (tini physei atheorētǫ)
(Exh.Mar. 46, K. 1:42. 14-17). This is a very deep and subtle matter
(pragmateia bathytatē kai anakechōrēkuia, Exh.Mar. 46, K. 1:42. 10-11;
in C.C. 1. 24 it is logos bathys kai aporrhētos, K. 1:74. 11).

---

[1]Though incantations are frequently referred to by Origen,
names seem to be the potent elements in them.

[2]Compare also his distinction between believing in Jesus' name
and believing in Jesus, and their results in Commentary on John (10.
44/[28]. 307, 310, 314).

Incantations. In the use of incantations, the same result is
reported. They are of force (energēsai) only in their proper languages,
and are "inefficacious and feeble [atonon kai ouden dynamenēn]" if translated, thus it is not the thing said but "the qualities and peculiarities of words [hai tōn phonōn poiotētes kai idiotētes] which possess a
certain power" (C.C. 1. 25, ANF 4:407, K. 1:76, 16-22).[1] Origen reports this as from "those who are skilled in the use of incantations
[hoi . . . epōdōn deinoi]" but does not seem to question its validity
in its own realm, though he denies that Christians are involved in
these areas (ibid., lines 16-17).

Christians are so far from this, that, contrary to Celsus's
charges (e.g., C.C. 6. 32, 40; 7. 40), they do not even use the precise Scriptural names of God,[2] but pray each in his own language, since
God hears them all (C.C. 8. 37, K. 2:252. 18-28; cf. 8. 61, K. 2:277.
3-13 -- those acceptable to God are those who trust Him, not those
curiously inquisitive about demonic names, etc.).

Spirits

The dominant element in Origen's theory of magic is one that

---

[1]Note also his emphasis on the proper sounding of names according to the numerous listed variables of pronunciation in Exh.Mar. 46
(K. 1:42. 14-15).

[2]This despite the fact that Origen elsewhere has argued against
Celsus's assertion of the indifference of the divine designation, and
attributed power to Sabaoth or Adonai which their translations would
not have (C.C. 5. 45, K. 2:50. 1-5; cf. also 1. 24, K. 1:75. 12-14).
In 5.45, however, Origen is referring to magical uses of these and
other names in incantations (which he appears to assume to be really
effective). In addition, in both these passages, Origen is speaking
somewhat pedantically, while in 6. 32 he is describing actual worship
practices of the unschooled (and the contrast does further emphasize
the non-magical view of prayer).

integrates it fully into his whole world-view--his theory of spirits.
The spiritual realm, of which man is a low-level component, is universally pervasive, highly organized, and at least partially subject
to human understanding and control.

The origin, but not the character, of spirits is in the creation of God; they came to their present statuses as a result of sin
(rebellion). The most guilty are demons, those with slight offense
are angels of various orders, etc. (C.C. 4. 65; De pr. 1. praef. 6;
1. 7. 2-3, 5; 1. 8. 1, 4; this includes the sun, moon, and stars
which are sentient, volitional beings, De pr. 2. 11. 7; On Prayer 7;
C.C. 5. 11). In this matter, the main emphasis is on the demons--
they are evil, daimōn is not a neutral·term (C.C. 5. 5; 7. 69; 8. 25;
respectively, K. 2:5. 15-16; 218. 10-11, 16-20; 242. 1-12)[1]--but Origen's controlling belief in free-will required that angelic status
and position also be determined by desert (De pr. 1. 8. 1, K. 5:94.
16-22; in C.C. 8. 25, there are angels of the devil as well as angels
of God). The demons (and angels) are assigned to, or choose, their
various areas of influence, geographical or otherwise, according to
their characters (De pr. 1. 5. 3; 1. 8. 1 and 4; 3. 3. 3; cf. C.C.
5. 29-30).[2] In addition, the natures of demons may bring them into

---

[1]Note also Hom. in Num. 13. 5: those who minister to magicians
are angeli . . . refugae, et spiritus maligni, et daemonia immunda
(PG 12: col. 672C), and can work only evil, never good (Hom. in Num.
13. 4, 5, 6).

[2]But this power is subject to certain restraints: only the
angels are assigned positive power over the good things of human life
(air, crops, etc.); the demons can affect them only negatively, as
executioners of divine judgments or discipline (C.C. 8. 31).

special relations with various animals (as in divination) (<u>C.C</u>. 4. 92,
93).

The demons have great power which is available to those who
can control them. The Magi had such control (<u>C.C</u>. 1. 60; etc.), as
did the Egyptians and those taught by them (e.g., 1. 68), and the
practice seems to have become widespread (4. 33, K. 1:304. 2). In
the first reference, Origen puts no limit to the demonic power in ordinary circumstances, but in the second he seems to imply that the
works are essentially fraudulent, appearances only. Further, in
<u>Contra Celsum</u> 8. 60, he pictures Celsus as backing down in his claims,
suggesting, in the final analysis, that the earthbound (<u>perigeiōn</u>)
demons responsible for magic can only heal the body, foretell the
future, and do other things related to mortal existence (K. 2:276. 15-
20), but Origen is not fully ready to concede the reality of even
these acts (lines 33-35). (Other acts--deceptive resurrection,
etc.--have been discussed above.) The appropriate control is achieved
by conjuration of the spirits using the proper names and other appropriate forms in the spells (as noted above under the discussion of
names). Especially powerful (and widespread) are those involving the
"God of Abraham" or "of Abraham, Isaac, and Jacob" (<u>C.C</u>. 1. 22, K.
1:72. 27-73. 1; see also 4. 33, 34; 5. 45). Other "barbaric names
of demons" were also used by practitioners, Origen again holding that
they must be kept distinct, the demons of the various nations are not
the same (6. 39, K. 2:108. 1-23). Celsus charged that Christians
were involved in this kind of action, citing certain "presbyters" whom
he found using barbarous books containing the names of demons and

marvels, which they professed to use for no good purposes, but to harm
mankind (6. 40, K. 2:109. 14-18; Origen replied by a denial supported
by popular knowledge of Christian character).

The demonic power, however, is two-sided, and the human may be
the one controlled (possessed) by the demon (e.g., De pr. 3. 3. 4-6).[1]
For this reason, even magic provides for the exorcism (exelaunein) of
demons in its repertoire (C.C. 1. 68, K. 1:122. 9; a rationalization
of their seeming success is presented in Comm. Mt. 13. 6). Further,
even when the human goētes appear to be in control, the demonic ends,
the furtherance of evil, are being served (C.C. 6. 45, K. 2:116. 23-
28). In the case of oracles, a prominent agency of the demons (8. 54),
their control becomes obvious (7. 3, 4).

There is thus no real boundary between magic and pagan worship.
In general, the same demonic forces are behind both (C.C. 3. 34, 36,
37), and specifically, the demons are bound to certain places or
images by "rites and incantations" (teletōn . . . kai manganeiōn) (3.
34, K. 1:231. 3; cf. also 7. 5, 64, 67, 69, respectively, K. 2:157.
2, 214. 10, 216. 20, 218. 30-32). Ptolemy's image of Serapis, for
example, was so prepared by magōn kai pharmakōn kai tōn epōdais autōn
kēloumenōn daimonōn (5. 38, K. 2:42. 28-43. 3). (The demons are especially attracted by the smoke, blood, etc., of the sacrifices,
which they need to survive [C.C. 4. 32; 7. 5; 8. 61, 63; De pr. 1. 8.
1; Exh.Mar. 45]. Angels apparently share this need, they are not
nourished on material bread [On Prayer 27. 10], yet they were attracted

---

[1]Note also the warning in Origen's arguments against invoking
angels in C.C. 5. 5.

to the altars of Israel and there were nourished [De pr. 1. 8. 1, K. 5:97. 8-11].)

On the other side, angels are associated with the worship of the Christian. They are at his side as he prays, even when unasked (aklētoi) aiding him against the demons (C.C. 8. 64); as he prays, they hear and do what they can for him as having received a general command (to minister to man) (On Prayer 11. 4), and also pray with him (11. 5). (They are, however, "listening in," the prayers are not addressed to them.[1]) The worshippers and the attending spirits form a double assembly, men and angels (On Prayer 31. 5), but if the men become lax and sinful, they may be accompanied by an assembly of wicked angels (31. 6, 7).

Celsus charged that Christians also worked by the use of demonic names and incantations (katakelēsesi) (C.C. 1. 6, K. 1:59. 8-10), as Jesus had worked by sorcery (goēteia) (lines 21-22). In reply, Origen states that the Christians use only the name of Jesus, along with the recital of the narratives concerning him (tēs apangelias tōn . . . historiōn) (ibid., lines 12-13).[2] Further, bypassing for

---

[1]See the further pictures of angelic aid and accompaniment of worship in C.C. 5. 4 and 5, and the irrationality of invoking them in the latter chapter.

[2]This could be seen as the magical use of a narrative (see, e.g., Alan H. Gardiner, "Magic[Egyptian]," Encyclopedia of Religion and Ethics, ed. Hastings, 8:265; cf. Bronislaw Malinowski, "Magic Science and Religion," in Science Religion and Reality, ed. Joseph Needham [New York: Macmillan Company, 1925], p. 69), but need not be. This is especially so in view of Origen's intellectualist bent; it is more likely to refer simply to a narration of Christ's power, to enlighten the subject and produce faith. This seems especially probable in view of the context; if Origen had considered any magical interpretation of the matter likely, he would hardly have introduced it into

the moment the source of Jesus' works, it is clear that the Christians
do not employ spells (epōdōn), but the name of Jesus and "other words
which are relied on according to the divine scripture" (lines 28-32).
The power of Jesus' name is such that even wicked men have on occasion
used it successfully for such purposes (lines 16-17). It has already
driven myriads of demons from the souls and bodies of men, exerting
power (energēsan) (C.C. 1. 25, K. 1:76. 13-15; also, On Prayer 12,
and 22. 3); and not only so, but even from animals (C.C. 7. 67, K.
2:216. 28) and from images (8. 43, K. 2:258. 20). Christians need not
fear the enmity of the demons (toward the human race, 7. 3; 8. 26) who
try to destroy Christianity (3. 29; 4. 32; 8. 27, 43), they are protected by the supreme God (8. 27, 36). The death of Christ has reduced the demons to impotence (7. 17; 8. 43; Comm. Jn. 1. 32/37).
But this also seems to be founded on a general principle, a sort of
natural law[1]; the death of Christ is unique, but there are analogies
to it in those who have died to remove a danger to their country:
"For it is probable that there is in the nature of things [en tē
physei tōn pragmatōn], for certain mysterious reasons which are difficult to be understood [kata tinas aporrhētous kai dysleptous . . .

---

the discussion, seemingly gratuitously (cf. also, C.C. 7. 67). Henry
Chadwick's notes on C.C. 1. 6 support this view in general, but do
note the other possibility (Origen, p. 10, notes 1 and 4).

  [1]Origen elsewhere speaks of a sort of "natural attraction" (tina
physikē holkē) of faith and the divine power (Comm. Mt. 10. 19;
Robert Girod, Origène: Commentaire sur l'Evangile selon Matthieu, vol.
1: Livres X et XI, Sources chrétiennes, no. 162 [Paris: Les Editions du
Cerf, 1970], p. 230, lines 20-23), though perhaps mutual interrelation
would be a better description; either is limited without the other
(ibid., p. 232, lines 43-46).

.logous] by the multitude, such a virtue [physin toiautēn] that one
just man, dying a voluntary death for the common good, might be the
means of removing [apotropiasmous empoiein] wicked spirits, which are
the cause of plagues, or barrenness, or tempests, or similar calami-
ties"[1] (C.C. 1. 31, ANF 4:409, K. 1:82. 24-30; also, Comm. Jn. 6.
54/36. 276-81, where the death of martyrs, including Jephthah's daugh-
ter, has similar powers).[2]

Materia magica

Origen's main concern with magic is in the areas of names (including incantations) and spirits, but he does evidence some knowledge
concerning the physical materials used in magic, but without information as to their specific manners of use.[3] In two passages he gives
abbreviated lists of items. The first occurs in a quotation from Celsus, of which Origen equivocally denied the accuracy, and unequivocally
denied the applicability to "us": ". . . images [or, noises: typous/
ktypous], or resemblances [schēmatismous] of demons, or the various

---

[1](See above also, p. 372.) A similar usage appears in modern
"apologetic" literature, but with an emphasis on its uniqueness, in C.
S. Lewis's chapter title, "Deeper Magic from Before the Dawn of Time"
(The Lion, the Witch, and the Wardrobe [London: Geoffrey Bles, 1950;
New York: Macmillan, 1950; reprint ed., New York: Collier Books, 1970],
chap. 15).

[2]A further interesting example of a specialized power, one also
negated by Christ, is that of the presumed angel who is hostile toward
the Jews (and all who worship the Creator) but has power only to harm
those of them who are not circumcised, a power abolished with Christ's
circumcision (C.C. 5. 48).

[3]In addition to the passages below, note also Selecta in Exod.,
cited by Bardy ("Origène et la magie," p. 142, n. 55 [PG, 12:col. 284B]),
where Moses is said to use his hand and voice, not only his staff, so
as not to allow belief that he worked by magical procedures.

sorts of antidotes against poison (to be found) in clothes, or in numbers, or stones, or plants, or roots, or generally in all kinds of
things?" (C.C. 6. 39, ANF 4:591, K. 2:109. 1-3). The second refers
to those who are "curiously inquisitive" about the demons, including[1]
the plants appropriate (botanas oikeias) to them and stones with inscriptions (glyphas) corresponding to their traditional forms, whether
symbolic or otherwise (C.C. 8. 61, K. 2:277. 7-10). A third passage
is probably related here also, though purely medicinal powers may be
meant (the context includes both natural and supernatural items):
among the things Paul (and any other Christian) will learn after death
is "the reasons certain properties are associated with certain roots
or herbs, and other herbs and roots, on the contrary, repel [or,
avert: depelluntur]" (De pr. 2. 11. 5, K. 5:188. 24-26). Further,
Origen has read in Numenius the Pythagorean that the Serapis image
partook of the essences of all the animals and plants governed by nature (C.C. 5. 38, K. 2:42. 26-29). This statement is connected with
the account of its preparation by magoi, etc., noted above (p. 381).

Origen denied that knowledge of natural antidotes and prophylactics by animals (specifically serpents and eagles) constituted
knowledge of sorcery by them, but he does not deny their power (C.C.
4. 86). He especially mentions (K. 1:357. 5 and 20)[2] the "eagle-

---

[1]Along with their names, powers, deeds, and appropriate incantations (lines 7-8).

[2]The alleged use of fennel by serpents (lines 14-15) is more
physic than magic. These items were presented as examples of the kind
of things known to animals by instinct (physis) or experience which
men learn only by reason and understanding.

stone," which supposedly preserves the young of the eagle in the
nest.

Discussion of related fields[1]

Oracles and divination

Origen, like his apologetic predecessors, and all other inhabitants of the ancient world, was aware of a large number of procedures
for learning the future. The nations employ numerous means of divination (manteiai): by portents, omens, birds, ventriloquists, professors
of the sacrificial art, of Chaldean casters of nativities (klēdonōn . . .
oiōnōn . . . ornithōn . . . engastrimythōn . . . tōn tēn thytikēn
epangellomenōn . . . Chaldaiōn genethlialogountōn) (C.C. 1. 36, K.
1:87. 26-29). These are besides the numerous established oracles
(chrēstēriai, theopropriai), the Pythian, Dodonian, Clarian, in
Branchidae, and in Ammon, and a myriad others (C.C. 7. 3, K. 2:154.
18-20; repeated at the ends of 7. 6 and 7).[2]

Origen's main point in the two preceding passages (especially
the former), is a contrast of pagan divination to Hebrew prophecy.

---

[1]Besides the major areas examined below, the field of music
appears in two incidental references. One of Celsus's informants regarding magic was an Egyptian musician, Dionysius (C.C. 6. 41, K.
2:109. 24). Then, in his discussion of Mithraic mysteries, Celsus al-
legedly added musical reasons for the order of the stars given by the
"Persian theology" and then added a second set, also with musical connections (C.C. 6. 22).

[2]C.C. 8. 45 (K. 2:259. 23-28) indicates a wide variety of ways
in which these oracles might be given. De pr. 3. 3. 3 includes a reference to the use of boys as recipients of a spirit (here a poetic
one), apparently a common magical operation (cf., e.g., the references
to this in Justin and Irenaeus [see esp. p. 351, with n. 1, above]).

The Jews shared in the normal human anxieties about the future (K.
1:87. 30-31), and so, to keep them from polytheism and pagan practices, God instituted prophecy among them, allowing the prophets even
to give predictions about events of no importance (C.C. 1. 36, note
esp. K. 1:87. 14-20 and 88. 2-4).

But this concession is almost the only point of similarity
between pagan divination and Jewish (and Christian) prophecy. The
oracles are the product of wicked spirits, who enter the bodies of
their spokespersons,[1] overpowering their minds, clouding them and
causing loss of self-control (C.C. 7. 3-5, esp. K. 2:155. 24-25 and
156. 10-12 regarding the effect on the subject). Those under the inspiration of the divine spirit, however, should have then the greatest
clarity (dioratikōteron) (7. 3, K. 2:155. 29-30). This is the case
with the Jewish prophets (7. 4, K. 2:155. 32-156. 9). In fact, they
were either wise men, or were made wise, and were chosen because of
the virtue of their lives (7. 7, K. 2:159. 1-6, 160. 5-8; see also
5. 42, K. 2:46. 19-22). This contrast was developed, in the present
tense, in De pr. 3. 3. 3 (K. 5:259. 18-260. 2), but in C.C. 7. 8,
Origen asserts that there are no significant[2] prophecies among the
Jews or the Christians of his time, despite Celsus's claim to have
heard some personally in Phoenicia and Palestine.

Origen also provides a rationale for divination, one in keeping with his other views expressed above. If there is anything to

---

[1] In a most unseemly manner in the case of the Pythian priest-
ess, Origen has heard (C.C. 7. 3, K. 2:155. 12-23).

[2] But he does allow himself some leeway: plēn kai nun eti
ichnē . . . autou par' oligois (K. 2:160. 26-27).

divination by birds and other animals (a prior question that Celsus

should have established before arguing from it: C.C. 4. 88, 89, K.

1:360. 13-14, 360. 22-361. 3),[1] it is due to the work of demons, not

because birds are more intelligent or more divine than man. The de-

mons, who, due to their lack of a material body, have some insight

into the future, indicate it by entering the bodies of the lower or

more savage animals and directing their movements (C.C. 4. 92; also

repeated at the end of 4. 97).[2] But the demons also work directly on

man, either by possession as in the noted oracles (C.C. 7. 3, etc.,

just above),[3] or through influencing dreams (C.C. 5. 6, K. 2:6. 1-2).[4]

The Jews recognized this and rejected all divination as vain (matēn),

a bewitching (kēlousēs) of men (C.C. 5. 42, K. 2:46. 18-19).

In any case, foreknowledge is non-probative, since it (like

the power of healing) is neutral (meson), neither good nor evil in

itself (C.C. 3. 25, and 4. 96, K. 1:221. 5-10, and 368. 23-369. 3).

Astrology

Origen manifests little interest in the somewhat magically

---

[1]But that was Celsus's responsibility, not Origen's, so while
pointing out that there were good arguments on both sides, he by-
passes it, assuming the existence of divination for the sake of the
argument (C.C. 4. 90, K. 1:362. 11-19). But, basically, the arguments
are theological versus testimonial (lines 14-19).

[2]As testimony of this, the unclean animals of the Mosaic leg-
islation are especially the divinatory, different species of demons
being similar to different species of animals, even weasels (!)
(C.C. 4. 93).

[3]Some are possessed from their earliest years, even from birth,
by a Pythonic daemon (De pr. 3. 3. 5, K. 5:262. 1).

[4]This occurs in a quotation from Celsus, but Origen makes no
specific objection to this element of the quotation.

related area of astrology. This lack of interest is despite his belief in the "personality" of the sun, moon, and stars (De pr. 2. 11.7;
etc.; see above under "Spirits"), and despite assertions of his belief in it by later detractors.[1] This attitude is, however, fully in
keeping with his emphasis on free-will (cf. De pr. 1. praef. 5).

He is, of course, not unaware of it and its theory. He re-
bukes Celsus for calling a "most divinely inspired nation" the Chaldeans "from whom the deceptive casting of nativities (genethlialogia)
came to use by men" (C.C. 6. 80, K. 2:151. 20-22). He also classes
"the astrology of the Chaldeans and Indians (Chaldeorum astrologia et
Indorum)" as part of the "wisdom of the 'rulers of this world'"
(De pr. 3. 3. 2, K. 5:257. 27).

This wisdom, however, is one which these "rulers" believe (De
pr. 3. 3. 3, K. 5:258. 15-21), and, presumably, act in accordance with.
This would give some, relative color to the charge of Theophilus that

> foreknowledge of events, . . . he . . . attributes to the motions
> of the stars, namely, that from their courses and the variety of
> their forms daemons can tell the future and either bring things
> to pass or else require them to be brought to pass by the stars[2]

---

[1]Theophilus of Alexandria, and charges quoted by an Anonymous
in Photius (cited by Koetschau, Origenes Werke, 5:259, on De pr. 3.
3. 3).

[2]Compare Origin's view of demonic operation in divination,
above. This impression is not weakened by the (somewhat lyrical)
expressions in On Prayer 7, to "the march and movement of the stars
that fits in with all the universe. . . . the free will of the stars
that dance in the heavens for the good of the universe" (K. 2:316.
6-7, 10-11; translation from John J. O'Meara, Prayer: Exhortation to
Martyrdom, Ancient Christian Writers, ed. Johannes Quasten and Joseph
C. Plumpe, no. 19 [Westminster, Md.: The Newman Press, 1954; London:
Longmans, Green and Co., 1954], p. 36), though these expressions probably refer only to the grand beneficient ordering of all things, not
to individual influences by sympathy or whatever. Further, does De

(Theophilus Alex. Ep. Synod. c.2; cited in K. 5:259, at De pr. 3. 3. 3).[1]

Origen does attribute significance (direct or indirect) to two possibly astrological items, establishing them on an empirical basis. Comets (such as the "star" at Jesus' birth, C.C. 1. 58) tend to appear, as observation shows, at times of great earthly changes, signifying either bad or good things (C.C. 1. 59, K. 1:110. 3-16). On a more mundane level, "lunacy," as physicians attest by their discussions, is connected to the moon. Contrary to their theories, however, it is not caused by moist humours in the head moved by sympathy with the moon, but by an impure spirit which observes the phases of the moon and varies his influence accordingly, to mislead men. If this is so, then why not other spirits operating in phase with the other stars? So,

> It is worth while, then, to listen to the casters of nativities
> [tōn genethlialogōn], who refer the origin of every form of mad-
> ness and every demoniacal possession to the phases of the
> moon.(Comm. Mt. 13. 6, ANF 10:478, Kl. 10:195. 13-14) [2]

---

pr. 1.praef.5, leave open the possibility that some things, those outside our freedom of will, are due to the course and motion of the
stars (K. 5:13, 3-5)? Note also Origen's discussion in his commentary on Genesis (in Eus. Prep. Gosp. 6. 11).

[1]G. W. Butterworth, trans., Origen On First Principles (London:
Society for Promoting Christian Knowledge, 1936; reprint ed., New
York: Harper and Row, Publishers, Harper Torchbooks, The Cathedral
Library, 1966), p. 225, n. 4.

[2]English translation by John Patrick, "Origen's Commentary on
the Gospel of Matthew," ANF 10:409-512; Greek text, Erich Klostermann,
ed., Origenes Werke, zehnter Band: Origenes Matthäuserklärung, I: Die
Griechisch erhaltenen Tomoi, unter Mitwirkung von Ernst Benz; Die
Griechischen Christlichen Schriftsteller der ersten drei Jahrhunderte,
vol. 40 (Leipzig: J. C. Hinrichs'sche Buchhandlung, 1935) (cited as
Kl. followed by volume [of Origenes Werke], page, and line[s]).

Other religions as magic

Pagan religion

Origen saw no sharp line dividing pagan worship from magic.[1]
The powers invoked in magic were the same as those worshipped, i.e.,
demons (C.C. 8. 61; 7. 67; also, 5. 46, K. 2:51. 2-3). They are addicted to the blood, etc., of sacrifices (Exh. Mar. 45; C.C. 3. 37;
4. 32; 7. 5, 6 [proof from Homer] and 35; De pr. 1. 8. 1), and they
can be influenced, their favor purchased by sacrifices (e.g., C.C.
8. 61, K. 2:277. 23-26, probably switching favor to the offerer of
the greater sacrifices). Not only so, but various "magical" rites
(manganeiai) are involved in the establishment of such worship (C.C.
3. 34, 36 [Antinous]; 5. 38 [Serapis]; 7. 5).

Heresies

Origen parried some of Celsus's charges of magic among Christians by attributing them to heretics or heretical groups. In the
past, Simon the Samaritan magos wished to seduce some by magic (tē
mageia) (C.C. 1. 57, K. 1:109. 6), because he and Dositheus, like
Celsus, thought Jesus simply did wonders (terateuesthai), and so
tried the same means to gain mastery over men (C.C. 6. 11, K. 2:81.
14-19). These groups, however, are obsolete, currently having either
none, or not even thirty members each (1. 57, not likely even thirty
Simonians in Palestine and none elsewhere; 6. 11, no Simonians, and

---

[1]He did, however, recognize a distinction between the broad
areas of religion and magic, as, e.g., his seeming view of magic as a
distinct tradition in C.C. 6. 32 (K. 2:102. 17-19), and a slight distinction between being carried away by magic, or by demons in 6. 41
(K. 2:110. 12-13).

not thirty Dositheans total); the current group that Origen (and Celsus) seem to know best is the Ophites. They are sorcerers (goētes) (C.C. 6. 31, 32; 7. 40; K. 2:100. 28; 102. 11; 190. 22), who profess a sort of magical sorcery (magikēn tina goēteian, 6. 38, K. 2:107. 23-24), but they scramble together elements (names) from magic and Scripture in their system (6. 32, K. 2:102. 17-19). The heart of their doctrine seems to be a set of secret charges to be addressed to the keepers of the various gates in the heavens (C.C. 6. 31 and 7. 40).

Christian practices

Origen, naturally, did not consider Christian practices as having any relation to magic, but Celsus did. There are thus a number of explicit discussions of the question.

Origen is emphatic on the point that Christian miracles are done by the power of God (C.C. 1. 38; 2. 9, 51; 3. 5, 24), by the name of Jesus (1. 6; 3. 24; etc.) not by magical means of any sort (1. 6, 38; 2. 9, 16; 3. 5) or demonic power (1. 6; etc.). But what evidence is there to support these assertions?

What distinguishes Christian miracles from magic or other miracles/marvels?[1] Origen's first stated criterion is the non-use of incantations (katakelēseis, katepadontes, epōdai, C.C. 1. 6, K. 1:59.

---

[1]Cf. Morton Smith's list (Jesus the Magician, pp. 83 and 92). Note also the three charges against miracle workers discussed by Anitra Bingham Kolenkow, "A Problem of Power: How Miracle Doers Counter Charges of Magic in the Hellenistic World," Society of Biblical Literature 1976 Seminar Papers (Missoula, Mont.: Published by Scholars Press for the Society of Biblical Literature, 1976), p. 107. The three charges are: subversion, use of power for evil purposes (maleficia), and use of miracles to gain riches or other power.

9, 10, 30) or other such means (hoiasdēpote hodou, 2. 49, K. 1:171. 1;

periergō kai magikō ē pharmakeutikō pragmati, 7. 4, K. 2:156. 14; note

also 2. 51).[1] Origen's next criteria are his most fully developed, a

series of interrelated moral arguments. The character of life (and

death, in 2. 44) of the one(s) performing the works (1. 68; 2. 32, 51;

3. 5; 8. 61), and the teachings connected with them (1. 38, 68; 2. 8,

44, 49; 3. 5 [Mosaic laws]; also, Comm. Mt. 12. 2) and their resulting

moral changes (C.C. 1. 43, 67, 68; 2. 44, 51; 3. 27, 42; 4. 5; 8. 47-

48) are all proofs that these works are not the result of magic.[2]

Further, their divine origin is confirmed by having been previously

prophesied (C.C. 2. 14, 55-56; De pr. 4. 1. 2; Comm. Jn. 2. 34/[28];

Comm. Mt. 12. 2). The results of such works are a crucial test (C.C.

2. 50, 51), and, besides the moral results in the individual, other

results also distinguish Biblical and Christian miracles from magic:

the existence of churches full of converts (1. 67), the founding of

(a) new nation(s) (2. 51, 52), curing of diseases not curable by man

or daemon (3. 24). In contrast to these results and to the reality of

the churches' miracles is the unreality of the works of magicians and

---

[1]This criterion has been frequently attacked (e.g., Hull,
Hellenistic Magic, pp. 54-55; and most recently by Morton Smith,
Clement of Alexandria, pp. 222-23, and Jesus the Magician, pp. 74-75),
but, apart from his distinction concerning of what and how miracles
are an attestation of a teacher/teaching (C.C. 2. 52; 3. 28 and 46;
8. 47-48; note also his distinction between belief in Jesus' name and
belief in Jesus, Comm. Jn. 10. 44/[28]. 307-14, cf. C.C. 1. 68, end),
it may be noted that Origen almost seems to anticipate some such objection: in C.C. 7. 4, he especially notes that it is the idiōtai who
commonly are involved in exorcisms.

[2]As a matter of fact, they are connected with the teaching
of the rejection of magic (C.C. 1. 38), and even the multitudes know
the Christians are not committed to the doing of evil (6. 40).

similar deceivers (1. 68, K. 1:122. 11-13, quoted from Celsus, but this part apparently accepted, note line 20, ei . . . apodeixeōs; 2. 49, phantasiai, K. 1:171. 3, and dokein . . . epitelein, 172. 13-14). But the ultimate test is, by what power are they done? Miracles are the result of divine power, magical results come from some other source; to this all other tests are only supportive (C.C. 2. 51; also 3. 46; 7. 4; 8. 54; Comm. Mt. 12. 2).

Hippolytus

A new dimension in the attack on magic is emphasized by Hippolytus--the concept of magic as fraud. This idea was not entirely lacking in the earlier writers,[1] and Hippolytus does not entirely abandon the demonic explanation of his predecessors, but there is a major shift to an attempt at a rational explanation of the phenomena.

Magic as fraud

Though Hippolytus begins his Refutation of All Heresies with a survey of the ancient philosophers (including the Brachmans, the Druids, and Hesiod) whose ideas underlay current religious error, many of which touched on magic,[2] his major contribution to the

---

[1]Is Hippolytus here perhaps following up a lead of his teacher, Irenaeus, who accused Marcus of adding the "buffooneries [paignia] of Anaxilaus to the craftiness [panourgia] of the magi" (Adv. haer. 1. 13. 1, ANF 1:334)?

[2]Ref. 1. Note especially the following chapters: 2, Pythagorus touched on magic; 3, Empedocles taught many things about the nature of demons; 4, Heraclitus's views were similar to Empedocles', he taught that the region around us, as far as the moon, was full of evil things; 11, Democritus studied with teachers of the various occult sciences in India, Egypt, and Babylon; 16, Plato taught the existence of demons; 17, Aristotle taught that evil is sublunary; and

discussion is in book four.[1] He there attempts to explain various

"magical" phenomena as being the result of fraud. The methods range

from fairly simple sleight of hand, or similar tricks,[2] to rather

large-scale productions,[3] some involving at least an empirical knowl-

edge of various aspects of physics or chemistry.[4] Unfortunately,

Hippolytus seems not to have gotten some of them quite clearly, but

the fault may be more in his sources than with himself.[5]

Other aspects of magic

General references to magic
(especially incantations)

As noted above, Hippolytus's opening survey of philosophers

shows that they also were tained with magic and related ideas. The

---

22, the Druids also resort to magical rites (taught by Zamolxis).
(The Brachmans are discussed in 21, and Hesiod in 23.)

[1]See the major discussion of these chapters by Ganschinietz,
"Hippolytos' Capitel gegen die Magier: Refut. Haer. IV 28-42."

[2]E.g., invisible writings and speaking through hidden tubes
(Ref. 4. 28), and reading sealed letters (4. 34).

[3]The divination by a cauldron, and various illusive appearances (4. 35-38).

[4]Such as the invisible writing and tricks with incense and
coals in 4. 28. Note also Marcus's displays with Eucharistic cups in
6. 39 and 40 [34 and 35] (cf. Iren. Adv. haer. 1. 13. 2). These were
supposedly explained in a preceding book (= bk. 4), but are not in the
extant portions of it. (The chapter numbers in brackets are those given
in ANF 5:9-153 ["The Refutation of All Heresies," trans. J. H. MacMahon].)

[5]Causing an earthquake sensation (vertigo in the observers?) by
burning weasel dung with a magnet on coals (4. 39; cf. Ganschinietz,
"Hippolytos' Capitel," p. 73). Also, in the realm of biology, the
killing of a goat by putting wax in its ears so it cannot breathe
(4. 31).

heresies developed from them follow this lead, and Hippolytus follows the lead of Irenaeus in generally labelling the heresiarchs as sorcerers and magicians.[1] The disciples of Simon Magus use magical rites and incantations (mageias epitelousi kai epaoidas), love spells and charms (philtra te kai agōgima), and demons who send dreams (tous legomenous oneiropompous daimonas), as well as those called Paredroi (Ref. 6.20 [15]; PG 16, 3:3226A).[2] The Carpocratians are similarly described (7. 32 [20]). The Elchasaites follow the teachings of these mathematicians, astrologers, and magicians (mathēmatikois kai astrologikois kai magikois),[3] teaching certain incantations and formularies (epaoidas te kai epilogous tinas), especially for those bitten by dogs or demon possessed (Ref. 9. 14 [9]; PG 16, 3:3390C; cf. 10. 29 [25]; see also, 9. 15-16 [10-11] for examples of their procedures in these and other cases). But the truth is not to be found in the wisdom of the Greeks, nor the tenets (dogmata) of the Egyptians, nor the results of the curiosity of the Chaldeans, nor the operation of demons in the irrational frenzy of the Babylonians (alogistō mania di' energeias daimonōn) (Ref. 10. 5 [1]; PG 16, 3:3414A/B).

---

[1]Ref. 6. 2, 7, 9, 19, 20 [contents, 2, 4, 14, 15], re Simon; 6. 5, 39 [contents, 34], re Marcus; 7. 32 [20], re the Carpocratians; 9. 14 [9], 10. 29 [25], re the Elchasaites. Similarly, the Peratics were devoted to astrology (5. 13 [8]; etc.).

[2]Greek text cited from PG 16, part 3: cols. 3017-3454 (published as Origen's Philosophoumena, ed. Emmanuel Miller [Oxford, 1851]). (Cited in the text by volume, part, and column of PG.)

[3]Note also 9. 4 [contents]: Elchasai devotes himself to the tenets of the Gnostics, or even the astrologers, and the arts of sorcery (mageias).

Spirits

Though Hippolytus treats magical displays basically as fraud, he does not entirely reject the idea of demonic activity. Empedocles and Heraclitus speculated concerning the nature and location of demons (i.e., sublunar) (Ref. 1. 3, 4; cf. also 1. 16 and 17, Plato and Aristotle). Though the invoking of Phryn (or, Phrēn; PG 16, 3:3090C and 3091A, respectively) or other demons in 4. 28 is part of the fraud, Marcus, for example, operates only partly by sleight of hand (dia kybeias, kybeuōn), it is also partly through demons (Ref. 6. 39 and 41 [34 and 36]; PG 16, 3:3258A and 3259B). It is not clear, however, what operations the demons perform other than inspiring Marcus and his followers. Similarly, it is not clear if Hippolytus accepts the actuality of the activity of the demons called oneiropompoi and paredroi whose use he charges on the Simonians and Carpocratians (Ref. 6. 20 [15] and 7. 32 [20]). Simon himself, however, seems to have operated by both. He was adept at sorceries (mageias empeiros), working his villainies (paixas) partly by the art (technēn) of Thrasymedes, as "explained above," and partly also by the assistance of demons. But he was a cheat (goēs) and full of folly (Ref. 6. 7 [2], ANF 5:74; PG 16, 3:3206D). In 6. 20 [15], the demons are "said to be 'senders of dreams,'" and in 7. 32 [20], the naming of those demons is followed by reference to "the rest of the tricks" (ta loipa kakourgēmata, PG 16, 3:3339A) of sorcery. On the other hand, a demon, while unable to call back the dead, could have conjured up the form of Samuel; further,

while the demon could infer Saul's fate, it could not really foresee
it.[1]

Amulets and drugs

The Egyptians claim to cure by the use of an amulet with the
name "Deity" (to theos), numerologically determined (psēphisas) written on it, or by an herb determined similarly (Ref. 4. 44, ANF 5:41;
PG 16, 3:3107C/D). Other references to drugs (and possibly amulets)
are less clearly occult. In 9. 12 [7], among the followers of Callistus (bishop of Rome, Hippolytus's rival) are women who resort (for
immoral purposes) to various birth-control or abortive procedures,
using drugs (pharmakois), and "gird[ing] themselves round" (perides-
meisthai) (= amulets, or some type of pressure bandage?).[2] In rather
different categories, the Esseni show great curiosity about plants
and stones (panu de periergōs exousi peri botanas kai lithous), busy-
ing themselves concerning their operative powers (periergoteroi ontes
pros tas toutōn energeias), arguing that they were not created in vain
(Ref. 9. 22 [17], ANF 5:135; PG 16, 3:3399B; expanded from Jos. B.J.
2. 8. 6 [Greek sec. 136]). Such interests on the part of a Jewish
sect would possibly be related to the tales of Solomon's knowledge in
these areas, tales concerning which another reference in Hippolytus
provides a variant. Solomon wrote of the physiology of plants, animals, and of the cure of diseases, but Hezekiah destroyed them because

---

[1]Fragment of a tractate "On the Sorceress" or "On Saul and
the Witch," ANF 5:169-70 (S. D. F. Salmond, trans., "The Extant Works
and Fragments of Hippolytus," ANF 5:163-258) (PG 10:605-8).

[2]ANF 5:131 (with n. 8); PG 16, 3:3387A.

the people looked to them, and not to God, for healing.[1]

Oracles, divination, and astrology

Those who attempt to prophesy by calculation and numbers (Ref. 4. 14) are closely related in Hippolytus's presentation to the Pythagorean calculations (4. 13). To Hippolytus, attempts at divination (specifically that by examination of foreheads) was rather madness (4. 15 [a manteia/mania paronomasia, cf. Clem. Alex. Exh. 2/11. 2-3]); but the pursuit of the idea led directly into astrology. Similarly, the Elchasaites, who claimed to have the "power of prescience," were charged with "bustling activity [sesobentai] in regard of astrological and mathematical science" (as well as sorcery, magikois) (Ref. 10. 29 [25], ANF 5:148; PG 16, 3:3442C). Only Essenes have the one interest ("practice of prophecy and prediction of future events," [to propheteuein kai prolegein ta esomena], Ref. 9. 27 [22]; PG 16, 3:3406B), without specific contamination with the other, at least in Hippolytus's account.[2]

---

[1]Fragment "On the Song of Songs," cited as found "In Gallandi, from Anastasius Sinaita, quaest 41, p 320" (ANF 5:176; PG 10:627-30 [629B]). Possibly a garbling of the tales of Solomon's occult knowledge with 2 Kings 18:4?

[2]Though both Pythagoras and the Stoics derived (parts of) their systems from them (Ref. 9. 27), and they show special reverence for the sun (9. 25 [20]). Josephus makes the point stronger: they prophesy by reading the holy books, by purification, and familiarity with the discourses of the prophets (Jos. B.J. 2. 8. 12; Gr. sec. 159). However, Josephus also attributes to them a strong belief in Fate (Ant. 13. 5. 9; Gr. sec. 172), which fits in with the discovery at Qumran (Cave IV) of a work containing horoscopes (A. Dupont-Sommer, The Essene Writings from Qumran, trans. G. Vermes [Cleveland and New York: World Publishing Company, Meridian Books, 1967], pp. 52 and 338).

Astrology itself receives special attention from Hippolytus,[1]
including several references connecting its practice with belief in
magic.[2] According to Hippolytus, the Peratics, especially, derived
their doctrines from it, their anthropology and soteriology as well
as their cosmogony/cosmology being based on variations of the sympathetic principle "as above, so below" (Ref. 5. 13, 17 [8, 12]).[3]

Alternate views as magic

Probably at least partially due to the nature of his surviving
works, Hippolytus does not connect pagan religion and magic as do his
fellow Christian writers. As noted above ("General References to
Magic," and "Spirits"), he does, however, draw a direct connection between many of the heresies and magic.[4] This in turn is related to a
contamination of even Greek philosophy by it. Many of these philosophers, in turn, had (occult) religious roots (note, e.g., Ref. 1. 2, on
Pythagoras).

---

[1]Especially in book four where it dominates the first twenty-
seven chapters and appears again in chaps. 46-50.

[2]Ref. 6. 39 [34], with 55 [50]--Marcus; 9. 14 [9], and 10.
29 [25]--Elchasaites (cf. also 1. 11--Democritus).

[3]The power of sympathy is supported by the analogies of naphtha "drawing" fire, and of magnetism and static electricity, in 5. 17
[12] (the magnet attracts iron alone; the backbone of a sea falcon, gold
alone; and chaff is moved by amber). This latter triad was also used
by the Naasenes (5. 9 [4] and the Sethians (5. 21 [16]) in explaining
the "mechanics" of their soteriologies. (Naphtha [Indian naphtha] appears again in 7. 25 [13] in Basilides' illustration of the nature of
the Son of the Great Archon.)

[4]Besides the references there, note also Ref. 7. 26 [14],
the Great Archon of Basilides is Abrasax; 7. 27 [15], Basilides says
Jesus was instructed by sages in Egypt.

Hippolytus's attitudes

While Hippolytus took a critical attitude toward many of the
"magical" displays of the heretics, he apparently could not explain
them all; and he was, after all, still a participant in the culture
and beliefs of his times. He thus accepted the possibility of demonic,
as well as divine, workings.

This ambiguity is visible in other areas also. While he manifested a fair amount of at least literary, empirical knowledge of
"scientific" matters (Ref. 4), he could also retail animal lore such
as those concerning the deer and the bird, "cemphus,"in his Commentary on Proverbs (7: 22; ANF 5:173). Also, while ridiculing the
numerical fantasies of Pythagoreans and Marcosians, and the astronom-
ical labors of such as Archimedes, he seems to correct the latter's
figures on a Platonic basis, because "That . . . they should not be in
harmony and symphony . . . this is impossible" (Ref. 4. 10, ANF 5:29;
with his own calculations in the next chapter). It may be that this
is an ad hominem argument, pitting philosopher against philosopher (unless it is a counter-presentation of Ptolemy's view; Ptolemy appears
suddenly, previously unannounced, in chap. 12), but Hippolytus manifests a similar sort of number mysticism elsewhere.[1]

---

[1]In his discussion of Christ's birth, he concluded that it
must have been in the year 5500, for the dimensions of the ark of
the covenant add up to 5 1/2 cubits; further, the end will come at
6000, the sixth day (On Daniel frag. 2. 5 and 6; cf. also 2. 4 [ANF
5:179]).

Latin Polemicists and Systematizers

Tertullian

Tertullian's view of magic is much like Origen's: there is a certain reality to magic, yet it is a fraud; but this is a demonic fraud upon mankind (including the magicians, etc.), not human fraud. The demons operate by various delusive means to turn men from God.

Introduction

Tertullian makes reference to a broad range of magical categories and related areas, viewing them all as bad. Astrologer and soothsayer (haruspices) and augur and magus are all equally consulted regarding Caesar's life, and all equally involve arts originated by angels who sinned (ab angelis desertoribus) (Apology 35. 12).[1] These things are perversions: though God created such things as iron, herbs, and demons (angeli), He is not responsible for their use in murder by iron, poison, or magical enchantment (ferro, ueneno, magicis deuinctionibus) (De spec. 2. 8; see also De pud. 5. 11 for further references to murder by poisoners and magicians, uenanarii . . . magi).

Discussions of magic

Origin and operations

Magic originated from fallen angels who taught various occult

---

[1] The Latin text has usually been given from Quinti Septimi Florentis Tertulliani Opera, Corpus Christianorum, Series Latina, vols. 1 and 2, 2 vols. (Turnhout: Typographi Brepols Editores Pontificii, 1954), but the traditional divisions of Tertullian's texts are short enough that more precise reference has not been deemed necessary in most cases. (Where needed, cited as CCSL, with volume, page, and line numbers.)

arts (metallorum opera . . . et herbarum ingenia . . . et incantationum uires . . . et omnem curiositatem usque ad stellarum interpretationem, CCSL 1:344. 6-9) to women (De cultu fem. 1. 2. 1; cf. 2. 10. 2, 3; also Apol. 35. 12).[1] (Astrology also comes from the same source, De idol. 9. 1.) But besides the ultimate demonic origin, there are also traditional human originators of magic: Ostanes, Typhon, Dardanus, Damigeron, Nectabis, and Berenice (De anima 57. 1).

The operations carried out by means of magic include producing apparitions (specifically, of Castor), carrying water in a sieve, pulling a ship by a girdle, reddening a beard by a touch (Apol. 22. 12);[2] in short, apparitions and various pretended miracles by juggling illusion (circulatoriis praestigiis, Apol. 23. 1, CCSL 1:130. 3). But there is an even darker side; they produce supposed souls of the dead, perhaps even kill boys for oracular purposes, and, at the least, work by the aid of demonic assistants to send dreams, or divine by goats and tables (Apol. 23. 1). Magic is also credited with some power in relieving scorpion stings (Scorp. 1. 2), and, in general, in exorcism and healings of various types (Apol. 21. 17 [= Jewish explanation of Jesus' acts]; see also Adv. Marc. 3. 6. 10).[3]

---

[1] Tertullian is aware that the Book of Enoch, on which this is based, was not universally accepted, but he argues for at least partial acceptance of it (De cultu fem. 1. 3. 1-3).

[2] At least some of these are apparently not "purely" magical: Minucius Felix connects the first and third with pagan religious rites (Oct. 7 and 27. 4; cf. also Lactantius Div.inst. 2. 7).

[3] Tertullian also refers, in two passages, to the idea of fascinatio (the "evil eye"), but rather ambiguously. In the one case he presents it in a sort of ad hominem argument, as a pagan idea which at least served to reinforce his ideas about virgins wearing veils (De virg. vel. 15. 1, 2). In the other, he quotes among Marcion's

There were various sub-divisions, and collateral fields, of
these magical operations. The calling up of the <u>ahoros</u> and <u>biaeothan-
atos</u> seemed to be for using them as familiars (<u>De anima</u> 57. 1 and 3),
while the supposed calling up of those who died naturally and were
properly buried (57. 2 and 6) was either for show or for purposes of
divining or both (like modern séances). Elsewhere Tertullian divided
magic, not too clearly, into astrology (<u>astrologis</u> and <u>mathematicis</u>,
alternately, throughout the chapter) and "the other species which operated by miracles" (<u>De idol</u>. 9. 1 and 6), and capped it by listing
various groups which appeared in the Gospels only to be condemned:
sophist, Chaldean, enchanter, diviner (<u>coniectores</u>), and magician
(<u>magos</u>) (<u>De idol</u>. 9. 7).

Spirits

The angels, like all creation, originated from God (<u>De spec</u>.
2. 8), but some of them fell through desire for earthly women (<u>De
virg. vel</u>. 7. 2; <u>Apol</u>. 35. 12; <u>Adv. Marc</u>. 5. 18. 14; <u>De idol</u>. 9. 1;
cf. also <u>De cultu fem</u>. 1. 2. 1; 2. 10. 2, 3). From this union the
daemons, properly speaking,[1] were produced (<u>Apol</u>. 22. 3; <u>Ad nat</u>. 2.
13. 19). The daemons are thus ill-disposed toward God, and work for
the ruin of mankind, trying to turn them from God (<u>Apol</u>. 22. 4; <u>De
bapt</u>. 5. 4; <u>Ad nat</u>. 2. 13. 19). Besides this, the evil spirits (both

---

objections to Luke's accounts of Jesus' nativity the remark, "Let the
old woman [Anna] be silent, lest she bewitch [<u>fascinet</u>] the child"
(<u>De carne Chr</u>. 2. 2).

[1]Because of this distinction by Tertullian himself, I have retained the spelling of "daemon" when this group of spirits is specifically in view.

angelic and daemonic) desire the fumes (nidoris) and blood of sacrifices for food (Apol. 22. 6; 23. 14; Ad Scap. 2. 8).

Their acts and manner of working are conditioned by this origin. As spirits, they do not have bodies of such a nature that they
can directly affect men physically (Apol. 22. 5 and 6; cf. Adv. Marc.
3. 8. 4; note also Tertullian's similar view of the soul, Res. mort.
17. 2; Adv. Prax. 7. 8; cf. De anima 5. 5, the soul "sympathizes"
with the body [passionum communione]),[1] but they can, and do, cause
diseases and distresses (Apol. 22. 4-6), and most dreams (De anima
46. 12; 47. 1; Apol. 23. 1). All spirits, angels or daemons, are
winged and thus can be everywhere in a moment (over all earth or up
to the heavens), and thus are able to appear to divine (Apol. 22. 8
and 10). Further, they cause diseases so they can then appear to relieve them miraculously, by "new or contrary remedies" (22. 11), and
they perform the various other deceptive, magical acts noted above
(22. 12; 23. 1). In the case of Pythagoras's recognition of Euphorbus's shield, Tertullian suggests various natural ways Pythagoras
could have gained the necessary knowledge, but then goes on to give a
magical explanation (Scimus etiam magiae licere explorandis occultis
CCSL 2:825. 48) which he seems to prefer. There are various types of
spirits, catabolicos and paredros and pythonicos; perhaps the same
daemon which had been in Euphorbus inhabited Pythagoras (De anima 28. 5).

It is, however, only a question of the level of the fraud, all
such operations, explicitly magical or otherwise, are simply deception

---

[1]On the other hand, angels have the power of assuming bodily
form temporarily (De carne Chr. 6. 9, 10).

by the spirits (De anima 57. 2).[1] The various categories of spirits
invoked, whether ahori or biaeothanati (57. 2 and 3), whether appearing
as deceased relatives, gladiators, bestiarii, or gods (sec. 5), or
even prophets (secs. 7 and 8), are all fallacy, impostures of daemons
(fallaciam/-ae; secs. 2 and 6). But their true nature is revealed in
conflict with the Christians; when exorcised they confess that they
are daemons (Apol. 23. 4), even though they had previously presented
themselves as deceased relatives, etc. (De anima 57. 5). What they
do when invoked is what they themselves do or desire to do naturally
(Apol. 23. 1).

Incantations, etc.

        Tertullian does not have a theory of incantation such as Ori-
gen developed.[2] In his discussion he simply uses various common terms
relating to this area: incantationum, incantatores (De cultu fem. 1.
2. 1; De idol. 9. 7), evocaturam, invocantur (De anima 57. 2, 3),
edunt, invitatorum (Apol. 23. 1; cf. De anima 57. 2, invitatoria operatione), and devinctionibus (De spec. 2. 8). In those cases where the
context makes the action clear (except the two incant- passages, in
which it is still a reasonable assumption), these refer to the calling
upon or the calling up of spirits, i.e., the incantations do not work

---

[1]The deception extends even to imitation of divine things, e.g.,
the special connection of unclean spirits with various types and bodies
of water (in malicious imitation of baptism) (De bapt. 5. 3-4).

[2]Indeed, his theory of demonic names is the opposite: they
lacked names until superstition provided empty names of gods which
they could seize on (De idol. 15. 5, 6).

directly, or "automatically," on "nature," but work indirectly,
through spirits.

Related fields

Drugs and medicine

In the area of medicine and healing, Tertullian agrees with
the general Christian view, against Tatian, that while the demons can
cause diseases and then withdraw them to gain credit for healing power
(Apol. 22. 4 and, esp., 11), there are other, good, sources of healing (remediis naturalis,[1] and medicina [alongside magia] in Scorp. 1. 2,
cf. also 1. 3; medicum, ibid., 5. 8). These may be further distinguished in that, in general, physicians employ remedies with like
properties (quod ferme pares adhibet qualitates medellarum aduersus
qualitates querellarum, Scorp. 5. 8, CCSL 2:1078. 27-28, i.e., a
"homoiopathic" approach to medicine), while the demons command
remedia . . . noua siue contraria (Apol. 22. 11, CCSL 1:130. 51-52;
= "antipathies"? or just contrary to accepted practice?). A possible
example of the latter would be the popular (?) remedy for epilepsy
(comitiali morbo), drinking the fresh-flowing blood of a criminal
slain in the arena (Apol. 9. 10).

The powers of herbs (herbarum ingenia) are among the things
the fallen angels taught women (De cultu fem. 1. 2. 1), but the herbs
themselves are a creation of God, so their use for evil (in poisoning,

---

[1]Somewhat related to this idea would be the remedies naturally
known to various animals (De pall. 3; De anima 24; De paen. 12), and
also the effects of the various materials of which wreaths were commonly
made (De cor. 7. 2-5).

etc.;[1] De spec. 2. 8; De pud. 5. 11; Apol. 43. 1), is a misuse (con-
versa; De spec. 2. 6 and 8).

Oracles, divination, and astrology

Foreknowledge. Tertullian regards the soul, by its very nature, as having some limited powers of divination (diuinationem inter-
dum, De anima 22. 1; diuinatricem, 22. 2; of an infant: praesciens
habenda, 19. 8; of every man: praesagam animam suam sentit, aut
ominis aut periculi aut gaudii augurem, 24. 10, CCSL 2:818. 79-80;
Recogita in praesagiis uatem, in omnibus augurem, in euentibus pros-
picem. Mirum, si . . . diuinare? Test. an. 5. 2, CCSL 1:180-81,
lines 12-13).   This is distinct from the special gift of prophecy
(prophetia, De anima 22. 1), more analogous to the general quality of
intelligence (De anima 19. 8; 22. 2; and Test. an. 5. 2), especially
enabling the soul to know God (Test. an. 5. 2). Dreams stand in a
rather complicated relation to this ability of the soul. Most dreams
are caused by demons, even though sometimes they are true and favorable
(De anima 47. 1; following extended examples in chap. 46), but some,
comparable to prophecy, come from God (47. 2), and a third class are
apparently created by the soul itself, for itself, from attention to
circumstances (ex intentione circumstantiarum, 47. 3). The possibility
of such action by the soul was not fully settled in Tertullian's mind,[2]

---

[1] Equally a misuse is the use of various mineral or other compounds to change the human appearance or even the color of clothing
(De cultu fem. 1. 8. 1-3; 1. 2. 1; 2. 6 and 10).

[2] Note also the final sentence of De anima 48. 2: dreams are
under the control of a man's will, if they can be controlled at all.

so he hesitates and suggests another, "ecstatic" possibility (47. 3,
4), but the third category would seem to be consistent with his view
of the "divinatory" capacity of the soul.

In any case, Tertullian's view of foreknowledge seems to fall
into these same three categories. Besides the limited natural fore-
sight of the soul, and the special divine gifts of prophecy, there is
the more visible, widespread phenomenon of demonic oracles and divination. These latter actually overlap with dreams (note, e.g., De anima
46, esp. secs. 11, 12, and 13; also, Apol. 23. 1). In the Apology,
Tertullian presents the actual operations of the demons in divination
(chap. 22) followed by their ostensive procedures (chap. 23). It
originates with certain fallen angels and their daemon offspring (22.
3; also 35. 12), who, because of their ubiquitous nature, can know and
report events anywhere in the world (22. 8). They know something of
the purposes of God from the pronouncements of the prophets,[1] and so
plagiarize His divination (dum furantur diuinationem, 22. 9). Dwell-
ing in the air and clouds, they sense the processes of the upper regions and so promise rain (22. 10). Publicly, however, they cooperate
with magicians, appearing as phantasmata, or as souls of the dead,[2]
operating in oracular responses obtained through boys slaughtered for

---

[1] But apparently they cannot read, since they must have heard
them, of old, from the prophets, or from their writings as they hear
them read (et tunc prophetis contionantibus exceperunt et nunc lec-
tionibus resonantibus carpunt; Apol. 22. 9, CCSL 1:129. 40-41).

[2] As noted earlier, they appear as ahori and biaeothanati, or
as other dead (De anima 57. 1-3, 6), or as catabolic, paredral, or
pythonic spirits (28. 5).

that purpose, sending dreams[1] when invoked, or making nanny-goats
and (sacrificial?) tables divine (23. 1; Tertullian then adds the
rhetorical question: How much more powerfully will they operate when
they do these same things for their own ends and will?).

     Their human "controls" (or, agents) appear with varying names
and procedures: astrologos et haruspices et augures et magos (Apol.
35. 12, CCSL 1:146. 59-60: those consulted about Caesar's life);
haruspices, harioli, mathematici[2] (43. 1; with magi, etc., those who
can justly complain about Christians), or, at the end of a list of
the early teachers of man who wore the mantle, et qui stellarem
coniectat et qui uolaticam spectat (De pall. 6. 2, CCSL 2:750. 14-15).
In the public oracles, acts indistinguishable from madness appear
(Apol. 23. 3, 5; also De anima 28. 5, re Pherecydes), perhaps induced
by the breathing of fumes from the altar (Apol. 23. 5).

     Astrology. Astrology, which appears in the lists in the pre-
ceding paragraphs under three different designations, not only shares
a place with magic in those lists, but in De idololatria is explicitly
classified by Tertullian as a species of magic (9. 7; note also 9. 3,
inter se societatem). It shares with magic both its "demonic" origin
and apostolic condemnation (9. 1-2, and 6-7; on its origin from fallen
angels see also De cultu fem. 1. 2. 1: stellarum interpretationem).

_____

     [1]Cf. the on(e)iropompoi of Justin (Apol. I 18. 3) and Irenaeus
(Adv. haer. 1. 23. 4). The whole of Apol. 23 appears to be a somewhat
garbled (and non-comprehending?) expansion of Justin Apol. I 18. 3-4.

     [2]The haruspice appears also, in concert with the undertaker
(dissignatore), as duobus . . . arbitris funerum et sacrorum, at the-
atrical exhibitions (De spec. 10. 2, CCSL 1:236. 6-8). (Is this perhaps a gruesome play on the meanings of dissignatore, "master of cere-
monies," and "funeral director"?)

Such origin means that this knowledge is evil, and Christians, as a
matter of fact, do not have recourse to it (Apol. 35. 12), but Tertullian does not clearly indicate whether he believes it untrue. He
can ridicule the astrologer for not seeing his own danger in the stars,
and for abusing the heavens with his finger or rod (digitus aut radius,
De idol. 9. 8), and ridicule Marcion's god in astrological terms, and
charge the Marcionites not only with addiction to astrology, but also
with supporting themselves by the Creator's stars (Adv. Marc. 1. 18.
1), but he also uses the practice of the ancient astrologers (ueteres
astrologi) as a proof of the origin of the soul at conception (De
anima 25. 9).[1]

The Sibyl. On the other hand, there is no question as to Tertullian's attitude toward the Sibyl: she is "our prophetess" whose
name has been usurped for the prophets/prophecies of "your" daemons/gods
(Ad nat. 2. 12. 35; Apol. 19. 10 [Fragmentum Fuldense, in CCSL 1:119-
20]).

Relation of other beliefs to magic

Paganism

Tertullian does not explicitly equate pagan beliefs and magic
as did some of his predecessors, but the same general attitude is

---

[1]This is, of course, something of an ad hominem argument, and
relates to a point (the time of origin of the soul) rather peripheral
to the main body of astrological beliefs. Further, the practice of the
ancient astrologers in determining the nativity (genituram) from conception was in opposition to the common practice of casting the horo-
scope from birth. This latter was a practical necessity, as Hippolytus
argued (Ref. 4. 3), though even the time of this was impossible to determine accurately (4. 4).

apparent. The demons who manifested themselves in magic as part of
their operations to deceive man are especially operative in pagan
religion[1] and the whole pagan culture. Men are born to and with idolatry as a result of the work of evil spirits to entrap the human race
(De anima 39. 1-3). Everyday practice is saturated with worship of
various demons, so it is impossible for a Christian to marry a pagan
without continuous danger of compromise (Ad ux. 2. 6. 1), and numerous
occupations are so closely involved with idolatry that they are im-
proper for Christians (De idol. 5-11). The whole of De idololatria and
De spectaculis are actually related to this question. The same fallen
angels who introduced magic (De cultu fem. 1. 2. 1; Apol. 22. 2, 3)
operate behind the idols (Apol. 22. 6). The deceptive operations
named by Tertullian (Castor apparitions, etc., Apol. 22. 12) are perhaps part of some religious ritual, rather than pure magic,[2] and certainly the operations described in Apology 23, either oscillate without distinction from magic to religious rite, or describe magical operations in connection with religion. Besides these, there may be noted
the various passages discussed above linking haruspices, etc., with
magic in one way or another. Further, a noted magician, Simon, had
been honored by the Romans with a statue and the title Sancti Dei
(Apol. 13. 9; cf. Justin Apol. I 26. 2, and 56. 2; Iren. Adv. haer. 1.
23. 1).

---

[1]Indeed the gods' names were empty until the demons seized on
them and began operating under them (De idol. 15. 5).

[2]Note the use of two of them (Castor apparitions and pulling a
small ship by a girdle) in such a pagan religious context by Minucius
Felix (Oct. 7 and 27. 4), and the further recounting of all of them by
Lactantius (Div. inst. 2. 7).

Heresies

The relation of the heresies to magic is stated explicitly and emphatically. Not only are various heretical teachers, individually, notable as magicians,[1] but, as a group, the heretics are notable for commerce with magicians, charlatans, and astrologers (besides philosophers!), because of their dedication to curious matters (commercia . . . cum magis . . . circulatoribus . . . astrologis . . . philosophis, curiositati scilicet et deditis, Praes. adv. haer. 43. 1, CCSL 1:222. 1-3). Their supporters, of course, claim that they deserve to be regarded as apostles since they have done the same things, raised the dead, healed the sick, foretold the future (44. 5); but such great miracles (uirtutes maximas) in support of deceitful, corrupt preaching was foretold, and proves nothing (44. 6). The heretical teaching disproves itself: Menander claimed his baptism gave immortality (De anima 50. 2), but no one can claim for magic such power as to exempt from death (Nec magiae tantum dabit quisquam, ut eximat mortem . . ., 50. 4, CCSL 2:856. 30-31).

Christian practices and magic

Charges against Christ and Christians

The Jews, being convinced that Jesus was only a man, regarded him as a magician because of the power he manifested (magum existimarent

---

[1]Simon magus, Apol. 13. 9, De anima, 34. 2, Praes. adv. haer. 33. 12; Manander, De anima 50. 2, 4; Carpocrates, ibid., 35. 1; "the magician Marcus," Adv. Val. 4. 2; also Marcion and the Marcionites as astrologers, Adv. Marc. 1. 18. 1, cf. De idol. 9. 3: "Astrology (mathesis) today concerns Christ, the stars preach Christ, not Saturn and Mars . . ."; note also Ps.-Tertullian Adv. om. haer. 1. 2, 3, re Simon and Menander.

de potestate), expelling demons, performing various healings, raising
the dead (Apol. 21. 17; cf. Adv. Marc. 3. 6. 10, planum in signis . . .
existimabant). This idea was refuted by Christ's acts and teaching:
he rebuked demons, but his highest glory was not destroying demons,
but saving mankind, an attitude he wanted the disciples to share
(Adv. Marc. 4. 7. 13; see also 4. 8. 4, 5, 7, and 4. 20. 1 and 4,
power over wind and wave, as well as over legions of demons); similarly, he raised the dead, but to teach men of a future resurrection,
not as a simple exercise of power; to raise men to die again is no great
thing (De res. mort. 38. 1, 2).[1]

The pagans take a similar attitude: if a Christian should ex-
pel the demon from a possessed or ecstatic person, will they not seek
to explain it as magic or some sort of trick (magia aut aliqua eius-
modi fallacia fieri dicetis, . . ., Apol. 23. 7, CCSL 1:131. 36-37);
and, as for Christ, "is he [not] an ordinary man, a sorcerer, one
whose body was stolen?" (si homo communis condicionis, si magus, si
. . . ., 23. 12, CCSL 1:132. 62-63).

Denial of magic and related practices

The various works, from astrology through magic, are forbidden
by God, and Christians do not consult them even about their own affairs, let alone the life of someone else (the emperor) (Apol. 35. 12).
Further, astrology should not even be spoken of (De idol. 9. 1). But

---

[1]Marcion's Christ, on the other hand, was such a figure,
tricking, deceiving, misleading the eyes and senses (fallit et decipit
et circumuenit omnium oculos, omnium sensus), not God-with-man, but a
magician, a conjurer (magum hominem . . . spectaculi artificem) (De
carne Chr. 5. 10, CCSL 2:882. 64-883. 71).

this may be something of an ideal; the equally tainted idol-makers,

for example, who should not even be admitted to the church, were being

chosen even for church offices (7. 3).

Astrology cannot be defended by reference to the "Magi and

astrologers" in the Gospels; astrology has not now become Christian

(De idol. 9. 3, in contrast to some group that asserted that it had;

perhaps the Marcionites, cf. Adv. Marc. 1. 18. 1?), the magi were

commanded to return another way, i.e., not to walk in their old ways

(De idol. 9. 5). Astrologers have no part in the kingdom of heaven

(9. 8). The other species of magic which operated by miracles (9. 6)

was equally condemned by the apostles and Gospels (9. 6-7).

This negative attitude extends to most aspects of pagan cul-

ture (note the various professions forbidden to Christians, De idol.

5-8), especially the theatre, which was opened by two ill-omened per-

sons, the undertaker and the soothsayer (dissignatore et haruspice:

De spec. 10. 2), and was claimed by a demon as his special territory

(26. 1 [at its exorcism from a "Christian" woman who became possessed

at a theatre]).

Exorcism

The hostility, and superiority, of Christianity to magic and

other demonic works is shown by the Christians' power over demons.

This is presented in the most sweeping terms at the beginning of De

anima: this new wisdom of the school of heaven does not introduce

new gods or demons, but expels (depellens) the old ones (1. 6).

Tertullian gives (even) less information about the actual pro-

cedures than did Origen,[1] but what he does say presents the same gen-

eral picture. The basic procedure is naming the name of Christ, and

reminding the demons of their impending divine fate by Christ as

judge (Apol. 23. 15).[2] This might be reinforced by fasts in battling

the more dreadful demons (aduersus diriora . . . proeliandum: De

jeju. 8. 3); and, in general, singleness of purpose and devotion to

spiritual things (as of one no longer having a wife) give, for example,

greater self-confidence if adjuring a demon (si daemonem adiurat,

---

[1]This is, of course, characteristic of the early Christian
writers, and fits well with their contention that such things were
simple acts of faith, the manifestation of the power of the true God,
not magic. Some sort of formal pattern may have been developing, but
there is no evidence of it, other than the fairly constant feature of
the use of the Name, et al.: even the use of the "sign" is not specifically brought into this connection by Tertullian. The account in
De spec. 26. 1 may refer to a formal act in the church, but such a
setting was not necessary; a courtroom, or any other setting, would
do (cf. Apol. 23. 4 and 15).

[2]This, also, has similarities to the magical use of "mythological narrative" (cf. above, p. 382, n. 2).
      The next section might suggest another procedure, "At our
touch and breath (contactu deque afflatu) . . . the demons leave,"
though the "breath" may be simply a graphic reference to the words
of the previous section. Compare Ad ux. 2. 5. 2 bis, immundum flatu
explodis, and De idol. 11. 7, fumantes aras despuet et exsufflabit;
unfortunately the former is without context, and the latter could
easily be interpreted as a physical quenching of the fire on an incense altar. But the blowing, like the spitting, could have a symbolic significance as well as a physical effect. [Were Tertullian
and his confreres becoming militant "anti-smokers"?] Franciscus
Oehler interprets both the spitting and blowing out as expressions
of contempt (Quinti Septimii Florentis Tertulliani quae supersunt
omnia, 3 vols. [Leipzig: T. O. Weigel, 1851-54], 1 (1853): 85, note
n [on De idol. 11. 7; cf. p. 690, note a, on Ad ux. 2. 5. 2]).

confidit sibi: De exh. cast. 10. 2).[1] (Anointing is also mentioned
in Ad Scap. 4. 5, but this is probably to be connected with cure of
disease in general, and not specifically with exorcism.)

Miracles and prophecy

Tertullian regards the power to heal as a proof of the validity of Christianity (besides the references to exorcism, above, see
also Scorp. 1. 3, 4; Ad Scap. 4. 5, cf. also De or. 29. 2, 3). He
also reports certain marvels in support of his views about the nature
of the soul (De anima 51. 6, 7), but he views these things somewhat
objectively. If miracles are not a sufficient proof for Marcion's
Christ (Adv. Marc. 3. 3. 1), and, as already shown, various apparitions
and wonders do not prove the truth of the magicians, then the same
holds true for Christianity. While signs may be useful in argument,
they cannot control our view of nature (signis . . ., naturam facere
non possunt: De anima 51. 8), and even Christ's deeds needed the support of prophecy to confirm them (Adv. Marc. 3. 3. 1, and bk. 4,
passim).[2] Even beyond this, miracles are overshadowed by the teaching
with which they are connected, the salvation of mankind (Adv. Marc.
4. 7. 13; cf. also 4. 8. 5).

---

[1]Later in the chapter, Tertullian reported a prophecy of
Prisca further exalting the power of purity, though there the result
was visions and other revelations (De exh. cast. 10. 5).

[2]In general, Tertullian uses the "proof from prophecy" much
less than his Greek predecessors, using it mainly against the Jews and
Marcion in his apologies against them (Adv. Jud. and Adv. Marc.).
There is limited use of it in Apol. 18-21.

Minor Latin Writers

Minucius Felix

The Octavius of Minucius Felix, rather naturally, does not
include the same breadth of references to magic as do the writings of
Tertullian, but such references as do occur in Minucius agree basically
with the views of Tertullian.

The actual successes of auspices and auguries or oracles are
not due to chance (Oct. 26. 1-7); rather, insincere and wandering
spirits, degraded from heavenly vigor, seek also to degrade others
(26. 8); these are the daemons of the poets (26. 9). The Magi work
their wonders by them,[1] though Hostanes, the first of the Magi, described the true God and angels and said the daemons were earthly,
wandering, and hostile to mankind (26. 10-11), as Plato also spoke of
angels and daemons (26. 12). These daemons work through rocks, entrails, etc. (27. 1), and produce disease and other evils that they
may appear to cure them when they release those afflicted (27. 2).
They produce other marvels, such as appearances of the Castors on
horses, and pulling a ship by a woman's girdle, and other wonders
(27. 4, also chap. 7). Not only are these events connected in one way
or another with the pagan religions (as are the demon-inspired auguries
and oracles), but the myths picture the gods themselves as using magic
and subject to it (22/23. 4, Jupiter enticed by the girdle of Venus).

---

[1]Here also, the performances are "real" (objective) yet fraud-
ulent--quicquid miraculi ludunt . . . ; illis adspirantibus et infun-
dentibus praestigias edunt, vel quae non sunt videri, vel quae sunt
non videri (Oct. 26. 10; text from Aloisius Valmaggi, ed., M. Minucii
Felicis Octavius, Corpus Scriptorum Latinorum Paravianum, [5] [Turin:
Io. Bapt. Paraviae et Sociorum (1916)], p. 34).

But many of the Romans know these things, since the daemons confess
their fraud when exorcised from their victims by the Christians,
driven out "by the torment of our words and the fire of our prayers,"
flying from the Christians when near at hand (27. 5 and 7); even pretended gods confess their true nature (27. 6).

Commodianus

The Instructions of Commodianus touch briefly on the same two
major points as noted in Minucius, the origin of evil spirits and
their connection to oracles. The offspring of the sinning angels and
women were giants. They taught the arts, dyeing of wool, etc.; and
after death, condemned never to be resurrected, they wandered about,
subverting many, being worshipped and prayed to as gods (Instr. 1. 3).
They are active in various types of augury and portents (1. 22, lines
1-8; cf. also 1. 18, 19), God being pleased to allow the daemons to
wander the world for our discipline (1. 22, lines 9-10).[1]

Pseudo-Tertullianica

The anonymous Adversus omnes haereses continued the charge of
magic against the heretics Simon Magus and Menander after him (secs.
2 and 3). The poetic "Five Books in Reply to Marcion" (Carmen aduersus
Marcionem) added Cerdo and Marcus (bk. 1, lines 157-58, 165-67, CCSL
2:1424-25; ANF 4:144, lines 198, 208-10). It amplified the charge
against the latter along the lines developed by Irenaeus: Marcus

---

[1]Commodianus also believed in the 6000 year duration of the
earth: 2. 39/80. 8), and perhaps alludes to the argument from prophecy
in 1. 6. 13: "There was none that predicted his [Jupiter's] previous
birth" (Robert Ernest Wallis, trans., "Commodianus," ANF 4:204).

used magic art (<u>in magicae formam</u>, line 166) for immoral purposes, and

also taught that he changed the Cup to blood by prayer (line 167).

The <u>Martyrdom of Perpetua and Felicitas</u> illustrates the pagan

suspicion of magic on the part of Christians: the tribune, apparently

incited by informers, at first feared that they would be withdrawn from

the prison by some sort of magic incantation (<u>subtraherentur . . . in-</u>

<u>cantationibus aliquibus magicis, . . . </u> , 5. 3/16. 2).[1] The writer of

the martyrdom himself holds a somewhat similar belief, that possibly

a woman such as Perpetua could not have been slain unless she herself

willed it, because she was feared by the impure spirit (6. 4/21. 10).

Certain metrical works, transmitted also along with Tertul-

lian's (or Cyprian's) works, include certain marvels relating to the

Dead Sea which, though not magical, relate somewhat to Africanus's

references to that region. The "Sodom apple,"[2] mentioned in <u>Jonah</u>

(CSEL 3, 3:297. 3-5; =lines 4-5 in <u>ANF</u> 4:127),[3] is amplified in <u>Sodom</u>

to include all fruits growing in the area (CSEL 3, 3:295. 133-37;

<u>ANF</u> 4:131, lines 182-90). The latter also includes, <u>inter alia</u>, the

---

[1]Text from Herbert Musurillo, The Acts of the Christian Martyrs, Oxford Early Christian Texts, gen. ed., Henry Chadwick (Oxford:
Clarendon Press, 1972), p. 124, lines 9-10. (Cited by traditional
chapter and paragraph numbers, and, following a virgule, by continuously
numbered paragraphs, with numbered sections.)

[2]Cf. Africanus, in Syncellus, ed. Dindorf, 1:188. 17-18; and
Cedrenus, ed. Bekker, 1:51. 13-14.

[3]Guilelmus Hartel, ed., S. Thasci Caecili Cypriani opera omnia,
Corpus scriptorum ecclesiasticorum Latinorum, vol. 3, parts 1-3, 1 vol.
in 3 parts (Vienna: Apud C. Geroldi Filium Bibliopolam Academiae,
1868-71) [cited as CSEL, followed by volume, part, page, and line(s)
in precise references]; ANF 4:127-41, "Appendix" [to Tertullian],
trans. S. Thelwall.

idea that a lighted torch floats, but sinks if extinguished[1] (CSEL
3, 3:296. 160-62; ANF 4:132, lines 221-25).

Syriac Writers

The major Syriac works that have survived from the Ante-Nicene
period do not show any great interest in magic,[2] though they have some
borderline value in this area.

One of Bardaisan's great interests was in the correlation of
Fate with divine providence and human freedom, in a Christian system.
He thus has some information about astrology, and refers to the books
of the Babylonians and the Egyptians, but has no references to magic.
Indeed, his allocation of causality for human experiences between Nature, Fate, and human Freedom[3] would seem to leave little room, or need,
for magical manipulations.

Later Writers

Latin Writers

Cyprian

Cyprian and his circle of correspondents do not speak directly

---

[1]Cf. Syncellus, 1:188. 14-15; Cedrenus, 1:51. 16-17.

[2]The most direct references to magic are found in the Apology
of pseudo-Melito, included above with the Greek apologists. This work
perhaps originated in the third century in Osrhoene (J. B. Segal, Edessa
'The Blessed City' [Oxford: Clarendon Press, 1970], p. 35).

[3]"Bardesan: The Book of the Laws of Divers Countries," trans.
B. P. Pratten, ANF 8:727-29; H. J. W. Drijvers, Bardaiṣan of Edessa,
trans. Mrs. G. E. van Baaren-Pape, Studia Semitica Neerlandica, no. 6
(Assen: Van Gorcum, 1966), p. 219.

of magic, though that may be largely because of more pressing problems. What they do say about demons presents the same basic views
found in the earlier writers.

Sinning and apostate angels taught women forbidden arts (De
habitu virginum 14, though in this case the arts are those of cosmetics, etc.). A demon inspired or possessed person may pretend to
cause an earthquake, though in actuality it is only foreseen by the
demon; it cannot cause such a physical event (Ep. 75. 10 [Firmilian to
Cyprian]).[1]

The one area where Cyprian goes beyond his predecessors, and
colleagues (cf. Firmilian, Ep. 75. 10), is in the rhetorical descriptions of exorcisms. Amplifying a theme suggested by Minucius Felix,
Cyprian pictures the demons as being forced, howling and groaning, out
of their victims, scourged and roasted with fire (Ad Don. 5; also Ep.
69. 15, and Ad Dem. 15). The rhetorical nature of this picture is
emphasized by the fact that all this is done calmly, soberly, with a
simple voice (castite sobria, mente integra, voca pura; Ad Don. 5,
CSEL 3, 1:7. 12-13); it is accomplished by the human voice and divine
power (Ep. 69. 15; Ad Dem. 15). Besides these exceptional cases, exorcism is a regular prelude to baptism, especially necessary in the
case of heretics[2] (repeatedly emphasized in the pronouncements of
various bishops at the Seventh Council of Carthage).

---

[1]With this is possibly to be compared the deceits and trickeries
(praestigias . . . et fallacias, CSEL 3, 1:362. 5) confessed by the
daemons, the heathen gods, at their expulsion by Christians (Ad Deme-
trianum 15).

[2]The demon-possessed "prophetess" in Firmilian's letter was a
heretic (possibly a Montanist) (Ep. 75. 10).

Pseudo-Cyprianica

Several of the treatises transmitted with the works of Cyprian,
and sometimes under his name, do speak specifically concerning magic.
The tractate On the Vanity of Idols, or That the Idols Are Not Gods
(Quod idola dii non sint), in a passage (chaps. 5-7) based largely on
Minucius Felix (Oct. 26 and 27), amplified (in chap. 7) from Cyprian
(Ad Don. 5, and Ad Dem. 15; compare esp. CSEL 3, 1:7. 19-20 with 25.
6-7, and more generally 361. 18-22 with 25. 4-9), presented the spirits
as misleading and deceiving and using tricks (fallit et decipit et
praestigiis, CSEL 3, 1:23. 10-11) to oppose the truth; by them the
Magi have power for harm or mockery (Quod idola 6). They hide behind
(sub) statues and images and cause the different effects of the various
types of augury and auspices, but, adjured by the true God, they are
driven out of possessed bodies, tortured, etc., by "our voice and
speech of hidden majesty" (Quod idola 7: nostra uoce et oratione
maiestatis occultae, CSEL 3, 1:25. 5-6).

The treatise De rebaptismate also presents the themes of demonic acts or trickery, and of exorcism. Some heretical groups contend
for the necessity of fire at baptism and claim to have it. The author
is unsure about this: it may possibly be effected by some trick, such
as those of Anaxilaus, perhaps by some natural means; or perhaps they
only think they see it; or perhaps "the work and magical poison of
some malignant being can force fire from the water" (chap. 16, ANF
5:676-77;[1] sicut . . . lusus Anaxilai esse, siue naturale . . . , siue

---

[1]English translation by Ernest Wallis, "Cyprian," ANF 5:261-
595, and "Appendix," ibid., pp. 651-78.

illi putant . . . siue maligni opus et magicum uirus ignem potest in
aqua exprimere: CSEL 3, 3:90. 5-8). The significance of invocation
of the name of Jesus is shown by the fact that in that name all kinds
of powers (including casting out demons, Matt. 7:22), are accustomed
to be worked (_uirtutes omnes solent fieri_), sometimes even by those
outside; even evil doers may possibly do good works by the super-
abounding energy of the name (_per nimiam uirtutem nominis_) (chap. 7,
CSEL 3, 3:78. 10-11, 18-19).

On the other hand, the miracles of Christ, done with commanding word and voice (_uerbo et uocis imperio_), caused the Jews to regard
him as a sorcerer (_existimabant magum_) (Quod idola 13, CSEL 3, 1:29. 10-
15).

Arnobius

The interests and views of Arnobius are much the same as those
of the Greek apologists of a century earlier. This is especially true
in regard to his views of magic and related areas.

References to magic

Magic goes back to ancient times, in the East. In a great
conflict between the Assyrians and the Bactrians, under Ninus and
Zoroaster, not only swords and physical power, but also the "magicians
and the mysterious learning of the Chaldeans" (_Magicis et Chaldaeorum_
ex reconditis disciplinis) were engaged in the struggle (_Adversus na-_
tiones [or _Adv. gentes_] 1. 5, CSEL 4:7. 15-18).[1] The Magian Zoroaster

---

[1]Augustus Reifferscheid, ed., _Arnobii aduersus nationes, libri_
VII, CSEL, vol. 4 (Vienna: Apud C. Geroldi Filium Bibliopolam Academiae,
1875).

appears also as one of several magicians named who are challenged to
give power to any (as Christ did), or even to actually work themselves
(1. 52). Among the effects of Christ's name are the overcoming of
evil spirits, soothsayers, augurs, and magicians (1. 46: <u>noxios spiritus, . . . uatibus, haruspices . . ., adrogantium magorum . . . ac-
tiones</u>, CSEL 4:31. 6-8).

Theory and praxis of magic

      One of Arnobius's longest passages on magic occurs in the con-
text of a discussion of the various means Christ did not use in working
his miracles. Christ was asserted to be a <u>magus</u> who worked by secret
arts, having stolen the names of angels of power from Egyptian shrines,
but were his deeds really the tricks of daemons and sports of magical
arts? (<u>Adv. nat</u>. 1. 43: <u>daemonum . . . praestigiae et magicarum
artium ludi?</u>, CSEL 4:28. 25-26). Are there any <u>magi</u> who did anything
the least similar, working without incantation (<u>carminum</u>), or juice
of herb or grass (<u>herbarum et graminum sucis</u>),[1] without regard to sacrifice, libation, or season (<u>sacrorum libaminum temporum?</u>)? (ibid.,
CSEL 4:28. 29-29. 1).[2] In 1. 52, he also will allow any challengers
to use their own rites with "whatever noxious herbs [<u>malefici graminis</u>]
. . . whatever powers [<u>uirium</u>] those muttered words and accompanying

---

   [1]In the area of material means, Arnobius elsewhere refers to
the <u>lamminae</u> sold by Psylli, Marsi, and others (apparently as protection against snakebite), apparently including Christians among their
users (2. 32).

   [2]The opening lines of chapter 44 reemphasize that Christ
worked without anything to assist, and without observing any rite or
rule (CSEL 4:29. 13-14; <u>sine ullius ritus obseruatione uel lege</u> [line
14]).

spells contain [*fremor ille uerborum atque adiunctae carminum*]" (*ANF*
6:428; CSEL 4:36. 2-4).[1] Following the brief list of materials in 1.
43, Arnobius also gives a list of the purposes of works of this
class: to know the future; to inflict disease; to sever affections,
or impure love; to open locks or seal mouths; or in chariot races, to
weaken, incite, or retard the horses; or, if they should attempt anything useful, to do it not by their own force (*ui*), but by the power
(*potestate*) of those they invoke (1. 43, CSEL 4:29. 4-13).

But such invocations (*inuocati*) would have to have a certain
force themselves, compelling the gods when summoned (*acciti*) by their
own names by diviners (4. 11). Even Jupiter himself was supposedly
dragged down (*tractum*) by charms and spells (*et quaenam . . . auocari
. . . ? . . . et nominum terribilium fremores? . . .*; 5. 1 and 3, esp.
the latter, CSEL 4:175. 27-176. 1). But how is it known that the
summoned power is the one who operates in the entrails, or lungs and
livers (4. 12)? The *magi*, who are brothers to the soothsayers, say
that at their incantations (*accitionibus*) pretended gods frequently
slip in instead of those summoned (*pro accitis*) (ibid.). Or, how is
it known that there is not one only who comes in place of all who are
invoked? If anyone doubts this, he can ask the Egyptians, Persians,
Indians, Chaldeans, Armenians, and all others[2] acquainted with the more

---

[1] Hamilton Bryce and Hugh Campbell, trans., "Arnobius," *ANF*
6:403-540.

[2] Elsewhere Etruria is specially noted in the origination of
divination and augury (2. 62; 6. 18; 7. 26).
   The Etruscans, together with the previously mentioned Psylli
and Marsi (2. 32), represent western (Roman) expansions of the traditional eastern (Greek) lists of ancient, mysterious races credited with
occult knowledge and power.

secret arts (<u>interioribus . . . artibus</u>) (4. 13).

Spirits

The passages introduced above all show the place of spirits
in magic and related practices. In addition, the Magi assert that
they have prayers which can win over certain powers and make access
to heaven easy for souls (ibid., 2. 62; this is perhaps similar to
certain mystic rites with a similar purpose referred to earlier, 2.
13).

Oracles, divination, and astrology

Various classes of fortune-tellers--augurs, dream interpreters, soothsayers, prophets, enthusiasts (<u>haruspices . . . , coniec-</u>
<u>tores harioli uates et . . . fanatici</u>, CSEL 4:16. 2-4)--are pictured in
<u>Adv. nat</u>. 1. 24 as extorting contributions from the devotees of these
arts, a livelihood threatened by the increase of Christianity. They
defend themselves as a part of "time-honoured rites of institutions
once sacred" (<u>sacrorum quondam ueterrimi ritus</u>, ibid., line 8) (<u>ANF</u>
6:419).[1] Various sources of omens are presented throughout Arnobius's
discussions: the sky or points of spears (2. 67), thunderbolts or
veins of sacrifices (2. 69), or their entrails, lungs, or liver (4. 12).

In a passage which credits the Etruscan Tages with discovering
the meaning in the fall of thunderbolts and in the veins of sacrifices, Arnobius also makes Theutis, the Egyptian, the beginning of

---

[1] A following chapter presents something of a roll-call of
the classic oracles: (Trophonius ?), Jupiter of Dodona, or Apollo,
whether Delian, Clarian, Didymean, Philesian, or Pythian (1. 26; <u>ANF</u>
6:419, with n. 3; CSEL 4:17. 12-17, with mg. re line 12).

knowledge of (the meaning of?) the motion of the stars and the calculation of nativities (ratio . . . genethliaca, CSEL 4:104. 3) (2.
69). Other than this, Arnobius makes no significant reference to
astrology, after his having presented it as being, if true, one of
several possible explanations[1] of the evils of the world (1. 8).

Further, Arnobius seems to lend some support to the idea that
divination/astrology have no logical connection with magic. In his
discussion concerning the Numa-Jupiter episode, he questions the ap-
propriateness of Jupiter-appointed means whereby what he has determined may be averted, and "pass away idly through the force of these
rites" (5. 2, ANF 6:490, CSEL 4:179. 19-24).

Magic and pagan religion

The Magi are still at least partially religious personages for
Arnobius. Part of their art concerns the fate of souls,[2] and there
are similar concerns in native religions, e.g., of Etruria (Adv. nat.
2. 62, cf. 2. 13). Certain of the Roman rites of aversion were obtained
by Numa by charming Jupiter, dragging him down with spells (5. 1), and
the priests have introduced relics (reliqua) connected with the Magian
arts (magorum cohaerentia disciplinis) into the secret laws of the
sacred rites (7. 24, CSEL 4:257. 9-11).[3] Augury and omen-watching (and

[1]Besides blaming them on the Christians.

[2]But they can soften and soothe only the lesser powers, not
the true God (2. 62).

[3]A large part of this section of book seven is devoted to
questioning the rationality of various aspects of the pagan rites.
This would have some implication that they are in essence superstitious
(magical), rather than religious, though this is never made explicit.

averting) have been regular parts of public service (e.g., 2. 67,
though Arnobius is here arguing that times have changed). In 2. 12,
Arnobius refers not only to the practices of king Numa and the superstitious observances of antiquity, but also to an arch-heretic, Simon.
Though Simon Magus had trusted in false gods, his chariot had been
blasted by the mouth of Peter, naming the name of Christ, and he had
fallen from the air, abandoned by them in their terror.

On the whole, Arnobius's attitude toward the pagan gods is
not clear-cut. They may exist, but if so, they are beings subordinate
to the Supreme God, and so will not desire worship belonging to Him
(e.g., 3. 2-4; 7. 2-3).[1] Thus Arnobius has little to say about demons
or evil spirits,[2] the passage cited in the preceding paragraph (2. 12)
being somewhat unusual.

Christian beliefs and practices

Arnobius seems to include himself and other Christians[3] among
those who use the plates (lamminae; =amulets?) sold by the Psylli,
Marsi, and others (Adv. nat. 2. 32, CSEL 4:74. 19-23).

---

[1]There is, however, a large ad hominem element in these passages.

[2]Thus, for example, the supposed giants' bones found in different places are taken as proof of the better state of men in ancient
times (2. 75); there is no attempt to connect them with the offspring
of the fallen angels whose souls became the demons in the theory of
other apologists. (Such a connection was made by the writer of the
Clementine Recognitions [1. 29; PG 1:1223B].) The approach of Arnobius
provides a parallel to the reconstruction, above, of Africanus's view
of the offspring of the fallen angels as being only giants (not demons),
a reconstruction based partially on silence.

[3]"We" apparently in contrast to "you" in the preceding and following passages, though here it may be all "we mortal and injury-liable
humans" in general.

He is aware that Jesus was charged with being a magician
(specifically one who worked by means of names of angels of might
stolen from Egyptian shrines, following a religious system of a remote country, 1. 43), but he denies the charge, attempting to refute
it by several arguments. Christ worked without material means or incantations (1. 43, 44), by audible and intelligent words (1. 45); his
work[1] was beneficial to man, not hurtful (1. 44), to convince men and
to show them the nature of a true god, not to boast himself in empty
display (1. 47). Further, his work continued, his inherent power was
such that he could give power to others (1. 50, 52);[2] he even now appears to righteous men and his name causes evil spirits to flee, si-
lences soothsayers and augurs, and frustrates the efforts of arrogant
magicians (1. 46).[3] In sum, Arnobius holds that there is "nothing
magical, nothing human, nothing deceptive (praestigiosum) or crafty
(subdolum), nothing of fraud in Christ" (1. 53). The ultimate proof
of the accounts of his deeds is that the whole world was filled with
such a religion in so short a time (1. 55).

Lactantius

Lactantius, the sometime student of Arnobius, exhibits the

---

[1]Arnobius's knowledge of the Gospel miracles is rather broad
(note the various items in 1. 45-47, 50; and 2. 11), but in 1. 46 he
includes some items that seem to be garbled accounts of the Day of
Pentecost and the transfiguration, unless they come from otherwise unknown apocryphal accounts.

[2]Magicians cannot really effect, by the aid of their gods,
what unlearned (rusticis) Christians have often accomplished by a
simple command (iussionibus . . . nudis) (1. 52, CSEL 4:36. 5-7).

[3]A great example of this power was the confrontation between
Simon Magus and Peter witnessed by the Romans (2. 12).

general attitude of Christians (and many others) of the ancient world
toward magic: sorcerers (uenefici) are to be classed with various
groupings of lowest types (Div. inst. 5. 1. 2--sacrilegious and
traitors; 5. 19 [20]. 30--gladiators, robbers, thieves, poisoners,
harlots; 6. 2. 10--assassin, adulterer, parricide).[1]

Discussions of magic

Lactantius, in defending Christ's works, distinguishes them
from the things worked by "magical tricks [praestigiis magicis],
which display nothing true and substantial," the "art of magic" (ars
magica) having skill of avail only for "deceiving the eyes" (ad circum-
scribendos oculos) (Div. inst. 4. 15. 4, 19; ANF 7:115, and 116 [with
n. 1]; CSEL 19:330. 2, 334. 1, 2).[2] On the contrary, Christ worked by
heavenly strength and power, "by a single word, and in a single moment"
(apparently in contrast to the elaborate incantations and lists of
names of the magicians) (4. 15. 6, ANF 7:115).

The Jews, besides calling these the works of a magician (magum,
4. 15. 1), attributed them to demoniacal power (4. 15. 12). The association of these ideas is natural; the art and power of the Magi

---

[1]References are given from the Latin text; where the chapter
numbers differ in the English version (Div. inst. 2 and later chapters
of 5, and in the Epitome), these appear in the first reference to each,
in brackets after the Latin chapter numbers.

[2]English translation by William Fletcher, "Lactantius," ANF
7:1-330; Latin text from Samuel Brandt and Georgius Laubmann, eds.,
L. Caeli Firmiani Lactanti opera omnia, part 1: Divinae institutiones
et epitome divinarum institutionum, ed. Samuel Brandt; part 2, fascicle
1: Libri de opificio dei et de ira dei, carmina fragmenta, vetera de
Lactantio testimonia, ed. Samuel Brandt; CSEL, vols. 19 and 27 (Vienna
and Prague: F. Tempsky, 1890, 1893; Leipzig: G. Freytag, 1890, 1893).

consist in the influences (adspirationibus) of the demons (2. 14[15].
10). When invoked (inuocati) the demons deceive the sight of men with
deceptive illusions (praestigiis obcaecantibus), so they "do not see
those things which exist, and think they see those things which do not
exist" (ibid., ANF 7:64; cf. Epitome 23[28]. 6). These demons had
assumed the names of the ancient kings, of whom they had caused images
to be made; but magicians, and those whom the people truly called
maleficii, in the practice of their arts (cum artes suas . . . exercent),
"call upon them by their true names, those heavenly names which are
read in the sacred writings" (Div. inst. 2. 16[17]. 4, ANF 7:65).
Magicians (magi) know that souls are called from the lower regions by
certain incantations (carminibus) so that they are at hand, seen by
human eyes, and speak, foretelling future events (this is presented as
a clear, convincing proof to those sceptical of the eternality of the
soul) (Div. inst. 7. 13. 7).

Divination of various sorts is presented as closely allied to
magic. They all--astrology,[1] soothsaying, divination and oracles,
magic art, and whatever else besides, whether done openly or in secret--
were invented by fallen angels/daemons to delude mankind (Div. inst.
2. 16. 1-2; Epit. 23. 5-9). Also, as noted above, part of the work
of magicians involves calling up souls who foretell future events.

---

[1]Astrology receives only passing attention here and elsewhere
in Lactantius. Even if the stars should hold the efficacy of all
things (which Lactantius allows provisionally only so as not to delay
the main discussion), still it is God (who made and ordered the stars)
who does all things (De op. dei 19. 7). A reference in De ira dei to
the other heavenly bodies (i.e., besides the sun and moon), at rising
and setting, supplying favorable times by their fixed positions (13. 5),
seems to refer to their marking of various seasons, and not really to
astrology.

The daemons (or angels) themselves practice deception, especially through oracles; having a presentiment of God's arrangements (since they had been His ministers), they interpose, that they may appear to do them, making promises or threats, and pretending to avert dangers, or contriving that the unavoidable dangers may appear to happen through disrespect shown toward them (Div. inst. 2. 16. 10, 13-19, referring esp. [2. 16. 11] to the series of prodigies [prodigia, CSEL 19:169. 9-10] given previously, in 2. 7[8]. 7-23).[1] These examples include dreams (cf. also De mort. pers. 44. 5). In general, dreaming was given by God for the sake of resting the body in sleep, but He has reserved to Himself the power of teaching men future events by means of dreams. There are remarkable narratives to testify of dreams which have had an immediate and remarkable fulfillment, though dreams are not always true, nor always false (De op. dei 18. 10-11).

Spirits

Like his predecessors, Lactantius ascribes the origin of the evil spirits in the world to the fall of certain angels; sent by God to protect and improve men, they had been corrupted and had had intercourse with women. There are, however, some differences in his emphases. He attributes their fall to the work of Satan, not just to their own degeneration and lust, and he regards only the daemons, the angels' offspring, as the active agents in the evils befalling man (Div.

---

[1]The middle part of 2. 7 provides details on several items referred to by Tertullian (Apol. 22. 12) and Minucius Felix (Oct. 7 and 27. 4).

<u>inst</u>. 2. 14. 5). It is through them that the Magi work,[1] invoking
them (ibid. sec. 10), calling upon them by their true names (2. 16.
4), names which they confess, along with their true nature, when adjured by the name of Christ (2. 15[16]. 3; cf. also, 4. 27. 2, and 5.
21[22]. 5). Their sole purpose (like that of their leader, 2. 14. 1,
5) is to injure man, since they can not harm God (2. 16. 9; cf. 5. 21.
6).

Magic and pagan religion

The Roman religion recognizes magic, at least to the extent of
having a goddess who watches over infants, keeping off witchcraft
(<u>fascinum</u>, CSEL 19:77. 20) (<u>Div. inst</u>. 1. 20. 36). The same powers
through whom the Magi work also represent themselves as the <u>genii</u>, receive libations, and are worshipped as gods and averters of evil, evil
they themselves cause (<u>Div. inst</u>. 2. 14. 10-13; 2. 16. 3-5, 9-20;
2. 17[18]. 10; cf. <u>Epit</u>. 23. 8; 25[30]. 1). They are, indeed, the in-
ventors of astrology, various sorts of divination, magic, and other
such arts (<u>Div. inst</u>. 2. 16. 1; <u>Epit</u>. 23. 5-8).

The pagan rites are frequented by all varieties of the low,
evil classes (<u>Div. inst</u>. 5. 19. 30), and the gods give aid to whoever
feeds them, whatever he may be (6. 2. 10). Sorcerers (<u>uenefici</u>) appear in both of these lists.

Christian beliefs and practices

In accord with his belief in the actions of the daemons,

---

[1]Appropriately enough, since magic, like astrology, etc.,
had been invented by them (2. 16. 1).

especially their inciting of persecution of Christians, Lactantius
gives prominence to exorcism among Christian practices: when adjured,
the daemons are put to flight by the divine name, crying out and confessing their true nature (Div. inst. 5. 21. 5; apparently based on
Cyprian (Ad Dem. 15, Ad Don. 5; cf. Min. Fel. Oct. 27. 5;[1] note also,
Div. inst. 5. 22[23]. 23).

    Not only the commands of Christians, but also their use of the
sign of the cross has this effect, even to the extent of interfering
with pagan rites (Div. inst. 4. 27. 1, 3, with Epit. 46[51]. 6-8;
and De mort. pers. 10. 2).

    The great proof of the truth of Christianity, however, is not
such works, or even the works of Christ, but the fact that they had
been previously announced by the prophets (Div. inst. 4. 5. 4; 4. 15.
4, 12; 5. 3. 18, 19).[2]

    Christ was regarded by the Jews as being a magician (magum),
working by demoniacal powers (Div. inst. 4. 15. 1, 12). The answer to
this, apart from the "proof from prophecy," is three-fold: (1) his
works were real ("true and substantive" [ueri ac solidi], by implication), (ibid., sec. 4); (2) he did not use elaborate rites, but worked
"by a single word and in a single moment" (ibid., sec. 6, ANF 7:115);

_____

    [1]Both Minucius and Cyprian (Ad Dem., specifically), as well as
Tertullian, were known and used by Lactantius (Div. inst. 5. 1. 22-24,
and 5. 4. 3).

    [2]Mainly the Hebrew prophets, but to some extent even the pagan
prophets, the Sibyls and Hermes (Div. inst. 1. 6; 4. 6-7, 9, 13-14;
Epit. 5. 1-3; 37[42]. 2-8), Sibyls and Hystaspes (Div. inst. 7. 15.
18-19), Hystaspes, Hermes, Sibyls (7. 18. 2-3, 5; cf. Epit. 68[73]. 1),
with prophecies of various Sibyls scattered throughout the following
chapters of Div. inst., bk. 7 (also, briefly, Epit. 65[70]. 6).

and (3) it is logically contradictory--if he was really a wonder-

working magician (magus . . ., quia mirabilia fecit, CSEL 19:408.

9-10), such as Apollonius or Apuleius, then he was an unskilful one,

since he did not escape as Apollonius did (ibid., 5. 3. 7, 9).

Summary

On the whole, Lactantius's views are much the same as those of

his predecessors. Compared to Arnobius, he exhibits greater Biblical

and theological knowledge, but this is balanced by losses in the area

of philosophy[1] and science. In a notable example, he retreats from

Arnobius's more advanced view of the universe (Arnobius Adv. nat. 1. 2

and 2. 58, earth revolving [CSEL 4:4. 11-13, and 94. 3-4]; use of "orb"

for the earth in 1. 52 [CSEL 4:35. 18]; reference to the heavens as

convex in 1. 55 [CSEL 4:37. 14]),[2] returning to a ridiculing of a round

earth and the consequent idea of antipodes (Div. inst. 3. 24. 1;

Epit. 34[39]. 2).[3]

Greek Writers

The Apostolic Constitutions, which, though a later work, re-

flects and develops ideas developing already in the Ante-Nicene period,

---

[1]Though Arnobius spoke sarcastically of the pride of the philosophers (e.g., Adv. nat. 2. 50) and of their conflicting opinions (2.
9-10), he could also use what he viewed as positive aspects of their
teachings to support his own views (e.g., 2. 13-14; note especially his
evaluation of Plato in the latter of these two chapters).

[2]On the idea of a round earth, see also Athenagoras Plea 8.
4; 13. 2; 16. 1 (earth in center, with vaulted heaven, in 13. 2).

[3]But, as Thorndike notes, Plutarch did the same (History, 1:
219, n. 6, citing De facie in orbe lunae, chap. 7 [924 A]).

includes wizards (pharmakous) among those brought to trial even before

secular courts (Const. apost. 2. 6. 52), while enchantments (epaoidas;

incantationes), various types of divination, and necromancies and in-

vocations (epiphoneseis) are among the indecent spectacles to be

avoided (2. 8. 62; PG 1:752B). The canon attributed to Paul excludes

from consideration for the church any who is a magician, enchanter,

astrologer, diviner, wild beast charmer, mendicant, charlatan, maker

of amulets, charmer, soothsayer, etc. (magos, epaoidos, astrologos,

mantis, therepodos, lotax, ochlagogos, periammata poion, perikathairon,

oionistes, . . .) (8. 4. 32; PG 1:1129A/B).[1]

Other than these references, magic does not receive great at-

tention in the later Greek writings of the Ante-Nicene period, but the

same general world view continues. Methodius, according to Photius,

was in agreement with Athenagoras regarding the fall of certain angels

who were enamoured with the daughters of men (Discussion on the Resur-

rection fragment 3. 1. 7 [ANF 6:370], from Photius Biblioth. 234).[2]

Apocrypha and Gnosis

The apocryphal and heretical writings (including the pseudo-

Clementines and the Nag Hammadi library) manifest all shades of belief,

ranging from those of the fathers themselves to those of the "heresies"

---

[1]Const. apost. 7. 1. 3, 6, 18, also repeat the prohibition
against magic from the Didache.

[2]About the same period, the Latin bishop, Victorinus of Petau,
credits magicians with working wonders (e.g., fire from heaven, Rev.
13:13) by the aid of such apostate angels "even to this day" (On the
Apocalypse, CSEL 49:128. 4-5; 129. 8-11 [Johannes Haussleiter, ed.,
Victorini episcopi Petavionensis opera, CSEL, vol. 49 (Vienna: F.
Tempsky, 1916; Leipzig: G. Freytag, 1916)]).

they attacked. But, as such, they represent only more developed forms
of the views already presented above, and so do not require further
explication. This is especially true since these developments (as
with most of the views themselves) are in the directions of beliefs
and attitudes apparently not held by Africanus.

Summary of Knowledge of Magic

Designations and Divisions of Magic

Terms used for magic

In their discussions of magic, the designations most commonly
used by the fathers generally are those of the mag- group (mageia,
mageuein, magos, magikos), but with a prominent use also of goē- forms
(goētēs, goēteia, goēteuein). As noted above in the discussions, two
of these writers present exceptions to this general rule: Clement of
Alexandria reverses this preference, giving greater prominence to the
more pejorative goē- forms, and Origen commonly substitutes the more
demeaning mangan- group.

Besides these terms, there are a few occurrences of the use of
technē and derived forms (especially in Justin and the other apologists,
and by Clement of Alexandria, and Hippolytus), as either general or
specific designations of the art. There is also a rather frequent use
of the pharmak- group (-eia, -euein, -os, -on), as either a synonym for,
or a sub-division of, the mag- realm.

All these terms, except the technē forms, have a somewhat negative connotation when used in this sense; of them, only the technē

forms were used by Africanus in a similar sense.

Divisions and correlates of magic

Within, and around, the realm of mageia, more specialized
areas were also sometimes designated. Prominent among these were
pharmakeia; the making or use of love charms or potions (philtra and
agōgima); and the uses of charms and enchantments (various of the
epaoid- forms, as well as a few compounds of -klēsis and -kelēsis;
also the use of periapt- forms by Clement of Alexandria and peri-
desmeisthai in Hippolytus).

Areas which the fathers relate to magic, despite some ancient[1]
as well as modern philosophical and logical objections, were the realms
of astrology (variously designated as astrologia, genethlia [in Origen;
cf. also the pseudo-Clementines], and mathēmatikos), and divination
(manteia, mantikē, and various synonyms and specialized types). The
varieties of this latter realm especially are detailed and attacked by
the fathers from Justin on.

Procedures of Magic

Certain of the fathers manifest a fair amount of knowledge
about magical procedures, though their knowledge would, in most cases,
probably have to be described as broad, rather than deep.

---

[1]Arnobius, for example, sets the ideas of portents, and their
magical aversion, in opposition to one another. Bardaisan, who has a
major place for Fate in his system of causalities, has no allusions to
magic (at least in the preserved fragments).

Goals

Two of the early fathers, Tatian and Arnobius, provide lists
of the goals sought by magical operations. Tatian's somewhat informal
listing includes healing and works of love, hate, and vengeance (Disc.
17). Arnobius's more extended list involves foreknowledge; infliction
of disease; severing affections or causing impure loves; opening, lock-
ing, or sealing mouths; weakening, inciting, or retarding horses in
the chariot races; or, occasionally, useful things, but by occult
powers (Adv. nat. 1. 43).[1]

Materiel

The same two passages just cited, especially Tatian's, also
provide listings of materials used (Tatian: "antipathies," leather
amulets, roots, sinews and bones, herbs, human remains; Arnobius:
juice of herb or grass, sacrifice, or libation; cf. also, Adv. nat. 1.
52, "noxious herbs"). Other, overlapping, lists are provided by Origen
(clothes, numbers, stones, plants, roots, all kinds of things: C.C.
6. 39; herbs, stones with inscriptions: 8. 61; cf. also De pr. 2. 11.
5); and Hippolytus (Ref. 4. 44; 9. 22).

Methods

The predominant type of methodology of the magicians is

---

[1]This list has numerous points of contact with the procedures
illustrated directly by the extant portions of Africanus, or reported
by Psellus to have been originally included.
    This type of listing reaches its extreme in the pseudo-
Clementines, in the naming of the various wonders either claimed by or
reported of Simon Magus (Recog. 2. 9; 3. 47, 57; 10. 66; Hom. 2. 32,
34). This list, however, was specially designed to demonstrate the
empty and non-beneficial nature of Simon's displays of power.

operations with/through demons. This is a constant theme of all the
Christian writers who refer to magic with any detail at all, at least
from Justin on. This factor is dealt with below in the discussion of
"Types of Magic."

Specifically, these operations involve the use of incantations,[1]
and, still more specifically, the use of names, to summon and/or control these demons. The theory of names[2] is especially emphasized and
discussed in Origen as part of his general theory of incantations and
magic (note especially C.C. 1. 24-25; 5. 45; 6. 39; Exh. Mart. 46).

Involvement of Other Areas

Inevitably, the discussion of these points overlapped with
other areas (as they still do in modern discussions), especially the
realms of science and religion.

In the realm of "science," illustrations were drawn from physics (especially magnetism and static electricity; e.g., by Clement),
biology (various wonders: Clement, Hippolytus, Tertullian),[3] and
medicine.[4] They were used as illustrations of spiritual lessons, but

---

[1]Note the corresponding sections of the discussions of the
Didache, Justin, Irenaeus, Clement of Alexandria, Origen, Hippolytus,
and Tertullian, above.

[2]Cf. also, the reference by Irenaeus to the use of "foreign"
words and the coining of names by various Gnostic groups (Adv. haer.
1. 21. 3, 5; 1. 24. 5, 7).

[3]Origen, on the other hand, denied Celsus's attempt to use
certain examples from this area as proof of knowledge of magic by
animals (C.C. 4. 86).

[4]Clement of Alexandria seems especially to have been relatively
knowledgeable and interested in this last area (cf. the discussion of
his view of "Biology and Medicine," above). Tatian, however, was a

with no real distinction of them from other unexplained or unexplainable wonders which were viewed as magical or demonic.

This lack of distinction is made especially apparent by the variety of references to the idea of sympathy and/or antipathy. It is variously viewed as a natural principle explaining such a range of items as that from physical properties of magnets and the "medical" properties of plants (in Clement) to whatever truth lies behind the claims of the astrologers (Clement and Hippolytus); or as the very essence of the demonic system (Tatian _Disc_. 17).[1] Of course, during this whole period (and for centuries before and after it), this view was one of the dominant theories of causation, a major element in the "philosophy of science" of the day.

Various aspects of religion, both pagan and Christian, were also compared to magic in these writings. Any real connection of Christ or Christianity with magic was, naturally, denied; but it was more than just denial. Extensive attention was devoted to various aspects of this topic by Justin, Origen, Tertullian, Arnobius, and Lactantius. A large part of their argumentation involved the so-called "proof from prophecy," but it was also dealt with extensively from the viewpoint of the nature, motivation, and results of the procedures involved. In all these areas, a distinction was seen between Christian practice and magic.

---

sort of negative "devil's advocate" in this realm, actually classifying all medical practices as demonic, and on a par with magic (_Disc_. 18).

[1]Perhaps comparable here is Tertullian's reference to the "contrary remedies" commanded by the daemons (_Apol_. 22. 11).

Conversely, almost all aspects of pagan religion (and various heresies) were attacked as being essentially the same as magic. Their origins and bases were the same, demonic inspiration, and their methodologies and goals could not be distinguished. The former involved irrational acts, rites, and words; the latter was connected with the fulfillment of base or irrational human desires, overtly for the human practitioners, covertly for the demonic powers really operating behind them.

Attitudes toward Magic

Types of Magical Operations

Indirect (daemonic) magic

In terms of the broad typology of magic used in the conclusion of the preceding chapter--direct/impersonal/automatic contrasted with indirect/personal/daemonic--the type of magic discussed and rejected by the fathers is almost exclusively the latter, the personal, daemonic type. The only exception would be in the case of some of Hippolytus's physical explanations (and some other charges of fraud, e.g., by Irenaeus), and those would probably be classed, even by Hippolytus and the fathers, as trickery, rather than magic (insofar as the two concepts were distinct in the ancient world; goēteia, for example, seems to have been used for both without a clear intent to distinguish the two meanings). While various materials and procedures were noted by the fathers in other areas, they were connected with manipulations of the demons (or, demonic manipulations), not as working directly to achieve the desired end(s) by natural, physical causation.

Theories of praxis

Within the broad category of daemonic magic, there were, however, two major competing interpretations of the actual praxis. The
first, which may be called the Tatianic, from its major (or, sole)
exponent, was a type of "conspiracy theory": the various materials,
acts, words, etc., had no significance in themselves; they had simply
been accorded meaning in an arbitrary system pre-determined by the
demons themselves. This was part of their over-all strategy to turn
man from, and against, God. Their system extended far beyond magic,
taking in pagan religion, medicine, and, potentially, all areas of
life.

The second theory of magical praxis may be termed the Origenistic, from its clearest enunciator. Following an essentially Platonic[1]
view of the nature of things, Origen argued that the factors underlying
the claims of the magicians were grounded in the "nature of things"--
certain sounds, certain words and names, were potent, and capable of
producing results in such usages. This was because they, like all lan-
guage(s), were essentially, "naturally," correct as the designation of
the things designated.[2]

---

[1]Origen himself called it the Stoic view, in contrast to the
Epicurean and Aristotelian (C.C. 1. 24, K. 1: 74. 10-75. 1).

[2]The other fathers do not really speak to such a question, but
in general, seem closer to the Origenistic, natural, theory, than to
the Tatianic conspiracy theory. Any deviations from this position
would probably have been in the direction of a more Aristotelian,
arbitrary-symbolizing-in-general view, than toward the more specific,
special-daemonic-sign-system view of Tatian.

Relation to Their Belief Systems

Spiritual realm

The fathers fairly uniformly view the spiritual realm as organized in a sort of hierarchy of three basic levels, but with several
variations at the middle level. At the top is God, the Creator and
Lord of all else, incomparably greater that the lower levels. At the
intermediate level are angelic beings, numerous both individually and
in types, as well as in natures. At the lowest level, at least at
present, are the human spirits.

The angelic beings are now divided in nature into the good
and the evil (the latter either identified or loosely associated with
the demons),[1] though this is the result of their own choice; they were
not created so. They are also typable into various ranks distinguish-
able by their power and/or special interests or areas of concern or
responsibility; this typology applies in general to both the good and
the evil ranks. The nature and the extent of the variations at this
level are capable of numerous variations. The Gnostic groups tended
to multiply them, and to expand them into a continuum running from God
down to the material realm. The "orthodox" writers tended to see a
sharp gap on each side of this level. Within the "orthodox" group,
Origen speculated the most about the extent and cause of the variations,

---

[1]The <u>daemons</u> were frequently identified as the souls of the
giants, the offspring of the fallen angels and human females. The
distinction of terminology was not always consistently maintained,
however, even by those who explicitly presented this view; sometimes
the fallen angels were also called <u>daemons</u>.

but still maintained the gaps separating the angels from God and from
man.[1]

The human spirit, while on a lower level than the angels, at
least at the present time, is not subordinated to them, but has direct
responsibility to God, and the possibility of direct communication with
Him.[2]

Thus, though the angels and demons were _higher_ than man in terms
of the "spiritual" nature of their existence, they were not _over_ them in
terms of power or organizational structure. They could have limited
contacts with man, but only as permitted or directed by God. Magic
could thus be viewed (as it was explicitly by Origen)[3] as a breaking of
the divine order by attempts to control, or enlist the aid of, the
lower level spirits (usually the demons) for personal, frequently
"this-world"-ly, ends. Such acts were also usually regarded as being
the result of deception by the demons; they are actually the ones in
control, despite the beliefs of the practitioners.

Material realm

Insofar as magical or comparable procedures were viewed as

---

[1]But he tended to narrow the internal gap between the "good"
and the evil angels, regarding the angels as only relatively less
guilty than the demons at the time of the primaeval rebellion (De pr.
1. praef. 6; 1. 7. 2-3, 5; 1. 8. 1, 4).

[2]In some systems, e.g., Lactantius (Div. inst. 2. 10-11, 15-17),
this status was an original cause of the angelic, i.e., diabolic and
demonic, jealousy and rebellion.

[3]Note C.C. 5. 5 (compare also the discussion in the preceding
chapter of the helpful, but limited, intermediary functions of angels
in relation to prayer and other aspects of human life and worship).

having any reality (apart from fraudulent procedures), they were
usually attributed to sympathetic principles. This principle was, of
course, not viewed as restricted to the realm of matter, but the visible (and less religiously suspect) examples of it come from this realm.

Physics

Some prime examples of this principle of sympathy are the mag-
netic stone; amber and chaff, and some related items (static electricity);
and the mutual attraction of fire and naphtha. All these items appear
in Clement of Alexandria, but others, either individually or in various
pairs or triads, appear in other writers, both orthodox and heretical
(e.g., both Hippolytus and various of the groups combatted by him--
Naasenes, Sethians, Basilideans). Origen suggests a connection of
celestial bodies with earthly events (e.g., the relation of the moon
and lunacy, which suggests other possibilities of influence; and comets
do seem to precede significant events).

Biology

The application of the principles of sympathy and antipathy in
the biological realm is illustrated also by Clement, especially in his
explanation of the effects of certain of the flowers or ointments.
Another way of viewing biological phenomena is presented by one passage
in Origen, though it seems to allow for (and actually overlap) the
"sympathetic" explanation in its use of the "eagle-stone" as an example. In the passage in question, C.C. 4. 86, Origen rejects Celsus's use of certain items as proof of knowledge of sorcery by certain

birds and animals--these things are simply remedies known by instinct (physis), not sorcery.[1]

Summary

Essentially the same explanatory options for "uncanny" phenomena were available to the ancients as are available to moderns: "spiritual" causation, fraud, or poorly understood "natural" causation. The major differences would be in the greater number of phenomena falling into the "uncanny" category in ancient times, and the greater tendency to propose the first explanation, compared to its almost total neglect by moderns in favor of the last explanation. But these differences in attitude and emphasis must not obscure the fact that the last option was available to the ancient Christian writers, and, further, was utilized by them on occasion.

---

[1]Similarly, Tatian, while rejecting such types of remedies as beneath human dignity and the divine resources available to man, does not seem to include them as part of his "demonic conspiracy" (Disc. 18).

CONCLUSION

THE PLACE OF JULIUS AFRICANUS IN EARLY CHRISTIANITY

The present chapter concludes the preceding study with an attempt to place Julius Africanus within the spectrum of beliefs of early
Christianity. Its main part is a descriptive style comparative study
of the relation of the views of Africanus concerning magic with those
of the other early Christian writers presented above. This study
parallels the conclusions of the two preceding chapters (following
generally the order of topics in the conclusion of Chapter III, where
the two orders differ). It combines and compares their results in the
areas of knowledge of magic and attitudes toward it.

Relation of Africanus's Views of Magic
to Those of the Early Church

Knowledge of Magic

Designations of the art

Terms used

Where Africanus uses a special term to describe his procedures
it is usually the term $\underline{\text{techn}\bar{\text{e}}}$, a term which he seems to use, at most,
only in a semi-technical sense. While Psellus uses the term $\underline{\text{go}\bar{\text{e}}\text{tik}\bar{\text{e}}\text{n}}$
to describe one of Africanus's procedures (mp 44$\underline{1}$; Vi., IX. 1. 34),
Africanus himself does not use any of the $\underline{\text{go}\bar{\text{e}}}$- or $\underline{\text{mag}}$- forms except
in the $\underline{\text{Chronography}}$ (mp 46/chr 1; Routh 2:242. 4; Syncellus 1:35. 2,

449

ed. Dindorf). In this passage he uses the terms in a negative sense in accord with their usage in the other early Christian writers.

These other writers, however, as noted in the conclusion of the preceding chapter, regularly use these and other pejorative terms by preference. They do make some use of the techn- forms as a designation of magic, but rather infrequently. On the other hand, they make rather frequent and pejorative use of the pharmak- group.

The use and non-use of these terms by Africanus is consistent with the views suggested in the thesis of this study. Africanus uses the term technē as a positive, or at least neutral term, to describe his procedures, but avoids any use in connection with them of the mag- or goē- forms, which he, like his Christian colleagues, regards (and uses) as pejorative. On the other hand, the pharmak- group, while used pejoratively by the fathers, is not necessarily such (and is not always so used even by them), and so Africanus has no hesitance in the use of pharmak- forms (pharmakon, pharmaxis) in and of his prescriptions, even using them of the destructive ones.

Divisions and correlates

Besides pharmakeia, presented just above, the early fathers included such areas as love charms or potions, and the uses of charms and enchantments, in the magical practices which they opposed. The specific terms used of the former, philtra and agōgima, are not used by Africanus; but Psellus (though not using these terms either) does suggest this type of operation in mp 44s ("kindles and quenches loves," Vi, IX. 1. 49) (cf. also the discussion of "love magic" in the summary of Africanus's knowledge of magic in Chapter III, above). In the area

of charms and enchantments, or spells, in general, two of the term-

groups used by the fathers, the epaoid- and periapt- stems, are used

explicitly of Africanus's procedures by Psellus (mp 44j; Vi., IX. 1.

31-32: periaptois . . . kai epasmasin; see also mp 44d, line 13:

epodē). In the preserved passages, Africanus does not use the epaoid-

forms of his own procedures,[1] but he uses periapt- forms, both verb

and noun (and other peri- forms) frequently in his prescriptions.[2]

Besides this, the term epiklētheisēs appears in mp 23a (Vi., III. 2.

13, p. 225), the invocation of Aphrodite. As noted in the discussion

of this whole passage (mp 23 a-e; and Vi., III. 2 in its entirety) in

Chapter III, its authenticity is uncertain. This uncertainty is in-

creased by, but not based solely on, this particular procedure. If it

is authentic, then it illustrates the fathers' charge of inescapable

ties of pagan worship to magic; but it also changes the problem con-

cerning Africanus from one of magic alone, to one of active promotion

of a pagan religious act.

The fathers also view astrology and divination as closely con-

nected with magic. Africanus has no major references to either of

these areas, and what he does say does not directly connect them with

---

[1] But two forms do appear in the Oxyrhynchus fragment: Oxy. Pap.
412 (Vi., V), lines 20 and 21--epaoide and epasai, and the whole interpolation is described as tēs epirrhēseōs (lines 45-46) in Africanus's
following comments. Elsewhere he uses the general term rhēsin in the
one instance where such an item is explicitly identified by him (mp 6;
Vi., I. 5. 4, p. 129). Besides this, as noted in Chapter III, under
"Inscriptions," he employs similar items in written form.

[2] See the discussion of "Amulets" in Chapter III, above.

magic. His views of them are, however, similar to his views of the
magical type items he presents. Insofar as there are other than natural senses involved in his discussion of divining fron horses (Vi., I.
8: mp 8 and the preceding paragraph), Africanus attempts a natural explanation of it.[1] He does use the word <u>astrologos</u> in at least one
reference, in the <u>Chronography</u> (Routh, frag. XXIV: Atlas as an <u>aristos</u>
<u>astrologos</u>, whence his reputation of bearing the heavens was derived),[2]
but it is not clear that he means astrologer rather than astronomer,
in terms of modern equivalents. Elsewhere the only evidence of his
interest in this area is the specification of certain times, usually
in relation to the moon, for some actions.

Methodologies of the art

Areas clearly within the realm of magical concern may be considered from the viewpoints of the goals of the procedures--the areas
of human concern to which they correspond--and of the procedures used--
the actual methods and materials used in the operations.

Goals

As noted in the "Summary of Knowledge" at the end of the preceding chapter, the goals of magical operations, as stated most fully
among the fathers by Arnobius, correspond roughly with the concerns represented by Africanus's magical passages, especially as summarized by
Psellus. The majority of the procedures in Africanus, however, relate

---

[1]As he does in the reverse situation in I. 16 ("Theft of Sound"),
in which the result of his non-magical procedure (provided with a "physical" explanation) is compared to the results from divination.

[2]<u>Rel. sacr.</u> 2:278. 22; Syncellus, ed. Dindorf, 1:283.

to the more neutral areas (at least socially, if not strictly legally
or ethically) of medical and agricultural magic, and the destructive
procedures are presented in a military context, thus preserving the
appearance, at least, of respectability.

Methods

Arnobius, in the introduction to the passage just mentioned,
also gives several methods of the magicians (Adv. nat. 1. 43). Two
of these methods, incantations and juice of herbs, are comparable to
some of Africanus's procedures, though the latter does not necessarily
appear in any of his really magical operations. On the other hand,
the method most stressed there by Arnobius, the careful observance of
divinations of various types to ascertain the future (and thus appear
to cause it), does not appear in Africanus. Indeed, as discussed
above, references to divination are rare in the Kestoi.

The main types of procedures used by Africanus,[1] however, are
among the things specifically noted by various of the fathers in their
attacks on magic. But other of his procedures (for example: the
right/left distinction, especially in relation to the production of
sexes; the significance of certain times;[2] the significance of certain
numbers) can be equally paralleled from the general views of the contemporary Christian writers.

---

[1]Manipulation, vocalization, graphic representations, and use
of special substances (see under the "Summary of Knowledge" in Chapter
III, above).

[2]E.g., the times for prayer in Hippolytus Ap. Trad. 36/41,
especially the "mythological" basis provided for prayer at midnight.

Materials

All of the main types of materials mentioned by the various

fathers in their denunciations of magic are represented by Africanus's

procedures, with the exception of the "human remains" mentioned by

Tatian (Disc. 17), and possibly the sacrifices and libations of

Arnobius (Adv. nat. 1. 43). Otherwise, in the animal realm, there are

examples of the leather amulets, the bones (even if not the sinews),

and human substances (though not "remains"); in the plant realm, there

are the roots, plants, herbs, or juices; of minerals, various types of

stones, though none inscribed, and especially none inscribed with the

names or symbols of demons (but there are some inscriptions, one on

metal, mp 37, if authentic); and, in Origen's words, "all sorts of

things" (C.C. 6. 39): numbers, "antipathies," and clothes (or at

least cloths).

Again, however, it may be noted that many of these things ap-

pear in prescriptions which are separated only by the narrowest of

lines, if at all, from other prescriptions in Africanus (or even some

of the animal wonders in the fathers). These other cases fall, at

worst, into Riess's "false belief" category,[1] and are really more

characteristic of Africanus than the magical proceedings.

Types of operations

Direct/indirect magic

As noted in the conclusions of the two preceding chapters, the

---

[1]"Aberglaube," col. 32: ". . . falschem glauben. . . . Aus
ungenügender und irriger Naturbeobachtung. . . ."

other early Christian writers uniformly class magic as a demonic operation. It is an indirect procedure operating through the intercession
or compulsion of demons, of one piece with the other demonic activities, including pagan religion. Africanus, on the contrary, while
manifesting a similar belief in the existence of demons, and of their
connection with the origins of magic, seldom, if ever,[1] connects them
with the operations he prescribes.

Theory of praxis

In terms of the theories of magical praxis presented by the
fathers, Africanus's view would, not unnaturally, be closer to that of
Origen than to that of Tatian. He goes beyond Origen, however, in
eliminating the daemonic role, even to the extent of eliminating them
from any active part in the procedures which he prescribes. Origen
argued that, "in the nature of things," there was some power in words
and sounds that compelled demonic obedience; Africanus's view seems
to be a sort of extension of that view to the inanimate realm, eliminating the animate (daemonic) "middle-man" from at least a conscious
part in his system. It could, perhaps, be validly argued that such a
system would be (logically) defective, but this is no argument against
the possibility of the existence of such a system of belief. Given
the prevailing belief in "sympathy," etc., and the pressures from his
Christian beliefs for the elimination of any idea of commerce with the

---

[1]The question here is largely that of the authenticity of mp
23 and the chapter in which it occurs, Vi., III. 2. The main points in
regard to the significance of this question, and the evidence concerning
it, have been presented above, in Chapter III, under the discussions
of "Fowls," "Rites," "Gods and Daemons," and "Indirect (Daemonic)
Magic? "

daemonic forces, such an intermediate link could easily be suppressed from at least conscious consideration. Given also the incipient and tentative nature of observation-based scientific knowledge and the tenuous nature of ancient knowledge of physical (chemical, etc.) causal links, such a suspension of emphasis on daemonic causation need not be viewed as an intellectual dishonesty. Africanus was not the modern ideal of the scientific observer,[1] resolutely resisting the formulation of inadequate theories till all the evidence was in; but neither does he appear to be the credulous dabbler in the occult that he is sometimes presented as being.[2]

Attitudes toward Magic

Religious/non-religious

As implied in the preceding discussion of "Types of Operations," the early Christian writers (including Africanus) considered "magic" to be related to religion, and of direct religious concern. Compared to pagan religion, it was essentially the same, and in many cases actually overlapped with it; but compared to true religion, the true worship of the true God, it was antagonistic. But this antithesis was because they both belonged essentially to the same thought realm, accepting most of

---

[1]But then, this modern ideal is still only an "ideal" even in modern times.

[2]Actually, he may have been something of a "nut" though: he was at least mildly egotistical, a name dropper, a dabbler in "one-upsmanship" (whatever the topic, almost, he could think up, or had heard of, an improvement). But why write, if he did not think he had something to offer?

the same basic views, but evaluating them differently.

At the same time, however, Africanus seems to have regarded his procedures as outside this realm, neither religious, nor yet anti-religious; they were, rather, non-religious, secular. Even when contrasted to the pagan gods, as in mp 11a, it was as a competing system, not as an opposing force within the same system.[1]

Relations to world-views

This topic has already been touched on in the discussion above, and thus the main lines of the position presented below are fairly obvious: at least those concerning the spiritual and the physical/material realms, and, to an extent, their civil and social involvement. Only the last area, possible functional values of the views, is new.

Spiritual realm

The views of Africanus and his fellow Christian writers are essentially the same in this area. Insofar as there was a consensus of Christian thought in various possible ramifications of this area, Africanus appears to be as close to the center as any of the others. In fact, he was closer than some, as, for example, Tatian, the fanatical "anti-magic"-ian, or even than Origen, with his speculations about the personality of the stars and the causes of the differences in

---

[1]The apparent exception to this, mpp 14a and 15b, are really rhetorical flourishes, personification and apostrophe, not actually challenges to a god conceived of as truly existent.

the ranks of spiritual beings.[1]

Physical/material realm

The views of Africanus and his fellow Christians separate somewhat here, but again, not more than do those within the ranks of the other writers themselves. Africanus was not much more interested in these realms than was Clement of Alexandria, and in some aspects of their study, perhaps less well versed than Clement or Hippolytus. The difference is mainly one of the area of concentration chosen for their writing; Clement, Hippolytus, and the others gave first consideration to those items from which they could draw spiritual benefit for their readers; Africanus was concerned with their material or intellectual benefit (including some concern for "entertainment value").

Some of the closest parallels between Africanus and the other Christian writers come, however, outside the fathers' discussions of magic, in their discussions of biology, or physics, or medicine, etc. In connection with this point, it may again be noted what a relatively small proportion of Africanus's surviving fragments are actually concerned with magic, and that, even in those passages, he frequently tries to provide a physical explanation of the procedures.

Civil and social areas

All the Christian writers by implication, and some, such as Lactantius, explicitly, classed magic and magicians with the criminal,

---

[1]This unity, of course, is not surprising, since much of the basic viewpoint was held in common with most of the ancient world. The differences appear largely in the different configurations of various elements in the systems, and in the "ethical" evaluations of them.

or at least the lower, elements of society, justly punished by the
civil authorities. Magical type operations were associated with persons of considerable status, leaders of religious groups, both pagan
and heretical; but such operations were presented as proof of the real
culpability and error of the persons or doctrines associated with
them.

Africanus, insofar as he speaks explicitly of magic, seems to
share such a general viewpoint, but he does not regard his prescriptions as falling into these categories. They are useful practical
knowledge, or handy tricks, or even valuable tactical procedures.
There is nothing criminal or low class here, only good practical, pa-
triotic advice. Some of the procedures might be regarded as a bit
ribald, or subject to misuse, but should an author be blamed for that?

His Christian colleagues would have objected to this type of
material, but from a Christian viewpoint; from a secular and/or literary viewpoint, Africanus's presentations were relatively mild by the
standards of that (or almost any other) age. Considering the semi-
medical nature of much of the material, only the excretion practical
jokes, and the horse-theft disguises, are really at issue in such a
discussion.

Functional values

Whatever functions magic, including divination, may have performed in the social systems (paganism, Gnosticism, etc.) which the
early Christian writers attacked—guidance in ambiguous situations,
reinforcement of resolve in threatening situations, help in situations

of "helplessness," reassurance that everything possible had been done

in situations of actual or potential loss[1]--would have been met in

their own context by Christ and/or the church. Thus magic was not

needed (and/or was attacked or rejected as pandering to evil desires).

Those who were "ensnared" by the heresies which used magic and who

afterwards returned to the church did so because the "magical dis-

plays" were not really functional from the perspective of their world

view. In some cases they were actually "dysfunctional," serving only

to lead those "ensnared" into situations of deeper conflict, especially

in relation to their system of moral values.[2]

Africanus, on the other hand, wrote always from a lay position,

and in the Kestoi from a secular one. It is in the Kestoi that any

positive magic appears, in contrast to the latent "magical world-view"

occasionally glimpsed in the Chronography (and shared with Africanus by

his Christian colleagues). In the situation addressed by the Kestoi,

Christ was not a viable functional solution, that was ruled out by the

terms of the "contract" (to borrow a structuralist term), so Africanus

tries to present functional solutions from the "science" of his sphere

of acquaintance. In such circumstances, Christian,[3] or other

---

[1]Concerning this last type of situation, note the excuses for
the use of amulets which are combatted at the end of the next century
by Chrysostom (Ad Col., hom. 8. 5; PG 62:357-58).

[2]E.g., Irenaeus Adv. haer. 1. 13. 4-5. But such conflicts were
not always recognized immediately; one such victim was reconverted only
after "no small difficulty" (ibid., sec. 5).

[3]Christianity would be a viable functional option only for
those at least open for conversion. But such persons need apologetic
or other missionary type presentations, and that Africanus leaves to
other writers or writings. In his Chronography, he had made some contribution of his own to that task, but that was not the role of the Kesto:

specifically supernaturalistic, solutions would have been dysfunctional, they would have lost him the audience that he thinks he can benefit by his accumulation of "fruitful helps."

Summary: Africanus and Early Christianity

Personal status of Africanus

Three of the more speculative thinkers of early Christianity, Africanus, Origen, and Bardaisan, were contemporaries. Of these three, Bardaisan was rejected by the "great church" even in his own lifetime, and Origen was condemned by a later generation; only Africanus escaped. Why should this be so, especially in view of the types of material attributed to the Kestoi?

Perhaps it is largely because his "non-orthodox" views were expressed mainly in a separable part of his works. Due to its "secular" topics, approach, and address it circulated largely to a different audience than his religious works. Further, it seems not to have circulated widely, and to have perished quickly; and it was a work which most readers in later generations did not (or would not) connect with the "most wise" Africanus of Emmaus.

But the secular and transitory nature of the Kestoi is probably not the full explanation; some allowance must also be made for Africanus's lay status. As a lay writer, he would be subject to less stringent inspection and standards of judgment.[1] Further, even if accused, and judged defective, not much could have been done in such a

---

[1] This is a fact of human existence which the Apostle James was neither the first nor the last to observe (cf. James 3:1).

case anyway (and especially in the case of an individual such as he?
Or of a work such as this, dedicated, and perhaps personally presented, to the emperor?).

Procedural implications for early church studies

To repeat a major question left unanswered by the history of
the study of Africanus: What do the contents and spirit of the Kestoi
tell us about the Christianity of the time of Africanus? The answers
are, Little, and Much. Explicitly, the Kestoi tells us little or
nothing, but potentially and by implication, it can provide a great
deal of information. As pointed out above, much of the Kestoi, and
thus much of the evidence, lies outside the bounds of magic, and thus
outside the bounds of this study. Thus only a few suggestions are
justified here. Since, however, the question of magic lies close to
the other aspects of the problem, these suggestions appear to have a
much broader field of application and validity.

As the denunciations of the Old Testament prophets warn us not
to read Israel's history in too ideal a light, as if in general conformity to the laws as promulgated in the various parts of the Penta-
teuch; so the sermons and tracts of the fathers should have warned us
not to read early Christian history in too glowing a light, as though
in uniform correspondence to the ideals presented in the Gospels. The
very remonstrances (De Corona) and boasts (Apol. 37. 4) of Tertullian,
for example, show us that there were Christians in the army, for example. They also tell us of the presence of Christians in some close
contacts with at least the Severan emperors (e.g., Ad Scap. 4. 5-6),

but would we take this seriously without Africanus?[1]

Africanus presents us with evidence of a Christian in the higher governmental and social circles of the empire, under at least the later Severans, and possibly under Severus himself. We also see him not only surviving, but apparently prospering, presumably with his Christianity essentially intact. Africanus might be unique in such a position, but the absence of explicit evidence of others is not a proof of that fact, and such hints as we do have suggest that he was not.[2] Also, we have no evidence to suggest that he secured his safety by any dishonorable means, but the survival of one so high in the circles of presumably greater danger may suggest that we should read in a new light charges or warnings against various types of evasion or escape from arrest and martyrdom. (Apparently some in the church thought they were justifiable [and were acting accordingly?].)

In the time of Septimius there was an intellectual circle (with at least mildly philosophic-religious tendencies)[3] which gathered around Julia Domna. Did such a circle continue under the succeeding

---

[1] Actually, even with Africanus, do we accept them as at least essentially valid, or write them off as rhetorical exaggeration (esp. in view of their association with the assertion of the Christian education of Caracalla and of the story of the "Thundering Legion," Ad Scap. 4. 6)?

[2] E.g., the Ad Scapulam references; or the later picture of the court of Diocletian in Lactantius De mort. pers. 10. 1, 2; 11. 3; 15. 1-2; cf. also 11. 1-2.

[3] Note Philostratus's Life of Apollonius of Tyana, both for the existence of this circle (1. 3), and something of its religious orientation.

Augustae, especially Mammaea? It seems not unlikely.[1] If so, was the

Kestoi an attempt by an "outsider" to gain status with such an inner

circle, or even to gain admission to it? Or was it written as a proof

of the intellectual capacity of a Christian, or even, of Christianity:

in a sense, a defense of Christian intellectual respectability? The

former possibility would seem more in keeping with the tone and the

individualistic character of the Kestoi,[2] but the two ideas are not

mutually exclusive.[3]

  Another consideration is related somewhat to the questions

raised in the discussion of Africanus's lay status and secular outlook:

despite the strong moral emphasis in Christianity, were certain types

of deviations in practice less objectionable than deviations in the-

ology? Extreme forms, of course, would not be tolerated, but would

lesser deviations,[4] and especially simply written discussion of them

---

[1]Alexander's religious and literary interests would seem to
make such a circle at court probable; but the names that actually come
to us are more those in the political and legal field (cf. Jean Reville, La religion à Rome sous les Séveres [Paris: Ernest Leroux,
1885], pp. 262-63, 274).

[2]But in addition to its speculative nature, such a specific
idea of the purpose of the Kestoi would fit better with Vieillefond's
view of Africanus as essentially a cosmopolitan courtier, than with
the more traditional view of him as basically a widely travelled Palestinian (of whatever original nationality).

[3]The latter view might appear farfetched, but it is not outside the realm of possibility, if the explicitly pagan passages are
non-authentic, and the strictly secular literary and "scientific" nature of the Kestoi is kept in mind.

[4]This both assumes and provides a further support for a negative decision on the authenticity of mp 23a (and its containing chapter, Vi., III. 2). Belief in demons was, and is, part of the official
teaching of the church, and thus magic, or some other sort of trafficking with evil, was theoretically possible (cf. Bardy, "Origène et la

(even positive ones), be overlooked? In the case of Africanus, there
is no evidence that his theological beliefs deviated significantly
from those of the other fathers, yet he was involved in some type of
magic. Further, some of his prescriptions (both magical and non-
magical) involve areas that (some of) the others spoke strongly
against, e.g., abortives, and love charms; and possibly horse-racing
and gladiatorial combats.

In some ways, the ethical questions raised, such as his prescriptions concerning warfare (of the most unrestricted kind) and
horse-thievery (at least aiding and abetting), are more problematic
than the questions raised by the type of "magic" which he apparently
propagated.[1]

Addendum: Relation of Africanus's Views
to Other Contemporary Attitudes

The examples cited in the discussions above have shown that
Africanus was not alone in his views. Many of his ideas and procedures
have explicit parallels, either in whole or in various parts, in roughly
contemporary writers. If the circle is extended to include influential
writers from the preceding centuries of the Christian era, especially

---

magie," p. 142, last paragraph; also, creedal testimonies to the existence of angels lend support to belief in their evil counterparts). But,
such trafficking has, I think, never been viewed as a minor deviation.
If anyone in the early church actually read the Kestoi, they must have
read it as presenting something other than "daemonic" magic.

[1]Perhaps the resolution of this dilemma in relation to Africanus
is found in the "separable" nature of the Kestoi and his other writings;
later generations, beginning at least with Rufinus and Jerome, condemned the work rather than the man.

Galen and Pliny, most of Africanus's ideas can be so paralleled.
These parallels include not only the types of items, but also much of
the spirit of the writings. This last was especially the desire to
present practical information, coupled with the wish not to be gullible,
but also not to omit potentially useful matters. Africanus added to
this a goal similar to that of his nearer contemporary, Aelian--a desire to do it in a pleasing literary form.[1]

<u>Conclusions</u>

The preceding studies seem to justify a slightly more precise
restatement of the beginning thesis: The difference in the attitudes
of Africanus and the early church fathers toward magic is due to their
views of what constituted it. They seem to agree that magic is evil,
and is a religious matter (as being anti-religious), but Africanus
does not regard his procedures as falling into the category of religion
(i.e., anti-religion), but rather as being a matter of tested practical
remedies: <u>technai</u> in the common, rather than the "technical" (i.e.,
magical) sense. This justification of the thesis thus extends also to
the "Amplification of the Statement," which follows it: the kind of
"mysterious, transhuman force" which Africanus would see lying behind
some of his procedures should also be characterized as "non-personal."

The "Related Aspects" presented under the "Statement of the
Thesis" seem also to be validated <u>in general</u>. Most of the items which
fit the description given there actually fall outside the area of

---

[1]Compare Aelian <u>N.A.</u>, "Epilogue," and Africanus's "Proem" to
<u>Kestos</u> 7 (Vi., I. proem, p. 103). Contrast with this Pliny's boasted
plainness of style (<u>N.H.</u> pref. 12-13).

possible magical involvement, and so have not been extensively considered above. In general, however, the areas of conflict are more in
the realm of moral evaluations than of theological beliefs.

In another realm, it has been suggested in the discussions
above that several of the questionable passages in Africanus are explainable as products of his literary interests and/or his dabblings
in "empirical science" (at least from a literary or theoretical [or,
speculational] approach, not an actual experimental one).

Finally, it may be remarked that the inhabitants of the age
of computer horoscopes, syndicated prophet(esse)s, and archepiscopal
séances can hardly look down too much on Africanus and his age.

SELECTED BIBLIOGRAPHY

Ancient and Medieval Texts

Julius Africanus

Duchesne, L. "III. Fragments métrologiques." Archives des missions
    scientifiques et littéraires (Paris), 3d ser., 3 (1876):
    378-85.

Grenfell, Bernard P., and Hunt, Arthus S. The Oxyrhynchus Papyri.
    Parts III and VI. Egypt Exploration Fund: Graeco-Roman
    Branch. London: Egypt Exploration Fund, 1903, 1908.

Lagarde, Paul de. Symmicta, I. Göttingen: Dieterichsche Verlags-
    buchhandlung, 1877.

Müller, K. K. "Zu Julius Africanus." Jahrbücher für protestantische
    Theologie 7 (1881):759-60.

Psellus, Michael. "Περὶ παραδόξων ἀναγνωσμάτων." In ΠΑΡΑΔΟΞΟΓΡΑΦΟΙ
    --Scriptores rerum mirabilium Graeci, pp. 143-48. Edited
    by Antonius Westermann. Braunschweig: Georgius Westermann,
    1839; London: Black & Armstrong, 1839; also, reprint ed.,
    Amsterdam: Verlag Adolf M. Hakkert, 1963.

Vieillefond, J[ean]-R[ené]. Jules Africain: Fragments des Cestes
    provenant de la collection des tacticiens grecs. Nouvelle
    collection de textes et documents publiée sous le patronage
    de l'Association Guillaume Budé. Paris: Société d'Edition
    "Les Belles Lettres," 1932.

_____. "Un fragment inédit de Julius Africanus." Revue des
    études grecques 46 (1933):197-203.

_____. Les "Cestes" de Julius Africanus. Etude sur l'ensemble
    des fragments avec édition, traduction et commentaires.
    Publications de l'Institut Francais de Florence, Ière série:
    Collection d'études d'histoire, de critique et de philologie,
    no. 20. Florence: Edizioni Sansoni Antiquariato, 1970;
    Paris: Librairie Marcel Didier, 1970.

Collections

The Ante-Nicene Fathers: Translations of the Writings of the Fathers
down to A.D. 325. Edited by Alexander Roberts and James
Donaldson. Amer. ed. Revised by A. Cleveland Coxe. 10 vols.
New York: Christian Literature Company, 1885-87; reprint ed.,
Grand Rapids: Wm. B. Eerdmans Publishing Company, 1951.

Berthelot, M[arcel Pierre Eugene] and Ruelle, Ch.-Em[ile]. Collec-
tion des anciens alchimistes grecs. 3 vols. Paris: Georges
Steinheil, 1888; reprint ed., 3 vols. in 1. London: Holland
Press, 1963.

Bueno, Daniel Ruiz, ed. and trans. Padres Apologistas griegos (s.
II): Introducciones, texto griego, versión española y notas.
Biblioteca de autores cristianos, no. 116. Madrid: La Edi-
torial Catolica, 1954.

Catalogue des manuscrits alchimiques grecs. 8 vols. in 3. Brussels: M.
Lamertin for Union Académique Internationale, 1924-32.

Catena patrum Graecorum in sanctem Ioannem. Ex antiquissimo Graeco
codice ms. nunc primum in lucem edita. Edited by Balthasar
Corderius. Antwerp: Ex Officina Plantianiana Balthasaris
Moreti, 1630.

Catenae Graecorum patrum in Novum Testamentum. Edited by John Anthony Cramer. Vol. 1: Catenae in evangelia S. Matthaei et
S. Marci. Oxford, 1840; reprint ed., Hildesheim: Georg Olms,
1967.

Corpus Christianorum. Series Latina. Turnhout: Typographi Brepols
Editores Pontificii, 1953-.

Corpus scriptorum ecclesiasticorum Latinorum. Editum consilio et
impensis Academiae Litterarum (Caesareae) Vindobonensis.
Vienna [et al.]: Apud C. Geroldi Filium [et al.], 1866-.

Corpus scriptorum historiae Byzantinae. Editio emendatior et co-
piosior, consilio B. G. Niebuhrii C. f. instituta. 50 vols.
Bonn: Ed. Weber, 1828-97.

Grant, Robert M. Second-Century Christianity: A Collection of Fragments. Translations of Christian Literature, ser. 6: Select
Passages. London: SPCK, 1957.

Griechischen Christlichen Schriftsteller der ersten [drei] Jahrhunderte. 40 vols. Issued by Der Kirchenväter-Commission
der Königlichen Preussischen Akademie der Wissenschaften.
Leipzig: J. C. Hinrichs'sche Buchhandlung, 1897-1936.
[Series continued by Deutschen Akademie der Wissenschaften
zu Berlin. Berlin: Akademie Verlag, 1953-.]

Kenyon, F. G., and Bell, H. I.   Greek Papyri in the British Museum:
    Catalogue, with Texts. 5 vols. London: British Museum, 1893-
    1917.

Migne, J.-P. Patrologiae cursus completus . . . series Graeca. 162
    vols. Paris: Garnier Fratres, 1857-66; reprinted 1880-1904.

_____. Patrologiae cursus completus . . . series Latina. 221
    vols. Paris: Garnier Fratres, 1841-1905.

Musici scriptores Graeci: Aristotoles, Euclides, Nicomachus,
    Bacchius, Gaudentius, Alypius et melodiarum veterum quid-
    quid exstat. Edited by Carolus Janus. Bibliotheca Scriptorum
    Graecorum et Romanorum Teubneriana. Leipzig: B. G. Teubner, 1895.

Musurillo, Herbert, ed. and trans. The Acts of the Christian Martyrs.
    Oxford Early Christian Texts, general editor, Henry Chadwick.
    Oxford: Clarendon Press, 1972.

Nag Hammadi Library in English. Translated by members of the Coptic
    Gnostic Library Project of the Institute for Antiquity and
    Christianity, James M. Robinson, Director. 1st U.S. ed.
    San Francisco: Harper & Row, Publishers, 1977.

New Testament Apocrypha. Edited by Edgar Hennecke. [3d (Ger.) ed.]
    Edited by Wilhelm Schneemelcher. English translation edited
    by R. McL. Wilson. 2 vols. Philadelphia: Westminster
    Press [1963-65].

Preisendanz, Karl. Papyri Graecae Magicae: Die Griechischen Zauber-
    papyri. 2 vols. Leipzig and Berlin: B. G. Teubner, 1928-31.

Routh, Martinus Josephus. Reliquiae sacrae: sive, auctorum fere jam
    perditum secundi tertiique saeculi post Christum natum quae
    supersunt. Editio altera. 5 vols. Oxford: E Typographeo
    Academico, 1846-48.

A Select Library of the Nicene and Post-Nicene Fathers of the Christian
    Church. [1st ser.] Edited by Philip Schaff. 14 vols.
    New York: The Christian Literature Company, 1886-90; reprint ed.,
    Grand Rapids: Wm. B. Eerdmans Publishing Company, 1956.

A Select Library of the Nicene and Post-Nicene Fathers of the Christian
    Church. 2d ser. Edited by Philip Schaff and Henry Wace.
    14 vols. New York: The Christian Literature Company, 1890-
    1900; reprint ed., Grand Rapids: Wm. B. Eerdmans Publishing
    Company, 1955-57.

Sources chrétiennes. [Early volumes add, Collection dirigée par
    H. de Lubac et J. Danielou.] Paris: Editions du Cerf, 1948-.

Individual Authors and Texts

Aelian. On the Characteristics of Animals. Translated by A. F.
    Scholfield. The Loeb Classical Library. 3 vols. Cambridge:
    Harvard University Press, 1958-59; London: William Heinemann,
    1958-59.

[Aelian.] Claudii Aeliani de natura animalium libri XVII. Edited
    by Rudolph Hercher. Bibliotheca Scriptorum Graecorum et
    Romanorum Teubneriana. Leipzig: B. G. Teubner, 1864.

Aeneae Tactici de obsidione toleranda commentarius. Edited by
    Richardus Schoene. Bibliotheca Scriptorum Graecorum et
    Romanorum Teubneriana. Leipzig: B. G. Teubner, 1911.

Aeneas Tacticus, Asclepiodotus, Onasander. Translated by The Illinois
    Greek Club. The Loeb Classical Library. Cambridge: Harvard
    University Press, 1962; London: Wm. Heinemann, 1962.

ΑΙΝΕΙΟΥ ΠΟΛΙΟΡΚΗΤΙΚΑ: Aeneas on Seigecraft. Edited and translated
    by L. W. Hunter; revised by S. A. Hanford. Oxford: Clarendon
    Press, 1927.

Agnus castus: A Middle English Herbal Reconstructed from Various
    Manuscripts. Edited with introduction, notes, and glossary
    by Gösta Brodin. The English Language Institute in the Uni-
    versity of Upsala: Essays and Studies on English Language and
    Literature, edited by S. B. Liljegren, no. 6. Upsala: A.-B.
    Lundequistska Bokhandeln, 1950; Copenhagen: Ejnar Munksgaard,
    1950; Cambridge: Harvard University Press, 1950.

The Apostolic Fathers. A Revised Text, with Introduction, Notes,
    Dissertations and Translations by J. B. Lightfoot. 2 parts
    in 5 vols. London and New York: Macmillan and Co., 1889-90.

The Apostolic Fathers. Translated by J. B. Lightfoot. Edited and
    completed by J. R. Harmer. London: Macmillan and Company,
    1891; reprint ed., Grand Rapids: Baker Book House, 1956.

The Apostolic Fathers. Translated by Francis X. Glimm, Joseph M.-F.
    Marique, and Gerald G. Walsh. The Fathers of the Church, a
    New Translation, editorial director, Ludwig Schopp [vol. 1].
    New York: CIMA Publishing Co., 1947.

[The Apostolic Fathers.] The Didache, the Epistle of Barnabas, the
    Epistles and the Martyrdom of St. Polycarp, the Fragments of
    Papias, the Epistle to Diognetus. Translated by James A.
    Kleist. Ancient Christian Writers: The Works of the Fathers
    in Translation, edited by Johannes Quasten and Joseph C.
    Plumpe, no. 6. Westminster, Md.: Newman Press, 1948.

The Apostolic Fathers: A New Translation and Commentary. Edited by
    Robert M. Grant. 6 vols. New York [before 1966] and Camden,
    N.J.: Thomas Nelson & Sons, 1964-68.

[The Apostolic Fathers.] Ignace d'Antioche, Polycarpe de Smyrne,
    Lettres, Martyre de Polycarpe. Texte grec, introduction,
    traduction et notes. Edited and translated by P. Th. Camelot.
    4th ed., rev. and corr. Sources chrétiennes, edited by C.
    Mondesert, no. 10. Paris: Editions du Cerf, 1969.

Arnobii adversus nationes, libri VII. Edited by Augustus Reiffer-
    scheid. Corpus scriptorum ecclesiasticorum Latinorum, vol.
    4. Vienna: Apud C. Geroldi Filium Bibliopolam Academiae,
    1875.

Athenagoras. Legatio and De resurrectione. Edited and translated
    by William R. Schoedel. Oxford Early Christian Texts, gen-
    eral editor, Henry Chadwick. Oxford: Clarendon Press, 1972.

[Bar-Hebraeus.] Gregory Abu'l Faraj Commonly Called Bar-Hebraeus,
    Commentary on the Gospels from the Horreum Mysteriorum.
    Translated and edited by Wilmot Eardley W. Carr. London:
    SPCK, 1925.

Chronicon paschale. Edited by Ludovicus Dindorfius. Corpus scrip-
    torum historiae Byzantinae, edited by B. G. Niebuhrius. 2
    vols. Bonn: Ed. Weber, 1832.

Clemens Alexandrinus. Edited by Otto Stählin. Die Griechischen
    Christlichen Schriftsteller der ersten drei Jahrhunderte
    [vols. 12, 15, 17, and 39]. 4 vols. [2d ed. of vol. 1.]
    Leipzig: J. C. Hinrichs'sche Buchhandlung, 1906-36.

Clemens Alexandrinus. Quis dives salvetur? Edited by K. Köster.
    Sammlung augewählter kirchen- und dogmengeschichtlicher
    Quellenschriften, edited by G. Krüger, vol. 6. Freiburg
    and Leipzig: Akademische Verlagsbuchhandlung von J. C. B.
    Mohr (Paul Siebeck), 1893; reprint ed., Frankfurt: Minerva,
    1968.

Clement d'Alexandrie. Le Protreptique. Introduction, translation
    and notes by Claude Mondesert. 2d ed., rev. and augm., of
    the Greek text, with the collaboration of André Plassant.
    Sources chrétiennes, edited by H. de Lubac and J. Daniélou,
    no. 2. Paris: Editions du Cerf, 1949.

Clement d'Alexandrie. Extraits de Théodote. Greek text, introduction,
    and notes by F. Sagnard. Sources chrétiennes, edited by H.
    de Lubac and J. Daniélou. Ser. annexe de textes hétérodoxe.
    Paris: Editions du Cerf [1948].

[Cyprian.] S. Thasci Caecili Cypriani opera omnia. Edited by
    Guilelmus Hartel. Corpus scriptorum ecclesiasticorum Latin-
    orum, vol. 3, parts 1-3. 1 vol. in 3 parts. Vienna: Apud
    C. Geroldi Filium Bibliopolam Academiae, 1868-71.

Dionysii Bar Ṣalibi commentarii in evangelica. Translated by I.
    Sedlacek, aided by I.-B. Chabot. Vol. 1. Corpus scriptorum
    Christianorum Orientalium, ed. I.-B. Chabot, et al.: Scrip-
    tores Syri, Versio, series secunda, vol. 98. Rome: Karolus
    de Luigi, 1906; Leipzig: Otto Harrassowitz, 1906.

[Dioscorides.] Pedanii Dioscoridis Anazarbei de materia medica libri
    quinque. Edited by Max Wellmann. Editio altera ex editione
    anni MCMVII lucis ope expressa. 3 vols. Berlin: Apud Weid-
    mannos, 1958.

Eusebius Werke. Die Griechischen Christlichen Schriftsteller der
    ersten [drei] Jahrhunderete [vols. 7, 9, 11, 14, 20, 23, 47,
    43, -]. 9 vols. Leipzig: J. C. Hinrichs'sche Buchhandlung,
    1902-13; Berlin: Akademie Verlag, 1954-75. Vol. 2, parts 1-3:
    Die Kirchengeschichte, edited by Eduard Schwartz; with Die
    Lateinische Übersetzung des Rufinus, revised by Theodor
    Mommsen. Vol. 5: Die Chronik: Aus dem Armenischen übersetzt
    mit textkritischen Commentar, edited by Josef Karst. Vol. 6:
    Die Demonstratio evangelica, edited by Ivar A. Heikel. Vol.
    7 [2d ed.]: Die Chronik des Hieronymus, edited and revised
    by Rudolf Helm. Vol. 8, parts 1-2: Die Praeparatio evangelica,
    edited by Karl Mras.

Eusebius. The Ecclesiastical History. The Loeb Classical Library.
    2 vols. Vol. 1, with an English translation by Kirsopp Lake.
    London: William Heinemann, 1926; and New York: G. P. Putnam's
    Sons, 1926. Vol. 2, with an English translation by J. E. L.
    Oulton. Cambridge: Harvard University Press, 1942.

Eusebius Caesariensis opera. Recognovit Guilielmus Dindorfius. Vol.
    1: Praeparationis evangelicae libri I-X. Bibliotheca Scrip-
    torum Graecorum et Romanorum Teubneriana. Leipzig: B. G.
    Teubner, 1867.

[Eusebius.] The Proof of the Gospel, Being the Demonstratio evan-
    gelica of Eusebius of Caesarea. Translated by W. J. Ferrar.
    Translations of Christian Literature, ser. 1: Greek Texts.
    2 vols. London: SPCK, 1920; New York: Macmillan Company,
    1920.

Eusebii Pamphili evangelicae praeparationis, libri XV. Edited by
    E. H. Gifford. 4 vols. Oxford: E Typographeo Academico,
    1903.

[Fulgentius.] Fabii Plancialis Fulgentii V. C. opera accedunt Fabii
     Claudii Gordiani Fulgentii V. C. de aetatibus mundi et ho-
     minis et S. Fulgentii episcopi super Thebaidem. Edited by
     Rudolf Helm. Bibliotheca Scriptorum Graecorum et Romanorum
     Teubneriana. Leipzig: B. G. Teubner, 1898.

[Galen.] Claudii Galeni opera omnia. Edited by C. G. Kühn. Medi-
     corum Graecorum opera quae exstant, vols. 1-20. 20 vols.
     Leipzig, 1821-33; reprint ed., Hildesheim: Georg Olms Verlags-
     buchhandlung, 1964-65.

Geoponica sive Cassiani Bassi scholastici de re rustica eclogae.
     Edited by Henricus Beckh. Bibliotheca Scriptorum Graecorum
     et Romanorum Teubneriana. Leipzig: B. G. Teubner, 1895.

Geoponika, Agricultural Pursuits. Translated by T. Owen. 2 vols.
     London: For the author by W. Spilsbury, 1805-6. (Typewritten
     copy, n.p., n.d.).

[Hieronymus.] Sancti Eusebii Hieronymi Stridonensis presbyteri operum.
     Edited by Dominicus Vallarsius. Editio altera. Vol. 1,
     part 1; vol. 2, part 1. Venice: G. Zerletti, 1766, 1767.

Hieronymus liber de viri inlustribus. Edited by Ernest
     Cushing Richardson. Texte und Untersuchungen zur Geschichte
     der altchristlichen Literatur 14, no. 1 (1896).

S. Hieronymi presbyteri opera.   Part I: Opera exegetica.
     Vol. 5: Commentariorum in Danielem libri III <IV>. Corpus
     Christianorum, Series Latina, vol. 75A. Turnhout: Typographi
     Brepols Editores Pontificii, 1964.

[Hippiatrica.] Corpus hippiatricorum Graecorum. Edited by Eugenius
     Oder and Carolus Hoppe. Bibliotheca Scriptorum Graecorum et
     Romanorum Teubneriana. 2 vols. Leipzig: B. G. Teubner, 1924,
     1927.

[Hippocrates.] Oeuvres complètes d'Hippocrate, traduction nouvelle
     avec le texte grec en regard, collationné sur les manuscrits
     et toutes les editiones; accompagnée d'une introduction, de
     commentaires medicaux, de variantes et de notes philologiques;
     suivie d'une table générale des matiérés. Edited by E.
     Littré. 10 vols. Paris: 1839-61; reprint ed., Amsterdam:
     Adolf M. Hakkert, Editeur, 1961-62.

[Hippolytus.] The Treatise on the Apostolic Tradition of St. Hippoly-
     tus of Rome. Edited and translated by Gregory Dix. [2d ed.]
     Reissued with corrections, preface, and bibliography by Henry
     Chadwick. London: SPCK for the Church Historical Society,
     1968.

St. Irenaeus. Proof of the Apostolic Preaching. Translated by Joseph
     P. Smith. Ancient Christian Writers: The Works of the Fathers
     in Translation, edited by Johannes Quasten and Joseph C.
     Plumpe, no. 16. Westminster, Md.: Newman Press, 1952; London:
     Longmans, Green and Co., 1952.

Saint Justin Martyr. The First Apology, the Second Apology, Dialogue
     with Trypho, Exhortation to the Greeks, Discourse to the
     Greeks, the Monarchy or the Rule of God. Translated by
     Thomas B. Falls. The Fathers of the Church, editorial direc-
     tor Ludwig Schopp [vol. 6]. New York: Christian Heritage,
     Inc., 1948.

[Lactantius.] L. Caeli Firmiani Lactanti opera omnia. Edited by
     Samuel Brandt and Georgius Laubmann. Part 1: Divinae insti-
     tutiones et epitome divinarum institutionum, edited by
     Samuel Brandt; part 2, fasc. 1: Libri de opficio dei et de
     ira dei, carmina fragmenta, vetera de Lactantio testimonia,
     edited by Samuel Brandt. Corpus scriptorum ecclesiasticorum
     Latinorum, vols. 19 and 27. Vienna and Prague: F. Tempsky,
     1890-93; Leipzig: G. Freytag, 1890-93.

M. Minucii Felicis Octavius. Edited by Aloisius Valmaggi. Corpus
     Scriptorum Latinorum Paravianum [no. 5]. Turin: Io. Bapt.
     Paraviae et Sociorum [1916].

Moïse de Khorène, auteur du Ve siècle: Histoire d'Armenie. Texte
     armenien et traduction française par P. E. Le Vaillant de
     Florival. 2 vols. Venice: Typographie Arménienne de Saint-
     Lazare, 1841.

Des Moses von Chorene Geschichte Gross-Armeniens. Aus dem Armenischen
     übersetzt von Dr. M. Lauer. Regensburg: G. J. Manz, 1869.

Nicander. The Poems and Poetical Fragments. Edited and translated
     with notes by A. S. F. Gow and A. F. Scholfield. Cambridge:
     University Press, 1953.

Novatiani opera: Quae supersunt nunc primum in unum collecta ad fidem
     codicum qui adhuc extant necnon adhibitis editionibus veteri-
     bus. Edited by G. F. Diercks. Corpus Christianorum, Series
     Latina, vol. 4. Turnhout: Typographi Brepols Editores Ponti-
     ficii, 1972.

Origenes Werke. Die Griechischen Christlichen Schriftsteller der
     ersten [drei] Jahrhunderte [vols. 2, 3, 6, 10, 22, 29, 30, 33,
     49, 40, 38, 41]. 12 vols. Leipzig: J. C. Hinrichs'sche Buch-
     handlung, 1899-1935; Berlin: Akademie Verlag, 1959-72. Vol. 1:
     Die Schrift vom Martyrium, Buch I-IV gegen Calsus, edited by
     Paul Koetschau. Vol. 2: Buch V-VIII gegen Celsus, Die Schrift
     vom Gebet, edited by Paul Koetschau. Vol. 5: De principiis

(ΠΕΡΙ ΑΡΧΩΝ), edited by Paul Koetschau. Vol. 10: Origenes Matthäuserklärung, part 1: Die griechisch erhaltenen Tomoi, edited by Erich Klostermann, assisted by Ernst Benz.

Origène. Contre Celse. Introduction, critical text, translation, and notes by Marcel Borret. Vol. 4: Livres VII et VIII. Sources chrétiennes, no. 150. Paris: Editions du Cerf, 1969.

Origène. Commentaire sur saint Jean. Greek text, foreword, translation, and notes by Cecile Blanc. Vol. 2: Livres VI et X. Sources chrétiennes, no. 157. Paris: Editions du Cerf, 1970.

Origène. Commentaire sur l'Evangile selon Matthieu. Introduction, translation and notes by Robert Girod. Vol. 1: Livres X et XI. Sources chrétiennes, no. 162. Paris: Editions du Cerf, 1970.

[Origen.] The Commentary of Origen on S. John's Gospel. The text revised with a critical introduction and indices by A. E. Brooke. 2 vols. Cambridge: University Press, 1896.

Origen. On First Principles. Translated with introduction and notes by G. W. Butterfield. London: Society for Promoting Christian Knowledge, 1936; reprint ed., New York: Harper & Row, Publishers, Harper Torchbooks, The Cathedral Library, 1966.

Origen. Contra Celsum. Translated with an introduction and notes by Henry Chadwick. Cambridge: University Press, 1953.

Origen. Prayer, Exhortation to Martyrdom. Translated and annotated by John J. O'Meara. Ancient Christian Writers: The Works of the Fathers in Translation, edited by Johannes Quasten and Joseph C. Plumpe, no. 19. Westminster, Md.: Newman Press, 1954; London: Longmans, Green and Co., 1954.

Papyrus Graecus Holmiensis (P. Holm.): Recepte für Silber, Steine und Purpur. Edited by Otto Lagercrantz. Uppsala: A.-B. Akademiska Bokhandeln, 1913; Leipzig: Otto Harrassowitz, 1913.

Pausanius. Description of Greece. With an English translation by W. H. S. Jones and [in vol. 2] H. A. Ormerod. The Loeb Classical Library. 4 vols. [with a companion volume prepared by R. E. Wycherley, containing maps, plans, and indices]. Cambridge: Harvard University Press, 1959-61; London: William Heinemann, 1959-61.

Photii bibliotheca. Edited by Immanuel Bekkerus. 2 vols. Berlin: G. E. Reimer, 1824-25.

Photius. Bibliotheque. Edited and translated by Renè Henry. Col-
lection byzantine publiée sous le patronage l'Association
Guillaume Budé. 2 vols. Paris: Société d'Edition "Les
Belles Lettres," 1959-60.

Pliny. Natural History. Translated by H. Rackham [vols. 1-4, 9],
W. H. S. Jones [vols. 6-8], and D. E. Eichholz [vol. 10].
The Loeb Classical Library. 10 vols. Cambridge: Harvard
University Press, 1938-63; London: William Heinemann, 1938-63.

Scriptores historiae augustae. Translated by D. Magie. The Loeb Classical Library. 3 vols. Cambridge: Harvard University Press,
1922-32; London: William Heinemann, 1922-32.

Σουΐδας: Suidae Lexicon, post Ludolphum Kusterum ad codices manu-
scriptos. Edited by Thomas Gaisford. 2 vols. Oxford: E
Typographeo Academico, 1834.

Suidae Lexicon. Edited by Ada Adler. Lexicographi Graeci, vol. 1.
1 vol. in 5 parts. Leipzig: B. G. Teubner, 1928-38.

[Syncellus.] Georgius Syncellus et Nicephorus CP. Edited by
Guilielmus Dindorfius. Corpus scriptorum historiae Byzantinae, edited by B. G. Niebuhrius. 2 vols. Bonn: Ed. Weber,
1829.

[Tertullian.] Quinti Septimi Florentis Tertulliani opera. Part 1:
Opera catholica, adversus Marcionem; part 2: Opera Montanis-
tica. Corpus Christianorum, Series Latina, vols. 1-2. 2
parts. Turnhout: Typographi Brepols Editores Pontificii,
1954.

[Tertullian.] Quinti Septimi Florentis Tertulliani quae supersunt
omnia. Edited by Franciscus Oehler. 3 vols. Leipzig: T. O.
Weigel, 1851-54.

Theophrastii Eresii quae supersunt opera. Edited by Jo. Gottlob
Schneider. 5 vols. Leipzig: Frid. Christ. Guil. Vogelius,
1818-21.

Victorini episcopi Petavionensis opera. Edited by Johannes Haussleiter. Corpus scriptorum eccleiasticorum Latinorum, vol.
49. Vienna: F. Tempsky, 1916; Leipzig: G. Freytag, 1916.

Modern Works

Amann, E. "Jules Africain." In Dictionnaire de theologie catholique,
8:1921-25. 15 vols. in 23. Paris: Librairie Letouzey et
Ané, 1903-50.

Assemani, Joseph Simonius. Bibliotheca Orientalis Clementino-
     Vaticana. 3 vols. in 4. Rome: Typis Sacrae Congregationis
     De Propaganda Fide, 1719-28.

Bandini, Angelo Maria. Catalogus codicum manuscriptorum bibliothecae
     medicae Laurentianae varia continens opera Graecorum patrum.
     3 vols. Florence, 1764-70; reprint ed., 3 vols. in 2;
     Leipzig: Zentral-Antiquariat der Deutschen Demokratischen
     Republik, 1961.

Barb, A. A. "The Survival of Magic Arts." In The Conflict between
     Paganism and Christianity in the Fourth Century, pp. 100-25.
     Edited by Arnaldo Momigliano. Oxford-Warburg Studies, gen-
     eral editors, T. S. R. Boase and G. Bing. Oxford: Clarendon
     Press, 1963.

Bardy, Gustave. "Origène et la magie." Recherches de science reli-
     gieuse 18 (1928):126-42.

_____. "Un encyclopédiste chrétien du IIIe siècle: Jules Afri-
     cain." Revue apologetique 56, no. 576 (1933):257-71.

Basnage, Jacobus. Thesaurus monumentorum ecclesiasticorum et his-
     toricum, sive Henrici Canisii lectiones antiquae, ad saeculorum
     ordinem digestae variisque opusculis auctae, quibus praefa-
     tiones historicas, animadversiones criticas, et notas in
     singulos auctores adjecit. Antwerp: n.p., 1725.

Bauer, Walter. Orthodoxy and Heresy in Earliest Christianity. Trans-
     lated from the 2d Ger. ed. by a team from the Philadelphia
     Seminar on Christian Origins. Edited by Robert A. Kraft and
     Gerhard Krodel. Philadelphia: Fortress Press, 1971.

Baumstark, Antonius. "Lucubrationes Syro-Graecae." Annalium philo-
     logicorum/Jahrbücher für classische Philologie, Supp. 21
     (1894):357-524.

Benedict, Ruth. "Magic." In Encyclopedia of the Social Sciences 10
     [5]:39-44. Edited by Edwin R. A. Seligman and Aloin Johnson.
     15 vols. in 8. New York: Macmillan Company, 1937.

_____. "Religion." In General Anthropology, pp. 627-55. Edited
     by Franz Boas. Boston: D. C. Heath and Company, 1938.

Berthelot, M[arcel Pierre Eugène]. Les origines de l'alchimie.
     Paris: Georges Steinheil, 1885.

_____. Introduction a l'étude de la chimie des ancien et du moyen
     age. Paris: Georges Steinheil, Editeur, 1889.

Bickerman, E. J. Chronology of the Ancient World. Aspects of Greek
    and Roman Life, general editor, H. H. Scullard. Ithaca, N.Y.:
    Cornell University Press, 1968.

Björck, Gudmund. "Zum Corpus Hippiatricorum Graecorum: Beiträge zur
    antiken Tierheilkunde." Uppsala Universitets Årsskrift:
    Filosofi, språkvetenskap och historiska vetenskaper, 1932,
    no. 5.

_____. "Apsyrtus, Julius Africanus, et l'hippiatrique grecque."
    Uppsala Universitets Årsskrift, 1944, no. 4.

Blass, Friedrich [Wilhelm]. Die Interpolationen in der Odyssee.
    Halle: Max Niemeyer, 1904.

_____. "Literarische Texte mit Ausschluss der Christlichen."
    Archiv für Papyrusforschung und verwandte Gebiete 3 (1906):
    255-99.

Bouquiaux-Simon, Odette. "Lucien, citateur d'Homère." L'antiquité
    classique 29 (1960):5-17.

Bratke, Eduard. "Das sogenannte Religionsgespräch am Hof der Sasani-
    den." Texte und Untersuchungen zur Geschichte der altchrist-
    lichen Literatur 19 (n.s. 4), no. 3 (1899).

Caras, Roger. Venomous Animals of the World. Englewood Cliffs, N.J.:
    Prentice-Hall, 1974.

Casaubon, Isaac. C. Suetonii Tranquilli de XII Caesaribus libri VIII.
    [Geneva]: I. Chouët, 1595. Reprinted in C. Suetonii Tran-
    quilli opera: Textu ad codd. mss. recognito cum Jo. Aug.
    Ernestii animadversionibus nova cura auctis emendatisque et
    Isaac Casauboni commentario, 3:77-4:314. Edited by Frid.
    Aug. Wolfius. 4 vols. Leipzig: Impensis Casp. Fritsch,
    1802.

_____. Aeneae vetustissimi scriptoris commentarius tacticus et
    obsidionalis quomodo obsessum resistere oporteat [Paris,
    1609]. Reprinted in Polybii Lycortae F. Historiarum quae
    supersunt, interprete Isaaco Casaubono ex recensione Jacobi
    Gronovii cum notis Casaubonorum, Ursini, Valesii, Palmerii
    et Jacobi Gronovii, accessit Aeneae Tactici comm. de obsidione
    toleranda cum interpr. et notis Isaaci Casauboni, 3:387-600.
    3 vols. Leipzig: Jo. Paul Krausium, 1763-64.

Cave, Guilielmo. Scriptorum ecclesiasticorum historia literaria, a
    Christo nato usque ad saeculum XIV. Geneva: Samuel de
    Tournes, 1694. Pars altera. Geneva: Fratres de Tournes,
    1699. Also, reprint edition, 2 vols., Oxford: Sheldon, 1740-
    43; Basil: Joh. Rudolph. Im-Hoff., 1741-45.

Conway, David. The Magic of Herbs. New York: E. P. Dutton & Co., 1973.

Cyclopaedia of Biblical, Theological and Ecclesiastical Literature. Edited by John M'Clintock and James Strong. S.v. "Julius Africanus." 10 vols. New York: Harper & Bros., 1867-81.

Dain, A[lphonse]. Les manuscrits d'Onésandros. Collection d'études anciens publiée sous le patronage de l'Association Guillaume Budé. Paris: Société d'Edition "Les Belles Lettres," 1930.

_____. "Cinq adaptations byzantines des 'Stratagèmes' de Polyen." Revue des études anciennes 33, no. 4 (1931):321-45.

_____. "Les manuscrits d'Enée le tacticien." Revue des études grecques 48 (1935):1-32.

_____. Review of Jules Africain: Fragments des Cestes provenant de la collection des tacticiens grecs, by J.-R. Vieillefond. Revue de philologie, de littérature et d'histoire anciennes, 3d ser., 9 (61 of the collection) (1935):328-30.

_____. La "Tactique" de Nicéphore Ouranos. Paris: Société d'Edition "Les Belles Lettres," 1937.

_____. Sylloge tacticorum, quae olim "Inedita Leonis Tactica" dicebatur. Paris: Société d'Edition "Les Belles Lettres," 1938.

_____. Le "Corpus perditum." Collection de philologie classique. Paris: L'Auteur, 1939.

_____. "Memorandum inédit sur la défense des places." Revue des études grecques 53 (1940):123-36.

_____. L'"Extrait tactique" tiré de Léon VI Le Sage. Bibliothéque de l'Ecole des Hautes Etudes, no. 284. Paris: Librairie Ancienne Homeré Champion, 1942.

_____. Histoire du texte d'Elien le tacticien. Paris: Société d'Edition "Les Belles Lettres," 1946.

_____, [Texte établi par]. Enée le tacticien: Poliorcétique. Traduit et annoté Anne-Marie Bon. Paris: Société d'Edition "Les Belles Lettres," 1967.

de Boor, C. "Neue Fragmente des Papias, Hegesippus und Pierius bisher unbekannten Excerpten aus der Kirchengeschichte des Philippus Sidetes." Texte und Untersuchungen zur Geschichte der altchristlichen Literatur 5, no. 2 (1889):165-84.

Dictionary of Christian Biography, Literature, Sects and Doctrines.
    Edited by William Smith and Henry Wace. S.v. "Africanus,
    Julius," by George Salmon. 4 vols. Boston: Little, Brown
    and Company, 1877-87.

Delatte, A. Herbarius: Recherches sur le cérémonial usité chez les
    anciens pour la cueillette des simples et des plantes magiques.
    2d ed., rev., enl., and illust. Liege: Faculté de Philoso-
    phie et Lettres, 1938; Paris: Librairie E. Droz, 1938.

Ditmars, Raymond L. Reptiles of the World: The Crocodilians, Lizards,
    Snakes, Turtles and Tortoises of the Eastern and Western
    Hemispheres. New rev. ed. New York: Macmillan Company, 1959.

Drijvers, H. J. W. Bardaiṣan of Edessa. Translated by Mrs. G. E.
    van Baaren-Pape. Studia Semitica Neerlandica, no. 6. Assen:
    Van Gorcum, 1966.

DuCange, Carolus du Fresne, D., ed. and trans. ΠΑΣΧΑΛΙΟΝ, seu
    Chronicon paschale a mundo condito ad Heraclii imperatoris
    annum vicesimum. Paris: E Typographia Regia, 1688.

Duchesne, Louis. Early History of the Christian Church from Its
    Foundation to the End of the Third Century. Translated from
    the 4th ed. 3 vols. New York: Longman, Green and Co.,
    1909-24; London: J. Murray, 1909-24.

Du Pin, L. Ellies. Nouvelle bibliotheque des auteurs ecclesiastiques.
    19 vols. in 8; 3d ed., rev. and corr. Paris: Chez André
    Prallard, 1693-1715.

_____. A New History of Ecclesiastical Writers. Translation
    from the French revised by William Wotton. 3d corr. ed.
    3 vols. Dublin: Grierson, 1723.

Edelstein, Ludwig. Review of Apsyrtus, Julius Africanus et l'hippia-
    trique grecque, by Gudmund Björck. American Journal of
    Philology 68 (1947):443-45.

The Encyclpaedia Britannica.
    Moore's Dublin ed. (1791-97). 18 vols. S.v. "Africanus
    (Julius)."
    9th ed. (1875). S.v. "Africanus, Julius."
    11th ed. (1910). S.v. "Africanus, Sextus Julius."
    1960 ed. S.v. "Africanus, Sextus Julius."

The New Encyclopaedia Britannica. 15th ed. (1974). Micropaedia.
    S.v. "Africanus, Sextus Julius." Macropaedia. S. v. "Magic,"
    by John F. M. Middleton.

Encyclopedia of Religion and Ethics. Edited by James Hastings.
    S.v. "Charms and Amulets," by B. Freire-Marreco, et al.;
    "Divination," by H. J. Rose, et al.; and "Magic," by R. R.
    Marett, et al. 13 vols. Edinburgh: T. & T. Clark, 1925.

Fabricius, Jo. Albertus. Bibliotheca Graeca, sive notitia scrip-
    torum veterum Graecorum. 3d ed. 14 vols. Hamburg: Chris-
    tian Liebezeit and Theodor. Christoph. Felginer, 1718-28.
    4th ed. Edited by Gottlieb Christophorus Harles. 12 vols.
    Hamburg: Carolus Ernestus Bohn, 1780-1809.

Farrington, B. Review of Apsyrtus, Julius Africanus et l'hippia-
    trique grecque, by Gudmund Björck. Journal of Hellenic
    Studies 64 (1944):121.

Fermald, Merritt Lyndon, rev. and ed. Gray's Manual of Botany:
    A Handbook of the Flowering Plants and Ferns of the Central
    and Northeastern United States and Adjacent Canada. 8th
    (Centennial) ed, illust. New York: American Book Company,
    1950.

Follet, Simone. Review of Les "Cestes" de Julius Africanus, by
    Jean-René Vieillefond. Revue de philologie 49 (1975):318-19.

Forbes, Robert James. Bitumen and Petroleum in Antiquity. Leiden:
    E. J. Brill, 1936.

_____. More Studies in Early Petroleum History, 1860-1880.
    Leiden: E. J. Brill, 1959.

Frazer, James George. The Golden Bough: A Study in Magic and Reli-
    gion. 3d ed. Part 1: The Magic Art and the Evolution of
    Kings. 2 vols. New York: The Macmillan Company, 1951.

Ganschinietz, Richard. "Hippolytos' Capitel gegen die Magier:
    Refut. Haer. IV. 28-42." Texte und Untersuchungen zur
    Geschichte der altchristlichen Literatur, 39, no. 2 (1913).

Ganszyniec, R. "Welches ist der ἰατρικὸς δάκτυλος?" Byzantinisch-
    Neugriechische Jahrbücher 1 (1920):342.

Gardthausen, V[iktor Emil]. Griechische Palaeographie. 2d ed.
    2 vols. Leipzig: Verlag von Veit & Comp., 1911-13.

Gelzer, Heinrich. Sextus Julius Africanus und die Byzantinische
    Chronographie. 2 parts in 3 vols. Erster Theil: Die Chrono-
    graphie des Julius Africanus; Zweiter Theil, erste Abtheilung:
    Die Nachfolger des Julius Africanus. Leipzig: B. G. Teubner,
    1880, 1885. Zweiter Theil, zweite Abtheilung: Nachtrage.
    Leipzig: J. C. Hinrichs'sche Buchhandlung, 1898. 2 parts in
    1 vol. Leipzig: J. C. Hinrichs'sche Buchhandlung, 1898;

reprint ed., Burt Franklin: Research and Source Works Series,
no. 169; New York: Burt Franklin, n.d.

_____. "Zu Africanus." Jahrbücher für protestantische Theologie
7 (1881):376-78.

Gemoll, Wilhelm. "Untersuchungen über die Quellen, den Verfasser
und die Abfassungszeit der Geoponica." Berliner Studien
für classische Philologie und Archaeologie 1 (1884):1-280.
Also published separately, Berlin: S. Calvary & Comp., 1883.

Goode, William J. Religion among the Primitives. Glencoe, Ill.:
The Free Press, Publishers, 1951.

Goody, Jack. "Religion and Ritual: The Definitional Problem." The
British Journal of Sociology 12 (June 1961):142-64.

Grant, Robert M. "Historical Criticism in the Ancient Church."
Journal of Religion 25 (1945):183-96.

Grieve, Mrs. M[aud]. A Modern Herbal: The Medicinal, Culinary, Cos-
metic and Economic Properties, Cultivation and Folk-Lore
of Herbs, Grasses, Fungi, Shrubs & Trees with All Their Modern
Scientific Uses. Introduction by the editor, Mrs. C. F.
[Hilda] Leyel. 2 vols. 1931; unaltered reprint ed., New
York: Dover Publications, 1971.

Grzimek, Bernard, editor-in-chief. Grzimek's Animal Life Encyclopedia. [Engl. ed.] 13 vols. New York: Van Nostrand Reinhold Company, 1968-72.

Harnack, Adolf. "Julius Africanus." In Real-Encyklopädie für protestantische Theologie und Kirche, 7:296-98. 2d impro. and
exp. ed. Edited by J. J. Herzog and G. L. Plitt. 18 vols.
Leipzig: J. C. Hinrichs'sche Buchhandlung, 1877-88.

_____. Reviews of Sextus Julius Africanus und die Byzantinische
Chronographie, by Heinrich Gelzer. Theologische Literatur-
zeitung 6 (1881):278-83; and 10 (1885):423-26.

_____. "Die griechische Übersetzung des Apologeticus Tertullian's
- Medicinisches aus der ältesten Kirchengeschichte." Texte
und Untersuchungen zur Geschichte der altchristlichen Literatur 8, no. 4 (1892).

_____. Geschichte der altchristlichen Literatur bis Eusebius.
2 vols. Leipzig: J. C. Hinrichs'sche Buchhandlung, 1893,
1904.

_____. "Julius Afrikanus Sextus." In Realencyklopädie für prot-
estantische Theologie und Kirche, 9:627-28. Founded by J. J.
Herzog. 3d impr. and exp. ed. Edited by Albert Hauck. 24 vols.
Leipzig: J.C. Hinrichs'sche Buchhandlung, 1896-1913.

Harnack, Adolf. Militia Christi: Die Christliche Religion und der
    Soldatenstand in dem ersten drei Jahrhunderte. Tübingen:
    J. C. B. Mohr, 1905.

_____. "Julius Africanus, Sextus." In New Schaff-Herzog Ency-
    clopedia of Religious Knowledge, 6:264-65. Edited by Samuel
    Macauley Jackson. 12 vols. New York and London: Funk and
    Wagnalls, 1908-12.

_____. "Julius Afrikanus, der Bibliothekar des Kaisers Alexander
    Severus." In Aufsätze Fritz Milkau gewidmet, pp. 142-46.
    [Ed. Georg Leyh]. Leipzig: Karl W. Hiersemann, 1921.

_____. "Über die Sammlung der Briefe des Origenes und seinen
    Briefwechsel mit Julius Africanus." Sitzungsberichte der
    Preussischen Akademie der Wissenschaften: Philosophisch-
    Historische Klasse, 1925, p. 266.

Heim, Ricardus. "Incantamenta magica: Graeca, Latina." Jahrbücher
    für classische Philologie, supp. 19 (1893):465-576.

Hefermehl, Ernst. "Der Homertext der Κεστοί des Julius Africanus."
    Berliner Philologische Wochenschrift 26 (1906): cols. 413-15.

Henderson, Isobel. "Ancient Greek Music." In The New Oxford His-
    tory of Music, vol. 1: Ancient and Oriental Music, pp. 336-
    403. Edited by Egon Wellesz. London: Oxford University
    Press, 1957.

Herwerden, H. van. "Observatiunculae." Rheinisches Museum für
    Philologie, n.s. 59 (1904):141-44.

Hopfner, Theodor. Griechisch-Ägyptischer Offenbarungszauber, I & II.
    Studien zur Palaeographie und Papyruskunde, ed. Carl Wessely,
    vols. 21 and 23. Leipzig: H. Haessel, 1921, 1924.

_____. "Mageia." In Pauly's Real-Encyclopädie der classischen
    Altertumswissenschaft, 14: cols. 301-93. New ed. begun by
    Georg Wissowa. Edited by Wilhelm Kroll. Stuttgart: J. B.
    Metzlersche Buchhandlung, 1893-.

Hopkins, R. V. Nind. The Life of Alexander Severus. Cambridge His-
    torical Essays, no. 14. Cambridge: University Press, 1907.

Horton, Robin. "A Definition of Religion, and Its Uses." The Journal
    of the Royal Anthropological Institute of Great Britain and
    Ireland 40 (July-December 1960):201-26.

Howes, F. N. A Dictionary of Useful and Everyday Plants and Their
    Common Names. Based on material contained in J. C. Willis,
    A Dictionary of Flowering Plants and Ferns (6th ed., 1931).
    Cambridge: University Press, 1974.

Hubert, H. "Magia." In Dictionnaire des antiquités grecques et romaines d'après les textes et les monuments, 3:1494-1521. Edited by Charles Daremberg and Edmond Saglio. 5 vols. in 10. Paris: Librairie Hachette et Cie., 1877-1919.

Hull, John M. Hellenistic Magic and the Synoptic Tradition. Studies in Biblical Theology. 2d ser., no. 28. Naperville, Ill.: Alec R. Allenson, 1974.

Hultsch, Fridericus. Metrologicorum scriptorum reliquiae. 2 vols. Leipzig: B. G. Teubner, 1864, 1866.

Ihm, Max. "Die Hippiatrica." Rheinisches Museum für Philologie, n.s. 47 (1892):312-18.

Jardé, Auguste. Etudes critiques sur la vie et la règne de Sévère Alexandre. Paris: E. de Boccard, Editeur, 1925.

Jastrow, J., and Wenley, R. M. "Magic and Divination." In Dictionary of Philosophy and Psychology, 2:35-36. Edited by James Mark Baldwin. New ed., with corrs. 3 vols. Gloucester, Mass.: Peter Smith, 1960.

Kenyon, F. G., and Bell, H. I. Greek Papyri in the British Museum: Catalogue, with Texts. 5 vols. London: British Museum, 1893-1917.

Klein, J. "Zu den Κεστοί des Julius Africanus." Rheinisches Museum für Philologie, n.s. 25 (1870):447-48.

Der Kleine Pauly: Lexicon der Antike auf der Grundlage von Pauly's Realencyclopädie der classischen Altertumswissenschaft unter Mitwirkung zahlreicher Fachgelehrter. Revised and edited by Konrat Zeigler, Walther Sontheimer, and Hans Gärtner. S.v. "Aberglaube," by Karl Preisendanz; "Zauberei, Zauberer," by Clemens Zintzen. 5 vols. Stuttgart and Munich: Alfred Druckenmüller Verlag, 1964-75.

Korzensky, Eleonore. Review of Jules Africain: Fragments des Cestes provenant de la collection des tacticiens grecs, by J.-R. Vieillefond. Byzantinische Zeitschrift 35 (1935):145-49.

Kotsones, Ier. Ier. "Ἰούλιους ὁ Ἀφρικανός, ὁ πρῶτος Χριστιανὸς χρονογράφος." Θεολογία 15 (1937):227-38.

Kroll, W., and Sickenberger, J. "S. Julius Africanus." In Pauly's Real-Encyclopädie der classischen Altertumswissenschaft, 10: cols. 116-25 [S.v. "Julius," no. 47.] New ed. begun by Georg Wissowa. Stuttgart: J. B. Metzlersche Buchhandlung, 1893-.

Kudlien, Fridolf. "Zum Thema 'Homer und die Medizin.'" Rheinisches
    Museum für Philologie, n.s. 108 (1965):293-99.

Labbe, Phil. Dissertationis philologicae de scriptoribus ecclesi-
    asticis quos attigit Eminentiss. S. R. E. Card. Robertus
    Bellarminus. 2 vols. Paris: Sebastian Cramoisy, 1660.

Lagercrantz, Otto. Papyrus Graecus Holmiensis (P. Holm.): Recepte
    für Silber, Steine und Purpur. Uppsala: A.-B. Akademiska
    Bokhandeln, 1913; Leipzig: Otto Harrassowitz, 1913.

Lambecius, Petrus. Commentariorum de Augustissim. Bibliotheca
    Caesarea Vindodonensi. Editio altera. Edited by Adamus
    Franciscus Kollarius. 8 vols. Venice: Joan. Thomae Nob.
    de Trattnern, 1766-1782. [1st ed. 8 vols. Venice, 1665-79.]

Lammert, F. "Julius Afrikanus und die byzantinische Taktik." Byz-
    antinische Zeitschrift 44 (1951):362-69.

Lardner, Nathaniel. The Works of Nathaniel Lardner, with a Life by Dr.
    [Andrew] Kippis. Vol. 2: The Credibility of the Gospel His-
    tory, part 2. London: William Ball, 1838.

LaRue, Carolus de, and LaRue, Carol. Vincent. de, eds. Origenis
    opera omnis quae Graece vel Latine tantum exstant. [4 vols.,
    Paris, 1733-59.] Denuo rencensuit emendavit castigavit
    Carol. Henric. Eduard. Lommatzsch. 23 vols. Berlin:
    Haude et Spener, 1831-47.

Lenain de Tillemont, [Sebastien]. Memoires pour servir a l'histoire
    ecclesiastique des six premiers siecles, justifiez par les
    citations des auteurs originaux. 16 vols. Paris: Charles
    Robustel, 1693-1712; 2d ed., 1700-1713.

Liddell, Henry George, and Scott, Robert, comps. A Greek-English
    Lexicon. Revised and augmented by Henry Stuart Jones and
    Roderick McKenzie. 9th ed., with a Supplement. Oxford:
    Clarendon Press, 1968.

Ludwich, Arthur. "Julius Africanus und die Peisistratos-Legende
    über Homer." Berliner philologische Wochenschrift 23 (1903):
    1467-70, 1502-4.

Malinowski, Bronislaw. "Magic Science and Religion." In Science
    Religion and Reality, pp. 19-84. Edited by Joseph Needham.
    New York: Macmillan Company, 1925.

Martin, Th. Henri. "Recherches sur la vie et les ouvrages d'Héron
    d'Alexandrie." Memoires présentés par divers savants à
    l'Academie des Inscriptions et Belles-Lettres de l'Institut
    Imperial de France, première série, tome 4 (1854).

Meurs, Johannes van. Ioannis Meursi operum. Ex recensione Ioannis
    Lami. 12 vols. in 11. Florence: Regiis Magni Etruriae
    Ducis Typis, apud Tartinum, et Franchium, 1741-63.

Miraeus, Aubertus. Bibliotheca ecclesiastica sive nomenclatores VII
    veteres. 2 vols. Antwerp: Apud Jacobum Mesium, 1639, 1649.

Naumann, Emil. The History of Music. Translated by F. Praeger.
    Edited by F. A. Gore Ouseley. 5 vols. London: Cassell &
    Co. [1886].

Neander, Augustus. General History of the Christian Religion and
    Church. Translated by Joseph Torrey. Rev. ed. Vol. 2.
    London: George Bell and Sons, 1890. [A translation of All-
    gemeine Geschichte der Christlichen Religion und Kirche.
    2 vols. in 6, Hamburg, 1825-31.]

The New Encyclopaedia Britannica. 15th ed. (1974). Macropaedia. S.v.
    "Magic," by John F. M. Middleton.

The New Schaff-Herzog Encyclopedia of Religious Knowledge. Edited
    by Samuel Macauley Jackson. S.v. "Amulet" by Johannes Ficker,
    and "Magic," by O. Zöckler. 12 vols. New York and London:
    Funk and Wagnalls, 1908-12.

Niclas, Io. Nicolao, ed. ΓΕΩΠΟΝΙΚΑ: Geoponicorum sive de re rustica
    libri XX. Cassiano Basso scholastica collectore antea
    Constantino Porphyrogenneto a quibusdam adscripti Graece
    et Latine post Petri Needhami curas [Cambridge, 1704.]
    ad MSS. fidem denuo recensi et illustrati. 4 vols. Leipzig:
    Sumtu Caspari Fritsch., 1781.

Norbeck, Edward. Religion in Primitive Society. New York and Evan-
    ston: Harper & Row, 1961.

Oder, Eugen. "Beiträge zur Geschichte der Landwirthschaft bei den
    Griechen." Rheinisches Museum für Philologie, n.s. 45
    (1890):58-99, 212-22; 48 (1893):1-40.

Pauly's Real-Encyclopädie der classischen Altertumswissenschaft.
    Neue bearbeitung begonnen von Georg Wissowa, herausgegeben
    von Wilhelm Kroll. [1st series] 24 vols. in 47 Halbbänder
    [1893-1963]; 2d series, 10 vols. in 19 Halbbänder [1914-72];
    Supplements, 1903-   [15 to 1978]. Stuttgart: J. B. Metz-
    lersche Buchhandlung, 1893-1972, 1903-.

Petavius, Dionysius. Opus de doctrina temporum. 2 vols. Paris,
    1627. Vol. 3: Uranologium sive systema variorum auctorum,
    1630. Reprint ed., 3 vols. Antwerp: Georgius Gallet, 1703.

Pettersson, Olof. "Magic-Religion: Some Marginal Notes to an Old
    Problem." Ethnos 22, nos. 3-4 (1957):109-19.

Pitra, J[oannes] B[aptista]. Spicilegium Solesmense complectens
    sanctorum patrum scriptorumque ecclesiasticorum anecdota
    hactenus opera, selecta e Graecis Orientalibusque et Latinis
    codicibus. 4 vols. Paris: F. Didot Fratres, 1852-58.

_____. Analecta sacra spicilegio Solesmensi. 4 vols. Typis
    Tusculanis, 1876-84; reprint ed., Farnborough, Hants, England:
    Gregg Press Ltd., 1966.

Plomteux, Hugo. "Le crapaud, magie et maléfice: à propos de quel-
    ques zoonymes italiens." Revue de linguistique romaine 29
    (1965): 132-40.

Politianus, Angelus. Miscellaneorum centuria una. Florence, 1489;
    reprint ed., Basil:[Apud Valent. Curionem, 1522]. Also
    reprinted in Omnium Angeli Politiano operum. 2 vols. in 1.
    [Paris]: [Jo. Badius Ascensius], 1512; and in Opera. Vol. 1:
    Epistolarum libros XII, Miscellaneorum centuriam I. Lugduni:
    Sebastianus Gryphius, 1533.

Pressel, Th. "Julius Africanus." In Real-Encyklopädie für protes-
    tantische Theologie und Kirche, 7:155-56. Edited by J. J.
    Herzog. 22 vols. Stuttgart and Hamburg: R. Besser, 1854-68.

Puech, Aimé. Histoire de la litterature grecque chrétienne depuis
    les origines jusqu'a la fin du IVe siecle. Vol. 2: Le IIe
    et le IIIe siècles. Paris: Société d'Edition "Les Belles
    Lettres," 1928.

Quasten, Johannes. Patrology. 3 vols. Utrecht and Antwerp: Spec-
    trum Publishers, 1960; Westminster, Md.: Newman Press, 1960.

Radin, Paul. Primitive Religion, Its Nature and Origin. New York:
    Dover Publications, 1957.

Real-Encyclopädia der classischen Altertumswissenschaft. Edited
    by August Pauly, Chr. Walz, and W. S. Teuffel. S.v. "Julius
    Africanus," by Christian Felix Bähr. 6 vols. in 7. Stutt-
    gart: J. B. Metzler, 1837-58.

Reville, Jean. La religion à Rome sous les Sévères. Paris: Ernest
    Leroux, 1885.

Riess. "Aberglaube." In Pauly's Real-Encyclopädie der classischen
    Altertumswissenschaft, 1: cols. 29-93. New ed. begun by
    Georg Wissowa. Edited by Wilhelm Kroll. Stuttgart: J. B.
    Metzlersche Buchhandlung, 1893-.

Robert, Louis. "La bibliothèque de Nysa de Carie." Hellenica:
    Recueil d'épigraphie de numismatique et d'antiquités grecques 1
    (1940):144-48.

Rosenmüller, Jo. Georg. Historia interpretationis librorum sacrum
    in ecclesia Christiana. Pars tertia continens periodum II.
    ab Origene ad Jo. Chrysostomum et Cypriano ad Augustinum.
    Leipzig: Io. Gottfr. Hanisch, 1807.

Salmasius, Claudius. Plinianae exercitationes in Caii Julii Solini
    Polyhistora. 2 vols. Paris, 1629; reprint ed., Utrecht:
    Johannem vande Water, 1689.

Sarton, George. Introduction to the History of Science. 3 vols.
    1927-48; reprint ed., Baltimore: For the Carnegie Institute
    of Washington, 1962.

Scaliger, Josephus Justus. Thesaurus temporum: Eusebii Pamphili
    Caesareae Palaestinae episcopi chronicorum canonum . . . in-
    terprete Hieronymo . . . reliquiae Graecae . . . notae &
    castigationes in Latinam Hieronymi interpretationem & Graeca
    Eusebii. Leiden: Thomas Basson, 1606; also, reprint ed.,
    Osnabruck: Otto Zeller, 1968.

Schalit, Abraham. "Die Frühchristliche Überlieferung über die Her-
    kunft der Familie des Herodes: Ein Beitrag zur Geschichte
    der politischen Invektive in Judäa." Annual of the Swedish
    Theological Institute 1 (1960):109-60.

Schmidt, Ernst. "Zu dem Zaubergesang in der Nekyia." Archiv für
    Religionswissenschaft 13 (1910):624-25.

Scullard, H. H. The Elephant in the Greek and Roman World. Aspects
    of Greek and Roman Life, general editor, H. H. Scullard.
    N.p.: Thames and Hudson, 1974.

Smith, Morton. The Secret Gospel: The Discovery and Interpretation
    of the Secret Gospel according to Mark. 1st ed. New York:
    Harper & Row, 1973.

_____. Clement of Alexandria and a Secret Gospel of Mark. Cam-
    bridge: Harvard University Press, 1973.

_____. Jesus the Magician. San Francisco: Harper & Row, Pub-
    lishers, 1978.

Stählin, Otto. Die altchristliche griechische Litteratur. Sonder-
    Abdruck aus W. v. Christ's Geschichte der griechischen Lit-
    teratur, zweiter Teil, zweite Hälfte, sechste Auflage.
    Munich: C. H. Beck'sche Verlagsbuchhandlung, Oskar Beck,
    1924.

Tarn, W. W. Review of Jules Africain: Fragments des Cestes proven-
        ant de la collection des tacticiens grecs, by J.-R. Vieille-
        fond. Classical Review 46 (1932):238.

Thevenot, Melchisedech. Veterum mathematicorum--Athenaei, Bitonis,
        Apollodori, Heronis, Philonis, et aliorum--opera, Graece
        et Latine pleraque nunc primum edita. Ex manuscriptis codi-
        cibus Bibliotheca Regiae. Paris: Ex Typographia Regia,
        1693.

Thiele, Waltharius. De Severo Alexandro imperatore. Berlin:
        Mayer & Müller, 1909.

Thomas, Keith. Religion and the Decline of Magic. New York: Charles
        Scribner's Sons, 1971.

Thompson, D'Arcy Wentworth. "Ancient Chemical Warfare." The Classi-
        cal Review 47 (1933):171-72.

Thorndike, Lynn. A History of Magic and Experimental Science. 8
        vols. New York and London: Columbia University Press, 1923-58.

Tylor, Edward B. Primitive Culture: Researches into the Development
        of Mythology, Philosophy, Religion, Language, Art and Custom.
        1st Amer. from the 2d Eng. ed. 2 vols. New York: Henry
        Holt and Company, 1874.

Valesius, Henricus. Eusebii Pamphili ecclesiasticae historiae libri
        decem. Eiusdem de vita imp. Constantini, libri IV. Quibus
        subjicitur oratio Constantini ad sanctos, & panegyricus
        Eusebii. Henricus Valesius Graecum textum collatis IV.
        MSS. codicibus emendauit, Latine vertit, et adnotationibus
        illustrauit. Paris: A. Vitré, 1659.

_____. The History of the Church from our Lord's Incarnation to
        the Twelfth Year of the Emperor Mauricius Tiberius, or the
        Year of Christ 594. As It Was Written in Greek by Eusebius
        Pamphilus . . . Socrates Scholasticus . . . and Evagrius
        Scholasticus. Translated from Valesius' editions of Paris,
        1659, 1668, and 1673. Translated by Ed. Wells. 2d ed.
        London: Printed by J. M. for A. and J. Churchill, 1709.

Vieillefond, J[ean]-R[ene]. Communication: "Sur deux signes magiques."
        Revue des études grecques 43 (1930):lix-lx.

_____. "Adaptations et paraphrases du Commentaire d'Enée le Tac-
        ticien." Revue de philologie, de litterature et d'histoire
        anciennes, 3d ser., 6 [58 of the collection] (1932):24-36.

_____. "De le Nekyia Homérique à l'Enfer de Dante." Revue des
        études italiennes, n.s. 11, nos. 1-2-3 (Jan.-Sept. 1965):
        439-53.

_____. <u>See also</u> texts of Julius Africanus, above.

Vincent, [A.-J.-H.]. "Histoire de la numération." L'Institut:
    Journal général des sociétés et travaux scientifiques de
    la France et de l'étranger. IIe section: Sciences historiques,
    archéologiques et philosophiques 6 (1841):173-75.

[_____]. "Histoire des Mathematiques. Sur un certain emploi
    que faisaient les Romains, des le IIe ou le IIIe siècle
    de notre ère, des valeurs de position pour l'expression des
    nombres. - Extrait d'une Lettre de M. Vincent." Comptes
    rendus hebdomadaires des séances de l'Academie des Sciences
    (Paris) 14 (1842):43-44.

_____. "Musique des grecs." Revue archéologique, IIe année
    (1845), pp. 453-55.

_____. "Extraits des Cestes de Jules l'Africain," with "Addi-
    tion: Communiquée par M. le Docteur Roulin relativ aux ani-
    maux mentioné par Jules l'Africain," in "Notice sur trois
    manuscrits grecs relatifs à la musiques, avec une traduction
    française et des commentaires." Notices et extraits des
    manuscrits de la bibliotheques du roi et autres biblio-
    theques 16, no. 2 (1847):344-63, 561-64.

_____. "Extraits des Cestes de Jules l'Africain," in "Extraits
    des manuscrits relatifs à la géométrie pratiques des Grecs."
    Notices et extraits des manuscrits de la bibliotheque im-
    periale et autres bibliotheques 19, no. 2 (1858):407-15.

Vincent, L.-H., and Abel, F.-M. Emmaüs, sa basilique et son his-
    toire. Paris: Librairie Ernest Leroux, 1932.

Vossius, Gerardus Joannes. De historicis Graecis liber IV. Editio
    altera, priori emendatior, & multis partibis auctior.
    Leyden, 1624; reprint ed., Leyden: Ex Officinâ Ioannis
    Maire, 1651.

Vossius, Isaacus. Cajus Valerius Catullus: et in eum Isaaci Vossii
    observationes. London: Apud Isaacum Littleburii, 1684.

_____. Justini historiarum ex Trogo Pompeio lib. XLIV cum notis
    Isaaci Vossii. Amsterdam: Ex Officina Elzeviriana, 1664.

Wallace, Anthony F. C. Religion: An Anthropological View. New York:
    Random House, 1966.

Wax, Murray. "Ancient Judaism and the Protestant Ethic." The Ameri-
    can Journal of Sociology 65 (March 1960):449-55.

Wax, Rosalie and Wax, Murray. "The Magical World View." Journal for the Scientific Study of Religion 1, no. 2 (1962):179-88.

Wax, Murray and Wax, Rosalie. "The Notion of Magic." Current Anthropology 4 (December 1963):495-518.

Weil, Henri. "Textes grecs trouvés récemment en Egypte." [Review of The Oxyrhynchus Papyri, part III, edited by Bernard P. Grenfell and Arthur S. Hunt.] Journal des savants, n.s. 2d année (1904), pp. 105-9.

Wellmann, Max. "Die ΦΥΣΙΚΑ des Bolos Demokritos und der Magier Anaxilaos aus Larissa, Teil I." Abhandlungen der Preussischen Akademie der Wissenschaften [Berlin]: Philosophisch-Historische Klasse, 1928, no. 7.

Wentzel, Georg. "Die Griechische Übersetzung der viri inlustres des Hieronymus." Texte und Untersuchungen zur Geschichte der altchristlichen Literatur 13, no. 3 (1895).

Westermann, Antonius. ΠΑΡΑΔΟΞΟΓΡΑΦΟΙ--Scriptores rerum mirabilium Graeci. Braunschweig: Georgius Westermann, 1839; London: Black & Armstrong, 1839; also, reprint ed., Amsterdam: Verlag Adolf M. Hakkert, 1963.

Wetstenius, M. Joh. Rodolfus. Origenis dialogus contra Marcionitas, sive de recta in deum fide; Exhortatio ad martyrium; Responsum ad Africani epistolam de historia Susannae . . . additis notis. Basel: J. Bertschius, 1674.

Wiesner, Julius von. Die Rohstoffe des Planzenreichs. 5th ed. Edited by Constantin von Regel. 7 vols. Weinheim: Verlag von J. Cramer, 1962-68.

Wünsch, Richard. "Deisidaimoniaka." Archiv für Religionswissenschaft 12 (1909):1-45.

Yalman, Nur. "Magic." In International Encyclopedia of the Social Sciences, 9:521-28. Edited by David L. Sills. 17 vols. N.p.: The Macmillan Company and The Free Press, 1968.

Youngken, Heber W. A Text Book of Pharmacognosy. 4th ed., rev. and enl., with 469 illust. containing about 1500 figs. Philadelphia: P. Blakiston's Son & Co., 1936.

INDEXES

A page number followed by an <u>n</u> indicates a reference to the
note(s) on the specified page; a number followed by a virgula and <u>n</u>
(e.g. 42/n) indicates a reference to that page and its note(s).

Index of Ancient and Medieval References

1. Julius Africanus

Mp 45=IX.4.1-4   (73), 103, 189, 218, 219, 240, 246, 299, 302
  IX.5 (Geoponica)   103
  IX.6 (Fulgentius)   103

From the <u>Chronography</u> (ed. Routh)
Mp 46/chr 1=frag. VII<a>   191, 199, 281, 307, 313, 367n, 449
Mp 47/chr 2=frag. XI, Dyn. IV, β   192, 199, 276, 292, 298, 312
Mp 48/chr 3=frag. XL (=Scholion On Manasseh's Escape, <u>see above</u>)   192, 199, 271

"Sylloge" (=Vieillefond, 1932, Appendix I)   222
  Chap. 3   206n
  Chap. 9   250n

"Ecloge" (=Vieillefond, 1932, Appendix II)
  Chap. 1   222n, 259n
  Chap. 2   206n, 208n

Pseudo-Africanian:

<u>Narratio in Perside</u> (mistakenly attributed to Africanus)   40n, 65-66

2. Bible, including Apocrypha

Old Testament

Genesis
  6:2, 4   282n

Exodus
  12:10, 46   243n

Deuteronomy
  20:19, 20   256n

Judges
  9:45   298n

2 Kings
  18:4   399

2 Chronicles
  33:11   271n

Psalms   80, 85
  34:8   43, 44, (80, 85)

Isaiah
  35:1-7   334

Daniel
  9:24   19n
  9:24   16n
  9:24-27   14n

Apocrypha

1 Enoch   403n
  6-10   282n
  7 and 8   357

Susanna   13, 14, 16, 21, 22, 23, 28, 54, 84n, 87/n, 95, 96n, 269

Prayer of Manasseh 271
  10   271n

New Testament

Matthew   14, 16, 17, 21, 25/n, 26n, 28/n
  1   28
  1:15, 17   25
  7:22   424
  17:9   25

Mark   364n

Luke   14, 16, 17, 21, 28n

John   25, 26n, 27n, 45n
  17:5   27n

3. Christian Writings, including Heretical

To Polycarp		Epistles	
5.1	318	70 (ad Magnum), sec. 4	
			15
Irenaeus	346–53, 364, 396,		
	419–20, 443	Comm. on Daniel	
Adv. haereses	316n	Bk. 3 (on Dan. 9:24)	
1.13.1	346, 347, 348,		16n
	349, 394n		
1.13.1-3	347	Latin translation of Eusebius	
1.13.1-6	348	Chronicle	15, 17
1.13.2	350, 395		
1.13.3	347, 348, 349,	Justin Martyr	329-36, 343,
	350		344-45, 438,
1.13.4	349, 350, 351,		439, 441, 442
	353, (460n)	Apology I	
1.13.5	346, 347, 460n	9-14	332
1.13.6	347, 348, 349,	9.1	333n
	351	14	332
1.14.3	346, 351	14.1	330, 331
1.15.6	347	14.2	329
1.21.3	351, 441n	18	331, 344
1.21.5	348, 351, 441n	18.2-5	330n
1.23.1	346, 347, 348,	18.3	331, 351/n, 410n
	351, 412	18.3-4	410n
1.23.4	346, 347, 348,	18.4	331
	349, 410n	18.5	331
1.23.5	346, 347, 348,	20.1	332
	351	26	348
1.24.1	346	26.1-4	333
1.24.5	346, 347, 348,	26.2	330, 331, 412
	351, 441n	26.4	330, 331
1.24.7	350, 351, 441n	30	333
1.25.3	346, 347, 348,	31.7	334n
	349	50.9	334n
1.25.4	347	56.1	330, 333
1.25.6	348	56.2	333, 412
1.26-31	346	66.4	333n
2.praef.1	346		
2.9.2	346	Apology II	330n
2.31.2	348, 349, 352	5	333
2.31.3	349, 352	5.2-4	330
2.32.3	349, 350, 351,	5.4	330/n, 332
	352	5.5	330, 332
2.32.4	350	5.6	333
2.32.5	352	6	331, 332, 344
4.29.2	353	6.5	335
5.28.2	349, 367n	6.6	332, 334/n, 335
5.28.3	367n		
		Dialogue with Trypho	
Jerome	15, 17, 38, 41,	3-8	333n
	71, 465n	7.2	336
De viris illustribus		7.3	336
chap. 63	16, 37	30.3	334
		35.8	334n

4. Secular and Other Sources

Index of Modern Authors and Works

Index of Subjects

309, 311-12, 460, 461; secular,
literary, (scientific), 311-12,
459, 464n
See also Africanus
Kestous, Tous, 137n
Kicking mule, 105, 129, 171n, 253
King: Phrygian, 136
Kitrion, 168
Kleptelenchon/thief-convicter, 187,
198, 217, 233
Klēsis: 331; -klēsis/-kēlēsis, 439
Kokytus, 182
Krithomanteis, 359
Krotonians, 124
Kybeias, kybeuōn, 397
Kyōn--kyō, 238
Kyprinē: 265; kyprinos, 264
Kypros, 265n

Lacedaemonians, 112, 121, 126
Laconian cap, 107
Lamminae, 425n, 429
Language(s), 356, 371, 377, 444
Latin: Africanus knew, 58, 64, 74
--translation of Africanus, 56
--expression, 119, 129, 190, 202n,
213, 267, 286, 289; prescription,
267n, 273n
Lead: 210n; plaque, 266
Left: side, 220, 278, 279-80, 303;
front hoof, 219, 272, 279, 287;
shoulder, 220, 279; hand, 264,
279, 288; with left hand, 287;
nostril, 279
Legume, 212
Lemnian: "certified", 153; earth,
166
Leōn (snake), 115, 223, 225
Leonidas, 110
Lēthē, 182
Libations, 425, 454
Librarian. See Africanus: profes-
sion, librarian
Library: in Rome, 66, 71n, 75, 79n
182; of Aelia, 270n
Libya: Africanus from, 22, 38, 41,
45, 56, 64, 79
--Felix, 145
--magical place, 276
Libyan: aromatic sap, 145
--Inaron the, 165, 228/n
Lice, 164, 215n, 238, 252
Lichanos, 118, 119, 120, 138
Lignite, 264, 279

Linen: frequent use of, 262; pen-
dant, 232, 233
Linozōstis, 255n
Literary interests, etc. See
Africanus; Kestoi
Liver: 217n-218n, 240n; hedgehog,
217, 239
Living: animal, 211, 212, 214-16;
frog's eyes, 232; wolf's tail,
235
Lizards, 230
Loosing, 284
Love: goal of magic, 337
--magic, 301; potions, 347, 350;
charms, 355, 439, 450, 465. See
also Agōgima; Charitesia; Charms
Luke. See in Index of Ancient and
Medieval References: 2. Bible
Lydian: mode, 112, 138, 203
--garum, 145; stone, 365/n

Macedonian(s), 107, 150
Macrinus, 13, 16, 21
Mad dog: bites, 165; saliva, 218,
237, 266
Madness, 410
Mag- forms, 344, 438, 449, 450
Mageia(i) 281, 317, 319, 354n, 368,
369n, 370, 391, 396/n, 397, 438,
439
Mageuō, 319, 438
Magi: 330, 331, 335, 337, 341, 342,
349, 354n, 355, 356, 357, 363,
373, 374, 380, 415, 418, 423,
427, 428, 431, 434; Magian, 341,
424
Magia(e), 348, 405, 407, 413, 414
Magia naturalis, 39, 70, 74, 242
Magic: 6, 8/n, 9, 193-315 passim
304n, 316-418 passim
--definition, 8, 194n; distinguished from superstition, 194n;
attitudes toward, 5, 466
--types of: 209; indirect/supplica-
tive/personal/daemonic, 9, 209,
443, 454, 465n; direct/imper-
sonal/automatic, 9, 209, 443,
454; compulsive, manipulative,
9; sympathetic, contagious, 9
--theory of: 337, 349, 425-27, 444,
455; Origen's, 376-86
--nature and origin: 247, 370n;
species of, 404, 410; astrology,
410; areas of, 300-03